OXFORD POLITICAL THEORY

Series Editors:
WILL KYMLICKA AND DAVID MILLER

Territorial Sovereignty

OXFORD POLITICAL THEORY

Oxford Political Theory presents the best new work in contemporary political theory. It is intended to be broad in scope, including original contributions to political philosophy, and also work in applied political theory. The series contains works of outstanding quality with no restriction as to approach or subject matter.

OTHER TITLES IN THIS SERIES

Strategies of Justice
Aboriginal Peoples, Persistent Injustice, and the Ethics of Political Action
Burke A. Hendrix

Immigration and Democracy
Sarah Song

Against Marriage
An Egalitarian Defense of the Marriage-Free State
Clare Chambers

Civics Beyond Critics
Character Education in a Liberal Democracy
Ian MacMullen

The Ethics of Immigration
Joseph Carens

Linguistic Justice for Europe and for the World
Philippe Van Parijs

Critical Republicanism
The Hijab Controversy and Political Philosophy
Cécile Laborde

National Responsibility and Global Justice
David Miller

Disadvantage
Jonathan Wolff and Avner de-Shalit

Levelling the Playing Field
The Idea of Equal Opportunity and its Place in Egalitarian Thought
Andrew Mason

The Liberal Archipelago
A Theory of Diversity and Freedom
Chandran Kukathas

The Civic Minimum
On the Rights and Obligations of Economic Citizenship
Stuart White

Reflective Democracy
Robert E. Goodin

Multicultural Citizenship
A Liberal Theory of Minority Rights
Will Kymlicka

Deliberative Democracy and Beyond
Liberals, Critics, Contestations
John S. Dryzek

Territorial Sovereignty

A Philosophical Exploration

ANNA STILZ

OXFORD
UNIVERSITY PRESS

Great Clarendon Street, Oxford, OX2 6DP,
United Kingdom

Oxford University Press is a department of the University of Oxford.
It furthers the University's objective of excellence in research, scholarship,
and education by publishing worldwide. Oxford is a registered trade mark of
Oxford University Press in the UK and in certain other countries

© Anna Stilz 2019

The moral rights of the author have been asserted

First Edition published in 2019

Impression: 4

All rights reserved. No part of this publication may be reproduced, stored in
a retrieval system, or transmitted, in any form or by any means, without the
prior permission in writing of Oxford University Press, or as expressly permitted
by law, by licence or under terms agreed with the appropriate reprographics
rights organization. Enquiries concerning reproduction outside the scope of the
above should be sent to the Rights Department, Oxford University Press, at the
address above

You must not circulate this work in any other form
and you must impose this same condition on any acquirer

Published in the United States of America by Oxford University Press
198 Madison Avenue, New York, NY 10016, United States of America

British Library Cataloguing in Publication Data

Data available

Library of Congress Control Number: 2019936878

ISBN 978-0-19-883353-6

Printed and bound in Great Britain by
Clays Ltd, Elcograf S.p.A.

Links to third party websites are provided by Oxford in good faith and
for information only. Oxford disclaims any responsibility for the materials
contained in any third party website referenced in this work.

For Hillel, Rachel, and our new baby

Acknowledgments

This book investigates the moral grounds for state rights over territory, exploring claims to land, self-determination, political legitimacy, border control, and natural resources. I have worked on these topics for nearly a decade, developing, refining, and often revising my views over the course of that time. While the book offers a qualified defense of a world order made up of independent territorial states, it does not justify the full set of sovereign rights that states claim, and that are currently recognized under international law. In that sense, it is a revisionist account.

Many people have made important contributions to my intellectual journey in writing this book. I am especially grateful to my colleagues at Princeton, including Chuck Beitz, Desmond Jagmohan, Melissa Lane, Alan Patten, Steve Macedo, Jan-Werner Mueller, and Philip Pettit. Each one of them has given me challenging critical comments, as well as companionship and moral support. I also received constructive questions and criticism from audiences at a number of universities where I presented parts of this work. Several people provided especially extensive feedback or useful suggestions on specific chapters, including (with apologies to those I have missed): Arash Abizadeh, Christian Barry, Eric Beerbohm, Corey Brettschneider, Shuk-Ying Chan, Thomas Christiano, Nico Cornell, Joshua Dienstag, Hasan Djindjer, David Estlund, Tweedy Flanigan, Katrin Flikschuh, Johann Frick, John Goldberg, Alex Gourevitch, Avery Kolers, Niko Kolodny, Chris Kutz, Seth Lazar, Isi Litke, Catherine Lu, Minh Ly, Chris Morris, Sankar Muthu, Peter Niesen, Shmulik Nili, Cara Nine, Liam Murphy, Jonathan Quong, Jennifer Pitts, David Plunkett, Lucia Rafanelli, Joseph Raz, Steven Ratner, Arthur Ripstein, Mathias Risse, Larry Sager, Debra Satz, Melissa Schwartzberg, Tim Scanlon, Scott Shapiro, Seana Shiffrin, Bas van der Vossen, Daniel Viehoff, Jeremy Waldron, and Jim Wilson.

I owe a particularly significant debt to those who participated in two workshops on the manuscript in May 2017, one of which was held at Princeton, the other at Georgia State University. I am especially grateful to Chuck Beitz, Michael Blake, Will Kymlicka, Alan Patten, Leif Wenar, and Lea Ypi for their feedback at the Princeton workshop, and to Andrew Altman, Andrew I. Cohen, Andrew J. Cohen, David Lefkowitz, Colleen Murphy, George Rainbolt, John Simmons, and Laura Valentini for their comments at Georgia State. Kit Wellman, Will Kymlicka, and David Miller also provided very helpful suggestions as manuscript reviewers, and Chuck Beitz and Lucia Rafanelli commented on Chapter 8 at a late date, and helped me to clarify crucial parts of the argument. I thank Alan Patten, as well, for his terrific comments on the penultimate version of Chapter 5. Ryan Born and

Ben Hofmann provided editorial assistance in assembling the final version of the manuscript, and Dominic Byatt was a very gracious and supportive editor.

Some parts of this book are based on previously published work. I am grateful to publishers for permission to draw on the following:

"Nations, States, and Territory." *Ethics* 121, no. 3 (2011): 572–601. © 2011 by University of Chicago.

"Occupancy Rights and the Wrong of Removal." *Philosophy & Public Affairs* 41, no. 4 (2013): 324–56.

"Decolonization and Self-Determination." *Social Philosophy and Policy* 32, no. 1 (2015): 1–24. © Social Philosophy and Policy Foundation 2015.

"The Value of Self-Determination." *Oxford Studies in Political Philosophy* 2 (2016): 98–127.

"Settlement, Expulsion, and Return." *Politics, Philosophy & Economics* 16, no. 4 (2017): 351–74.

As always, I owe the greatest debts to those who are most special to me: my family. I thank my Dad, Pam, Coley, JP, Amber, Bobby, and Caroline for the love and support they have given me over many years. I also owe a great deal to my mom, who passed away as this was being written, and who is missed. Finally, I thank Hillel and Rachel for doing their best to distract me from working on this book. They are the light of my life, and I dedicate my book to them both and to our new baby, who will be born just as this book is finally being put to rest.

Table of Contents

1. Introduction: The Normative Bases for Territorial Sovereignty	1
PART I. OCCUPANCY	
2. Occupancy Rights	33
3. Challenges to Occupancy	59
PART II. SELF-DETERMINATION	
4. Legitimacy and Self-Determination	89
5. Refining the Political Autonomy Account	119
PART III. EXCLUSION	
6. Territorial Distribution	157
7. Is There a Right to Exclude?	187
PART IV. LOOKING FORWARD	
8. Resource Sovereignty and International Responsibilities	219
9. Conclusion: Territorial Sovereignty and Global Institutions	249
Bibliography	259
Name Index	275
Subject Index	277

1
Introduction: The Normative Bases for Territorial Sovereignty

A deep fact about our political world is that it is a world of sovereign territorial states. According to the 1933 Montevideo Convention, a state under international law is an entity that possesses a permanent population, a defined territory, a government, and the capacity to enter relations with other states.[1] Familiar debates about political legitimacy, authority, and obligation focus on whether these states have the right to make, interpret, and enforce law vis-à-vis their subjects. Does the state have a permission to use coercion or force to regulate its subjects' conduct? Does the state have a right to be obeyed when it issues directives? Do citizens have a right to engage in civil disobedience or, in seriously unjust circumstances, to attempt violent resistance or revolution? These well-worn controversies all address the state's internal legitimacy—its right to exercise political power over its own members.[2]

But modern states do not only claim rights against their own members. They also claim rights against outsiders and, especially, rights to independent control over a particular territory. These claimed rights take four principal forms. First, sovereign states claim the right to *territorial jurisdiction*: the right to issue legal directives and to coercively regulate the activities of people situated in a particular geographical space. Second, states claim the right to *nonintervention*: the exclusive right to govern an area and its population free from interference or efforts at "regime change" on the part of foreign states, individuals, or groups. Third, states claim the right to *control their borders*: to regulate the movement of people and goods across their territories. Fourth, states claim *resource rights*: most states attempt to regulate the use and extraction—and sometimes to profit from the sale or taxation—of minerals, oil, and other natural resources in their territories.[3] Many of these claimed territorial rights exclude foreigners from undertaking various activities within a particular portion of the globe. Yet while there is a long tradition

---

[1] Seventh International Conference of American States, *Montevideo Convention on the Rights and Duties of States* (1933).

[2] I define the state's "members" as its citizens and permanent residents, including unauthorized migrants long resident on the state's territory, who, in my view, have a moral claim to become citizens. "Outsiders" include foreign individuals not resident on the state's territory, as well as foreign states.

[3] For a similar typology, see David Miller, "Territorial Rights: Concept and Justification," *Political Studies* 60, no. 2 (2011): 252–68.

of debating the grounds for the state's internal legitimacy, much less has been said, by comparison, about the grounds—if any—for these territorial rights.

Unlike their internal claims, states' territorial claims have to be understood against the backdrop of the modern states system. As a mode of political organization, the states system is distinctive in the essential structuring role that it grants to geographical boundaries.[4] Modern states exist as part of a broader global order in which autonomous units are represented as both spatially limited and coexisting side by side with rival units. In normal cases, the units claim jurisdictional exclusivity: the modern state claims to be the sole legitimate maker, enforcer, and interpreter of legal rights and duties within its recognized boundaries.[5] Rival power wielders are for the most part excluded from interfering inside its territory. Finally, the states system structures opportunities for individuals, since it partitions people into separate, partly closed, territorial groupings. Boundaries are markers of both the limits of state authority and the rights, duties, and statuses of the individuals who make up those states.

1.1 The Contingency of the Territorial State

Though today it is hard to imagine life without the states system, as a political form, it is relatively new. We can find several alternative modes of political organization just by looking back through human history. Many of these historical alternatives did not accord the same structuring role to geographical boundaries as the modern states system does. Reflecting on this history makes clear that organizing our world as a system of sovereign territorial states is neither necessary nor inevitable.

Early hunter-gatherer societies took the form of *bands*, small groups (perhaps 25 to 150 people) of nomadic families.[6] Many indigenous groups in North America were organized this way before first European contact. Indeed, some groups, such as the Inuit or the Australian Aborigines, still preserve aspects of this organization. Band societies are usually highly egalitarian, lacking formal political leadership, and featuring an economy based on sharing.[7] They do not exhibit private property, exchange, or a specialized division of labor. To the extent they possess political leaders, these are informal arbiters or military commanders temporarily chosen according to need. For most precontact groups in North America, political organization was limited to villages of a few extended families in which day-to-day

---

[4] Hendrik Spruyt, *The Sovereign State and Its Competitors* (Princeton: Princeton University Press, 1996), 35–6.

[5] Exceptions include federations like the EU, where member states have created supranational law through treaty.

[6] Francis Fukuyama, *The Origins of Political Order* (New York: Farrar, Straus, and Giroux, 2011), 53–5; Ted C. Lewellen, *Political Anthropology* (South Hadley: Bergin and Garvey, 1983), 19.

[7] Lewellen, *Political Anthropology*, 17.

leadership was provided by a *sachem*. But the *sachem* had no binding legislative authority: he could not impose legal obligations on the members of his band. Unanimity rule, or at least the suppression of visible dissent, was a common feature of band decision-making. Nor was there any centralized coercive enforcement power: a *sachem* could not rely on a police force to carry out his directives.[8] Band societies lack characteristic features of a modern state, such as written law, courts or judges, and a monopoly of coercion. Though they are nomadic within loosely defined areas, bands do not claim exclusive control of a territory, but rather rights to move around in a given migratory pattern.

Once agriculture was invented, nine to ten thousand years ago, many societies came to be organized into *tribes*. Tribes are decentralized systems in which authority is distributed among a number of kinship-based groups, which occasionally join into larger units (usually for purposes of warfare).[9] Agriculture allows for higher population densities: a square kilometer of land can support 40 to 60 people in the average agricultural society, compared with 0.1 to 1 person in a hunter-gatherer society.[10] Agriculture also created the need for land ownership, which initially took the form of common, rather than private, holdings. Many precolonial groups in Mexico, South America, and the American Southwest were agricultural tribes, with recognizable common property systems. Tribes claimed distinct territories (with boundaries specified by natural landmarks), and within that territory, they allocated exclusive land rights to individuals.[11] Families had the privilege of cultivating their land, though they lacked a right to alienate it, and their title reverted to the tribe if they stopped using it.[12] Like hunter-gatherer bands, tribal societies typically lack centralized authority, rule of law, or third-party enforcement mechanisms. Disputes are instead resolved through self-help by tribal segments: kinsmen have obligations to seek revenge or restitution for wrongs committed against fellow kin, through vendettas. Unlike modern states, tribal societies also lack centralized coercive power; instead, the right to use force belongs to each clan.[13]

A third alternative is the *empire*. Empires are large, expansionist political units that incorporate a number of distinct social groupings within a single overarching governance structure. As Jane Burbank and Frederick Cooper put it, "empire reaches outward and draws, usually coercively, peoples whose difference is made explicit under its rule."[14] Empires often feature government by elites who are

---

[8] See Bruce Trigger, ed., *The Handbook of the North American Indians, Vol. 15: Northeast* (Washington, DC: Smithsonian Institution, 1978). A general overview is Robert H. Lowie, "Some Aspects of Political Organization among the American Aborigines," *The Journal of the Royal Anthropological Institute of Great Britain and Ireland* 78, no. 1/2 (1948): 11–24.
[9] Lewellen, *Political Anthropology*, 25.   [10] Fukuyama, *Origins of Political Order*, 55.
[11] Linda Parker, *Native Estate* (Honolulu: University of Hawaii Press, 1989), 16.
[12] Parker, *Native Estate*, 10.   [13] Lewellen, *Political Anthropology*, 28.
[14] Burbank and Cooper, *Empires in World History: Power and the Politics of Difference* (Princeton: Princeton University Press, 2009), 8–11.

socially distinct from the groups they govern.[15] Empires can control vast physical spaces, and often shape far-flung economies of trading and production. Both the Roman and the Ottoman Empires lasted for over 600 years, longer than the period since the modern state's invention. A key difference between empires and territorial states lies in how they conceive of their external relations. While empires do have boundaries—the *limes* of the Roman Empire or the Great Wall of China—they do not think of themselves as coexisting alongside other units that together make up a wider *territorial system*. Instead, their frontiers were simply the present limits of the empire's expansionary thrust. As Friedrich Kratochwil notes, "the Roman Empire conceived of the *limes* not as a boundary, but as a temporary stopping-place where the potentially unlimited expansion of the *Pax Romana* had come to a halt."[16] Unlike the states system, the empire does not allocate authority according to recognized territorial boundaries, and it does not organize people into distinct, partly closed jurisdictions.[17]

A final alternative is *personal* political authority. In medieval Europe, a variety of authorities—including towns, lords, kings, emperors, popes, and bishops—claimed rights over different people located in roughly the same geographical space. Political obligations were based not on an individual's presence in a given area, but rather on (often-crosscutting) personal ties. A political unit was composed of those people who recognized bonds of allegiance to the same superior: in the twelfth century, one spoke of the King of the French rather than the King of France.[18] To ensure his security, an individual needed to affiliate himself with a lord who could provide protection, usually in exchange for military service. Yet often a vassal would undertake military obligations to many lords at once: "one could simultaneously be the vassal of the German emperor, the French king, and various counts and bishops, none of whom necessarily had precedence over the other."[19]

A key characteristic of the feudal system, by contrast to the modern state, was that it lacked *jurisdictional exclusivity*. Lines of jurisdiction in this system were highly unclear: competence depended on the issue, and since military power was in the hands of decentralized local strongmen, enforcement often required private war. While peasants might be subject to a lord's jurisdiction by virtue of residing on his manor, the lord himself stood in various personal relations of vassalage to conflicting authorities: "the land of the feudal nobility in the late Middle Ages was often not contiguous; a village could depend on more than one lord; lords could owe allegiance to more than one ruler; manorial courts, royal

---

[15] Christopher Morris, *An Essay on the Modern State* (Cambridge: Cambridge University Press, 1998), 30. See also Ernest Gellner, *Nations and Nationalism* (Ithaca: Cornell University Press, 2009), ch. 2, for this point.
[16] Kratochwil, "Of Systems, Boundaries, and Territoriality: An Inquiry into the Formation of the State System," *World Politics* 39, no. 1 (1986): 35–6.
[17] For this point, see also Spruyt, *The Sovereign State and Its Competitors*, 16–17.
[18] Spruyt, *The Sovereign State and Its Competitors*, 40.
[19] Spruyt, *The Sovereign State and Its Competitors*, 39.

courts, and ecclesiastical courts dispensed customary, statutory, and church law to the same populations."[20] In this world of fragmented and spatially cross-cutting authorities, the very idea of *international* relations failed to apply, depending as it does on a distinction between internal and external politics. "In a Europe without states and without boundaries," as Joseph Strayer puts it, "the concept of 'foreign affairs' had no meaning."[21]

I mention these historical alternatives to the territorial states system not because they represent real options for us today: for the most part, they depend upon social and economic preconditions that no longer obtain, and they lack contemporary advocates. Nor will I offer a detailed examination of the relative costs and benefits of these modes of political organization in this book. Still, considering these alternatives makes clear that however deeply rooted it may be at present, the territorial states system is not a natural or an unavoidable political form. Past political orders have not always given geographical boundaries the structuring role granted them by the states system; they have not always allowed for jurisdictional exclusivity; and they have not always organized individuals into separate and partly closed associations.

This leads me to the first general question with which this book is concerned: is there any compelling *moral* justification for organizing our world as a structure of autonomous, bounded, spatially defined jurisdictional units? Should we see this mode of political organization as just a firmly rooted historical contingency? Or are there ethical principles that might support or legitimate it? Since engaged efforts to transform the territorial states system may be possible, it is worth considering the evaluative stance we should take toward it. Is the states system an institution we should endorse, in some or all of its features? Or is it instead something we should work to radically restructure?

1.2 A Morally Justified System?

Increasingly, cosmopolitan theorists offer systemic critiques of the territorial states system. They point to various moral problems that are sustained and reproduced by this system and, particularly, by the structuring role it grants to geographical boundaries. These problems include:

(1) *War.* While a classic argument for sovereignty is that the state is necessary to specify, interpret, and enforce the rights of its members, the formation of a states system may paradoxically make individuals less secure by creating

---

[20] Malcolm Anderson, *Frontiers: Territory and State Formation in the Modern World* (Cambridge: Polity, 1996), 17.
[21] Strayer, *Medieval Origins of the Modern State* (Princeton: Princeton University Press, 2005), 27; see also Spruyt, *The Sovereign State and Its Competitors*, 36.

the threat of interstate war. The evils associated with war may be even worse than the perils a legitimate state is designed to solve.

(2) *Unfreedom.* The modern states system assigns individuals to a territory at birth, and grants states the right to restrict free movement, coercively excluding those who might like to live in another part of the world. These arrangements limit individuals' freedom to live their lives as they choose, to associate with others, and to take advantage of the globe's shared resources.

(3) *Inequality.* There are vast material inequalities among existing states, and many people live in extreme poverty. Since the range of opportunities and advantages varies so dramatically with territorial membership, the state one is born into has a major impact on one's life prospects. State boundaries effectively assign people to an international class hierarchy, preventing them from achieving better lives.

(4) *Collective Action.* By dispersing authority among many constituent units, the modern states system makes it difficult to mount a successful response to pressing contemporary problems, such as climate change, or refugee crises, that require policy coordination at the global level.

Because of these problems, some cosmopolitan theorists hold that the territorial states system is radically unjust and, ideally, should be replaced by something better.[22] On these views, a world without states (perhaps a world organized into nonterritorial or overlapping political jurisdictions), a world state (perhaps a unitary global democracy or world federation), or a world in which state sovereignty was drastically curtailed (perhaps by extensive supranational regulatory institutions or mandatory open borders) would be a morally preferable state of affairs. Unlike the historical alternatives to the states system canvassed earlier, these cosmopolitan options increasingly have vocal and sophisticated defenders.

One cosmopolitan proposal that has seen much discussion is global democracy. Global democracy's proponents often cite the fact that state decisions have significant cross-border externalities; the impacts of decisions made in one place affect people in other places.[23] Some invoke an All-Affected Interests Principle, which holds that everyone who is affected by a decision should have the right to participate in making that decision.[24] According to Robert Goodin, properly interpreted, this principle requires that every person on the globe (and possibly future persons) be enfranchised on virtually every political decision taken anywhere. In practice,

---

[22] Not all cosmopolitans take this view. Some are *moral cosmopolitans*, who argue that duties of justice extend globally, but hold that these principles need not be implemented through transformed political institutions. See Charles Beitz, *Political Theory and International Relations* (Princeton: Princeton University Press, 1979), 182–3.

[23] Raffaele Marchetti, *Global Democracy: For and Against* (New York: Routledge, 2008), 2–3.

[24] For defenses, see Robert Dahl, *Democracy and Its Critics* (New Haven: Yale University Press, 1989); David Held, *Democracy and the Global Order* (Stanford: Stanford University Press, 1995); Iris Marion Young, *Inclusion and Democracy* (New York: Oxford University Press, 2000).

Goodin concedes that the best feasible approximation to the principle is a "world government, federal in form."[25]

Others have advocated global democratic institutions via a different argumentative route, appealing to the "All Subjected Principle," according to which each person *subject* to a law ought to have a say in its making. According to Arash Abizadeh, one is "subjected" when one is threatened with coercion. Abizadeh points out that "borders are one of the most important ways that political power is coercively exercised over human beings."[26] He concludes that foreigners ought to be included in global decisions about the demarcation and control of state boundaries. Abizadeh holds that "the self-determination of differentiated democratic polities" should be viewed as "*derivative* of the self-determination of the 'global demos' as a whole."[27] A global democratic institution is required to legitimately demarcate the boundaries of the territorial states system's constituent units.

Still other thinkers appeal to the possibility of nonterritorial, "polycentric" forms of political order. Such political authorities might be issue specific or functionally delineated and exhibit territorial overlap with one another. Archon Fung has argued for a system of multiple, overlapping memberships that applies not only to governments, but also to non-state associations and organizations (such as churches, corporations, and universities), and in which each specific issue and organization would have its own relevant voting public.[28] Niko Krisch defends a "pluralist" order of postnational law in which local, national, regional, and international authorities and networks regulate the same issues, competing with one another for jurisdiction.[29] Terry MacDonald argues for a global "stakeholder" democracy in which nongovernmental organizations, transnational corporations, and international organizations would be held to account by multiple overlapping democratic constituencies.[30]

A final proposal holds that "borders should generally be open and people should normally be free to leave their country of origin and settle in another."[31] Joseph Carens argues that a human right to immigrate is logically entailed by the domestic commitment to the right of free movement within states.[32] Kieran Oberman has likewise argued for a human right to immigrate on the basis that

---

[25] Goodin, "Enfranchising All Affected Interests, and Its Alternatives," *Philosophy & Public Affairs* 25, no. 1 (2007): 40–68.

[26] Abizadeh, "Democratic Theory and Border Coercion," *Political Theory* 36, no. 1 (2008): 46, and "On the Demos and Its Kin: Democracy, Nationality, and the Boundary Problem," *American Political Science Review* 106, no. 4 (2012): 121–30.

[27] Abizadeh, "Democratic Theory and Border Coercion," 49. See also Marchetti, *Global Democracy*, 81.

[28] Fung, "The Principle of Affected Interests: An Interpretation and Defense," in *Representation: Elections and Beyond*, edited by Rogers M. Smith and Jack H. Nagel (Philadelphia: University of Pennsylvania Press, 2013).

[29] Krisch, *Beyond Constitutionalism: The Pluralist Structure of International Law: The Pluralist Structure of International Law* (Oxford: Oxford University Press, 2010).

[30] MacDonald, *Global Stakeholder Democracy: Power and Representation Beyond Liberal States* (Oxford: Oxford University Press, 2008).

[31] Carens, *The Ethics of Immigration* (Oxford: Oxford University Press, 2013), 225.

[32] Carens, *The Ethics of Immigration*, 236–45.

people have a vital interest in being free to access the full range of existing "life options."³³ Open borders advocates do not necessarily dispute the division of the world into separate jurisdictions, but they do maintain that states' territorial rights should be significantly diminished compared to the current *status quo*.

Of course, these cosmopolitan institutional proposals seem politically unviable at present. But it would be misguided to dismiss these ideas as illusory or uninteresting simply because they are unachievable in current circumstances. An opponent of the states system can acknowledge that an alternative global arrangement may not be feasible right away: the territorial state is too deeply rooted and too difficult to transcend. Still, perhaps we should consider reorganization of our international system to be a valid long-term goal. After all, as our reflections on past political forms showed, there have been many far-reaching organizational transitions over the course of human history. The radical reorganization of our institutions might be worth pursuing, even if it is "a distant ideal that cannot be realized in the near future."³⁴ And reflecting on alternatives to the territorial states system allows us to gain an evaluative perspective on existing social arrangements that is itself important.

Faced with this systemic critique of the states system, noncosmopolitan thinkers (apart from liberal nationalists) have generally had little to say. As mentioned earlier, despite a long tradition in modern political philosophy of justifying the state's internal sovereignty, little has been said about the moral bases, if any, for the territorial states system as a whole. Most political theorists have instead adopted an *institutionally conservative* approach to this issue, taking current states and their boundaries "as given."³⁵ Commentators have often noted John Rawls's neglect of the sovereign state's boundaries, a neglect reflected in the opening assumption of *Theory of Justice* that the society for which principles of justice are to be constructed is a "closed system isolated from other societies," a structure "we enter only by birth and exit only by death."³⁶ Rawls simply sets aside all questions about how that society's boundaries might be properly constituted.³⁷

---

³³ Oberman, "Immigration as a Human Right," in *Migration in Political Theory: The Ethics of Movement and Membership*, edited by Sarah Fine and Lea Ypi (Oxford: Oxford University Press, 2016), 32–56.

³⁴ Laura Valentini, "No Global Demos, No Global Democracy? A Systemization and Critique," *Perspectives on Politics* 12, no. 4 (2014): 790.

³⁵ For defense of the institutionally conservative methodology, see Michael Blake, *Justice and Foreign Policy* (Oxford: Oxford University Press, 2013), 47.

³⁶ Rawls, *A Theory of Justice*, 2nd ed. (Cambridge, MA: Harvard University Press, 1999), 7; Rawls, *Justice as Fairness: A Restatement* (Cambridge, MA: Harvard University Press, 2001), 40. Both Moore, *A Political Theory of Territory* (Oxford: Oxford University Press, 2015) and A. John Simmons, *Boundaries of Authority* (Oxford: Oxford University Press, 2016), 8–9, call attention to Rawls's neglect of territorial boundary issues.

³⁷ While much of Rawls's work is consistent with institutional conservatism, important aspects of the *Law of Peoples* show that Rawls did not ignore boundary legitimacy completely. There he argues for "preserving significant room for the idea of a people's self-determination," and strongly criticizes external intervention into the affairs of decent peoples. Rawls, *The Law of Peoples* (Cambridge, MA: Harvard

To be sure, there is a commonsensical element to Rawls's institutional conservatism. In evaluating a political order, we do well to begin from the structures that now exist. Only then can we assess—with appropriate attention to empirical realities—whether there are strategies of action that might lead to normatively desirable reforms. Yet by presuming that existing boundaries are worthy of respect, the institutional conservative goes beyond this commonsense insight. For the institutional conservative, territorial states are simply *given to us* by history, and we must try to theorize justice, and implement it, within existing structures. What matters morally is that current states provide just rule for the populations and territories they now control. This approach accepts that the states system as a whole—as well as the boundaries within it—is (and can only be) shaped by historical processes beyond the domain of justice, including long-term historical forces of institutional selection, as well as more contingent events like conquest, settlement, and colonialism.

Yet the gravity of the moral problems highlighted by the cosmopolitan critique shows the need to address the territorial states system's justification, rather than simply assuming it as a background fact that unavoidably structures our world. This should lead us to abandon the institutionally conservative approach. By treating existing institutions as presumptively acceptable, institutional conservatism is overly biased in favor of the status quo. Perhaps the cost of reform gives us some reason to accept an arrangement simply because it is now in place, but this reason is weak, and it may not suffice to legitimate our acceptance of deeply inequitable institutions, as the territorial states system is increasingly alleged to be. Further, it is not obvious that the classic justifications of the state's internal sovereignty will suffice to justify its external boundary claims. States' claimed territorial rights impose burdens on outsiders, and the fact that a state provides just or beneficial governance to its members says nothing about the legitimacy of a given way of dividing the earth's spaces into autonomous territorial jurisdictions. Finally, the institutional conservative provides no principled way to resolve territorial disputes, while failing to acknowledge that the way we draw boundaries often determines substantive political outcomes, by specifying who gets a say in these outcomes. To address these questions, we instead need a theory that asks whether a system of territorially bounded political authorities can be justified in the first place, and if so, how we might properly demarcate geographical and membership boundaries within that system. This book offers such a theory.

Thus, I agree with cosmopolitan critics that our territorial states system should not be taken "as given," and indeed, that it cries out for moral justification. Unlike them, however, I believe central aspects of our current system can be defended (though I will also advocate important reforms to it). Significant moral values, in

---

University Press, 1999), 61 and 84. But whatever Rawls's views on boundary legitimacy might have been, it is certainly correct to say that the issue was never the central focus of his work.

my view, are served by organizing our political world as a structure of self-governing territorial units. Though I will offer a revisionist view of the nature and moral basis of territorial sovereignty in this book, I hold that some central structural tendencies of our states system are morally justified. Three core values, in my view, tell in favor of maintaining an international order of self-governing, spatially defined units demarcated by territorial boundaries, even were it one day to become politically feasible to change this.

The first core value is that of allowing people to use specific geographical places to realize the social, economic, and cultural practices they care about, free from interference, so long as they do not encroach on others' reciprocal rights to do likewise. This limited, "property-like" entitlement to use geographical space I call the *right of occupancy*. In my view, the right of occupancy provides us good reason for allocating political authority in a *spatial fashion*, a mode of political organization that is particularly distinctive of the territorial state by comparison with its rivals. A legitimate function of the international system is to specify and protect people's preinstitutional claims to specific places.

The second core value, *basic justice*, requires the existence of states with functioning legal systems, property and contract schemes, courts, police, and other institutions necessary for the specification, interpretation, and enforcement of individual rights. States are essential to securing justice among us: they are necessary to provide a unitary interpretation of rights that binds everyone, and to enforce those rights consistently with individuals' reciprocal independence from one another. There are important reasons—to do with the state's role in establishing clear definitions of property, contract, and tort—to believe that to carry out these tasks, states need to be territorially defined. Yet states also wield enormous power. To wield such power rightfully, the state must protect certain fundamental rights, including security, subsistence, core elements of personal autonomy, and deliberative freedom, for all its subjects.

While the second core value sees the state as necessary for basic justice, by itself it is not sufficient to decide whether to prefer a plurality of states to a single world state. It is the third core value, *collective self-determination*, that gives us moral reason to favor a system of states. I argue that to have a right to rule a population and territory, a state must represent its subjects' *shared political will*. A group shares a political will when they are jointly committed to a common political enterprise and to certain values and procedures by which they believe their enterprise should be structured. When members participate in a group's shared will, and government imposes laws and policies that reflect that will, individuals are ruled in a way that partly reflects their own priorities and judgments. Collective self-determination, on my account, serves individual interests, particularly interests in *self-direction*, in establishing social order through our own free agency, and *nonalienation*, in being governed in a manner that reflects our convictions about how society should be arranged. For that reason, where institutionally feasible and consistent with basic justice, groups with common commitments ought to be allowed to govern themselves. By guaranteeing self-determination, the territorial states system can protect people against alien domination, safeguarding their claim to live according to their own beliefs. This, I believe, is one of the most compelling arguments in its favor.

Of course, many will object to my language of "shared political will." All modern political communities feature deep and intractable political disagreements. Given this, can there be any such thing as a "shared political will?" While I will return to this objection later, it is important at the outset to distinguish three meanings of "shared will." A group might (i) share a political will with a certain substantive content—a will to enact certain laws or promote certain shared values. It is the existence of such a substantive shared will that critics contest. But a shared will could also take the form of (ii) a will to support certain political institutions (to recognize Parliament or the Constitution, say, as a source of valid law). A commitment to support institutions may also entail a commitment to the higher-order values that structure these institutions (e.g., a commitment to representative democracy, say, or to constitutional principles). This procedural will is more likely to be shared even among a group of people who have deep-seated substantive disagreements. Finally, even those who contest certain aspects of prevailing institutional arrangements (i.e., those who favor reforming the Constitution or instituting a presidential rather than a parliamentary system) may still (iii) share a will to associate politically with their fellow-citizens under *some* common set of institutions. Such a dissenter remains a willing member of the political community, who voluntarily accepts and complies with its decisions. So a shared will may take a thicker or thinner form. Still, as long as any of (i)–(iii) obtain, we can say of this group that they share a will to govern themselves together, and that it would be wrong, other things equal, for outsiders to interfere with their joint decisions.

The three core values of occupancy, basic justice, and collective self-determination that underpin the states system are not so many disparate considerations: instead, they are implications of a more fundamental natural duty of justice, which requires us to respect and protect individuals' *autonomy*. By "autonomy," I refer to the capacity to reflect upon, and to endorse or revise, one's own life-commitments for what one authentically judges to be good reasons, and to carry out these commitments in action. Each of the core values highlights a distinct institutional implication of autonomy. *Occupancy* stresses the way in which individuals' central life projects are often bound up with specific geographic locations, so that interference with their use and possession of these places undermines the lives people have built. *Basic justice* highlights core state protections necessary to guarantee individuals the ability to form, revise, and carry out self-endorsed commitments in central areas of their lives. And *collective self-determination* suggests that the process by which political institutions are imposed on subjects must respect their autonomy, ensuring that institutions properly reflect the values and priorities of those they govern. Because autonomy has these distinctive facets, I argue that our natural duty to respect and protect the autonomy of others is best fulfilled through a pluralistic and decentralized order of self-governing territorial units.

The three core values, in my view, show that our international system is not a mere historical contingency, but exhibits some structural tendencies that are morally justified, including its central institution of jurisdictional boundaries. I do not claim that our territorial system of states is the very best system we might have developed—indeed, I will advocate important reforms that I believe might bring us closer to a better world. But I do argue that it serves important human interests and should not be abandoned in favor of a cosmopolitan system of global governance. Because of the core values, an acceptable international system should allow political authority to be dispersed among (i) self-governing jurisdictional units that (ii) are spatially defined. Ideally, the current states system will continue to evolve in ways that maintain these features.

As noted, the view of territorial sovereignty I defend in this book is also a revisionist one. Once we understand the core values that best justify a system of territorial states, I believe that we will see reason to work for certain reforms to the sovereignty rights that states now claim under existing international law. As currently constituted, our international order serves the core values only imperfectly, and it ought to be regulated and reformed to better instantiate them. This leads me to propose important changes to states' sovereign prerogatives in the later sections of this book, particularly with respect to internal autonomy for political minorities, immigration, and natural resources.

First, I propose that states should be required to adopt a decentralized, pluralistic structure that facilitates self-determination for their indigenous peoples and various substate minorities. While self-determination is a cardinal principle of international law—one that I argue plays a crucial role in justifying a system of self-governing territorial units—our interstate order as it is currently constituted does not fully realize that principle. If the states system is to be brought into line with its legitimating ideals, then states must abandon a unitary structure. As I argue in Chapter 5, states' decisions about whether to grant self-governance to their minorities should not be seen as a purely internal matter. Instead, this is a subject of legitimate global concern, and the international community can intervene in proportionate ways to ensure that states recognize minority self-determination claims.

Second, I propose that states' territorial rights should be conceived in a less exclusionary fashion than they traditionally have been. On my view, states lack the discretionary right to exclude outsiders, at will, from accessing or settling on their territories, or sharing in the value of their natural resources. To justify exclusion, a state must show that (i) access for outsiders would significantly harm its inhabitants, and (ii) these outsiders lack any urgent interest in accessing the territory. Often, this justificatory burden cannot be met. Additionally, I argue that states have a duty to cooperate in establishing international institutions that can guarantee the fundamental territorial interests of outsiders who might otherwise be harmed by their territorial claims. So though the core values of my view do ground some territorial sovereignty rights, I hold these are less robust, and less exclusionary, than those that have traditionally been attributed to states.

Though the international order that is justified in this book shares certain elements with the status quo, then, it is not the territorial states system we actually have. In this respect, the book's normative position is compatible with the important changes to the structure of the world political and legal order embodied in the UN Charter and the Universal Declaration and subsequent human rights covenants. These changes had the effect of imposing some limits on the traditional rights of state sovereignty, and I will suggest that we should move further in this direction.

Can sovereignty be limited, in the manner I propose? Sovereignty is traditionally thought to have two dimensions. *Internal sovereignty* is a political community's right that its legal order be supreme within its territory. *External sovereignty* is a community's right to immunity from interference by outside powers. In assuming that sovereignty has limits, I am opposing a traditional view that conceives sovereignty as absolute, indivisible, and unqualified—a view that holds "sovereignty is about each state's doing entirely as its current government pleases."[38] But such a construal of sovereignty has never been plausible.

First, a legitimate state's internal sovereignty can only be conceived as limited. Territorial sovereignty is not tied to the notion—associated with early modern absolutists like Bodin and Hobbes—that sovereignty is located in a unitary ruler whose will cannot be bound by law.[39] To guarantee basic justice, a legitimate state's constitution should contain provisions to ensure the rule of law, including the separation of powers, checks and balances, and the protection of essential human rights.[40] Most modern representative democracies exhibit such self-limiting provisions, while remaining sovereign over their territories.

More central to this book is the state's external sovereignty—its immunity from unauthorized interference by outside agents with decision-making within its territory. But external sovereignty must also be conceived as limited. Though it recognizes states' "sovereign equality," the UN Charter also places states under duties to refrain from aggressive war and unauthorized intervention into other states' internal affairs. Indeed, only by imposing such duties can states' internal sovereignty be secured. These duties protect the sovereignty of states, but they also constrain

---

[38] Henry Shue, "Limiting Sovereignty," in *Humanitarian Intervention and International Relations*, edited by Jennifer Welsh (Oxford: Oxford University Press, 2004), 13.

[39] For discussion of the absolutist notion, see F. H. Hinsley, *Sovereignty* (Cambridge: Cambridge University Press, 1986), 121–5, 140–4; Stephen Krasner, *Sovereignty: Organized Hypocrisy* (Princeton: Princeton University Press, 1999), 11–12.

[40] On sovereignty's compatibility with constitutionalism, see Hinsley, *Sovereignty*, 156–7; Jean Cohen, *Globalization and Sovereignty: Rethinking Legality, Legitimacy, and Constitutionalism* (Cambridge: Cambridge University Press, 2012), 30.

their activities.[41] So if external sovereignty is to be a recognized right, it must be limited, at a minimum by duties to respect the reciprocal sovereignty of other states. Thus, as Daniel Philpott argues, "a holder of sovereignty need not be sovereign over all matters."[42] Parts III and IV of this book will propose additional limits to a state's external sovereignty, in the form of distributive constraints on state territory, duties to refugees, and duties of environmental justice.

I should stress several qualifications to my argument. First, in defending core aspects of the territorial states system, I am not claiming that the four problems highlighted by cosmopolitan critics are not genuine problems needing to be solved. To the contrary: I believe there is an urgent need to create authoritative global institutions to address climate change, refugee resettlement, interstate war, and other issues of global concern. Yet there is an important question about how these institutions should be designed: should they build on territorial states or try to radically transform them? In general, I believe that such solutions should place secondary responsibilities on states to cooperate in international bodies that can coordinate a response to common concerns. This institutional response may be more fragile and less successful at addressing global issues than a sweeping reform of the states system might be. But while drastically reconfiguring the states system may succeed at addressing the four problems mentioned earlier, it is my view that it would throw up other, worse moral difficulties. Thus, the core values protected by territorial sovereignty justify addressing these problems in a more indirect way than might otherwise be desirable.

Second, to guard against misunderstanding, I should specify that in using the term "state" in this book, I do not imply that an institution that qualifies as "a state" need be organized along the lines of the Weberian, bureaucratic states we are familiar with today. By "state," I mean a public-law making authority with the power of enforcement. To qualify as a "state," on my view, an institution must feature (i) binding collective rule setting and (ii) the ability to enforce its determinations in case of disputes. But traditional indigenous decision-making procedures, operating by compromise and consensus, would count as "states" on this definition. So too would local self-organized schemes that typically operate on a much smaller scale than nation-states.[43] From now on, I will use the term "state" to refer to any institution that meets the above conditions. Unlike some critics of bureaucratic states, however, I believe that it is not impossible for a large, impersonal institution to exhibit respect for norms of occupancy and basic justice and to guarantee collective self-determination.

---

[41] Shue, "Limiting Sovereignty," 15.
[42] Philpott, *Revolutions in Sovereignty* (Princeton: Princeton University Press, 2010), 19.
[43] For one view of local "common pool resource schemes," see Elinor Ostrom, *Governing the Commons: The Evolution of Institutions for Collective Action* (Cambridge: Cambridge University Press, 1990).

Third, I accept that modern states do not have an unblemished history with respect to the core values. Critics of the state have often highlighted that its establishment involved acts of violence, colonization, conquest, displacement, and cultural homogenization that were at odds with these values. These critics stress that our modern interstate system and the configuration of states within it is in large part the product of European colonialism.[44] Much of my discussion will be concerned with how we should respond to such past acts. Still, I do not think this history makes it impossible for modern states to be reformed to live up to the core values here and now. Sometimes an institution that was started in an initially unjust and illegitimate way can be restructured, over time, to render it morally acceptable. My account focuses on the changes that would be necessary to make modern states justifiable despite their unjust history.

Fourth, as already noted, I am not arguing that the three core values are sufficient to justify all the territorial prerogatives currently claimed by existing states. Instead, I offer a *reformist* account of territorial sovereignty. The moral values that best justify a system of self-governing territorial units, in my view, also demand that territorial sovereignty take a more modest form than has traditionally been conceived. Though important moral purposes are indeed served by a states system, not all extant sovereignty rights are equally well-justified in terms of these purposes. States' territorial rights should be seen as subject to modification in light of our best interpretation of international ideals, and the later chapters of the book propose several such modifications.

Finally, I am not arguing against global distributive justice. While I reject theories (such as global equality of resources or welfare) whose implementation would require overriding the three core values, many accounts of global justice are quite consonant with my views, and indeed, are plausibly required for a system of states to fully realize the core values. Though I do not attempt to develop a theory of global distributive justice in this book, let me outline five global justice duties that I see as compatible with my argument:

(1) *A Duty to Eradicate Global Poverty.* Individuals around the globe should reach a threshold where they have the material resources necessary to lead a decent life and to establish just political institutions.[45] This is a sufficientarian duty to assist "burdened" societies facing unfavorable domestic conditions.[46]

---

[44] Catherine Lu, *Justice and Reconciliation in World Politics* (Cambridge: Cambridge University Press, 2017), 267–9.

[45] Miller, *National Responsibility and Global Justice* (Oxford: Oxford University Press, 2007), 52. There is broad consensus on such a duty, including Blake, "Distributive Justice, State Coercion, and Autonomy," *Philosophy & Public Affairs* 30, no. 3 (2001): 257–96; Pablo Gilabert, *From Global Poverty to Global Equality* (Oxford: Oxford University Press, 2012); Mathias Risse, *On Global Justice* (Cambridge, MA: Harvard University Press, 2012); Andrea Sangiovanni, "Global Justice, Reciprocity, and the State," *Philosophy & Public Affairs* 35, no. 1 (2007): 3–39; and others.

[46] Rawls, *The Law of Peoples*, 118.

(2) *A Duty to Ensure Fair Terms of Economic Cooperation.* Many theorists argue that international interdependence (e.g., practices of trade or foreign investment, and the new international organizations that regulate these practices) widens our duties of distributive justice.[47] International economic cooperation generates requirements of socioeconomic fairness analogous to, but distinct from, the requirements of social justice that apply within domestic states. This includes principles regulating relative inequalities in the distribution of goods and resources whose production and distribution depends upon the global market. Participation in the global economy generates responsibilities to ensure the benefits and burdens created by international trade and investment are justly distributed, and that all states have a fair opportunity to develop.[48] This requires reforming international organizations and instituting redistributive transfers to share the gains of global capitalism more equitably.

(3) *A Duty to Ensure Fair Background Conditions for Self-Determination.* Gross inequalities of power and wealth among states may undermine the conditions for self-determination. These inequalities allow wealthy states, multinational corporations, and international organizations to exercise undue power over poorer countries' internal policies, undermining their ability to shape their own futures.[49] Supranational regulatory institutions are plausibly required to forestall these interferences, securing an international order that safeguards collective self-government for all.

(4) *A Duty to Contribute to Morally Mandatory Collective Action.* Many issues facing the world today can only be addressed through coordinated global action. Climate change and refugee crises are two of the most salient. States and their citizens have a duty to establish and sustain international institutions that can mount an effective response to these problems.

(5) *Duties of Corrective Justice.* Theorists of race and imperialism have long emphasized the contribution that economic exploitation, forced labor, and political domination of the Global South have historically made to the development of global capitalism and to the wealth of industrialized

---

[47] Beitz, *Political Theory and International Relations*, Part III; Joshua Cohen and Charles Sabel, "Extra Rempublicam Nulla Justitia?" *Philosophy & Public Affairs* 34, no. 2 (2006): 147–75; A. J. Julius, "Nagel's Atlas," *Philosophy & Public Affairs* 34, no. 2 (2006): 176–92. There is also some textual support for a duty of this sort in Rawls, *The Law of Peoples*, 42.

[48] For one proposal of what these duties might amount to, see Aaron James, *Fairness in Practice* (Oxford: Oxford University Press, 2012). For another discussion of the distribution of the gains from global trade, see Risse, *On Global Justice*, chs. 14 and 18.

[49] For proposals of this sort, see Adom Getachew, *Worldmaking after Empire* (Princeton University Press, 2019); Miller, *National Responsibility and Self-Determination*, 76; Miriam Ronzoni, "The Global Order: A Case of Background Injustice?" *Philosophy & Public Affairs* 37, no. 3 (2009): 229–56.

countries. Reparations and structural reforms to overcome these practices are necessary to create the conditions for a just world order, and for formerly subject peoples to have genuine chance to determine their own destiny.[50]

Taken together, these five duties add up to a demanding conception of socioeconomic justice between countries, with several reasons for supporting regulation and economic redistribution at the global level. These distributive duties, moreover, are not extraneous supplements to a theory of territorial sovereignty: instead, their fulfillment is plausibly seen as a condition for a territorial states system to be morally justified. By dispersing power in a pluralistic and decentralized way, the international system generates predictable risks, and states must address these risks for this system to be reasonably acceptable to those who live within it. Hence, this book is not a critique of global distributive justice as such, or of all versions of a cosmopolitan political program. Though I do not accept that the requirements of justice between societies are the same as the demands of justice within them, I believe that there are far-reaching duties of global justice and that implementing them requires significant reforms to the international order.

Yet there is a distinct, and more radical, strand of cosmopolitanism that places the normative presuppositions of the modern states system itself into question, critiquing boundaries and political membership as "morally arbitrary."[51] For these thinkers, the division of the world into a plurality of states is an obstacle to justice. By assigning people at birth to states that possess substantial authority over what goes on within the territories they govern, on this view, the territorial states system shapes people's life prospects, their aspirations, and their relationships in unjust ways. I disagree: in my view, the territorial states system instead protects moral values we have reason to care about and to preserve. If this book's central argument is correct, the institution of territorial boundaries is *not* morally arbitrary, since there are important moral reasons for favoring an international order that is structured in this way. But my argument against the radical critique of boundaries and membership does not mean I deny the attraction of more moderate forms of cosmopolitanism, many of which highlight genuine and pressing problems and propose progressive forms of international organization that might ameliorate these problems.

---

[50] See Frantz Fanon, *The Wretched of the Earth* (New York: Grove Press, 1963), 52–62; Walter Johnson, "To Remake the World: Slavery, Racial Capitalism, and Justice," *Boston Review*. February 20, 2018. See also Daniel Butt, *Rectifying International Injustice* (Oxford: Oxford University Press, 2009); Lu, *Justice and Reconciliation in World Politics*.

[51] See, among others, Beitz, *Political Theory and International Relations*, 179; Simon Caney, *Justice Beyond Borders* (Oxford: Oxford University Press, 2005), 107; Thomas Pogge, *Realizing Rawls* (Ithaca: Cornell University Press, 1989), 254; Philip Cole, *Philosophies of Exclusion* (Edinburgh: Edinburgh University Press, 2000), 5–6; Philippe van Parijs, "International Distributive Justice," in *The Blackwell Companion to Political Philosophy*, edited by Robert Goodin, Philip Pettit, and Thomas Pogge (Oxford: Blackwell, 2007).

1.3 Existing States and Their Current Boundaries

Suppose for a moment that the three core values defended in this book do justify our endorsement of some central features of the territorial states system. How might a state demonstrate a right to control a population and geographical area within that system, especially in the face of challenges from foreign powers or separatist groups who dispute its title? This second question does not concern the general legitimacy of the territorial state, but rather asks how a *particular* state might go about justifying a claim to this or that *particular* territory.[52] This too seems a difficult issue. After all, few states can show a "clean" historical title to their land. States have gained territory largely through unjust processes, including dispossession, dynastic union, conquest, settlement, and colonial rule. So do current states have valid claims to rule the territories and populations they now control? What could ground such claims?

To see how challenging this question can be, consider the case of Poland. From its first recorded mention as a political entity in the tenth century, Poland became the spatially largest state in Europe by 1492, covering 435,547 square miles, with 11 million inhabitants.[53] Yet after partitions by Austria, Prussia, and Russia—in 1773, 1793, and 1795, respectively—Poland vanished from the world map, not to be resurrected until after the First World War. Following a brief interlude as an independent republic, it was annexed again during the Second World War. Poland's territory underwent reconfiguration following the peace in 1945, and its borders have remained stable since. But looking back through all these historical vicissitudes, as Norman Davies puts it, "it is impossible to identify any fixed territorial base which has been permanently, exclusively, and inalienably, Polish."[54]

Let me zoom in on the most recent of these many reconfigurations, during the Second World War. By the end of the war, Poland's territory had been moved about 150 miles to the west of where it was situated in 1939. The Polish government also ruled a society with a transformed demography and social structure, in which almost all its former Jewish, German, and Ukrainian populations had been eliminated.[55] In the space of just 6 years, nearly half the prewar Polish population was killed or expelled.[56]

These dramatic changes were the result of Nazi Germany's war aims, which involved the extermination or redistribution of Poland's inhabitants, and the

---

[52] For similar distinctions between the general justification of territorial rights and the claims of particular states to particular territories, see Simmons, "On the Territorial Rights of States," *Philosophical Issues* 11, no. 1 (2001): 304; Olivero Angeli, *Cosmopolitanism, Self-Determination, and Territory* (New York: Palgrave Macmillan, 2015), 15.

[53] Norman Davies, *God's Playground: A History of Poland* (New York: Columbia University Press, 2005), 23.

[54] Davies, *God's Playground*, 24.

[55] Davies, *Heart of Europe: The Past in Poland's Present* (Oxford: Oxford University Press, 2001), 71.

[56] Mark Mazower, *Dark Continent* (New York: Random House, 1998), 218.

settlement of millions of Germans in former Polish territory. A network of concentration camps was established to liquidate Poland's Jewish population. Following the war, even those Jews who had managed to survive for the most part did not try return to their homes and villages, which had generally been confiscated in any case; instead, they fled to Palestine, the United States, or Western Europe under the auspices of Zionist organizations. This meant Poland lost virtually its entire Jewish population, formerly the world's second largest. The Nazi plan for Poles was that they were either to be Germanized—to serve as a useful labor force for the Reich—or expelled further east. The Polish intelligentsia and political leadership were murdered, and less prominent Poles were slated to be removed from their homes to make way for new German colonists. These resettlement efforts briefly got underway in 1942–1943, before being partially halted to stem the Soviet advance.

Following its victory, the Soviet Union then implemented its own plans for reconfiguring Polish territory and demography. The USSR annexed what had previously been Poland's Eastern provinces—including major centers like Lviv and Vilnius—and expelled 2 million Polish-speakers west. In 1945, the Allies compensated Poland for its territorial loss by granting it the formerly German territories of Silesia and Pomerania. The settlement at Yalta sanctioned the expulsion of nearly all ethnic Germans within Poland's newly configured borders, in a process that involved widespread brutality and confiscations of property. By 1950, about 7 million ethnic Germans had been forced to leave. Many of their farms and houses were taken over by Poles who had previously been removed from the Soviet annexed areas further east. Between the expelled Germans, the transplanted Poles, and the surviving Jews scrambling to find new homes, the end of World War II saw one of the largest population movements in history. As Mark Mazower highlights, "in the summer of 1945 the roads of Europe were packed with long lines of civilians straggling . . . in all directions."[57] Hundreds of thousands of people died during these exchanges.

The Polish case shines a spotlight on the brutal processes through which territorial boundaries have been established. Poland is not especially exceptional: nearly any other region of the world would provide material for a similar story. Consider the United States: much of its land was acquired from Native Americans by force and fraud. It also annexed the Republic of Texas in 1845, captured the Southwest from Mexico in 1848, purchased Alaska from Russia in 1867, and acquired Hawaii, Puerto Rico, and Guam in various colonizing ventures in the 1890s. If one looks closely, nearly every existing state has established its boundaries through violent conquest, expulsion, or fraud. Given this, do existing states like Poland or the United States have any *moral right* to their current territories? If the processes

---

[57] Mazower, *Dark Continent*, 215.

that gave rise to existing boundaries involved such disquieting events, why not redraw them?[58]

Three extremely common challenges to current boundaries derive from *colonial settlement, conquest,* and *separatism*. First, consider colonial settlement, which often involves expulsion or dispossession of prior inhabitants. In 1838, US troops forcibly removed the Cherokees from their ancestral homeland in Georgia, and relocated them to Indian Territory (current-day Oklahoma). Their previous homes, lands, and businesses in Georgia were reallocated to white settlers in a land lottery. Though the Cherokee Removal occurred long ago, there are several more recent similar cases, including the expulsions in Poland just detailed, and the displacement of Palestinians in 1948, at the moment of Israel's creation. Projects of colonial settlement that do not involve expulsion but still subject prior occupants to foreign rule are also quite common, including the French settlement of Algeria, the ongoing Han Chinese settlement in Tibet, and Jewish settlement in the West Bank. Can states legitimately claim territory acquired through colonial settlement and/or expulsion?

A second challenge comes from *conquest*, including but not limited to colonial conquest. In 1893, a group of American plantation owners—backed by a shipload of US Marines—overthrew the Hawaiian monarchy and imprisoned its queen. Their coup d'état was precipitated by a proposed Constitution that would have strengthened the monarchy and weakened the power of American business elites. Five years after this coup, Hawaiian territory was legally annexed to the United States. Similar stories might be told about the Scramble for Africa, or the recent Russian annexation of Crimea. Should conquered, annexed, or colonized territories be restored to independence?

Finally, challenges to the state's control over territory do not come only from the past. They are also voiced by disaffected groups in the present. Secessionist groups—including popular regional parties in places like Scotland, Catalonia, or Quebec—challenge the state's control over the regions they occupy. Can the state legitimately claim authority over such groups? If separatists seek to appropriate part of the state's territory to found a new political unit, can the state prevent them from doing so? Might we sometimes be required to redraw state boundaries in the face of separatist challenges, or to create new internal autonomy arrangements?

Despite their often-violent history, I believe that current boundaries can sometimes be given a moral justification. This book articulates criteria that can guide a response to the challenges of colonial settlement, conquest, and separatism. I hold

---

[58] One might object that redrawing boundaries can only occur through violence. But peaceful boundary reconfigurations have often occurred, including, inter alia, the secession of Norway from Sweden in 1905, the 1936 US Indian Reorganization Act granting partial sovereignty to Native Americans, the 1993 dissolution of Czechoslovakia, and some cases of decolonization. Recent referendums in Quebec, Scotland, and Catalonia raise the possibility of future peaceful boundary reconfigurations.

that an existing state has a right to rule its current territory and population if it properly lives up to the three core values I outlined in the last section. To do so, a state must satisfy the following conditions:

(1) *Rightful Occupancy*. First, the state's inhabitants must have a moral claim to occupy the geographical space it governs. I explain in subsequent chapters how such claims can sometimes be established in the face of an unjust history, and why rightful occupants must comply with a *fair use proviso* that respects others' interests in the earth.

(2) *Basic Justice*. Second, the state should effectively implement a system of law in the area, which protects the basic rights of its own subjects and respects the rights of outsiders; and

(3) *Self-Determination*. Third, the state must represent the shared will of a significant majority of its rightful occupants, under conditions where those who dissent from this shared will lack any right to an institutional alternative. Again, "a shared will," as I define it, is, at a minimum, a commitment to associate together politically, usually accompanied by a commitment to support specific institutions. It need not extend to a shared commitment to enact specific laws or common values.

A state that satisfies these three criteria, in my view, has *legitimate territorial jurisdiction*. Such a state has a permission to govern its constituents and territory, as well as an immunity, vis-à-vis potential competitor organizations (domestic or foreign), from interfering with its rule or attempting to reconfigure its territorial boundaries.

It is important to stress that a state can be *justified* in ruling a territory and population *pro tempore*, even while lacking legitimate territorial jurisdiction. If an institution is the only available means for providing decent rule to a population, or if reconfiguring its boundaries would jeopardize urgent interests or entail unreasonably high costs, then that organization may be justified in governing a particular territory and its population on a temporary basis.[59] Occupying forces, humanitarian interveners, or minimally just states that lack legitimate territorial jurisdiction fall within this category. But a merely justified state lacks any rights against replacement by a rival regime or against future boundary reconfiguration(s) that might better satisfy the above three criteria.

---

[59] Several theorists have argued for a weak notion of political legitimacy as a liberty to exercise coercive power, which does not correlate with obligations on subjects to refrain from competing with the state's enforcement or to obey its directives. My use of the phrase "justified rule" is meant to capture this weaker concept. A state may have a liberty to exercise coercive power without having a right against interference on the part of outsiders or insiders who could potentially establish an alternative regime. Arthur Applbaum, "Legitimacy without the Duty to Obey," *Philosophy & Public Affairs* 38, no. 3 (2010): 215–39; Allen Buchanan, "Political Legitimacy and Democracy," *Ethics* 112, no. 4 (2002): 689–719.

I also argue that even states *satisfying* these three criteria possess only *limited* rights to control their borders and to profit from their natural resources. In Chapter 6, I show that there is a strong right to relocate for people whose fundamental territorial interests, connected to the three core values, are threatened. This relocation right functions as a proviso on the state's territorial holdings and may sometimes require redistributing territory away from historic homeland groups. Chapter 7 argues that states have only a *conditional* right to exclude would-be migrants whose fundamental territorial interests are not threatened. To be justified in limiting immigration, the state must show that migrants' settlement would significantly harm its existing inhabitants. Finally, in Chapter 8, I contend that citizens do not own the natural resources situated in their territory, and that they have enforceable obligations to co-manage certain resources to address urgent problems like climate change. Hence, my view of territorial sovereignty is a revisionist one: to a significant degree, my theory revises the territorial prerogatives traditionally attributed to states.

1.4 Plan of the Book

Part I of the book develops my account of the territorial state-system's first core value, *occupancy rights*. I believe the state's territorial sovereignty rests in part on a prior "property-like" entitlement to the area it governs. But this prior entitlement does not belong to the state itself. Though states exercise rights over particular spaces, they do so on behalf of another party. It is the state's inhabitants who are the underlying possessors of rights to their geographical area. The state gets its right to territory indirectly, as an agent of its members, who hold what I call *occupancy rights* in these spaces. As I explain further in Chapter 3, I conceive occupancy rights as *use-rights* that are compatible with common ownership of our shared earth. An occupancy right is a preinstitutional claim of those who do not unjustly inhabit a place to reside there permanently; to make use of the area for valued social, cultural, and economic practices; not to be expelled or removed; and to return if occupants leave temporarily or are wrongly dispossessed. Only if the citizens represented by a state rightfully occupy their geographical space does their state have legitimate jurisdiction over it. Part I of the book develops this idea of occupancy rights, their grounding, and limits in more detail.

As I conceive it, occupancy shares some features of a property right. For that reason, the book engages with foundational questions in property theory, including the question of whether unilateral appropriation can create land claims that others are obliged to respect, and the question of how to specify appropriate distributive limits to territorial occupancy. This link between property and state sovereignty might seem strange to contemporary ears, but it was a commonplace of early modern political thought. The account of occupancy I defend in Part I is therefore developed in part in dialogue with theorists from this period, including Grotius, Pufendorf, Locke, and Kant. Part I of the book also spells out the implications of my theory for current boundaries, by considering cases of colonial settlement, expulsion, and dispossession. Once wrongful settlement or expulsion has occurred, can states legitimately claim territory acquired through these unjust processes? Should countries ever take steps to *undo* settlement and dispossession by requiring settlers to repatriate or granting their expelled victims the right to return? Finally, does the case for correcting these wrongs retain force indefinitely or is it only time limited?

Part II of the book develops my account of the states system's second and third core values, *basic justice* and *collective self-determination*. Most traditional liberal theories hold that the justice of a state's institutions suffices to ground a right to govern its population and territory. I argue that these theories face an important challenge: they are unable to distinguish between domestic and foreign rule, and they may even license benign colonialism. I argue that we should revise these theories, recognizing the importance of a second dimension to state legitimacy. The state's right to rule depends not only on its provision of justice to its population but also on its fulfilling their interest in being the "authors" or "makers" of their institutions. To be legitimate, state institutions must express the population's willing engagement in a joint political venture.

This account of self-determination, which I call the *political autonomy theory*, draws in important ways on Kant's argument that the rules governing our collective political life ought not to be enforced *unilaterally*. Kant instead holds that to have the right to make and enforce law and policy for a population, the state must represent its subjects' *omnilateral will*, that is, their shared judgments about how, and by whom, they should be governed. I suggest that we should understand an omnilateral will as an *actual* popular will. To legitimately enforce law and policy on behalf of a population, a state needs to reflect its people's shared intention to cooperate to establish justice through specific institutions. A group of individuals who share such intentions constitutes a collectively self-determining people.

Collective self-determination matters, on my view, because it can afford individuals an important form of autonomy within the coercive institutions that rule them. The key idea behind my theory is that state coercion potentially threatens a basic moral claim to lead our lives in accordance with our own evaluative and moral judgments. The importance of political autonomy, I believe, is particularly clear in cases of *alien* coercion, that is, coercion that bears no relationship to the goals or purposes of those subjected to it. When one is pervasively subject to alien coercion, substantial aspects of one's life can come to seem hostile, threatening, and beyond one's grasp. For this reason, I think individuals have a strong interest in avoiding alien coercion. Though political autonomy is ultimately an interest of individuals, I argue that it can be furthered through the individual's participation in a collectively self-determining group. When an individual intentionally participates in a self-determining group, the "alien" quality of government coercion is at least partially neutralized because the individual shares a commitment to common purposes underwriting this coercion. It is because of this connection to individual interests that collective self-determination is morally important.

I also address a key worry about political autonomy: it is unrealistic to think that all citizens in a territory will unanimously affirm their membership. My response to this worry is that we should not aim at complete unanimity, since there are compelling reasons for discounting nonunanimity in some cases. Exploring these reasons, I argue for a novel, *endogenous* approach to the question of "who are the people?" On the endogenous approach, there is no Archimedean point for delineating "peoples" outside our existing structure of political institutions. Instead, we delineate a new "people"—when we do—because we believe that renegotiating our institutional arrangements will afford greater political autonomy for some individuals at reasonable cost to other values. The "people" is thus a mutable entity, and drawing and redrawing its boundaries is a process that will be ongoing. I conclude by assessing what my account of self-determination implies for the rights of states to their current boundaries. On my view, persistently alienated internal minorities will often have moral claims to collective self-governance. The international community should do more to recognize those claims, by incentivizing states to negotiate autonomy arrangements for their minorities.

Parts III and IV of the book then apply these foundational ideas to generate an account of states' *morally justified exclusionary rights*. My approach to theorizing this issue is to draw on the core international values defended in Parts I and II. I ask: which exclusionary sovereignty rights would be granted under a system of international rules narrowly tailored to safeguard these core values? I suggest that the exclusionary rights that can plausibly be justified on the basis of the three core values are more limited than has traditionally been thought. Examining the case of future climate refugees, I argue that states may have a duty to redistribute territory to migrants who relocate out of necessity, affording political autonomy and cultural rights to groups not previously associated with a particular area. I also contend that states have extensive duties to allow settlement by immigrants whose fundamental interests are not threatened in their home country, so long as prior inhabitants are not significantly harmed by the influx. Finally, I argue that citizens lack any exclusive property entitlement to the full value of their natural resources. This part of the book takes seriously the objections pressed by cosmopolitan critics and attempts to show how we can respond to many of their concerns while still defending an international order composed of a plurality of self-governing territorial units.

1.5 Alternative Views

In international law, states' territorial sovereignty has traditionally been grounded in a principle of effective control. Though other principles such as discovery, conquest, and cession have been recognized in earlier eras, since the nineteenth century, sovereignty over territory has most often been acquired simply by effectively administering it.[60] Effective control is a relative concept: when two states press competing claims to sovereignty, it is necessary to decide which of the two claimants has done more to exercise sovereign governance over the territory. An organization gains territorial rights when it has been the most effective at physically controlling the territory and exercising governmental functions within it.

Yet the effectiveness standard is unsatisfying, since it permits territorial disputes to be settled by sheer force. Whichever power can maintain physical control for a sufficiently long period of time gains title to the territory. As Leif Wenar emphasizes, such a rule allows "might to make right."[61] Effectiveness eradicates the distinction between violent conquest and legitimate rule. When there is a discrepancy between the law of territorial jurisdiction and the "facts on the ground," effectiveness holds that we should adjust the law to fit the facts, rather than vice versa.[62]

Because this seems to make a mockery of rights, political theorists have proposed moral criteria for territorial sovereignty that go beyond effectiveness. While I say more about these alternative views later in the book, it is helpful to begin by differentiating my own theory from three other approaches. While I reject each of these as comprehensive theories of territory, my own account has learned much from other views, as should gradually become clear. At this stage, I briefly introduce these alternatives, returning to them in greater depth later. My departures from each alternative will be justified as the book proceeds.

The first view I call the *functionalist theory*. This theory holds that that the state has a right to its territory insofar as it actually rules an area and population, and its rule is sufficiently just. This view is a straightforward extension of liberal concerns with the justification of state power to individuals. Going back to Hobbes, Locke, and Kant, a traditional argument for the state has been that owing to problems with an anarchic state of nature, states are necessary to specify, adjudicate, and securely enforce individuals' moral entitlements. So long as an existing state provides an adequate level of protection for these entitlements, its use of political power is justified. The functionalist theory simply extends this account of internal sovereignty to issues of boundaries and territory.[63] While the functionalist tradition has a distinguished history, including luminaries like Hume and Sidgwick, Allen Buchanan is perhaps the most prominent functionalist in recent literature.[64]

---

[60] Peter Malanczuk, *Akehurst's Modern Introduction to International Law* (London: Routledge, 1997); Malcolm Shaw, *International Law* (Cambridge: Cambridge University Press, 2008), 487–552.
[61] Wenar, *Blood Oil* (Oxford: Oxford University Press, 2016), 67–79.
[62] See Malanczuk, *Akehurst's Modern Introduction to International Law*, 152–3.
[63] Simmons, *Boundaries of Authority*, 101.
[64] David Hume, *A Treatise of Human Nature*, edited by L. A. Selby-Bigge and P. H. Nidditch (Oxford: Clarendon Press, 1978), 534–67; Henry Sidgwick, *The Elements of Politics* (London: MacMillan, 1908). Other functionalists include the early Beitz, Blake, and Jeremy Waldron. See Beitz, *Political Theory and International Relations*, Part II; Blake, "Territorial Rights: In Defense of the Naïve View," presented colloquium paper, Eastern-APA, Washington University in St. Louis, 2014; Jeremy

He argues that a state is morally justified in exercising political power over a population and territory if it "(1) does a credible job of protecting at least the most basic human rights of all those over whom it wields power and (2) it provides this protection through processes, policies, and actions that themselves respect human rights."[65] To this core theory of state legitimacy, Buchanan also adds a "Non-Usurpation" requirement, holding that "an entity is not legitimate if it comes into being by destroying or displacing a legitimate state by a serious act of injustice."[66]

I agree with many elements of the functionalist theory. Like the functionalist, I demand that a legitimate state should protect a set of basic human rights. Yet in Chapter 4, I argue that a pure functionalist theory has difficulty explaining why a state may claim jurisdiction only over a specific territory and its population. So long as a state protects human rights, or provides reasonably just governance, why can't it extend its boundaries simply by extending its effective control? An important worry about the functionalist approach, then, is that it may legitimize benign colonialism. Its theory of state legitimacy is retrospective: it tells us that if a sufficiently just state exerts control, it has a right to rule, but it cannot explain which areas and populations that state should govern.

Buchanan attempts to avoid these difficulties through the addition of a "Non-Usurpation requirement." But this requirement is not based in his human rights account of legitimacy, and it is unclear to what additional value(s) it appeals. Unlike a pure functionalist view, my account incorporates rights of occupancy and self-determination that allow me to explain the proper boundaries of the legitimate state in a less ad hoc manner. To explain why usurpation is wrong, in my view, we need to invoke values beyond human rights protection, and my theory gives due weight to these values.

A second alternative is the *proprietarian* view. This view holds that like individual property owners, states have historical claims to territory that can be traced back to originally just acts of acquisition. Most proprietarians draw inspiration from Locke's political philosophy, which holds that individuals can acquire private property rights through first labor in a state of nature, and can transfer aspects of these rights to the state.[67] By consenting to form a political society, on the Lockean view, property owners give up certain jurisdictional incidents included within their

---

Waldron, "Two Conceptions of Self-Determination," in *The Philosophy of International Law*, edited by John Tasioulas and Samantha Besson (Oxford: Oxford University Press, 2010). There are also many *hybrid* views of territorial rights that give at least some weight to functionalist concerns, but combine them with other considerations. These views include my own theory; Andrew Altman and Christopher Wellman, *A Liberal Theory of International Justice* (Oxford: Oxford University Press, 2009); Cara Nine, *Global Justice and Territory* (Oxford: Oxford University Press, 2012).

[65] Buchanan, *Justice, Legitimacy, and Self-Determination* (Oxford: Oxford University Press, 2004), 247.
[66] Buchanan, *Justice, Legitimacy, and Self-Determination*, 264–5.
[67] Simmons is a prominent defender of the proprietarian account. See Simmons, "On the Territorial Rights of States" and *Boundaries of Authority*. My discussion here draws on remarks from my earliest paper on this topic, "Why Do States Have Territorial Rights?" *International Theory* 1, no. 2 (2009): 185–213, in which I criticized the Lockean view.

natural property.⁶⁸ One plausible view of this process understands it by analogy to a land covenant in modern law.⁶⁹ In covenanting to set up a state, initial contractors attach permanent conditions to any later use of their land. Future users must "take it with the condition it is under; that is, of submitting to the government of the commonwealth, under whose jurisdiction it is . . ."⁷⁰ So individual consent to establish political society, on this view, at the same time generates the state's jurisdiction over territory: the state has a claim to jurisdiction over that land (and only that land) that is owned by its consenting citizens.

There is a variety of familiar criticisms of the proprietarian account.⁷¹ Since it is possible for some of the individuals occupying a territorial space not to consent, the state's territory might take on a "patchwork" quality, with holes formed by the property of those who refuse subjection. Further, since no current state's territorial claims have been legitimated through the agreement of original appropriators, the proprietarian account implies that no current state has territorial rights.⁷² Finally, the Lockean theory of territory is only as convincing as the account of strong natural rights to property on which it rests. Most contemporary theorists hold instead that property rights are conventional.

While I am sympathetic to many of these criticisms, I argue in Part I of this book that proprietarian views contain an important kernel of truth. Proprietarians have one crucial insight: that we must begin from some preinstitutional claim to space if we are to justify the state's right to its territory. Some account must be given of the basis on which a set of people have a privileged claim to live within a particular area, and why their state should exercise political rule over that area. I call this the question of *foundational title*. I also believe the proprietarian is correct in thinking that however we choose to characterize a state's foundational title, it has "property-like" qualities. There are striking similarities between the rules governing territorial membership, on the one hand, and the rules governing property, on the other.⁷³ Much like property rules, territorial boundaries create and protect title bearers, establishing spatial demarcations backed by coercion or force. These are rights over *material resources*, and they raise important questions of acquisition and distribution. While my account of foundational title differs from the proprietarian one, I have nonetheless benefited from their key insight about the need for such a theory.

Let me now turn to the third family of competing views, which I call *collectivist theories*. These theories see territorial rights as accruing in the first instance not to

---

⁶⁸ Locke, *Second Treatise of Government*, edited by Donald Cress (Indianapolis: Hackett, 1980), 64.
⁶⁹ Beitz, "Tacit Consent and Property Rights," *Political Theory* 8, no. 4 (1980): 487–502.
⁷⁰ Locke, *Second Treatise of Government*, 64.
⁷¹ I articulated many of these objections in "Why Do States Have Territorial Rights?" For similar criticisms, see Moore, *A Political Theory of Territory*, 19–21.
⁷² Simmons recognizes and embraces this conclusion. See "On the Territorial Rights of States," 315.
⁷³ Ayelet Shachar, in *The Birthright Lottery* (Cambridge, MA: Harvard University Press, 2009), draws attention to these similarities.

the state, but rather to a self-determining group that, in principle, can be identified apart from representative political institutions. There are two branches within this family. The *nationalist* argues that self-determination is a claim of a *nation*, a group defined by cultural features its members believe themselves to share. The *peoplehood* view holds that a self-determining group need not share *cultural* features, but is defined by some other tie.

On the nationalist view, a nation is more than a group of people who happen to be thrown together in one political institution or who share an aspiration to constitute a state: it is a transhistorical group of people united by shared traits.[74] These traits will centrally include "a common public culture, a set of understandings about how their collective life should be led," and an aspiration to be or become politically self-determining.[75] The nation acquires rights to a specific territory, on this view, by transforming the land in ways that add both material and symbolic value to it.[76] Nations add material value to land by cultivation, creation of buildings, roads, and waterways, in ways that enable the space to better meet the needs of its inhabitants. These collectives have an entitlement to keep and enjoy the material value they have historically created.[77] In addition, over time, places or areas within that territory acquire symbolic significance for that nation. Specific events in the group's history may have occurred in the area, and rituals and practices mark out sites or natural formations as sacred.

According to David Miller, cultural nations have claims to self-determination over the territories they have so transformed, because (i) individuals have an important interest in the preservation of their national culture; (ii) that culture has imprinted itself on a certain territory; and (iii) a national culture is best preserved though the group's self-governance over its own territorial unit. In the ideal case, the relevant political unit would be a *nation-state*, since "where a state exercises its authority over two or more nationalities, the dominant group has a strong incentive to use that authority to impose its culture on the weaker groups."[78] But in cases where nations are intermixed, other arrangements (e.g., confederal institutions, internal autonomy, special representation rights, or devolution) ought to be considered.

The second branch of collectivist theory, the *peoplehood* view, likewise attributes territorial rights to a self-determining collective that exists independently of the state.[79] But peoplehood theorists define this collective without reference to cultural

---

[74] Miller, "Territorial Rights: Concept and Justification," 7.
[75] Miller, *National Responsibility and Global Justice*, 124.
[76] For a similar argument, see Tamar Meisels, *Territorial Rights*, 2nd ed. (AA Dordrecht, Netherlands: Springer, 2009).
[77] Miller, "Territorial Rights: Concept and Justification," 8. See also Miller, *National Responsibility and Global Justice*, 218–19.
[78] Miller, *On Nationality* (Oxford: Oxford University Press, 1997), 88.
[79] Other "peoplehood" theorists, discussed later in the book, include Rawls, *The Law of Peoples*; Philip Pettit, "Rawls's Political Ontology," *Politics, Philosophy, and Economics* 4, no. 2 (2005): 157–74;

characteristics. Cara Nine defines "a people" as a group that shares a common conception of justice and has the capacity to establish minimally just institutions.[80] Margaret Moore holds that "a people" is a "group that aspire[s] to create or continue to maintain shared rules and procedures together."[81] Peoplehood theorists stress that political peoples, so defined, strongly *desire* self-government: they grant it tremendous subjective weight, connecting it to their personal identity. They further emphasize that political peoples stand in valuable *relationships*, which give rise to associative obligations, and ought to be protected.

As with proprietarian views, there is an important kernel of truth in collectivist accounts. Collectivists correctly recognize that a good theory of territorial boundaries must incorporate a concern for self-determination. While I agree that self-determination is an important value, I doubt that national culture plays any necessary role in defining it. Unlike liberal nationalists, I do not accept that modern states should be nation-states or that the value of a decentralized and pluralistic international order is rooted in the importance of preserving or promoting national cultures. Liberal nationalism will be a frequent interlocutor in the book, as I distinguish its implications from those of my own view.

My own account, on the other hand, has significant affinities with the peoplehood view. But, to date, I think peoplehood theorists have not clearly explained why the self-determination of peoples is of moral importance. Their explanations of the value of collective self-determination—explanations rooted in subjective identity or associative relationships—are often weak and not compelling. This opens the door to cosmopolitan skepticism. As noted above, cosmopolitans tend to think that our modern system of separate bounded communities is one that we should be working to overcome, in favor of a more global system of governance.[82]

To adjudicate this dispute, I believe we need a better understanding of self-determination. One of the key aims of this book is to provide an account of self-determination and its value that is superior to those offered to date. I ground this account in the significance, for individuals, of enjoying political autonomy under coercive governing institutions. If I am right, self-determination is a fundamental good, closely connected with our ability to lead lives we can appropriately see as our own. My autonomy-based account, I believe, does a much better job than alternative views at explaining why self-determination is something we have deep reason to care about, and something we ought to prioritize in the design of our international institutions.

Pettit, *On the People's Terms* (Cambridge: Cambridge University Press, 2012), ch. 5; Altman and Wellman, *A Liberal Theory of International Justice*. But I focus here on recent theories of the people applied to territorial rights.

[80] Nine, *Global Justice and Territory*, 67.   [81] Moore, *A Political Theory of Territory*, 54.
[82] See Marchetti, *Global Democracy*, 18–19; Abizadeh, "On the Demos and its Kin"; Sofia Näsström, "The Challenge of the All-Affected Principle," *Political Studies* 59, no. 1 (2011): 116–34.

As should now be clear, my aim in discussing these alternatives has not been to refute them conclusively. To the contrary, my own account makes use of key insights from each of these schools of thought. The positive argument I offer here is thus not some radical invention. Rather, it is by articulating more plausible versions of the core insights of other approaches, placing them on a more secure philosophical foundation and showing how they can be made to fit together into a theory that is coherent and compelling, and has plausible implications, that I aim to make my contribution. Elaborating that positive argument is the task to which I now turn.

PART I
OCCUPANCY

2
Occupancy Rights

As I noted in the introduction, there are striking similarities between the rules governing territorial membership, on the one hand, and property rules, on the other.[1] Citizens have a "property-like" claim to remain in their country and to return to their country. Just as property owners claim to use and control objects, states and their members claim rights to use and control parts of the globe.

Proprietarian theories typically draw our attention to these property-like aspects of the states-system. Robert Nozick, for example, suggests that:

> ...those believing that a group of persons living in an area jointly own the territory...must provide a theory of how such property rights arise; they must show why the persons living there have rights to determine what is done with the land and resources there that persons living elsewhere don't have (with regard to the same land and resources).[2]

In the introduction, I called this the question of *foundational title*: what, if anything, gives a particular set of people a special claim to live in a given area, including the right to establish a state that governs and controls that space?

To see why some foundational title is necessary, consider the following case:

> *Forced Removal.* Suppose a group of settlers gets together, overthrows the state of Chad and drives out all its inhabitants, who become refugees in neighboring states. The settlers then up a perfect state on the territory: it rules justly, implements a fair distribution of property, and enjoys the unanimous consent of all its inhabitants.

We will still want to say that this perfect state does not have a right to its territory, at least not at its founding. This is because the settlers lacked any claim to construct a state there in the first place: they lacked foundational title. If the state's members have no right to settle and inhabit the spaces it governs, then their state's rule over these areas is illegitimate. So some account must be given of the inhabitants' prior title to the lands that they occupy.

Typically, proprietarians conceive foundational title as a natural right to property. On the standard Lockean view—recently rearticulated and defended by A. John Simmons—the state's territory is an amalgam of individual natural property

---

[1] Shachar, *The Birthright Lottery*, draws attention to these similarities.
[2] Nozick, *Anarchy, State, and Utopia* (New York: Basic Books, 1974), 178.

rights, constructed through the agreement of original appropriators "to submit both themselves and the land on which they live and work to the state's authority."[3] A more collectivist version of the view is sometimes defended by nationalists. Strong collective proprietarians see foundational title as held by a *group* that "jointly owns" its territory.[4] On both these views, the state's land is conceived as "belonging" to its inhabitants in much the same way property belongs to its owner. Since full rights of property typically confer robust claims to things that are owned, including rights to control the good, to exclude others from it, and to exploit it for the owner's benefit, proprietarians argue that states and their citizens have strong discretionary rights to exclude others from the use and material value of their territory.[5]

As noted, I have benefited from the important proprietarian insight about the need for some account of foundational title. Like them, I will argue that a state's territory "belongs" in a certain sense to its inhabitants. Yet, as I will show, this sense of "belonging" is much weaker than a traditional property right. Instead, as I will argue, individuals who (not unjustly) inhabit a place have a right to *occupy* their area. This chapter develops my account of occupancy and its connection to individuals' important interests in well-being and personal autonomy. In the next chapter, I say more about what *kind* of right occupancy is, and how it differs from the more familiar claims to property.

2.1 The Concept of Occupancy

To capture the notion of an occupancy right, consider three different "property-like" entitlements that could apply to roughly the same location. First, there are rights of private ownership, such as my right over my house and the lot on which it rests. My property right in my house encompasses a bundle of incidents: the claim to possess, use, and alienate it; to exclude others from it; to enjoy the income if I rent it; the right to manage it (e.g., to make decisions about its upkeep); to bequeath it to my heirs; and to consume or waste it.

My private ownership right is not the only "property-like" entitlement that applies to the space in which my house is situated, however. A second right also applies here: the right of territorial jurisdiction. Both the United States and the state of New Jersey claim the right to make and enforce law in the space where I live. This includes the power to change my rights over my house, by modifying property rules (say, enacting new zoning laws), or by exercising the power of eminent domain and taking my house with compensation. States have the power to determine what

---

[3] Simmons, *Boundaries of Authority*, 171.
[4] A weaker version of collectivism is also possible. This weaker view sees a group as acquiring title to its territory through means analogous to property acquisition, though in content, the territorial rights acquired may be more restricted than rights of property.
[5] Moore, *A Political Theory of Territory*, 16; Simmons, *Boundaries of Authority*, 240–1.

kind of control, over which aspects of which material objects, can be exercised by the holders of property rights within their legal systems.

Yet private ownership and territorial jurisdiction do not exhaust our entitlements with respect to geographical space. Instead, I believe that people have a third "property-like" claim in their territory: the right to reside permanently in that place, to participate in the social, cultural, and economic practices ongoing there; to be immune from expropriation or removal; and to return if they leave temporarily. Thus, I have a right to reside on US territory, and when I go abroad, I do not just have a right to return to my own private land, I have a right to reenter this territory and to move around within it. My occupancy right allows me to access various places within civil society that are important to me, like my workplace, my house of worship, shops, restaurants, and public spaces, such as roads or parks. Occupancy is more geographically capacious than private ownership is, though it confers a more limited control over resources. Children, non-property owners, and homeless people also possess occupancy rights that entitle them to reside in a place, to travel freely through that area, and to participate in social, cultural, and economic practices there, even though they lack private property. We can thus distinguish at least three different entitlements to geographical space: rights of private ownership, rights of territorial jurisdiction, and rights of occupancy.

What exactly is an occupancy right? As I understand it, an occupancy right is composed of two main incidents. First, it comprises a liberty to reside permanently in a particular space and to make use of that area for social, cultural, and economic practices. This extends to the liberty to travel freely through the area to access the places in civil society where those practices take place. Occupancy rights do not grant the freedom to access others' private property, but they do confer access to public spaces (such as parks, roads and byways), as well as businesses or buildings that offer services to the public, whether these are publicly or privately owned. Second, occupancy rights also include a claim-right against others not to move one from that area, to allow one to return to it, and not to interfere with one's use of the space in ways that undermine the located practices in which one is engaged.

On my view, the state's foundational title to land consists in a bundle of moral rights of occupancy held by the inhabitants of a place. Occupancy does not extend to full liberal ownership of a territory. As I will argue, it does not include rights to income from the natural resources situated there, nor does it involve the power to alienate or bequeath the territory. Occupancy does not necessarily extend to a right to exclude outsiders from access to the territory, if their access is not disruptive to one's residence there and one's ability to participate in shared social practices. Yet while less robust than a private ownership right, occupancy does confer some of the incidents typically associated with property, including rights to secure access to and use of a geographical area. In addition, as I develop later, a state that appropriately represents rightful occupants may be entitled to exercise some control over the area on their behalf. Since property is a concept that admits of a wide variety of forms, it seems reasonable to interpret occupancy as a very weak form of property. This raises important questions as to the relationship between occupancy and more familiar private property rights that I will return to in the next chapter.

There is an obvious question as to the identity of the bearers of occupancy rights: are they groups or individuals? Occupancy could be primarily grounded in the collective claim of a group to its "homeland," and then derivatively attributed to the group's members. Or occupancy could be primarily grounded in the claims of individuals to reside in a particular place, and derivatively attributed to the groups in which they participate. I believe that occupancy is an individual right, though the justification for the right is in part that it enables individuals to participate in collective social practices. I say more about this important issue in Section 2.5.

2.2 The Limits of Institutionalism

If occupancy is a weak form of property in the earth, what is its grounding? Is it best understood as a preinstitutional moral right, or as a conventional right conferred by legal or social institutions? While *institutionalists* understand property as a right conferred by social practices or systems of law, *preinstitutionalists* see property as a moral right that binds independently of law and convention. (Various hybrid views also exist, which see some aspects of property as preinstitutional, while others depend on law or convention).

While all institutionalists see property as dependent on background social rules, there are different ways to interpret this dependence: some hold that the relevant rules are the joint social conventions of a community, whereas others invoke the laws promulgated by a state. The first, *social institutionalist*, approach is exemplified by David Hume. Hume argues that property is determined by social conventions that assign ownership of objects and define the conditions for valid contracts and transfers. These conventions develop because humans have needs that must be met through social cooperation, and because the scarcity and instability of goods pose an obstacle to stable cooperative enterprises.[6] As each individual is sensible of the benefit to society of these rules, each conforms to property conventions provided others are willing to do so, and, over time, the members of society acquire a disposition to approve of rule-conforming conduct.

A second, *legal institutionalist*, view holds that property depends on a background system of positive law. According to Hobbes, "*Propriety* is an effect of Common-wealth...the act onely of the Soveraign; and consisteth in the Lawes."[7] Bentham offers a similar account, arguing that "property and law are born and die together. Before the laws, there was no property: take away the laws, and all

---

[6] Hume, *A Treatise of Human Nature*, 484–513.
[7] Thomas Hobbes, *Leviathan*, edited by Richard Tuck (Cambridge: Cambridge University Press, 1996), 171.

property ceases."⁸ On this view, positive law is required to generate rules with sufficient publicity, determinacy, and assurance of enforcement to ground property rights. Only a legal system can create the commonly shared and secure expectations necessary for property to exist.

Institutionalist approaches have two important virtues. First, institutionalists appropriately recognize that property rights can be structured differently in different times and places. To have common rules concerning property, we must solve many coordination problems. Different systems may recognize different configurations of holdings (e.g., the means of production may be collectively or privately owned), or specify rights in different ways (e.g., one can own a condominium in some countries but not in others). The duration of property rights can also be more-or-less extensive, and the right to transfer more-or-less limited.

Second, institutionalists also appreciate that many forms of property depend on the complex background of a modern society, including rules about contract, tort, corporate and inheritance law, fiscal and monetary policy, zoning, and environmental regulation. Consider intellectual property, like patents or copyrights; rights to bequeath one's estate; or rights over complex financial instruments, like bonds or securities. These forms of property extend far beyond any rights we could imagine obtaining in a "state of nature." Moreover, since different definitions of these rights will have important social consequences, the rules regulating them ought to be designed with the justice of these social outcomes in mind.

Although institutionalists are therefore correct to point out that property depends significantly on a background of social and legal convention, we can distinguish between a stronger and a weaker institutionalist thesis. The strong thesis holds that there can be no rights to material goods outside shared social or legal institutions. On this view, a moral duty to respect others' property is activated only with the development of background laws or conventions.⁹ The weaker, hybrid institutionalist thesis holds that there can be limited forms of property outside shared social institutions and these limited rights partly constrain how conventional institutions should be designed. But preinstitutional property rights are underspecified: they leave many aspects of property undetermined, including the solutions to various coordination problems, the rules that should regulate transfer and bequest, and the forms of complex private ownership mentioned above. For that reason, they require the construction of further conventions to be fully fleshed out.

I believe the weaker, hybrid position is the more attractive one. To see why, consider the problems that strong institutionalism faces in theorizing what is wrong with *territorial removals*. Take an example: in 1864, the US Army removed 10,000

---

⁸ Jeremy Bentham, "Principles of the Civil Code," in *The Works of Jeremy Bentham*, edited by John Bowring (New York: Russell and Russell, 1962), 309.

⁹ Even strong institutionalists accept that there can *some* moral rights and duties independent of shared institutions, for example, the right not to be assaulted and the duty of nonaggression; but they do not believe these preinstitutional rights extend to rights of *property*.

Navajo Indians from their homeland in Arizona to a reservation in New Mexico. Two hundred people died on the trek, which the Navajos still refer to as their "Long Walk." The removal was not a success: the Navajos were unused to farming, and their crops failed; they were required to live in adobe villages rather than their traditional hogans; and they had to share their reservation with the Apaches, tribal enemies. Finally, in 1868, the United States allowed the survivors to return to their lands in Arizona, unlike most other tribes it relocated during the War for the West.

Think of how a legal institutionalist, like Hobbes or Bentham, might approach this case. Their theory presupposes the existence of a system of positive law, and then, in a second step, it defines property entitlements with respect to the rules laid down by this system. But this overlooks some important questions. First, what about people who lack legal institutions, such as non-state tribes? Do they have rights to the land they occupy? Or is their land *res nullius*, available for acquisition by some sovereign state? The Navajos did not form a state with a defined territory and a mature legal system, so their removal did not obviously violate any state's jurisdiction.[10] And although the Navajos recognized some private property rights, like rights over livestock and dwellings, these rights were very limited and did not extend to property in land.

Second, what if the legal institution that defines property rights in an area itself came to exist *wrongly*, through the dispossession of a prior state or group? Surely these facts about how an institution came to exist are relevant to the legitimacy of the entitlements it creates. The legal institutionalist approach thus seems incomplete, since a state can put into place a perfect *internal* system of distribution for its subjects and still be participating in an expropriation with respect to prior occupants. Suppose—as occurred in the aftermath of many colonial removals—that Arizona had distributed what were formerly Navajo lands to poor settlers. Further, suppose that it performed this distribution in accordance with the correct principles of distributive justice: say (for the sake of argument) Rawls's two principles. In that case, its internal property system would have been fully just. But intuitively, the entitlements of its citizens would have remained defective. A rancher who drew forty acres should not have regarded himself as having title to his new farm since the state that granted him title was dispossessing people with continuing claims over the area.

Of course, if we adopted a more informal, Humean institutionalism, we might explain why the Navajos held property rights against one another, even though they

---

[10] The Navajos were not a politically organized group. Their fundamental unit was the clan, an extended family group that often operated independently of other bands. The Navajo nation did not exist as a political entity until 1923. See L. R. Bailey, *The Long Walk: A History of the Navajo Wars, 1846–68* (Los Angeles: Westernlore Press, 1964); Gary Witherspoon, "Navajo Social Organization," in *Handbook of North American Indians 10*, edited by William C. Sturtevant, general editor, and Alfonso Ortiz, volume editor (Washington, DC: Smithsonian Institution, 1983), 533.

lacked a state: these property rights were rooted in their own social conventions. But this more informal approach is still unable to show why the forced removal was wrong. Though it can explain why the *Navajos* were bound to recognize one another's property claims, it cannot explain how *an outsider* should regard their practices. Are the land rights established by Navajo conventions normatively binding on this outsider such that it would be wrong for him to dispossess them? If so, it is not because he is a party to their social practices.

A Humean might further invoke an *international* convention requiring states and their citizens to respect the territorial rights of other groups, but this response too is problematic. Nineteenth century international law recognized a right to territory conquered in war, which was thought to apply with special force to the territory of "non-civilized peoples."[11] So it seems that a strong institutionalist, who sees the moral duty to respect others' property as wholly dependent on background social rules, must concede that the settlers could displace the Navajos without wrongdoing. But this is surely wrong: an outsider ought to respect the Navajos' occupancy of their land, whether there is a shared convention to that effect or not.

These reflections give us reason to adopt a hybrid institutionalist account. On a hybrid view, limited forms of property can obtain in the absence of social institutions, though these claims are underspecified and leave many incidents of ownership undetermined. If we understand occupancy as a preinstitutional claim, we can explain why it binds even people who do not share a community's conventions. On this approach, Christopher Columbus ought to have recognized the occupancy rights of the inhabitants of Hispaniola in 1492, though he shared no social practices, conventions, or legal institutions with them.[12]

On the hybrid view, not all rights to place are the conventional products of a state's laws or of a community's social practices. At least one *preinstitutional* right precedes these: the right of individuals to live in a certain area; to make use of that space for their valued social, cultural, and economic practices; and, together with others, to authorize a legal institution to enforce rules regarding ownership or to engage in social practices defining their ownership. By a "preinstitutional right," I mean a claim that could logically exist prior to a legal system or social practice, and whose binding force is moral, not legal or conventional. (This is more-or-less equivalent to a natural right: a claim that could be possessed by persons even in a

---

[11] See Sharon Korman, *The Right of Conquest* (Oxford: Clarendon Press, 1996).

[12] One might object that the contrast between institutionalism and preinstitutionalism is not as sharp as I have drawn it, since most institutionalists hold that we have moral interests we are entitled to see protected by a scheme of property. But for an institutionalist, people do not have duties to respect these interests unless a system of conventions has arisen among them. On a preinstitutional account, however, the duty to respect others' interests is a *moral* duty, whose binding force does not depend on its being generally recognized and respected by a given population. For a similar argument with respect to promises, see T. M. Scanlon, *What We Owe to Each Other* (Cambridge, MA: Harvard University Press, 1998), ch. 7.

"state of nature," and that is independent of legal recognition).[13] Preinstitutional rights also constrain institutional schemes: whatever legal or social institutions are set up, they ought to respect the claims to land that already exist. Such claims may not morally determine all aspects of legal regulation regarding land, but they determine some of them. Finally, this preinstitutional claim is *particularized*: it is a claim, not to some general slice of geographical space somewhere in the world, but to a specific area.

2.3 Interests in Occupancy

How might we ground such a preinstitutional right of occupancy? I begin from the observation that occupancy of a particular place is of central importance for an individual's life plans and projects.[14] What is most arresting about the Navajo removal is that territorial dispossession severely disrupted the Navajos' ability to enjoy the lives they had built in Arizona. As many theorists argue, our personal well-being depends substantially on our success in pursuing the morally reasonable projects and relationships that we adopt.[15] The endeavors a person is committed to play an important role in determining what counts as a flourishing life for that person. My theory of occupancy builds on this idea, highlighting the connection between a place and people's comprehensive goals and pursuits. The basic thought is that stable territorial occupancy is a necessary background condition for well-being and personal autonomy.

On an interest-based theory of rights, "'X has a right' if and only if an aspect of X's well-being (his interest) is a sufficient reason for holding some other person(s) to be under a duty."[16] In order to show that our interest in pursuing life plans grounds occupancy rights, we must therefore show two things: first, that people have an interest in occupancy of a particular place, derived from their interests in

---

[13] Sometimes further meta-ethical premises are associated with the term "natural right," implying that such a right is inscribed in the fabric of the natural universe or is binding because it derives from human nature itself. I do not mean to endorse any of these meta-ethical premises, and the term "preinstitutional right," as I use it, does not rely on them. For more on natural rights, see A. John Simmons, *The Lockean Theory of Rights* (Princeton: Princeton University Press, 1992), 87–92; Charles Beitz, *The Idea of Human Rights* (Oxford: Oxford University Press, 2009), 48–72.

[14] Jeremy Waldron, "Superseding Historic Injustice," *Ethics* 103, no.1 (1992): 17–18. This account is similar to what Jeremy Waldron sketches as "the most plausible account of initial acquisition" (18). It is also close to John Simmons's reinterpretation of Locke's labor theory as "bring[ing] things within our purposive activities" (*The Lockean Theory of Rights*, 273).

[15] See Joseph Raz, *The Morality of Freedom* (Oxford: Clarendon Press, 1986), 288–320; Scanlon, *What We Owe to Each Other*, 119–26. The qualification "morally reasonable" is meant to accommodate our intuition that a Nazi's commitment to the goal of exterminating the Jews does not make his life go better. But to be "reasonable," a goal need not be the most valuable pursuit available to a person: it need only be nonharmful. Though some nonharmful pursuits are more valuable than others are, these pursuits do not contribute to a person's well-being unless he endorses them. For more on this, see Ronald Dworkin, *Sovereign Virtue* (Cambridge, MA: Harvard University Press, 2000), 267–74.

[16] Joseph Raz, *The Morality of Freedom*, 166.

carrying out their comprehensive life projects, and in controlling and revising their commitments to these projects; second, that this interest is of sufficient weight to hold others under a duty to respect their occupancy.

How are a person's life projects connected to his occupancy of a place? Most complex goals and relationships require us to form expectations about our continued use of, and secure access to, a place of residence. Geography and climate may affect the economic and subsistence practices we take up, making it difficult for us to reconstitute these practices in some very different place. Suppose you run a dairy farm, an economic practice that structures much of your life. You could not continue to pursue this practice if you were moved, say, to Siberia or the American Southwest. Our religious, cultural, or recreational activities also often have territorial components: think of how sled-dog racing belongs in the Arctic, and surfing in coastal areas, or of how religions incorporate places or natural formations into their rituals of observance. The Pueblo Indians' rituals center around Blue Lake in New Mexico, and the Black Hills have religious significance for the Sioux. Finally, people form personal bonds and enter work, religious, educational, and friendship relations in part because they expect to remain spatially arranged in certain ways: we structure our daily activities and associate together under the assumption that current patterns of residence will not be massively disrupted. We can call these situated goals, relationships, and projects our *located life plans*.

The interest in carrying out located life plans does not depend on those plans' having been autonomously chosen. Each individual has a broad well-being interest in carrying out the (morally reasonable) projects that person happens to have, whether or not these projects were acquired through a process of critical evaluation and choice. Consider a Navajo herdsman who was simply socialized into the pastoral traditions of his people. As long as his pursuits are not harmful to others, and as long as the Navajo endorses them, he has an interest in continuing these practices. Thus, even those who reject autonomy as a fundamental value have an interest in occupancy of their territory. The ability of a person to act on the values that make life meaningful for him is morally significant, even where he has not arrived at his values through critical reflection and choice.

Beyond its connection to well-being, however, stable territorial occupancy is also important for personal autonomy. "Autonomy," as I defined it in Chapter 1, is the capacity to reflect upon and to endorse or revise one's own life commitments for what one authentically judges to be good reasons, and to carry out these commitments in action. Many people—particularly in modern, pluralist societies—hold that individuals should freely select their goals from among a range of options, based on their own critical evaluations. An autonomous person creates his own conception of a worthwhile life through successive decisions to embrace goals and relationships. Personal autonomy in this sense has important preconditions, including access to an adequate range of options and the reflective mental abilities necessary to critically evaluate and assess these options. But another crucial precondition of personal autonomy is the secure ability to shape and direct one's life according to the values and commitments one actually holds. By protecting our ability to carry out the life projects to which we are currently committed, stable territorial occupancy also contributes to our ability to author our lives autonomously.

Not all located life plans are equally significant in grounding a claim to territorial occupancy. Our life projects are hierarchically organized: our immediate goals are means to achieve longer-term aims, which are in turn subordinate to our highest-order commitments.[17] These are our *comprehensive* projects: they organize many choices; they give meaning to our lives and provide a standard for its success; they often reflect an agent's deepest moral and evaluative convictions; and they integrate a person's plans over time in a way that constitutes her distinctive narrative identity. Comprehensive projects sometimes present themselves as imposing nonnegotiable obligations, and they often bear a close connection to intimate personal relationships. These plans are fundamental to our sense of our lives as our own. Careers or economic pursuits; family, friendships, and other personal relationships; and religious and cultural activities are all good examples of comprehensive projects where autonomy has special weight. But other life plans are *peripheral*: they do not structure many choices and do not contribute to our sense of our lives as our own. What color to paint my house or which supermarket to shop in are examples of peripheral plans. Our autonomy and flourishing are not threatened by interference with peripheral plans since they are normally of little weight. But loss of territorial occupancy is very likely to undermine these values when it destroys people's comprehensive plans.

Most located life plans, for most people, involve shared practices. For a person to undertake a religious, recreational, educational, or work activity means being able to participate in the social practices that constitute these options. A key reason why occupancy of a place is important for us, then, is that it facilitates our access to social practices and to the physical spaces in which they unfold. Especially important are spaces like the workplace, the place of worship, the leisure or recreational facility, the school, and the meetinghouse. Of course, this list is culturally biased, and it reflects life in a modern industrialized society. But even though the types of shared space will differ across societies, some shared spaces will be necessary within any society. This is an implication—for territory—of the fact that many of our projects depend upon collective social forms.[18]

While social practices are essential for most people's projects, it is not *necessary* to participate in social practices to have located life plans. Some located life plans are purely individual. Joseph Carens argues, along somewhat similar lines, that long-term residents who have strong social ties in an area have a claim to remain

---

[17] For this point, see Raz, *Morality of Freedom*, 292; Scanlon, *What We Owe to Each Other*, 122.

[18] See Raz, *Morality of Freedom*: "A person can have a comprehensive goal only if it is based on existing social forms, i.e. on forms of behavior which are in fact widely practiced in his society" (308).

in the place where they have become deeply rooted.[19] While my account is broadly similar to Carens's, unlike him, I believe that located life plans need not *necessarily* have a social dimension: even Robinson Crusoe had plans involving his island. Similarly, a reclusive individual who has few social ties may still have located life plans involving the place where she keeps her home and has her daily routine. So while located life plans do commonly involve social practices, we should not take the additional step of making social ties a necessary condition of such plans.

We can distinguish several significant features of located life plans:

(1) *Economic Practices.* Many economic practices can only be carried on in a territory with certain geographical, ecological, or infrastructural characteristics. The mainstay of the Sioux Indians' economy was hunting wild buffalo, so they had an interest in living somewhere that could sustain these animals. Many modern Americans work in white-collar professional jobs, so they have an interest in living where there is office space, copy machines, broadband Internet, etc. People are significantly dislocated by having to move where they cannot maintain their economic practices.

(2) *Membership in Religious, Social, and Cultural Organizations.* Many located life plans require individuals to have access to associational spaces shared with other people. For a person to have the option to undertake a religious, recreational, educational, or work activity means being able to access the physical spaces and infrastructure (e.g., churches, mosques, schools, meetinghouses, etc.) where these activities occur. These first two features of located life plans usually require access to a *type* of place, though not necessarily to a specific place.

(3) *Personal Relationships.* People are engaged in networks of relationships—with colleagues, family, and friends—that are fundamental to their well-being. They have an interest in continuing these relationships with the people that matter to them, and that requires living near enough to do so. Since each individual is tied to differing associations, friends, and networks, it is hard to draw bounds around a community such that one could move all and only the members of that community without breaking personal ties. Sustaining people's important personal relationships will often require maintaining their current spatial arrangements to a significant degree.

(4) *Attachment to Locality.* Some people have projects based on a special identification with a unique locality. As mentioned above, the Taos Pueblo's religious rituals center on Blue Lake, the Sioux attribute spiritual significance to the Black Hills, and the highland culture of Switzerland is focused on the Alps. Such projects are closely linked to attitudes that people direct

---

[19] Carens, *The Ethics of Immigration*, ch. 8.

specifically at the physical objects around them, and these projects are hard to keep intact without sustaining people's occupancy of that unique location. The last two features can typically only be satisfied in a specific place.

Taken together, these reflections show that the people who live on a territory have important *plan-based interests* in continuing to occupy that place, and in using it for the located social, cultural, and economic practices that they value.

Along with these *plan-based interests* in a place, I believe individuals have a more generalized *control interest* in being the agent in charge of revising the commitments that are fundamental to their lives. Our located life plans must take account of other people's legitimate claims, and this means we must sometimes revise them in ways that we would not otherwise choose. But for your life to be meaningfully your own there must be some central range of decisions concerning it that are yours alone to make. Many important rights serve not only our goals and well-being, but also our ability to exercise control over these factors, and occupancy is no exception.[20] When other people interfere with your chosen occupation, your religion, or your intimate friendships and family relationships, this jeopardizes your authorship over your life. One extreme form such interference can take is expulsion from territory.

Let me now consider several objections to my argument connecting territorial occupancy to our interest in located life plans. First, one might object that our social practices could theoretically be translocated to a different spatial location without disruption. Perhaps the university where I work could be taken down and reconstructed, brick by brick, somewhere else. Perhaps the inhabitants of the area could be carefully resettled in a way that precisely reproduces the patterns of residence people now inhabit. Would there then be any harm in relocation?

I believe it is sometimes possible to move people without damage to their located life plans. Occupancy requires security in one's central life commitments, with a sufficient geographic scope to ensure access to an adequate range of opportunities for revising these commitments. Occupancy is violated only if a person is moved in a way that disrupts these central life projects. But not all forms of forced movement do this. If the state takes my home in order to build a new road, requiring me to move a few streets away, this does not necessarily violate my occupancy rights, so long as it did not prevent me from working in my job, attending my church, or associating with friends and family.[21] Similarly, we might imagine that a self-contained group (such as an Amish settlement) could be instantly relocated, to a different, but geographically similar place, where their social infrastructure had already been replicated, and their lives could immediately resume. In such a case, I believe the group members retain a general claim not to be forced or coerced without sufficient justification. If there are no competing social values at stake,

---

[20] See David Lefkowitz, "Autonomy, Residence, and Return," *Critical Review of International Social and Political Philosophy* 18, no. 5 (2015): 529–46.

[21] For a similar view, see Moore, *A Political Theory of Territory*, 39.

we ought not to move them against their will. But the case against territorial removal will be significantly weaker here. The example highlights that our interests in specific geographical locations are largely indirect. What makes a place my "home" is not that location's GPS coordinates, but my plans involving the place, and my attachments to the people and practices there. Competing social values may more easily suffice to justify relocating people in "pure" cases, where no harm to their located life plans is involved.

Still, I find such "pure" cases difficult to imagine on any very large scale. The *process* of removal usually involves significant disruption, even if the removed group is eventually able to reconstruct their lives and practices somewhere else. Ethnographic accounts speak of "upheaval" and "uprooting": people tell of losing their family and friends on the journey, of being detached from their workplace and associations, and of reconstructing these things only with much effort, and after a difficult process of adjustment. Further, short of relocating humanity to a new planet, there is nowhere to put people that will not involve transforming their life plans, by the simple fact that a different social world already exists there, since most places on earth are currently inhabited. The translocation objection shows that the connection between territorial occupancy and personal autonomy is not a logical one, but rather it depends on certain empirical facts. Still, I believe that in a world like ours, the interest in located life plans grounds an interest in secure occupancy of a specific place.

A second worry is that perhaps the stability of located life plans may not be fundamental to all people. Some people may have only very generic located life plans, as for example, an individual who lives in a cookie-cutter suburb, telecommutes, and needs only fiber-optic cable and an Internet connection to feel at home. Would this "loner" be harmed by removal from his territory? I should emphasize that, on my view, it is not only the inhabitants of traditional communities who have located life plans. Even this suburban loner would be dislocated by a requirement to move, say, to an Amazonian tribal region, which shows that his life plans are not as generic as they seem. Instead, they are highly tied to the geography and environment of a modern, urban, industrialized society. Mastering a new social organization and cultural environment is costly, and we should not require people to pay these costs unless they choose to do so.[22]

Still, there is a plurality of modern, suburban, English-speaking social settings, and perhaps it does not matter to the loner which one he inhabits. While that conclusion may be correct in his case, it does not show that the stability of located life plans does not matter for modern people generally, nor does it undermine the argument for a right of occupancy. A peculiar feature of the loner is that he has no social ties. He is indifferent between suburban environments primarily because he has no family, friends, workplace, or other personal connections anywhere.

---

[22] See Will Kymlicka, *Multicultural Citizenship* (Oxford: Oxford University Press, 1995), 85.

There may be some individuals as disconnected as this person. But clearly most people are not as socially disconnected as this, nor can we expect them to be. Social ties are essential to a fulfilling human life, and it would be unreasonable to ask people to forego them. Even the loner should enjoy the background preconditions for forming stable social ties, should he revise his life plans and decide to do so. Since rights are grounded on broadly shareable interests, the idiosyncrasies of the loner's case do not affect the argument for occupancy rights.

Third, we might wonder whether my account emphasizes too strongly the interest in staying in place. The experiences of migrants show that relocation does not always result in significant setbacks. This might make us suspect that staying put is not a strong interest. While I agree that people often move, I do not think this shows that people lack a strong interest in the *right* to stay put. It is a very different thing to move voluntarily than to move because one is not allowed to stay. Undocumented migrants, for example, are not allowed to remain in their host country permanently, even when they came as young children and even when they have lived in a place for a long time. As a result, they find it difficult to commit to relationships, to undertake education, start a business, or participate fully in the community because at any moment they might be required to leave. So one can have a strong interest in the protections that enable one to form located life plans in a place, even if one in fact chooses to waive these protections and to move somewhere else.[23] These protections grant one security in one's plans and commitments, and make the choice to move meaningfully one's own.

Fourth, one might ask: is it necessary that someone now live in a place, or have previously lived there, to have located life plans involving that place? While living in a place is the most common way of developing a life plan tied to a specific location, there may be other ways. Sometimes it is possible to have an occupancy right to a place one has never been, if (a) an individual's central life commitments can only be protected through residence there, and (b) that individual's interest is not outweighed by countervailing costs to prior occupants. This has implications for the ethics of migration, about which I say more in Chapter 7.[24] In the clear majority of cases, however, living in a place is what makes occupancy of that location essential to one's personal well-being and autonomy.

Fifth, one might object that attributing people occupancy rights based on their located life plans places too much moral weight on existing expectations regarding resource use. In response, I stress that located life plans have normative weight

---

[23] See Kieran Oberman, "Immigration, Global Poverty, and the Right to Stay," *Ratio Juris* 30, no. 2 (2017): 144–57.
[24] One might object here that individuals can rightly be expected to take into account certain constraints on geographic mobility in forming their life plans. Rawls argues, in this vein, that individuals are responsible for shaping their plans to the resources they can expect to have in a just distribution. But, as I will argue more extensively in Chapters 3 and 7, territorial occupancy rights do not extend to a moral claim to exclude outsiders from the territory at discretion. Thus, it is not clear that, in forming their life plans, outsiders can reasonably be expected to take the prospect of exclusion into account.

only within the bounds of a fair-use proviso, about which I say more as the book proceeds. My plans involving an immense area do not give me any claim to the portion that extends beyond my fair share. This expresses the idea—familiar from Locke—that to be justified, our appropriation of geographical space must leave "enough, and as good" for others. Occupants must comply with this fair-use proviso.

Yet within the bounds of the fair-use proviso, I believe located life plans do have moral weight: later comers ought to respect them. Suppose it is Sunday afternoon and my family and I have packed up a picnic and headed to our favorite shady spot in the park. When we get there, we find another family already picnicking under our preferred tree (the spot is too small to accommodate us both, so there is no option to share). Should we demand they flip a coin for the right to be there? No: all else equal, our moral freedom to take this spot is limited by the fact that they are already using the area. If there are other picnic spots available, we should keep walking.

The *ceteris paribus* clause is important: if there are no other spaces available, or if using these other places would involve serious harm to us, then we might be justified in appropriating the spot, even though the other family was there first. But having already built important life projects around a particular thing gives one an interest of a different weight than a mere desire to use it. Those who are already living in a place typically rely on that location in the structure of their central life commitments, while those who merely desire to live there do not. This is one reason why it is generally worse to deport people from a territory than to prevent would-be newcomers from settling there. While frustrated in their desires, would-be relocators generally do not suffer the destruction of the lives they have already built, and they can often seek out other attractive options for pursuing their projects.

2.4 Justifying an Occupancy Right

Showing that people have an important interest in the area fundamental to their located life plans is the first step in an argument that they have a preinstitutional *right* to occupy this place. But while residents of an area certainly have an interest in it, we have not yet shown that their interest is of sufficient weight to hold others under a duty. Claim-rights declare that it is reasonable to expect other individuals or institutions to bear responsibilities for protecting, respecting, or promoting the locational interest in specific ways.[25] To argue for a moral *right* of occupancy, we must compare the strength of the interests protected under the proposed right

---

[25] These remarks are indebted to T. M. Scanlon's remarks on rights in *The Difficulty of Tolerance* (Cambridge: Cambridge University Press, 2003), especially chs. 2, 5, and 6; and his contractualist account of morality in *What We Owe to Each Other*, ch. 5.

against the strength of possible countervailing considerations. Once a right has been justified, it grounds duties with pre-emptive force: these duties exclude our direct consideration of the underlying merits case by case.[26] The assertion of a right sums up our assessment, from a general perspective, of several more fundamental, intersecting, and potentially competing, value considerations. Since the interest in located life plans is just one such consideration, we must assess whether it is defeated by conflicting reasons.

Viewed in this way, however, the occupancy interest seems quite robust. Removing someone from his territory destroys many of his life plans at once; it harms not just his peripheral plans, but also his most comprehensive endeavors; and his projects tend to be rapidly and thoroughly undermined in ways that are difficult to compensate. Since imposing duties on others to respect occupancy rights involves costs, however, we must also consider their interest in being free from such duties. In most cases, it is difficult to conceive of a weighty interest in being able to remove or expel others, or to interfere with their occupancy in ways that undermine their shared social practices. Nor does compliance with duties to respect others' occupancy seem especially burdensome: so long as an outsider enjoys flourishing life plans where she lives, depriving her of the liberty to interfere with others' occupancy does not seem unduly costly to her. It is worth recalling here that I am arguing for a quite limited entitlement to geographical space: namely, the right to reside permanently in an area, and to make use of it for social, cultural, and economic practices, immune from removal or expropriation. The limited nature of the right is important, since outsiders may have weightier interests in other aspects of territorial control. For example, they may have an interest in access to other areas of the globe, or they may have an interest in sharing in the value of the earth's resources. Rights to exclude outsiders from a territory or to control its natural resource wealth face a higher burden of justification, and I will investigate these claims in Parts III and IV of the book.

There is an important class of cases, however, where imposing duties to respect others' occupancy does seem unduly burdensome. When someone is unable to enjoy flourishing located life plans where he now is, he has a significant interest in acquiring some space in which to pursue these plans, even if that space is now occupied by someone else. Again, this suggests that we should impose a fair-use proviso on occupancy. Imposing distributive constraints does not undermine our assertion of an occupancy right, since rights need not exclude all conflicting reasons. Duties to respect occupancy rights exclude many potential reasons for interfering with occupancy, such as the fact we could increase economic efficiency by removing people; that we could enable other, desirable uses of an area; that we

---

[26] Raz, *Morality of Freedom*, 186. A right, as Raz defines it, grounds not only a first-order reason to act, but also a second-order, *exclusionary* reason not to act for certain other reasons. Duties to respect rights thus support reasons not to act on considerations that would ordinarily count against respecting the rights-grounding interest in the case at hand.

could alleviate social conflicts; and so on. The assertion of an occupancy right means we ought to refrain from acting on these competing considerations, even where, on balance, they seem to outweigh the occupancy interest in the case at hand.

So long as the fair-use proviso is respected, then, I believe that the interest in located life plans is significant enough to justify imposing duties on others not to remove us from our territory, and not to interfere with our use of it in ways that undermine our shared social, cultural, economic, and political practices. This is because (i) the increased security afforded to located life plans by recognizing such duties is of great benefit to us, and (ii) our interest in not having such a duty imposed is quite weak by comparison.

I should stress, however, that I do not understand occupancy rights as absolute. While rights are normally sufficiently stringent to override competing considerations (such as economic efficiency or aggregate welfare), sometimes there will be countervailing concerns of such moral weight as to justify infringing occupancy. I do not here attempt to specify these, though I believe they would involve truly grave costs to other values. Even where a right is justifiably infringed, it persists and deserves some acknowledgment, such as an apology or compensation.

A final worry I wish to consider is whether recognizing an occupancy right—based on an interest in stable located life plans—would entail undesirable implications for other aspects of our economic and social life. Consider a group that has historically practiced mining in a particular location and has evolved a way of life based around it. If mining becomes economically unprofitable, do these people have a right against the state to subsidize their dying industry, so as not to disrupt their located life plans?

In response, I deny that an occupancy right extends to a duty to subsidize dying industries. But I do think that where technological change or economic restructuring have dramatic impacts, devastating people's lives in ways akin to territorial removal, individuals have a right that others act to cushion these dislocations, assisting them in maintaining their located life plans.

It is doubtful that the occupancy right grounds a duty to subsidize dying industries, for two reasons. First, located life plans are typically less drastically affected by economic restructuring than by territorial removal. If there are alternative jobs available in their community, the miners' loss of their occupation—though a significant blow—need not undermine all their other located commitments, including their relationships with friends and family and membership in religious, cultural, and social organizations. A second reason against subsidy is that other people have strong countervailing interests in not bearing the burdens required to maintain dying industries. Citizens have an interest in a market economy that affords them significant benefits—including dynamic innovation, lower consumer prices, and greater opportunities.

Still, when economic restructuring is sufficiently thoroughgoing, it can undermine people's fundamental plans and projects in a way that is similar to territorial removal. If there are no jobs available in their community, the miners may be effectively forced to move, abandoning the lives they have built in a place. Here, I believe inhabitants have a right to be assisted in maintaining the locational continuity of their plans. Though their industries need not be subsidized, inhabitants of disadvantaged areas ought to be provided sufficient economic options to allow them to stay in place, through social welfare benefits, publicly funded investment, or worker retraining schemes. This affords them some security in their central life commitments, ensuring that they need not move out of necessity.

2.5 Compulsion and Removal

On the view I endorse, the primary wrong of territorial removal is the way it undermines our fundamental plans and projects and our ability to control these commitments. But is this correct? An alternative view would highlight the fact that removals often involve physical force or coercion. This view holds that our interest in being free from coercion or force captures all that is at stake in territorial occupancy, without any reference to located life plans.

Adapting Nozick's well-known analysis, stipulate that P coerces Q when he communicates to Q that he intends to bring about some seriously undesirable consequence if Q does A (something Q might otherwise do), and as a result, Q does not do A.[27] Following Nozick, "coercion" is usually used to refer to communicative threats: however, we can define a broader category of *compulsion* that includes both coercion and physical force. Coercion and force are two modes of a single activity, compelling someone to do something against her will.[28]

I do not deny that territorial removals are typically wrong in part because they feature compulsion. But I do deny that the wrong of compulsion captures all that is problematic here. Relatedly, I believe that a general claim to freedom from compulsion is insufficient to explain why we have a right to permanently occupy a geographical space. We cannot reduce the distinctive injustice of territorial removal to the wrong of coercion or force.

A common view of compulsion is that it is always *pro tanto* wrong, though it may be justified, all things considered, in the presence of a compelling rationale. Why is compulsion *pro tanto* wrong? A plausible explanation holds that it is wrong because it subjects someone else's will to our own. When one person coerces another, she deliberately changes the circumstances of his choice—by attaching serious disadvantages to an otherwise desirable option—to place sufficient pressure on his will to induce him to take the action she desires him to take. She "makes" him do what she wishes. But subjecting someone's will dominates that person and

---

[27] See Robert Nozick, "Coercion," in *Philosophy, Politics, and Society: Fourth Series*, edited by Peter Laslett, W. G. Runciman, and Quentin Skinner (Oxford: Blackwell, 1972), 101–35.
[28] See Scott Anderson, "Coercion," in *The Stanford Encyclopedia of Philosophy* (Winter 2017 edition), edited by Edward N. Zalta. https://plato.stanford.edu/entries/coercion/.

violates the ideal of interpersonal relations in which we think people ought to stand. Similarly, using physical force against another person's body makes him serve as a direct instrument of one's desires and intentions. Because it is *pro tanto* wrong to dominate people in this way, it is *pro tanto* wrong to coerce or force them.[29]

Although the typical case of territorial removal involves coercion or force, there are cases in which people are deprived of their occupancy rights without compulsion. I believe that an uncompelled removal is almost as wrong as its more forceful variant. Just like the victim of a typical removal, the victim of an uncompelled removal suffers the rapid and thoroughgoing destruction of her located life plans. The difference between the two cases is that in a typical removal, the victim also suffers an additional indignity: he is necessitated, by coercion or force, to do something he does not want to do.

To illustrate, consider the situation of Palestinian refugees at the moment of Israel's independence. As Benny Morris shows in his landmark history of this event, not all refugees left for the same reasons, and their exodus occurred in stages. In the first stage, many Palestinians fled to nearby countries voluntarily. These people were eager to ensure their security and safeguard their wealth: they felt that their persons and property might be vulnerable in an uncertain scenario. They did not think in terms of a permanent emigration abroad; instead, they expected the imminent defeat of Israel by surrounding Arab states, and they intended to return to their homes after the war was over.[30] On the definition outlined above, this group was not compelled to move.

Then, from April–July 1948, the Jewish armed forces implemented a plan to secure the emerging state of Israel against an Arab invasion. This plan involved clearing potentially hostile "fifth column" elements—namely, Arab Palestinians—from the new state's territory, cleansing large areas of their historic inhabitants. At this stage, many Palestinians were directly forced out by the Jewish army, which burned villages, harassed local populations, and drove them from the area. In this wave, as Morris illustrates, "the most important single factor... was Jewish attack."[31] On the above definition, this second group did suffer compulsion. They were pressured to move by threats or the application of direct physical force.[32]

---

[29] My discussion here draws on Raz, *The Morality of Freedom*, 150–7 and 418–19, and Grant Lamond, "The Coerciveness of Law," *Oxford Journal of Legal Studies* 20, no. 1 (2000): 39–62, although it does not duplicate either author's views exactly.

[30] Benny Morris, *The Birth of the Palestinian Refugee Problem* (Cambridge: Cambridge University Press, 2004), 133–9.

[31] Morris, *Birth of the Palestinian Refugee Problem*, 265.

[32] One might wonder whether national defense could conceivably outweigh the duty not to interfere with occupancy rights. In response, I distinguish two questions: first, whether the interest in occupancy grounds a generally valid duty not to evict people, and second, whether that duty can ever be overridden in extraordinary circumstances. I believe the occupancy interest does ground a general duty not to evict others, even in the face of countervailing security concerns. Assuming that occupancy rights are not absolute, however, it is possible that this duty could be overridden where the infringement of occupancy was the only reasonable means to protect other, stronger rights, or to avoid a terrible calamity. Yet even where occupancy rights are justifiably infringed, the displaced

Whether they fled voluntarily or were compelled, however, all Palestinian refugees were deprived of their occupancy rights. This is because after the exodus, Israel banned the return of displaced persons to their homes and villages. Among the measures taken to forestall Palestinian return were destroying their residences; demolishing their religious and associational infrastructure; obstructing economic practices, like cultivating fields or harvesting previously planted crops; settling new immigrants in previously Arab areas; and prohibiting free movement along public roads. This deprivation of occupancy had grave consequences for the Palestinian Arab community: they became scattered in refugee camps throughout the West Bank, the Gaza Strip, Jordan, Syria, and Lebanon. Their businesses and sociocultural associations were decimated, and many Palestinians lost contact with relatives, who fled to other areas. But the refugees suffered these consequences regardless of whether they evacuated voluntarily or were evicted by the Jewish army.

One might object that since the Palestinian refugees were forcibly prevented from returning, this example does not prove the intended point, viz. that there is more at stake in removal than compulsion. But I believe it does. Palestinians were prevented from returning to their *homes*, and that is very different from their being prevented from visiting a foreign land, such as Japan or Sweden. To be sure, some theorists argue that border coercion is presumptively wrong.[33] But even if border coercion is wrong, surely it is a much more *serious* wrong to prevent people from returning to their homeland than it is to prevent them from entering some country to which they have no important ties. Unlike third-party uses of border coercion, Israel's exclusion destroyed the lives the refugees had built for themselves. We cannot appreciate the gravity of this harm unless we suppose that the Palestinians had important interests in this specific place that they do not have in the territories of Japan or Sweden.

So my theory of occupancy is not equivalent to the simple view that individuals have a liberty-right to move freely across the globe as long as they do no wrong or harm to others, and claim-rights not to be coercively expelled from the location where they now are, provided they satisfy these conditions. In addition to a claim against wrongful coercion, occupants have a moral right to *return* to the place they rightfully occupy even when they leave it voluntarily. This moral right of return protects the security of occupants' located life plans.

I believe the Palestinian case shows that though the *pro tanto* wrong of compulsion often features in territorial removal, and certainly contributes to its wrongness, it does not fully account for it. Removal is wrong not simply because it is compulsive, but also because it dispossesses people of the place that is central to their lives. Undermining people's economic pursuits, destroying their homes

---

individuals are still wronged: they are entitled to have their occupancy restored after the fact, and to be paid compensation for the harm of displacement.

[33] See Abizadeh, "Democratic Theory and Border Coercion."

and meeting places, and dislocating their social ties are harms of a different type than compulsion. Objections to removal are objections to the deprivation of an especially important good: the use of the geographical space that is fundamental to one's life.

2.6 A Group or Individual Interest?

As noted earlier, our interest in territorial occupancy is in part an interest in spaces where we participate in collective practices together with others. Though it is possible for a solitary individual to form located life plans, for most people, most of the time, such plans involve shared social practices. We might therefore wonder: is occupancy a right held by individuals? Or is it a collective right of the group whose practices take place in these spaces? Liberal nationalists (including Chaim Gans, Will Kymlicka, Tamar Meisels, and David Miller) argue that occupancy rights belong to *nations*, groups that share a common culture and a special attachment to a territorial homeland.[34] Margaret Moore also attributes the right of occupancy to groups (though she grants individuals moral rights of *residency*, as well, based on their personal projects, aims, and relationships). Moore stresses that groups see themselves as "attached to specific areas, specific bits of land, which form an important source of the group's identity."[35] Expulsion, she argues, is wrong not only because it inflicts harms to individuals' projects, relationships, and aims, but also because it is "profoundly disruptive to collective identities as people of a particular kind, which in turn is partly defined by the location of the group."[36] This identity relation gives the group an interest in controlling the geographical location to which they are attached.

Unlike liberal nationalists, I do not understand territorial occupancy as a right belonging to corporate groups. While most located life plans involve group activities, I have stressed that located life plans *can* be purely individual: a solitary homesteader, for instance, has plans involving his cabin and the cultivation of his fields. And while it is true that occupancy is valuable in part because it facilitates our participation in social practices, the *bearer* of an occupancy right need not be a group. Freedom of association is similarly valuable because it facilitates social activity, yet we attribute this right to individuals.

I believe there are important reasons to eschew the nationalist approach, since it is rarely the case that everyone who is settled on a territory belongs to the same cultural group. Territories everywhere are inhabited by diverse populations, including authorized and unauthorized immigrants and refugees. To be sure, unlike more extreme versions of ethnic nationalism, liberal nationalists typically do not

---

[34] See Chaim Gans, *The Limits of Nationalism* (Cambridge: Cambridge University Press, 2003), 83; Will Kymlicka, *Multicultural Citizenship*, 30–1; Meisels, *Territorial Rights*, 126; Miller, "Territorial Rights: Concept and Justification."
[35] Moore, *A Political Theory of Territory*, 40.   [36] Moore, *A Political Theory of Territory*, 43.

see the whole of the state's territory as belonging to one national group alone. Instead, they extend homeland rights to indigenous peoples and other minority groups historically associated with a territory, not only to the national majority. Still, most liberal nationalists draw a sharp distinction between the rights of homeland groups—who have strong claims to occupancy, including the right to see their culture protected and promoted by the state—and the rights of non-homeland groups, such as immigrants and refugees, which are much weaker. The fact that these groups are not members of the core self-determining nation(s) gives them a lesser claim to inhabit the area and to participate in the political community. So even the most liberal nationalist view still creates two classes of residents; those who belong to the recognized homeland group(s) and who have privileged claims on the land—including the claim to organize that area's public spaces in accordance with their cultural preferences—and those who do not, despite having built their lives in their area, and whose claims are more questionable. This sends the message that some residents are outsiders, not full members of the community. By attributing occupancy to groups, we risk marginalizing those who do not belong.

Instead of attributing occupancy rights to nations, I believe we should attribute occupancy to the individual residents of a place, and only derivatively to the various cultural and other practices in which those people participate. Each person will require access to the shared spaces on which her located life plans depend, but persons living in close proximity may have interests in different spaces and participate in different practices. A Cuban immigrant may have an occupancy right in Miami because it contains his family, his workplace, his Catholic church, and his Spanish-speaking co-ethnics, while a Jewish Miamian may have an occupancy right in the same area because it contains his soccer club, his synagogue, and his school. Though there is little overlap between the "cultures" of these two individuals, each has an occupancy right *in Miami* because it contains shared spaces that are fundamental to him.

My approach can make space for some derivative group rights to territory, grounded in the importance of located social, cultural, and political practices for their participants.[37] To illustrate, consider a town inhabited by a religious community (Hutterites), members of a majority national group (Canadians), and an immigrant subculture based around a shared language (Somali). Alongside their individual interests in occupancy, members of these communities also have interests in their groups' use of public and civil society spaces for their shared purposes. They may wish to hold meetings in a local coffee shop or gather in the park, to speak their language or celebrate their holidays in public places.[38] While some of

---

[37] For this notion of collective rights, see Raz, *The Morality of Freedom*, 207–8; Peter Jones, "Group Rights and Group Oppression," *Journal of Political Philosophy* 7, no. 4 (1999): 353–77.

[38] Since different groups will likely wish to use the area in potentially incompatible ways, this may give rise to disputes. In Chapter 4, I argue that when people come into conflict about the use of material resources, they are obliged to set up a state that can fairly regulate these matters. Following Kant,

these activities may be adequately protected by standard individual rights, others will require group rights to access and use public spaces that are recognized by the town's other inhabitants, and by outsiders. We should allow that such groups have derivative rights to use the territory's public spaces, grounded in their members' interests in the shared practices that matter to them.

So my account can still recognize some group occupancy rights, based on the joint interests of residents in located social practices. But unlike nationalist views, my approach does not derive individuals' occupancy rights from the prior right of a nation to its "homeland"; instead, individuals hold occupancy rights directly. And my approach allows that as residents' participation in social and cultural practices shift, so too will the distribution of groups that have occupancy rights in a territory. If some residents of Quebec begin to engage in a Swahili-speaking subculture, that subculture will possess occupancy rights alongside the Quebecois nation.

2.7 Deriving Territory from Occupancy

One worry about my account is that the spaces with which individuals' located life plans are connected can vary greatly in their scale. The satisfaction of most people's located life plans does not obviously require access to the entire territory of the modern state. So how should we understand the domain that an occupancy right protects?

Occupancy rights, as I see them, are grounded in individuals' interests in residing in and accessing the localities where they have built their lives. The boundaries of this area are somewhat vague, and will be different for each individual, but they center on her primary place of residence and extend out to those places where she has important projects, associations, and connections. So my occupancy right includes not just Pennington, New Jersey, where my house is, but also Princeton, New Jersey, where my job is, and Philadelphia, where my husband works and many of our friends live, and Kentucky and New Mexico, where we grew up and have extensive family ties. But it does not include Alaska or Hawaii, where I have never set foot. Prior to the state's establishment, then, we must imagine an overlapping web of individual attachments to land, with dense nodes formed by social practices where many people share located plans together.

If most people's plan-based interests can be satisfied in a smaller "space" than their state's entire territory, then how do we move from individual occupancy rights to state-level territorial rights? How do individual occupancy rights whose domains may not map onto the entire territory of an existing state add up to a title to all the territory enclosed within a state's borders? In Part II of this book, I will

---

I accept a *natural duty of justice* to enter a juridical state that can stabilize people's expectations about the use of resources (by instituting a regime of property law), and serve as an impartial arbiter for resolving their conflicts. The disputes generated by diverse occupants may therefore generate moral pressure to construct a more formal property system.

argue that a state acquires jurisdiction over territory when it legitimately represents rightful occupants, in accordance with the following conditions:

(1) The state effectively implements a system of law in that territory that meets the requirements of basic justice.

(2) The state's institutions reflect the *shared political will* of a significant majority of cooperators among those rightful occupants.

(3) Those who dissent from this shared will lack any right to an institutional alternative.

If a state meets these conditions, then it can assert jurisdiction over the entire aggregate of places its subjects rightfully occupy. When constituted, the state's jurisdiction is assembled like a jigsaw puzzle: because a legitimate state has the authority to specify, interpret, and enforce its subjects' rights (including their occupancy rights), it also has authority over the various spaces that those subjects justly occupy. It is important to stress here that land need not be inhabited to be subject to occupancy rights—keeping land in an unaltered state to serve as a hunting ground or grazing pasture, to conduct religious practices, or to maintain a public park are all ways of incorporating that land into one's located life plans. But inhabitants must have ongoing, temporally extended projects involving a specific place to rightfully occupy it. Land that is rightfully occupied by its legitimate subjects, then, forms the state's *core territory*.

Though rightfully occupied areas form its core territory, a state can also legitimately claim jurisdiction over what I call *ancillary territory*. One worry about the preceding account is that the jurisdiction of the state might take on a "patchwork quality," with holes formed by unoccupied spaces. For example, 4.9 million out of 11 million US Census blocks are unpopulated: the US claims territorial jurisdiction over deserts, tundra, and many other areas of uninhabited wilderness. While I do not claim that the United States has strong moral rights to all these areas, control over some of them may be necessary for the state to protect rights, provide public goods, and secure justice for its legitimate subjects. As I will explain in Chapter 4, there are important reasons—to do with the state's role in establishing clear definitions of property, contract, and tort, and in coordinating its subjects' activities—to believe that the state must exercise jurisdiction over a reasonably continuous area. If control over an unused space is essential to providing national defense, for example, the state may claim jurisdiction over that space as a means of protecting its citizens against external invasion. Jurisdiction over unoccupied spaces may also be necessary to facilitate economic exchange. There would be many more transaction costs if, when traveling from Princeton to San Francisco, one had to cross several countries, applying for a visa, asking for overflight permission, and so on.[39] So the state may also claim jurisdiction over *ancillary*

---

[39] I thank Minh Ly for discussion of the ideas in this paragraph.

territory to the extent that such control is necessary to carry out its morally mandatory functions.

Still, it is easy to imagine that many unoccupied areas currently controlled by states (consider Arctic regions, vast wilderness areas, or uninhabited islands) are not in this way essential to the state's ability to provide justice for its subjects, and for that reason, states' moral rights to jurisdiction over some of these areas may be weak. In Chapter 6, I will argue that such lands may be particularly good candidates for territorial redistribution under the fair-use proviso.

Once a group of individuals is legitimately subject to a territorial state, we can expect their occupancy rights to be somewhat malleable, since located life plans will be shaped in part by existing legal and conventional structures. A "core" pre-institutional occupancy right extends to one's place of permanent residence and to security in the comprehensive life commitments one has formed nearby, with a sufficient geographic scope to provide an adequate range of options for revising these commitments. But once people access wider areas than this "core" space, they can be expected to form life plans that extend over these wider areas. A "core" preinstitutional right may therefore be broadened in various ways through expectations shaped by conventional structures. For example, citizens have a membership interest in being able to move around freely within their state, and this will lead them to form attachments and relationships in farther-flung locations. Similarly, free movement in the EU has led many people to form life plans involving other countries. So we can distinguish "core" preinstitutional occupancy rights from "broadened" claims shaped by legal and conventional institutions.

Once formed, I believe these "broadened" occupancy claims are also worthy of respect, so long as they are compatible with the fair-use proviso. One ought not to reshape or reform institutional structures in ways that unduly disrupt people's locational expectations.[40] Suppose that in the future, Alaska were to secede from the United States. It would be wrong for Alaska to close its borders to people from other US states who have family ties or associational or occupational commitments in the area: it ought to allow these people to continue to come and go freely, reside there, and so on. But after the secession occurs, there may be a long-term reshaping of expectations, such that—within a generation or two—very few people from the continental United States retain meaningful ties in Alaska. In that case, the occupancy rights of those in the continental United States would no longer extend to Alaska. Hence, although occupancy has a "core" domain that institutional schemes are morally constrained to respect, it is also malleable in ways that depend upon conventional structures. Changes in legal and conventional

---

[40] In a relevant discussion, Catherine Lu highlights the ways in which the establishment of state boundaries has often disrupted the located life plans of transboundary indigenous groups. In my view, unless states cooperate to ensure access for such migratory groups, their boundaries are unjust, since they fail to respect prior occupancy rights. See Lu, "Decolonizing Borders, Self-Determination, and Global Justice," in *Empire, Race, and Global Justice*, edited by Duncan Bell (Cambridge: Cambridge University Press, 2019), 251–71.

structures can lead to a broadening or narrowing of these rights. Where they exist, these broadened expectations have moral weight, so long as they do not entail use of more than a fair share.

2.8 Conclusion

This chapter outlined my account of foundational title to land, explaining the basis on which certain people have a special claim to live in an area, including the right to set up a state that governs that space. I argued that *foundational title* is a bundle of individual occupancy rights held by the state's inhabitants. An occupancy right comprises two main elements:

> *First*, a liberty to reside permanently in a particular geographical space, and to make use of that space for social, cultural, and economic practices.
>
> *Second*, a claim-right against others not to remove one from that area, to allow one to return to it, and not to interfere with one's use of the space in ways that undermine the located practices in which one is engaged.

Occupancy rights protect our *plan-based* interests in the locational continuity of our central life commitments, as well as our more generalized *control* interest in being the agent in charge of revising and reshaping these commitments.

I also argued that while foundational title is held by a space's rightful occupants, this title can come to be interpreted and enforced on their behalf by a legitimate state, if the state appropriately represents these occupants. While the state's *core territory* is composed of land that its legitimate subjects rightfully occupy, the state may also claim jurisdiction over *ancillary territory*, when necessary to establish justice for these subjects. Once subject to a state, inhabitants' preinstitutional occupancy rights will typically be "broadened" by the institutional structures it establishes.

While weaker than a traditional ownership right, occupancy does confer at least some of the incidents associated with property, including rights to secure access to, use, and control of a particular area. This raises important questions about the kind of right occupancy is meant to be. Is it a claim of ownership, or something weaker, like a use-right? How is it related to the more familiar rights of property? Can "property-like" rights of any kind be unilaterally established, through the appropriation of particular places, or the formation of attachments to these areas?

Further, as highlighted in the introduction, most states have acquired (parts of) their territories through invasion, displacement, conquest, and other past wrongs. No state has a "clean" historical title to its land. So can present-day occupants claim foundational title to the spaces they now inhabit? Can the moral right of occupancy legitimate any territorial claims in the world today? The next chapter turns to these issues.

3
Challenges to Occupancy

Chapter 2 argued for a right of occupancy: a preinstitutional, "property-like" right to use a particular area of the earth. I held that a state has a right to rule a territory only if it represents inhabitants who hold moral rights to occupy its spaces.

However, my account raises important questions about whether such prepolitical occupancy rights can be justifiably established. Can the unilateral formation of life plans and projects place others under a duty to respect land claims made on this basis? Many cosmopolitans are skeptical of privileged claims to lands or resources. They often challenge such claims by appealing to common ownership of the earth. It is plausible to think that initially the earth's spaces would have been available to all, and that anyone's right to be in a given area would be as good as anyone else's. So how might we legitimately move from a scenario where the earth is freely available to everyone to a scenario where some people hold special rights over certain areas? Is this simply the usurpation of resources that rightfully should remain open to all?

Often, cosmopolitans argue that rights to land and territory can only be legitimately established through the consent of all the earth's common owners, or—failing that—through global democratic institutions that could legitimately legislate for humanity.[1] Otherwise occupation of territory is "a theft of what rightly should (have continued to be) held in common."[2] In this vein, Lea Ypi draws on Kant's political theory to argue that "the status of territorial rights remains in question" until a universal political association has been constituted.[3] On her view, territorial states that have been built on the occupancy of particular geographical spaces "remain illegitimate," since the original unilateral appropriation of these spaces was wrongful.[4] Ypi argues that states "can continue to exercise territorial rights if and only if their citizens are also politically committed to the establishment of a global authority realizing an all-inclusive principle of right."[5]

---

[1] Jakob Huber, "No Right to Unilaterally Claim Your Territory: On the Consistency of Kantian Statism," *Critical Review of International Social and Political Philosophy* 20, no. 6 (2016): 677–96; Kieran Oberman, "Immigration and Equal Ownership of the Earth," *Ratio Juris* 30, no. 2 (2017): 144–57.

[2] G.A. Cohen, *Self-Ownership, Freedom, and Equality* (Cambridge: Cambridge University Press, 1995), 73.

[3] Ypi, "What's Wrong with Colonialism," *Philosophy & Public Affairs* 41, no. 2 (2013): 176. Similar views about the need for cosmopolitan democratic institutions are expressed in Abizadeh, "Democratic Theory and Border Coercion," 46, and "On the Demos and Its Kin."

[4] Ypi, "What's Wrong with Colonialism," 184.

[5] Ypi, "A Permissive Theory of Territorial Rights," *European Journal of Philosophy* 22, no. 2 (2012): 293.

Drawing on Hugo Grotius, I argue in this chapter that even in the absence of global political institutions, or the consent of common owners, we can acquire limited exclusive rights over geographical space. Certain rights over material goods, including land, arise in virtue of our moral duties to respect the self-preservation and autonomy of other people. I call these *primitive rights*. Occupancy rights, as argued for in the last chapter, are primitive rights of this kind. Therefore, I reject the cosmopolitan premise that if the world is commonly owned, it is always impermissible to appropriate parts of it.

Still, the cosmopolitan critique does contain an important element of truth—in the absence of common consent or legitimate global institutions, exclusionary rights over territory are limited. The moral claims that can be justified in the absence of law and convention do not extend to the discretionary right to exclude others from accessing an area, or to prevent them from sharing in the material value of its resources. These limits will be important for my argument—developed in Parts III and IV of the book—that territorial rights should not extend to the full complement of exclusionary claims states currently make.

Primitive occupancy rights differ from property rights in three important ways. First, occupancy rights are not permanent titles, but rather *use-rights* that are limited in ways that express a common property background. Since these constraints can shift as background circumstances change, I argue in Chapter 6 that this may sometimes justify *redistributing* territory away from historic homeland groups.

Second, rightful occupants have only a limited right to exclude outsiders in cases where their settlement threatens significant harm to prior inhabitants' legitimate interests, and where those outsiders lack an urgent interest in coming. I argue for this *conditional* account of the right to exclude in Chapter 7.

Third, occupancy rights are not historically transmissible. This has the consequence that occupants cannot bequeath territory to their descendants, and bearers of occupancy rights will change as people's located life plans change. For this reason, this chapter also rejects challenges to current-day occupancy deriving from the fact that few inhabitants can show a "clean" historical title to their lands. I argue that an unjust past does not necessarily invalidate present-day occupancy, and that primitive occupancy rights can often be established in the aftermath of historic dispossession.

3.1 Grotius's Primitive Right

To defend these claims, I draw on Hugo Grotius's argument that individuals can bring about limited moral rights to geographical space through unilateral appropriation, even in the absence of a background system of property conventions or global political institutions. The goal of this section is to show that such primitive, property-like rights are plausible, and that accepting them does not commit us to full-blown naturalism about property.

Grotius stakes out an intriguing position with respect to common ownership—he claims that some exclusive rights are *consistent* with common ownership, on its best interpretation. Common ownership must be understood as the thesis that the inhabitants of the earth are equally entitled to use it for their own self-preservation and life projects, without interference from others, so long as they confine their use within reciprocally justifiable limits. Even prior to the invention of private property, Grotius argues, humans would have some moral rights over material resources. As he puts it, "a certain form of ownership did exist" prior to the institution of private property, "but it was ownership in a universal and indefinite sense" (*DJP*, 317), which he further glosses as "the power to make use rightfully of common property" (*DJP*, 315).[6] "[T]o have made use of Things that were then in common, and to have consumed them, as far as Nature required, had been the Right of the first Possessor: and if any one had attempted to hinder him from so doing, he had been guilty of a real Injury" (*DJBP*, 1.2.1).

William Blackstone, a later expositor of the Grotian view, argues that common ownership:

> seems ever to have been applicable, even in the earliest stages, to aught but the substance of the thing; nor could it be extended to the use of it. For, by the law of nature and reason, he who first began to use it, acquired therein a kind of transient property, that lasted so long as he was using it, and no longer... Thus the ground was in common, and no part of it was the permanent property of any man in particular; yet whoever was in the occupation of any determined spot of it, for rest, for shade, or the like, acquired for the time a sort of ownership, from which it would have been unjust, and contrary to the law of nature, to have driven him by force: but the instant that he quitted the use or occupation of it, another might seize it, without injustice.[7]

I call this right to use our commonly owned earth without interference a *primitive right*. What arguments might be given in its favor? I believe the primitive right is best justified on grounds that it is instrumental to protecting other, more fundamental rights. Every plausible moral theory holds that we are bound by general duties that we have done nothing voluntarily to incur, including duties to respect others' self-preservation and autonomy. Certainly, natural law thinkers take this view: they hold that we are bound by the law of nature to respect others' sphere of sovereign decision-making, their *suum* (*DJBP*, 1.1.5). Grotius argues that this sphere of sovereignty is partly preinstitutionally defined: thus, "our Lives, Limbs, and Liberties had... been properly our own, and could not have been (without manifest Injustice) invaded" (*DJBP*, 1.2.1).

---

[6] *DJP* stands for *De Jure Praedae* (composed 1604, but unpublished until 1868); and *DJBP* stands for *De Jure Belli ac Pacis* (first published 1625). I cite Grotius's works from the Liberty Fund editions, by book, chapter, and section number. *DJP* = *Commentary on the Law of Prize and Booty*, edited by van Ittersum. *DJBP* = *The Rights of War and Peace*, edited by Tuck.

[7] Blackstone, *Commentaries on the Laws of England*, edited by George Sharswood (Philadelphia: Lipincott, 1893), Bk. 2, ch. 1.

Yet it is difficult to see how we could fulfill these basic duties to others without sometimes also respecting their possession of material goods, when those goods are currently serving as essential supports for life, limb, and liberty. Clearly, it is necessary to appropriate some material goods (at the very least: food and drink, clothing, shelter, and the means of producing them) in order to guarantee self-preservation. Further, it also seems necessary to appropriate external things in order to enjoy the freedom to pursue our lives and projects. To exercise personal autonomy, an individual must dispose of some independent sphere—free from interference by other agents—in which to pursue her own life plans. Natural law thinkers called this sphere the *suum*.

How do external objects figure in our personal autonomy? Consider that almost any temporally extended project that we might undertake requires the use of external objects. Suppose I want to paint a landscape. To carry out this project, I need rights over the paint, brushes, and canvas sufficient to enable me to execute it without fear of someone else coming in and interfering with my work.[8] If we were unable to use anything without the permission of other common owners, we would be pervasively subject to their authority in our choices about what to do. They would exercise a veto power on our ability to set our own goals. Thus, if there is a background moral requirement to respect others' self-preservation and autonomy, it seems that there ought to be a background requirement to respect at least some claims to use and possess external things.

How extensive is this primitive right? Grotius says that this right gives us a claim to use things "as far as Nature required." Since each human being has a natural right to self-preservation, she also has the right to the necessary means for it. Some interpreters have read Grotius as limiting primitive right to basic survival needs, but he speaks more expansively of it: some external goods, he says, "are necessary to being, while others are necessary only to well-being; or, one might say that they relate respectively to safety and comfort" (*DJP*, 23). He refers to many uses of things that are not directly tied to survival, e.g., our right to use the sea to sail from place to place.

Grotius stresses that there are limits to the primitive right, although these remain vaguely defined in his work: "there was an equality to be observed in that state, where all things were common, that one as well as another might have the liberty of using what was common" (*DJBP*, 2.10.1.2). Why would there be such limitations? Note that the duty to respect others' personal autonomy—which, alongside self-preservation, grounds respect for primitive rights—is itself a limited duty. One does not have a duty to respect another's life projects full stop. Instead, one has such a duty only insofar as those projects are compatible with the autonomy of other people, including their enjoyment of an opportunity to form similarly

---

[8] See Arthur Ripstein, *Force and Freedom* (Cambridge, MA: Harvard University Press, 2009), 64; Anna Stilz, *Liberal Loyalty: Freedom, Obligation, and the State* (Princeton: Princeton University Press, 2009), 42.

valuable plans and projects. Any act of legitimate appropriation for one's own use, then, must be consistent with a rule that would allow others a similar use. This expresses the idea—again, familiar from Locke—that our appropriation must leave "enough, and as good" for others. I say more about the implications of this fair-use proviso for territory in Chapter 6.

Does the primitive right impose correlative duties? Grotius suggests so: "no Man could justly take from another, what he had thus first taken to himself" (*DJBP*, 2.2.2). As long as it is consistent with the fair-use proviso, our use of a thing places others under a moral duty to respect that use. Grotius illustrates this with a famous analogy from Cicero: "though the theater is common for anybody that comes, yet the place that everyone sits in is properly his own" (*DJBP*, 2.2.2). The theater remains common, but each theatergoer has a right against the others to his seat for as long as he is using it. Like the theater, the world in "early times" is common, according to Grotius, but anyone who has laid hold of a good may claim it as his, for the period of his own use. This holds at least so long as he dispossesses no one and respects the fair-use proviso.

Is the primitive right reducible to a simple duty to respect someone else's body? Kant argues that some material objects may fall within the compass of our duty not to assault others when they are physically attached to those objects (6:248).[9] He calls this a title to "empirical possession." But Grotian primitive rights seem more extensive than this, as the analogy to the theater suggests. In the theater, you may get up to get a drink or use the restroom and return to your seat without losing your claim—your "use" does not cease as soon as you are no longer physically attached to the space. That seems appropriate, for otherwise our claims to external things would be too limited to guarantee self-preservation and autonomy. Consider shelter: under an "empirical possession" system, one could claim only as much space as one's body took up. Others could come and share other bits of your cave, say, so long as they could do so without touching you. Were our claims to use material things so minimal—constrained to what we could physically touch or hold, for the time we were holding it—it is unlikely we could secure our other rights in a preinstitutional scenario. For that reason, I think our basic duties to others give us reason to respect uses of things that are more extensive than Kant's right of empirical possession.

What is the proper scope of a person's primitive rights? There is always a *pro tanto* reason, on my view, to respect an individual's use of space or objects for her life projects. Although this reason can be outweighed by the stronger competing interests of others, the reason for respecting someone's existing projects is especially weighty in cases where that life project is an *essential* means to carrying out a person's *comprehensive aims*. Again, these are aims that structure many choices and

---

[9] For explanation, see Ripstein, *Force and Freedom*, 94. For an interpretation of Grotius's primitive right that makes it coextensive with Kantian empirical possession, see John Salter, "Grotius and Pufendorf on the Right of Necessity," *History of Political Thought* 26, no. 2 (2005): 288.

activities and are closely related to a person's sense of her life as her own. Reasons of autonomy vary in their weight and stringency, however. Sometimes a project is a peripheral one, relatively unconnected to an agent's comprehensive aims. Sometimes, although a particular project is connected to a person's comprehensive aims, other means for achieving those aims are available. The reason against interfering with someone's use is less forceful in these cases, and the competing interests of others may outweigh it. So the scope of primitive rights is defined by the urgency and weight of our interests in a place or good, when assessed by comparison with the competing claims of others.

I find Grotius's primitive right plausible. The basic argument is that even absent the social convention of (full liberal) property, political institutions, or an act of collective consent, we can acquire limited moral rights over material goods, when those goods serve as essential supports for our other rights, playing an integral role in our self-preservation and life projects—so long as we confine our use within reciprocally justifiable limits.[10] Suppose I come across a plot of land where you have built a hut, are tending a small garden, and have installed various art projects. Does the fact that these goods are necessary to your sustenance and plans give me reason to refrain from interfering with them? I believe so. The fact that a material good is an essential support for someone else's preservation and projects grounds a *pro tanto* moral duty on me to respect her use of it, even if I did not consent to her possession. If I have (or can procure) a place to live and food to eat somewhere else, then I ought to leave your hut, garden, and art projects alone. On the other hand, the strength of these *pro tanto* duties depends greatly on the background situation. If I am starving or lack space in which to pursue my own projects, then I may be justified in interfering with "your" goods to obtain sufficient resources for myself. In this situation, interference is not a failure to respect your personality, but a justified attempt to appropriate the resources necessary for my own.

3.2 The Unilateralism Objection

A potential objection to primitive right—typically pressed by cosmopolitan critics—is that the unilateral appropriation of things wrongly interferes with the freedom of other common owners. I now want to investigate this objection, asking what kind of infringement of freedom might be at stake.

Samuel Pufendorf is the first to articulate this worry: he objects that "*taking* must not presently be construed *acquiring*: the former being a bare natural Action, whereas the latter includes a moral Effect."[11] Pufendorf holds that:

---

[10] Simmons, *A Lockean Theory of Rights*, 273–5, offers a similar interpretation of Locke.
[11] Pufendorf, *Of the Law of Nature and Nations*, translated by Basil Kennett (London: Carew, 1729), Bk. 4, ch. 6, §7.

upon supposition that all men had originally an equal power over things, we cannot apprehend how a bare corporal act, such as seizure is, should be able to prejudice the right and power of others, unless their consent be added to confirm it; that is, unless a covenant intervene.[12]

Even the most basic rights to food and shelter, according to Pufendorf, must be created by human agreement: "all Dominion, capable of producing any Effect against the claims of others, takes its rise from some Act of Men."[13] Before people could consume anything, a first covenant was necessary to introduce what Pufendorf calls "qualified communion," where "the substances of things belong to none, but their fruits become a matter of property when gathered."[14] Otherwise, as Richard Tuck puts it, "even goods picked for personal consumption could legitimately be snatched from the mouth of the prospective consumer."[15]

Yet if unilateral appropriation seems potentially problematic, Pufendorf's position seems equally so. This is the truth in Locke's dictum that "if such a consent as that were necessary, Man had starved, notwithstanding the Plenty God had given him."[16] Being unable to appropriate anything—even for our own use—in a commonly owned world would undermine our other rights and claims.

To put Pufendorf's view in its best light, we should note that by "agreement," he has in mind a rule-bound practice or convention, not an explicit compact. Pufendorf holds that property conventions evolve in stages, beginning with the initial rule allowing people to privately consume food and drink; then moving to property in moveable goods, like clothing, houses, and stores of provision; then to property in things that require industry and improvement, like household goods, cattle, tools; and finally to property in land, money, and exchange. Still, there are costs to Pufendorf's strong institutionalist position: as we saw in the last chapter, this kind of view has trouble handling cases of territorial removal. Given that Christopher Columbus shared no conventions with the inhabitants of Hispaniola, it would seem that on Pufendorf's view Columbus was morally free to dispossess them of their island.

Given these costs, it seems especially important to get clear on the nature of Pufendorf's moral objection to unilateral appropriation. Consider four interpretations of Pufendorf's worry that unilateral appropriation is prima facie objectionable:

(1) *Constraint*: it removes from other common owners the option of using a particular good.

(2) *Distribution*: other common owners might lack a fair share of what was initially possessed in common.

---

[12] Pufendorf, *Of the Law of Nature and Nations*, Bk. 4, ch. 4, §5.
[13] Pufendorf, *Of the Law of Nature and Nations*, Bk. 4, ch. 5, §8.
[14] Pufendorf, *Of the Law of Nature and Nations*, Bk. 4, ch. 4, §13.
[15] Richard Tuck, *The Rights of War and Peace* (Oxford: Oxford University Press, 2011), 155.
[16] Locke, *Second Treatise of Government*, §28.

(3) *Robbery*: it violates the property rights of other common owners of the good.

(4) *Authority*: as a moral equal, no individual has the authority to impose new obligations on another that this other person does not accept.

First, consider *Constraint*. On this view, consent to appropriation is necessary because taking a space for one's own use removes from others the option of using it. Yet others often *permissibly* interfere with our options through perfectly legitimate exercises of their rights, some of which involve using physical space. As Jeremy Waldron puts it, "everything that is done has to be done somewhere."[17] The fact that you are standing in this space may interfere with my ability to stand there now, removing that option from my choice set. But surely you do not need my permission to take up space with your body. You do not need such permission because the ability to stand somewhere, free from assault, is already covered under your general right to bodily integrity. If our rights to self-preservation and autonomy similarly "cover" the right to use external things necessary to secure these rights, then others' consent to our use is not necessary.

Consider next *Distribution*. On this view, taking *too much* space might interfere with the autonomy of other common owners. Autonomy requires a fair share of opportunity to engage in valuable activities, and an appropriator who hoards resources may deprive others of such opportunities. This is a very plausible worry. But the distributive objection could potentially be met by a system in which people were allowed to use only a fair share, highlighting once again the importance of the fair-use proviso. Of course, how to define a "fair share" is a fundamental question, and I return to it in Chapter 6. But fundamental as it is, *Distribution* does not rule out unilateral appropriation as such. If proper limits can be specified, and if individuals can respect them, there is no further objection to appropriation itself.

Consider next *Robbery*. Should we think that an appropriator commits a kind of theft? For this to be the case, we would have to conceive the initial common ownership scenario in such a way that all exclusive use of space without others' consent was ruled out. But that would leave people unable to secure their self-preservation and autonomy, since they could not perform even the most basic acts without others' permission. So we should not conceive the initial common ownership scenario that way. Everyday examples of common possession support this: at a family-style meal—where all the food is the common possession of all the guests—we do not ask the consent of the other guests before serving ourselves a portion, so long as we leave enough for others to eat; at the movie theater, we do not ask the consent of all moviegoers before sitting down, so long as there are enough seats. Instead, so long as an appropriator respects reciprocally justifiable limits on appropriation, he simply *particularizes* the common, in a way that is already morally permissible.[18] In the primordial scenario, the division of the

---

[17] Waldron, "Homelessness and the Issue of Freedom," *UCLA Law Review* 39, no. 295 (1992): 296.
[18] James Tully, *A Discourse on Property* (Cambridge: Cambridge University Press, 1980), 3.

common may not yet have *historically* occurred, but there is nothing in the morality of the situation that should *prohibit* its occurrence.

The best way to interpret Pufendorf's worry, I believe, is *Authority*. The thought is that by appropriating, I create new rights that did not exist before, deliberately imposing a duty on others to respect my possession. Were I to have this ability, it would make me a kind of *legislator* for others, placing their moral duties under my control.[19] By a bare act of will, I could change their moral situation. Pufendorf argues that such unilateral authority is at odds with the natural freedom and equality characteristic of a state of nature, in which no one is marked out as superior to anyone else (*DJNG*, 5.13.2). An agreement works to counteract this concern, ensuring that individuals together impose duties to respect property on themselves.

But is *Authority* successful against Grotius's primitive right? I do not think so. Notice that on the Grotian account, it is not the *appropriator* who legislates the duty to respect others' use of space. Instead—so long as that use helps to secure background moral rights—pre-existing morality legislates that duty. I respect your possession of this area not because of your arbitrary choice to seize it, but rather because morality requires respecting your possession of space in cases where that possession secures your self-preservation and autonomy and is consistent with my own. Of course, by taking up a space, the appropriator does *trigger* these background moral duties, but this need not be problematic. We trigger particular "applications" of others' moral duties all the time: when I cross the street, I trigger a requirement that drivers slow down to stop, thus "applying" their general duty not to unjustly threaten my life; when I post a flyer on a common message board, I trigger a duty on others not to post their flyers on top of mine, thus "applying" their general duty to respect my legitimate projects; and so on.[20] Likewise, by taking up and using part of the world, an appropriator activates a particular application of others' moral background duties, viz. the duty to respect his self-preservation and autonomy. But the appropriator does not claim any moral power to create *sui generis* duties for other people that they would not already have had.

We should distinguish the four worries just examined from a fifth, related, objection:

(5) *Interpretation and Enforcement*: No individual has the standing to enforce her interpretation of primitive rights upon an equal who reasonably disagrees with that interpretation.

---

[19] For this way of putting it, see Bas van der Vossen, "Imposing Duties and Original Appropriation," *Journal of Political Philosophy* 23, no. 1 (2013): 4.

[20] For further discussion, see David Estlund, *Democratic Authority* (Princeton: Princeton University Press, 2008), 143; Ripstein, *Force and Freedom*, 151; van der Vossen, "Imposing Duties and Original Appropriation." Of course, if the moral duties triggered are unduly costly or burdensome to others—as they would be, say, if I sat down in the middle of the street, blocking the free flow of traffic—they may have an objection to my act. But the mere triggering of a duty itself does not seem to ground a weighty objection.

I attribute this objection—to which I am sympathetic—to Kant's *Doctrine of Right*. But notice that unlike the other four possibilities just canvassed, *Interpretation and Enforcement* is not an objection to *appropriation*. To the contrary, Kant argues that appropriation is morally permitted.[21] However, Kant maintains that land and goods can only be held "provisionally" in the state of nature, because the definitive shape of the rights we acquire through appropriation remains a matter of dispute, since each individual lacks the rightful authority to force others to submit to her moral judgments. As independent equals, individuals have a right not to be politically "ruled" by other private persons. For this reason, such claims hold "conclusively" only once an *omnilaterally authorized* state is established. I say more about Kant's account in the next chapter.

At this point, I want to stress that the fact that primitive rights cannot be legitimately enforced in the face of disagreement does not mean that they are not valid *moral* claims, or that individuals lack duties to respect them. We should distinguish between two questions: how good a moral claim of right is, and whether, in case of dispute, that moral claim can be enforced consistently with everyone's standing as independent equals.[22] As Jeremy Waldron puts it, "the trouble with the application of acquisition principles is not that, in theory, no right answer exists, but that there is no basis common to the parties for determining which answers are right."[23] Kant argues that legitimate institutions are necessary to resolve disagreements consistently with our reciprocal independence. But he does not imply that there are no moral principles of justice independent of a legitimate authority's decision that govern rights to property and territory. Even in the absence of legitimate institutions, individuals should guide their actions by (their best interpretation of) these moral principles, respecting others' possession of land in cases where it appears to them that this possession is essential to others' self-preservation and autonomy, and consistent with their own.

I fully concede that these primitive rights are subject to pervasive problems of indeterminacy and disagreement, which render them fragile, unstable, and subject to dispute in a state of nature, and require authoritative adjudication to solve. It is especially unlikely that agents will converge in their interpretations of the fair-use proviso, for example. Yet even fragile and unstable moral claims can pre-exist the institutions necessary to legitimately adjudicate and enforce them.

---

[21] See Kant's "Postulate of practical reason with regard to rights" (*Metaphysics of Morals*, 6:257).

[22] Unfortunately, many Kantians have failed to distinguish adequately between these two issues. Instead, they have implied that, for Kant, strictly speaking, there are no moral claims to external goods outside a civil condition, and that individuals commit a prima facie wrong when they appropriate in a state of nature.

[23] Waldron, "Kant's Legal Positivism," *Harvard Law Review* 109, no. 7 (1996): 1550.

3.3 The Extent of Primitive Right

Let me briefly summarize my argument up to this point. I have claimed that it is permissible to unilaterally appropriate geographical space even in the absence of a global political institution or social convention regulating the use of land. Our background moral duties to respect others' self-preservation and autonomy license an additional requirement to respect at least some claims to material goods. Controversially, I have held that all this is *consistent* with common ownership, on its best interpretation.

I now want to ask: how extensive are these primitive rights? How many incidents of ownership do they encompass? Following Honoré, I define "full liberal ownership" as "the greatest possible interest in a thing which a mature legal system recognizes."[24] Nozick glosses full liberal ownership as involving "a permanent bequeathable property right."[25] I believe the interest acquired through a primitive occupancy right would fall considerably short of full liberal ownership. There are two relevant differences: first, primitive rights confer more limited claims to exclude; and second, primitive rights do not extend to contractual transfer or bequest.

Let me first consider exclusion. Full liberal ownership specifies criteria for acquiring permanent legal title to things regardless of the role those things play in the owner's life, and it allows the title-holder to exclude others from the good at will.[26] If you enjoy full liberal ownership of a theater seat, you may keep others out of it even when you are not sitting there, and even if you do not like seeing plays. You may simply be an investor who buys theater tickets to sell them at a profit. As Pufendorf puts it, "such is the force of dominion that we are able to dispose of things, which belong to us as our own, at our pleasure, and to keep all others from using them..." (*DJNG*, 4.4.2).

Yet primitive rights, as I interpret them, confer a claim to exclude others from space or good only insofar as that space or good (i) serves as an essential material support for a person's normal life activities; (ii) these activities would be set back by another's competing use; and (ii) the fair-use proviso is satisfied. This means that primitive right does not license exclusion in cases where the use of a space is not essential to a person's life plans, where the space can be used by others without detriment to these plans, or where the fair-use proviso is not satisfied.

Why doesn't primitive right extend to discretionary exclusion? Consider a "state of nature" case: suppose I come across a hut and plot of land where someone once lived but which has gone unused for some time. It is clear, however, that the would-be "owner" wishes me to refrain from "his" land, as is apparent from the "No

---

[24] See Tony Honoré, *Making Law Bind* (Oxford: Clarendon Press, 1987), 62.
[25] Nozick, *Anarchy, State, and Utopia*, 178.
[26] T. M. Scanlon, "Nozick on Rights, Liberty, and Property," in *Reading Nozick*, edited by Jeffrey Paul (Oxford: Blackwell, 1981), 125.

Trespassing!" signs. Is it self-evident that I am morally obliged to refrain from trespassing—say, that I have a duty not to shelter in the hut for the night? I deny that it is. The "natural" duty to respect others' possession is based on a prior moral requirement to respect someone's self-preservation and life projects, so long as these are compatible with the reciprocal claims of others. In this case, it is not clear how my use of the area would constitute an interference with anyone's life projects. Of course, my use may contravene the would-be owner's *intentions*, but natural morality does not require me to respect anyone's intentions.

The primitive right does license some exclusionary claims, however. To the extent that a space is essential to our personal privacy and daily life activities, primitive right generates a *pro tanto* claim to exclude others from it. Return to our earlier example, in which I come across a plot of land where you have built a hut, a small garden, and art projects. The purpose of that example was to suggest that I ought morally to recognize a duty not to trespass on your land, because (a) you are physically occupying it, and you require some protected sphere of choice in order to enjoy personal independence; (b) it is essential to your daily activities and life projects, even if you are not currently present there; and (c) my use of this area would risk setting back these projects (it may interfere with your current or future plans, or leave traces that disturb you, or you might come back and find me, causing distress). So we should conceive of a primitive right as comprising two elements: first, a claim not to be forcibly interfered with in our uses of commonly owned things, so long as we confine that use to a fair share, and second, a claim to *possess* those goods essential to personal privacy and daily life activities.[27] Typically, this means that individuals should be able to exclude others from private dwellings and the objects kept therein.

More controversial is whether primitive right can ground a claim to exclude others when privacy and personal independence are not at stake, and it is certain that a person's life projects *will in no way be harmed* by a given competing use.[28] Suppose you leave your canvas, paints, and brushes to go for a walk. Knowing you will be gone for the next hour, I come along and—leaving absolutely no trace— use one of the brushes to sign my name to a birthday card.[29] I deny that primitive right grounds a claim to exclude here. But I also fail to see how this use infringes your autonomy, since it does not damage any of the temporally extended, future-directed commitments that structure your life. One might object here that

---

[27] See Rawls, *Justice as Fairness*, 114, who endorses a basic liberty of personal property, which he says "would include certain forms of real property, such as dwellings and private grounds."

[28] Arthur Ripstein argues that nothing short of full liberal property suffices to guarantee individual freedom. See Ripstein, *Force and Freedom*, 19. In one prominent example, he asks whether I can take a nap in your bed, leaving absolutely no trace, if I am sure that you will never find out. See Ripstein, "Beyond the Harm Principle," *Philosophy & Public Affairs* 34, no. 3 (2006): 215–45. I think the example draws heavily on our fundamental interests in privacy and control over intimate space, and does not tell in favor of a more general right to property.

[29] Thanks to Daniel Viehoff for discussion of this example.

respecting personal autonomy involves more than simply respecting people's existing life commitments: it also requires that individuals have adequate opportunity to revise their plans. I agree. But I am not convinced that the opportunity to revise requires robust claims to full property. Suppose a squatter takes up residence in the overgrown back corner of my yard, a spot which I am not presently using and for which I have no plans. Would this competing use of my property jeopardize my autonomy? I deny that it would: no existing project of mine has been set back, I still have access to an adequate range of options for reshaping my life commitments, and I retain a protected domain of choice over my home and personal possessions. So the primitive right does not extend to a claim to exclude others from goods purely at will, when no setback to life projects is at stake.

Full liberal ownership also differs from the primitive right in a second way: it involves powers of contractual transfer, including rights to alienate, loan, rent, bequeath, and to derive income, all of which enable the possibility of market exchange.[30] As Grotius puts it: "the law of nature gave indeed a right to use things; as for instance, to eat or keep them, which are natural acts, but not to alienate them. This power was introduced by the fact of men, and therefore it is by that we must judge of its extent" (*DJBP*, 2.6.6). The natural duty to respect uses of material goods that are essential to others' life projects applies centrally to *nonexchange* uses. If you appropriate land for the sole purpose of giving others an incentive to exchange with you (i.e., you are not otherwise using this area for your life projects), then you lack primitive rights over it. I do not deny, of course, that there can also be duties to respect the possession of goods, including land, for economic exchange, but the shape and scope of these duties, I believe, depends on further conventional institutions.

Why shouldn't primitive right extend to the claim to transfer, to earn income, to exploit a good for market exchange, and so on? I do not deny that there might be a limited natural right to alienate. Even in a state of nature, one might promise one's goods to someone, and morality might require one to follow through on that promise. And, surely, if I come across two people in the forest bartering their nuts and apples, it would be wrong for me to run up and snatch the goods as they are passing between them.[31] If later, the recipient comes to incorporate those goods into her central life activities, I ought to respect her use and possession of them.

But the institution of contractual exchange differs significantly from the prepolitical morality of promise keeping and noninterference. Contract grants the donor a power to create a new right in a recipient, altering the duties of third parties so that they are now required to respect the recipient's—and not the donor's—possession of the thing. Moreover, this new right is meant to bind independently of any role that the thing might play in the donor's or recipient's projects, *other than the project of exchange*. To form a plan for market exchange, then, I must *assume* that both

---

[30] Tully, *A Discourse on Property*, 88.   [31] I owe this example to Nicolas Cornell.

my recipient and I have the right to exclude others from things apart from personal use. Yet I have argued that primitive rights protect only plans that we would have reason to adopt independently. Plans that I might form *for the sake of excluding others*—not for my own personal use—are not plans that we are required, as a matter of primitive right, to respect. Again, I concede that there can be duties to respect projects of contractual exchange, but those duties, in my view, depend upon a justified system of background conventions.

To sum up this account, I believe that even in a state of nature, and as a matter of minimal human morality, we would recognize certain rights over material goods, including land, that allow us to meet our needs, and to engage in (largely noneconomic) personal plans and projects. But I doubt that our recognition of this interest would extend to recognition of full liberal ownership, in the modern sense. Liberal private property depends on an agreement to establish new conventions—allowing for discretionary claims to exclude apart from use, to alienate, to derive income, and so on—that are *added* to the natural primitive right.

One might object that while there may indeed exist some prepolitical claims of the kind postulated by my "primitive right" thesis, these do not amount to "property" as that term is normally used.[32] Property is usually taken to involve direct rights over a thing itself. Primitive rights, on the other hand, involve only indirect rights to things. Primitive rights are generated insofar as certain moral duties to *persons*—in specific empirical circumstances—create a derivative requirement not to interfere with a person's use of a good or space. Primitive rights, we might say, are not really *rights to the thing*; instead, they are other rights that (indirectly) *happen to concern the thing*.

This objection is correct, and it highlights a key way in which primitive right falls short of full property. For my purposes, whether we wish to label the primitive right "property" is morally unimportant, so long as we recognize that it protects some "property-like" interests. I have argued that the primitive right goes beyond familiar duties not to interfere with another's body, grounding duties to respect others' possession of goods and spaces that are essential to their temporally extended plans and projects. Since many scholars use "property" to describe any bundle of rights over objects or resources, it may be reasonable, on this broad view, to describe primitive occupancy rights as a weak form of property. For others, who wish to reserve the term "property" for a more specific set of entitlements—including discretionary rights to exclude and alienate—I have no objection if they withhold the label here.[33]

---

[32] Again, I thank Nicolas Cornell for the objection.
[33] For this dispute over the meaning of "property," see Waldron, *The Right to Private Property* (Oxford: Oxford University Press, 1988), ch. 2; J. W. Harris, *Property and Justice* (Oxford: Oxford University Press, 1996).

3.4 Territory and Exclusion

I turn now to the implications of this account of primitive right for territory specifically. I argued in the last chapter that the state's foundational title to land consists in a bundle of rights, held by individual inhabitants, to occupy those areas essential to their comprehensive life projects, to enjoy security in these projects, and to access a range of options for revising them. In this chapter, I have argued that occupancy rights should be understood as primitive rights, not full property claims.

On this Grotian understanding, foundational title to land is rather thin. The inhabitants of a place cannot claim the discretionary right to exclude others from their territory at will. Claims to exclude, under primitive right, depend on showing that outsiders' settlement would harm the social, cultural, and economic practices of the locals (and, further, that these practices are consistent with the fair-use proviso). In the absence of such a showing, outsiders are permitted to use land that the local inhabitants are also using, so long as they do so in ways that do not undermine the inhabitants' legitimate activities.

Nor can local inhabitants necessarily claim the right to bequeath land to their successors. If the same land remains essential for the life activities of their descendants, then those descendants too can claim primitive rights to it. But if the descendants move elsewhere, or their social, cultural, and economic practices substantially change, then their ancestors' land may no longer be essential to their lives. If so, they lack any claims to the area. So primitive rights to geographic space can be expected to shift as people's attachments and activities change. On this view, the earth's land *itself* should not be thought of as an object of full proprietary control. Instead, land remains in common ownership, though—as we have seen—we should understand common ownership as compatible with limited exclusionary practices.

An important criticism of the "primitive right" tradition is that it may license colonial settlement.[34] It is true that under primitive right, claims to exclude settlers are more limited than they would be in a full property system. But some moral claims to exclude do exist, and these can be drawn upon to defend local inhabitants against unwanted colonization. Specifically, as I argue in Chapter 7, would-be migrants can permissibly be excluded where (i) they come with intent to politically control the population against their will *or* (ii) where they possess an adequate territorial base somewhere else, lack an urgent interest in moving, and seek to settle in a new place under conditions that would significantly harm the projects

---

[34] Tuck, *Rights of War and Peace*, 108; Ypi, "What's Wrong with Colonialism," 163. For a contrasting view, which holds that occupancy has equally often been wielded to defend the claims of native peoples, see Andrew Fitzmaurice, *Sovereignty, Property, and Empire* (Cambridge: Cambridge University Press, 2014), 68.

and practices of prior occupants. Since primitive right can ground claims to exclude in these "limit cases," my view does not endorse colonial settlement or expropriation. I say more about the implications of primitive right for colonial injustice later in this chapter.

Further, primitive right is also limited by the fair-use proviso. Even granting the expansive definition of "use" outlined in Chapter 2—on which keeping land in an unaltered state to maintain a public park, say, might count as "use"—local inhabitants may only claim a fair share of space for their practices. Space over and above that fair share can permissibly be settled and used by others, no matter how central the projects and attachments associated with it. So inhabitants are not permitted to deny outsiders access to areas kept for, say, recreational purposes (or indeed, for any purposes) if this involves claiming more than their fair share of land. Is this "proviso" a license for colonial settlement?

While any distributive limit will justify the entry and settlement of outsiders in some cases, I believe this is a consequence we have moral reason to accept. No right to exclude outsiders can be made compatible with each person's equal common right to the earth unless it rests on some comparative assessment of the urgency and weight of competing claims to space. This means we will have to balance the risk of harms to prior occupants' life projects against the interests of would-be migrants in settling. As I develop in more detail in Chapter 6, when incomers have urgent reasons to settle, this will outweigh the risk of trivial harms to local inhabitants. So one needs to think about (a) the urgency of the entrant's interest in coming, as well as (b) whether she has access to another territory that would fulfill this interest, and then (c) weigh these concerns against the potential setback to the locals' plans. Any right of locals to use part of the earth's surface to maintain a specific way of life must be suitably limited if it is to impose moral duties on others.

3.5 Past Dispossession

I turn now to whether the primitive right of occupancy is capable of grounding any real-world territorial claims. As noted in the introduction, the inhabitants of most existing territories did not come to be where they are through blameless first occupancy of previously uninhabited lands. Instead, territorial settlement has usually involved wrongdoing of various kinds, including the conquest and expulsion of prior occupants. If current residents have kicked out prior inhabitants, do they possess a moral right of occupancy in the new territory? Does the answer depend on how long ago the wrong occurred? Should settler states ever take steps to undo the effects of these past wrongs, and if so, what should these steps be?[35]

---

[35] Tamar Meisels, "Can Corrective Justice Ground Claims to Territory?" *Journal of Political Philosophy* 11 no. 1 (2003): 66.

In occupying a place, one must not remove or expel prior occupants who had a right to be there. For this reason, the primitive occupancy right grounds a presumption of repatriation and return in first-generation cases. By this, I mean that living wrongdoers who unjustly expelled people from their territory are morally required to restore the territory to the living victims they harmed. To see why, consider the following case:

> *Trail of Tears.* In 1838, US troops removed the Cherokees from their homeland in Georgia and relocated them to Indian Territory, in what is now the state of Oklahoma. Their homes, lands, and businesses were reallocated to white settlers, in a land lottery held by the state of Georgia.[36]

Suppose it is 1839: do the settlers have occupancy rights where they now reside? I believe they do not: located life plans do not confer occupancy rights when the establishment of those plans involved dispossessing people with prior claims. Like other moral rights, the right to occupancy may be forfeited through wrongdoing.[37] Just as someone who commits an assault renders himself liable to bodily harm by his victim or the police, so too wrongful dispossessors make themselves liable to territorial removal.[38] This is despite the fact that they may have formed located life plans in the area, and they may have an interest in sustaining those plans. Wrongful dispossessors have no complaint if they are expelled by way of their victims' reclaiming their place of residence.

In the Cherokee case, settlers forfeited their occupancy rights for two reasons: (i) they were aware that the Cherokees had a right to their lands, and (ii) they voluntarily chose to contribute to the violation of that right. In a well-publicized decision, the US Supreme Court upheld the Cherokees' title, so the settlers could not plead ignorance of Cherokee claims.[39] And most white settlers willingly contributed to their dispossession: while the Cherokees were still living there, Georgia began to distribute their territory through a lottery system, and hundreds of eager settlers purchased tickets for plots of Cherokee land. The excited lottery winners were not content to wait until a removal treaty was negotiated to take possession of their winnings. Instead, squatters invaded Cherokee lands: even the Chief of the Cherokee nation, John Ross, arrived home from Washington in 1835 to find a strange family living in his house.[40] So though they established flourishing farms, businesses, and associations in the area, these settlers had no

---

[36] Theda Perdue and Michael Green, *The Cherokee Nation and the Trail of Tears* (New York: Viking Penguin, 2007), 124–5; Tim Garrison, *The Legal Ideology of Removal: The Southern Judiciary and the Sovereignty of Native American Nations* (Athens: University of Georgia Press, 2009), 2–33.

[37] For a contrasting argument that even wrongdoers can acquire occupancy rights, see Lefkowitz, "Autonomy, Residence, and Return," 11.

[38] For discussions of forfeiture, see Jeff McMahan, *Killing In War* (Oxford: Oxford University Press, 2009), 1–37; and Christopher Wellman, "The Rights Forfeiture Theory of Punishment," *Ethics* 122, no. 2 (2012): 371–93.

[39] *Worcester v. Georgia*, 31 U.S. (6 Pet.) 515 (1832).

[40] Perdue and Green, *The Cherokee Nation and the Trail of Tears*, 105.

moral complaint about being removed, since they bore contributory responsibility for the wrong.

Do first-generation expelled victims have a right to come back? Generally, they do have a right to return, for two reasons. First, consider that return would have enabled the Cherokees to significantly reconstitute their located life plans. If they can reclaim their homes, businesses, and associational infrastructure, expelled victims have the right to do so.[41] The Cherokees' early years in Indian Territory were very hard. They initially had no fixed dwellings and lived in tents, and they faced challenges in rebuilding their schools, political institutions, and businesses.[42] This tells in favor of their continued claim to return to their lands, and to repossess the infrastructure there.

What about cases—unlike the Cherokee one—where victims' located life plans cannot be easily reconstituted? Often settlers destroy the victims' homes and infrastructure, so that all the nongeographical features that connected them to that place are gone. Do they still have a right to return? I believe they do. As I mentioned in Chapter 2, beyond the *plan-based* interest in occupancy, individuals also have a *control-interest* in being the agent in charge of revisions to their comprehensive life projects. This interest in authorship of one's own life can be radically set back through territorial expulsion. The control-interest is important in justifying a right to return in cases where victims will have to rebuild their lives from scratch. Even if their life plans have been destroyed, it ought to be the victim's decision whether to accept this change. Allowing them to decide whether to return mitigates the effect of an alien transformation of their lives and restores a sense of their own self-authorship. The interest in controlling revisions to one's life projects grounds a disjunctive right for first-generation victims:

(1) to go back if they wish or
(2) to waive their right of return and accept compensation/aid for building a new life somewhere else.

For these two reasons, I believe that first-generation victims will nearly always have the right to return if they choose.

While the Cherokee case is relatively straightforward, not all first-generation cases are so clear. Some settlers have excuses or even justifications.[43] While the Georgia settlers freely signed up for the land lottery, duress was involved elsewhere, as when Britain transported large numbers of convicts to Australia. Some cases of settlement may also be justified on grounds of necessity, as in the case of Jews fleeing persecution and settling in Mandatory Palestine under the auspices of Zionist organizations. In yet further cases—as perhaps, the indentured servants

---

[41] Alon Harel, "Whose Home Is It?" *Theoretical Inquiries in Law* 5, no. 2 (2004): 352.
[42] Perdue and Green, *The Cherokee Nation and the Trail of Tears*, 141–64.
[43] Chaim Gans, *A Just Zionism* (Oxford: Oxford University Press, 2011), 40–42, discusses justification and excuse for wrongful settlement.

who came to pre-Revolutionary America—settlers may have been ignorant of the injustice of the process in which they participated.

These considerations show that sometimes settlers should not be blamed for their participation in a wrongful colonization process, and that some have morally justified occupancy rights in the new place, especially where they have no homeland to which to return. Still, I doubt these complications are sufficient to undermine the presumption of first-generation remedies. Even where duress or ignorance was involved, excused settlers are under a duty to repatriate if they can do so at reasonable cost. They are wronging others by retaining their lands, and though they are not blameworthy, they can still be held liable to correct the injustice to their victims. Consider a recent immigrant to Israel—largely unaware of the situation in the West Bank—who moves to a settlement in search of cheap housing. Once he becomes aware of the injustice of the process in which he is participating, it does not seem unreasonable to hold him under a duty to move back within the Green Line.[44] In other cases where first-generation settlers have nowhere to go, they may not be obliged to repatriate, but this does not undermine the victims' right to return. It is not justified to destroy the lives of the occupants of a territory, even in order to rescue oneself from a desperate plight. It is also not necessary, since most territories can accommodate additional residents without expelling the old ones. Generally, then, a group of justified settlers should expect to share territory with the original occupants, not to expel them. If they instead engaged in removal, they have a special responsibility to facilitate their victims' return, and to compensate them.

A final complication for first-generation remedies is that innocent newcomers will quickly be born among the wrongful settlers. It may take these newcomers time (say, until their adolescence) to establish located life plans in the area. But the fact that they cannot be held responsible for the place of their birth means that once their life plans are established, second-generation settlers will have legitimate occupancy rights in the area. Moreover, the located life plans of these young people will depend on practices that are shared with first-generation wrongdoers. We cannot repatriate the wrongdoers, while allowing their offspring to stay (at least not without seriously harming the offspring). But how many newcomers does it take before a wrongful act of settlement is superseded, and all the settlers gain rights to stay? If one baby is enough, then repatriation will hardly ever be required.

In situations like this one, I believe we must balance the interests of the settlers' children with those of the expelled victims. If the prior inhabitants are refugees, they have especially strong claims to return. Moreover, the encroachment of

---

[44] For useful discussions of the settler movement, see Gershom Gorenberg, *The Accidental Empire: Israel and the Brith of Settlements* (New York: Times Macmillan, 2007); Idith Zertal and Akiva Eldar, *Lords of the Land: The War over Israel's Settlements in the Occupied Territories, 1967–2007*. While some settlers move for cheap housing, many are ideologically driven members of religious-nationalist groups, who explicitly endorse the aim of expelling or subjugating Palestinians and replacing their practices with Jewish institutions.

settlers often forms part of a project of colonial oppression, determined to subject the natives to alien rule or expropriate their lands. If this is the case, then repatriation may be justified even though it infringes some second-generation rights. This will be especially true if the second-generation population is small; if they have robust ties to a sending country, where they can move without too much disruption; and if they receive state aid for the dislocation they have to endure. Especially when the dislocation to nonculpable settlers can be minimized, such relocations can be justified despite the fact that they involve infringing rights.

There are other cases where the second-generation population is large and entrenched, and where they lack ties to any sending country to which they can return. In these cases, it may not be appropriate to repatriate *any* settlers—even the first-generation wrongdoers. Here, the best that can be done is to constrain wrongdoers to pay compensation in lieu of repatriating, to allow the expelled victims to return, and to require the two groups to share the territory. Of course, this sharing will often involve populations who wish to use the territory's resources in incompatible ways. In such cases, each side will have to make concessions in their way of life to allow those on the other side to enjoy at least core elements of their social and cultural practices: I say more in Chapter 6 about how this process might work.

The crucial point, however, is that even though it falls short of a full property right, the primitive claim to occupancy does have some remedial implications: it justifies a presumption of repatriation and return in the first generation. In many scenarios, there will be complicating factors—including excuses and justifications—that can weaken or rebut the presumption. Yet the primitive occupancy right can still support a principle of repair much like ordinary tort law. Where someone has been unjustly harmed by expulsion, the wrongdoer has a responsibility to "make her whole" again.[45] This principle of repair, however, applies only within the lifetimes of actual wrongdoers and their actual victims. The question now is whether this is sufficient, or whether we need to go beyond it. Can this limited principle of repair support our full range of intuitive judgments about settlement and return?

3.6 Beyond First-Generation Remedies?

In many cases, I believe the limited, first-generation principle is enough. Often the descendants of an expelled group do not plausibly inherit their parents' claim to return. Consider Jews who were expelled from Eastern Europe two generations ago, but whose children have grown up in America and Israel, or the children of Germans expelled from Poland who have grown up in Germany. It does not seem

---

[45] Leif Wenar, "Reparations for the Future," *Journal of Social Philosophy* 37, no. 3 (2006): 397, defends a similar "Limited Reparative Principle."

that these people have a claim to return to their grandparents' homes. A past expulsion may still ground other, ongoing moral duties in these cases: to issue an apology or other form of acknowledgment, and to pay compensation for stolen property or displacement. But return and repatriation do not seem appropriate here because the descendants' interest in territorial occupancy is not suffering a continued setback in the present. They have occupancy rights—and perfectly adequate life projects—in the places they now reside.

This illustrates that on my approach, occupancy rights are not heritable. As I have emphasized, occupancy rights should not be understood as permanent, bequeathable property titles, but rather as *primitive rights*: nontransmissible claims to use our commonly owned earth. Occupancy rights may be *contingently* transmitted to the next generation, if descendants form located life plans in the same area their parents did. But where no such connection exists, descendants will not inherit rights to their ancestral territory. Instead, the bearers of occupancy rights in a place will change as people's located life plans change. This is because what justifies occupancy in the first place is a certain class of personal values: the fundamental goals and relationships that structure individuals' lives. Expelled descendants whose lives are very different from their ancestors therefore lack claims to their ancestors' lands.[46] And while the first-generation has a waivable right—based on their control-interest in self-authorship—to reoccupy territory even where they cannot reconstitute their way of life, second and higher generations never suffered such wrongful interference with their lives, and so cannot claim a right of return on this basis.

Of course, many theorists and political actors have understood occupancy differently, as a property entitlement that can be bequeathed to subsequent generations. To explain why I reject this approach, let me briefly consider three prominent arguments for transmissibility, based on *inheritance, national identity*, and *political struggle*.

On the *inheritance* view, just as descendants inherit their forbears' property, so too they inherit the right to occupy their ancestors' lands. A. John Simmons argues that land rights are heritable and "descend down family lines." Further, he suggests that the original owner's (or his heirs') right to an unjustly taken thing can "remain through any number of unjust transfers of the thing over any period of time."[47] I am skeptical that territorial occupancy can be passed down perpetually through the generations in this way. Instead, I have suggested that occupancy is a primitive right that does not include claims of contractual transfer, such as bequest. The best reasons for allowing inheritance, in my view, turn on the consequences for social investment of a legal institution that incentivizes people to save for

---

[46] Waldron also argues that some entitlements can fade over time due to a change in "the basis of the rights themselves." Waldron, "Superseding Historic Injustice," 16.

[47] See Simmons, *Boundaries of Authority*, 164. For a similar view, see Wellman, "Occupancy Rights and the Right of Return," unpublished manuscript (2015).

future generations.[48] Yet these considerations do not apply to occupancy rights, which are moral claims to noninterference with uses of space fundamental to our self-preservation and autonomy.

It might be objected here that even if they are innocently born in an area from which previous inhabitants had been expelled, second-generation settlers could become culpable once they discover that their ancestors had wrongly occupied the land and they do nothing to restore it to the descendants of expelled victims. But this objection assumes without argument that those descendants would have a persisting right to their ancestors' homeland. In many cases—like the descendants of Jews and Germans mentioned earlier—I deny that expelled descendants have such persisting claims. On my view, primitive occupancy rights are rather like rights to a carrel in the library, or a picnic table in the park. If one not unjustly occupies a carrel or a picnic table, one may use these areas, and others should respect one's use (so long as other carrels or tables are available for them). But one cannot claim to bequeath a carrel or picnic table to one's descendants. To be sure, there will often be intergenerational transmission via overlap, as descendants who grow up in the same place their ancestors lived form located life plans there. Similarly, I might start a picnic at a table in the park with a couple of friends, and as time passes, some might leave, while others drop by. At a certain point, neither any of the original group nor I may be there—yet the people who are now sitting round the table will have a right against being ousted. Still, where a chain of overlap has been broken, one cannot claim a "right of return" to a picnic table from which one's grandfather was wrongly kicked out 50 years ago, though one may have a general right to access some picnic table for one's own use. So the inheritance view begins by assuming what needs to be shown: viz., that absent the unjust expulsion, descendants would have inherited a claim to their ancestors' lands. If those descendants have established flourishing lives elsewhere, then on the primitive right view I espouse, there is no reason to think they would inherit such a claim.

According to the *identity* view, the right of occupancy is a *group* claim. A group preserves a collective attachment to its ancient homeland for a long time—longer than three generations, and perhaps forever.[49] But I doubt that an identification with a territory based in collective narrative, rather than in members' lived experiences, can ground an entitlement to *reoccupy* that territory, especially at the expense of its present inhabitants. This is particularly true where the group has built a flourishing cultural life somewhere else: the claim that a nation centers its existence on a place

---

[48] See David Lyons, "The New Indian Claims and Original Rights to Land," in *Reading Nozick*, edited by Jeffrey Paul (Totowa: Rowman and Littlefield, 1981), 355–79; D.W. Haslett, "Is Inheritance Justified?" *Philosophy & Public Affairs* 15, no. 2 (1986): 122–55.

[49] Waldron, "Superseding Historic Injustice," 19. Moore argues that occupancy is a group right based on collective identification. It would seem that this corporate right could persist over time, even as individual life plans change, a conclusion Moore seems to want to deny in her discussion of rights of return. See Moore, *A Political Theory of Territory*, 153.

must be reasonably verifiable. Though the Serbs are strongly identified with the territory of Kosovo, their claim to reoccupy it is not credible, given that most of their cultural practices now take place in Serbia. A group does not have a claim to reside on its preferred territory, and certainly not to expel other people, just because it plays a central role in their national story.

Finally, Victor Tadros has recently argued for inherited rights of return based on *intergenerational political struggle*. He holds that Palestinian children have joined their parents' struggle for return, which gives them a valuable relationship to their ancestral territory.[50] Tadros may be correct that the intergenerational relationships of Palestinians are based around a political struggle that descendants find meaningful. But the fact that people identify with a political project is not sufficient to give them a right to see that project succeed. Zealous aspirations and strong convictions are not, in themselves, bases for moral claims. One must instead ask: (i) is it reasonable for descendants to grant this project such weight? And (ii) is this project's value generally recognizable enough and significant enough to ground a duty on others to enable its success? I am skeptical that—where other avenues for flourishing are easily accessible to them—it is reasonable for descendants to insist that their own lives must be based on the fulfillment of the political struggles of their ancestors. We are all born into lives that must inevitably differ from those of our ancestors. As Rawls puts it, we should assume that "people are able to control and to revise their wants and desires in light of circumstances and that they are to have the responsibility for doing so."[51] As long as the descendants grow up with a sufficiently wide range of options from which to build valuable lives, and so long as (unlike their parents) they suffer no wrongful interference with the lives they have in fact built, they lack any specific entitlement to the option they most prefer, namely the opportunity to lead those valuable lives on their ancestral territory.

So on my view there is no general presumption that in cases where people have been expelled, occupancy rights to their ancestral lands will persist through generations. Still, I think my occupancy theory should allow for some cases where rights of return *do* persist beyond the first generation, despite this general presumption. Especially worrying are cases where (i) the victims' descendants remain refugees or second-class citizens, who fail to establish flourishing located life plans in their new place of residence or (ii) where descendants lack lands that are fundamental to their ongoing religious or cultural projects. Consider Palestinians who live in refugee camps in Lebanon. It does not seem that their claim to return has been "superseded": they are still suffering in ways that are causally connected to the expulsion of their ancestors in 1948. Intuitively, we are concerned about the situation of these people in a way we are not in the case of a German whose

---

[50] Victor Tadros, "The Persistence of the Right of Return," *Politics, Philosophy, and Economics* 16, no. 4 (2017): 382–3.
[51] John Rawls, "A Kantian Conception of Equality," *Cambridge Review* 96, no. 225 (1975): 97.

grandparents were exiled from Poland. Return seems like a potentially appropriate remedy here.

When claims of return persist, I think they do so only because descendants of expelled victims lack a reasonable opportunity to establish flourishing lives where they now are. Though the wrong to their ancestors occurred long ago, I believe that Palestinian descendants continue to be harmed by that wrong, and that—because of its causal role in creating the refugees' plight—Israel bears a continued special responsibility for their suffering, and ought to be *first in line* when it comes to addressing their situation. Just as I have a greater responsibility than an innocent bystander to rescue a child I have pushed into a river, settler states have a greater responsibility to deal with the plight of their expelled victims than do third-party countries.

It seems clear that Israel's past expulsion continues to harm second- and third-generation Palestinian refugees, by causally contributing to their bad present-day condition.[52] The fact that they were born in refugee camps is due to Israel's decision not to allow their ancestors to return to their homes. People who lack access to a territory where they can reside permanently and engage in their social, cultural, and economic practices without fear of expulsion, deportation, or severe oppression lack one of the most essential preconditions for a fulfilling life.

I also believe the state of Israel bears an ongoing liability to repair this harm. Israel is a persisting, transgenerational organization that can be held responsible for past wrongs it inflicted. Analogously, we hold states responsible to pay their debts or to keep their treaties, even when these agreements were entered into long ago. This responsibility is attributed to the state itself, viewed as a collective agent. Of course, the costs of repair—in the form of a responsibility to integrate returning descendants or higher taxes to subsidize their resettlement—will eventually fall on current citizens, including many who played no role in the expulsion. These citizens are not blameworthy for what happened. But they are *liable* to repair these harms, within certain limits, much as they are liable to repay their public debt. Attributing them this liability reflect their status as members of a beneficial collective organization, and it gives them an incentive to act to *control* that organization, exercising their political rights to ensure that similar wrongs do not occur again.[53] So in cases where the descendants of expelled victims are unable to form flourishing life plans where they now reside, their interest in territorial occupancy

---

[52] While I find this claim intuitively plausible, this argument is subject to important philosophical challenges that turn on the metaphysics of harm. While I do not have space to explore these challenges here, I believe they can be overcome. See Lukas Meyer, "Intergenerational Justice," in *The Stanford Encyclopedia of Philosophy* (Summer 2016 edition), edited by Edward N. Zalta. https://plato.stanford.edu/entries/justice-intergenerational/.

[53] For further elaboration, see Anna Stilz, "Collective Responsibility and the State," *Journal of Political Philosophy* 19, no. 2 (2011): 190–208.

remains unfulfilled, and the settler state that expelled their ancestors may have a continuing duty to ensure their access to a permanent residence.

Suppose this argument for the extension of some remedies beyond the first-generation succeeds. What policies are appropriate in these second- or third-generation scenarios? I believe that the case for a right of return to a *particular* place is weaker for second- or third-generation descendants than for first-generation victims, so alternative remedies may be more appropriate here. Indeed, Israel may have significant discretion over how it discharges its responsibility to contemporary Palestinian refugees.

Why does Israel have this discretion? In my view, the Palestinian descendants are suffering primarily because they lack a permanent territorial residence *of any kind*, not because they lack *Palestine*. The descendants have not had a chance to form life plans involving the territory of their ancestors since they have never been there. Nor have they had much chance to form projects involving the territories where they now reside, since they generally lack citizenship in these places and they are subject to various rights restrictions there.[54] So they seem to have an outstanding *general* claim to form stable located life plans *in some decent place*. But it is not clear that this claim gives them the right to return to Israel *in particular*.

To soften this conclusion, I add one caveat. While in most cases the particularity of the claim to return has become diluted by the third generation, there may be a few cases where descendants have ongoing attachments to their ancestral territory that are grounded in *their own* life projects, not in narratives about their ancestors. Sometimes a locality plays a unique role in religious or cultural practices, and these projects are significantly impaired because descendants lack rights to that specific place. Such unique claims are often made by indigenous peoples. They may be unable to carry out their religious observances (say, as the Taos Pueblo claims to worship at Blue Lake) or to engage in economic or cultural practices tied to a specific ecological environment (say, reindeer herding for Saami people in Scandinavia). In such cases, descendants' claims to be restored to occupancy may carry greater weight. But this requires showing that descendants are truly impaired in leading their lives because they cannot engage in central religious, cultural, or economic practices without that specific location. This is a high bar: it is not sufficient simply to show that descendants strongly desire to live in the area or that the place plays a role in their narratives or myths. Which territory a person has a right to occupy

---

[54] One might object here that it is the states where Palestinian refugees now reside—not Israel—that are responsible for wronging them: these states should have granted them permanent residence. Yet I believe both parties are responsible for the Palestinians' plight. Responsibility is not zero-sum. In ordinary criminal law, when two parties together commit a crime, we hold each fully responsible: we do not "divide" the criminal responsibility between them, or absolve one by attributing responsibility to the other. Certainly, the Palestinians' situation would be much less tragic had Israel not refused to recognize their claim to return.

thus depends on objective facts about his actual pursuits, not on his subjective desires and aspirations.

I conclude with a sketch of how my account might apply to the second- and third-generation Palestinian refugees. I believe that Israel is responsible for ensuring that Palestinian refugees have access to a sufficiently good place of residence, one where their rights are protected; they can engage in the cultural, social, and economic practices that matter to them; and they can exercise political autonomy. But there are various ways this might be done: Palestinians might return to parts of Israel (in some cases, different places from the villages their parents once inhabited) and be granted political autonomy there, or they might be settled in a future Palestinian state in the West Bank and Gaza Strip, with compensation for their long exile, or Israel might aid them in acquiring a territory where they could enjoy political and cultural autonomy in some other part of the world. I believe Israel, in principle, could meet its historic responsibility to the Palestinians by undertaking any of these measures. While it is important for the third-generation Palestinians to possess a territory, I do not think that this must be the exact territory of their ancestors.

3.7 Conclusion

To sum up the account developed in Part I of this book, I offer a formal statement:

> *Occupancy Rights.* A person has a preinstitutional right to occupy a particular area if (1) access to spaces in that area is fundamental to his located life plans and (2) his connection to the territory was established without any wrongdoing on his part, involving (at a minimum) no expulsion or wrongful interference with prior occupants or infringement of others' claims to an equitable distribution of geographical space.

In this chapter, I argued that occupancy should be conceived not as a full property right, but rather as a primitive right to use our commonly owned earth, free from interference. Following Hugo Grotius, I held that these primitive rights arise from prior natural duties to respect others' self-preservation and life projects. I therefore rejected cosmopolitan challenges to occupancy that would suggest that unilateral appropriation of geographical space necessarily violates common ownership. Even if the earth is owned in common, I argued that there is nothing wrong with people asserting claims to specific areas of it, so long as they respect the fair-use proviso. I further argued that these primitive occupancy rights are limited in scope and do not extend to the discretionary claim to exclude outsiders, at will, from accessing the territory. This has implications for the right to control borders and natural resources that will be further explored in Parts III and IV.

Since primitive rights are nontransmissible, I also rejected an additional challenge to present-day occupancy that derives from the history of dispossession.

I held that the validity of present-day occupancy does not necessarily depend on showing a historically "clean" chain of title. Unlike property rights, primitive rights of occupancy can sometimes be established even in the face of an unjust past. Still, this is no charter for thieves: despite its nonhistorical character, occupancy has some remedial implications and can provide a plausible basis for theorizing rights of return. On my view, first-generation expellees will nearly always have a right to return, and so will descendants of higher generations who have failed to establish flourishing lives elsewhere.

PART II
SELF-DETERMINATION

4
Legitimacy and Self-Determination

In Part II, I turn to the question of how a state might acquire legitimate territorial jurisdiction over a population of rightful occupants. What gives a state the right to rule a specific territory and group of people? Let me define "legitimacy" as the state's possession of an exclusive moral right to make law and policy on behalf of a specific group and to use coercion or force to implement those laws and policies. The concept of *legitimacy*, which focuses on the state's right to make and enforce law, is distinct from the concept of *justice*. A theory of *justice* addresses the question: what scheme of rules about rights ought a political community (ideally) to adopt and enforce? Justice is about content. A theory of *legitimacy* addresses a different question, namely: who has the right to *decide* what scheme of rules a political community will adopt, as well as the right to enforce that scheme? Legitimacy is concerned with procedure.

Because legitimacy and justice are importantly distinct values, someone may have the correct view about justice, yet lack the right legitimately to enforce that view. Suppose, for example, that Rawls's theory of justice is correct. By any reasonable estimation, current property laws in the United States are far from satisfying his difference principle. Yet were my fellow Rawlsians and I to arm ourselves and—taking to the streets—strip the rich of their goods and give them to the poor to satisfy Rawlsian requirements, others would have an important objection to our actions. As private individuals, we lack the proper standing to make and enforce property law. Normally, only our legitimate government may do that.

Moreover, sometimes a legitimate government may permissibly implement political decisions that are not perfectly just. It may be acceptable for the United States to enforce property laws that do not realize Rawls's Difference Principle, provided those laws are legitimately enacted. Sometimes it can be illegitimate to impose a just policy (because the imposer lacks the proper standing to do so). And sometimes it can be legitimate to impose an unjust policy (because the policy, while not perfectly just, is not so unjust as to undercut the imposer's right to decide).

The concept of legitimacy is contested: some see legitimacy as correlative to subjects' obligations to obey the state's directives, whereas others define "legitimacy" as a mere liberty to enforce. The definition I adopt here is agnostic about whether the subjects of a legitimate state always have duties to obey the law, but it does hold that legitimacy correlates to at least *some* obligations—namely, the obligation not to interfere with, compete with, or resist the state's efforts to issue and enforce its directives. Outsiders ought to refrain from interfering with a legitimate state, through efforts at intervention or regime change. And insiders ought to defer to its legal system and forgo vigilante enforcement.

When a state has legitimate jurisdiction over a group and their territory, it will have a right to specify, interpret, and enforce its subjects' occupancy claims, as well as a right to make new rules governing conventional property (including rights to exclude apart from use, alienate, loan, rent, bequeath, and derive income) within the area it governs. It will also have the power to exercise compulsory adjudication over disputes between individuals, to provide public goods, and to apprehend and punish criminals.

What could give a state the standing to do these things? I hold that a state has a right to rule a territory and population if and only if it: (i) protects certain essential private rights (including security, subsistence, core elements of personal autonomy, and deliberative freedom) for all its subjects and respects these rights in outsiders, and (ii) it reflects the shared will of its population as to how (and by whom) they should be ruled. To gain the right to rule, a state must serve the second and third core values that underpin the states system: *basic justice* and *collective self-determination*.

In emphasizing collective self-determination, my account departs from traditional liberal theories, many of which hold that the state's right to rule is determined solely by its ability or record in securing justice. Unlike these theorists, I hold that legitimacy has two dimensions.[1] To be legitimate, a state must not only provide minimum conditions of justice to its population (*basic justice*); it must also satisfy their interest in being authors of their political institutions (*collective self-determination*). Only if a state facilitates its subjects' collective self-determination can its enforcement powers be reconciled with their *autonomy*, their claim to shape their lives by their own judgments. I argue that respecting individual autonomy requires not only that people enjoy certain rights over their personal lives, but also that they are part of a collective that pursues justice through rules they choose by the exercise of their own deliberative agency.

4.1 Functionalism and Colonialism

Many traditional liberals instead take a *functionalist* approach to state legitimacy. As outlined in the introduction, the functionalist holds that a state has a right to rule a population and territory insofar as it governs in a reasonably just manner.[2] Recall Allen Buchanan's view, introduced in Chapter 1. Buchanan claims that a

---

[1] Simmons, *Justification and Legitimacy*, (Cambridge: Cambridge University Press, 2001) 122–57, also distinguishes a state's legitimacy from what he calls its *justification* (roughly synonymous with what I refer to as "justice"). For a similar argument, see Pettit, *On the People's Terms*, ch. 3.

[2] Simmons, *Boundaries of Authority*, 60.

state is morally justified in exercising political power over a population and territory if it "(1) does a credible job of protecting at least the most basic human rights of all those over whom it wields power and (2) it provides this protection through processes, policies, and actions that themselves respect human rights."[3] Functionalist accounts of state legitimacy often appeal to a natural duty of justice that requires us "to support and comply with just institutions that exist and apply to us" and "constrains us to further just arrangements not yet established, at least when this can be done without too much cost to ourselves."[4] This duty to participate in a just state is binding on us independently of any special relationships we have, or any voluntary transactions we have engaged in.

Functionalism comes in both *maximizing* and *threshold* variants. The maximizing variant holds that a particular state has a right to rule a territory if—compared with its rivals—it can do *best* at delivering justice. The threshold variant holds that the state has a right to rule a territory if it achieves a *decent* level of success in that task.[5] Meeting the threshold gives it a claim against interference by foreign powers that would do an even better job.

An important worry about functionalism, however, is that it may license benign colonialism, the unilateral imposition of political institutions onto unwilling groups.[6] The charge is not that functionalists will endorse colonialism in all cases. Colonialism and annexation frequently involve unjust rights violations and may be ruled out on these grounds. Allowing states to annex territory also promotes war, which has predictably bad consequences for international peace and security.[7] Further, functionalists would likely condemn most historical instances of colonialism. Colonial rulers dispossessed indigenous populations and sometimes exterminated them; they engaged in forced labor and economic exploitation, and they institutionalized systems of racial and cultural discrimination. Functionalist commitments to human rights explain why these acts were wrong.

Still, the functionalist does not rule out a *benign* colonial regime if it did a reasonable job at providing good governance. Indeed, functionalism might be invoked to support "civilizing" colonialism: particularly in the later colonial period, European colonizers often relied on arguments grounded in liberal principles to justify their practices.[8] Colonial rule was defended on the basis that it would abolish the slave trade in Africa, further the moral and material well-being of native populations, or advance commerce and development. The US occupation of the Philippines, for example, supposedly aimed to improve "the well-being, prosperity,

---

[3] Buchanan, *Justice, Legitimacy, and Self-Determination*, 247.
[4] Rawls, *Theory of Justice*, 99; Buchanan, *Justice, Legitimacy, and Self-Determination*, 85.
[5] See, e.g., Buchanan, *Justice, Legitimacy, and Self-Determination*, 70.
[6] For this charge, see David Miller, "Neo-Kantian Theories of Self-Determination: A Critique," *Review of International Studies* 42, no. 5 (2016): 858–75.
[7] See Buchanan, *Justice, Legitimacy, and Self-Determination*, 275–88, 355–7.
[8] For a similar critique, see Ypi, "What's Wrong with Colonialism," 168.

and the happiness of the Philippine people" and to establish "an enlightened system of government."⁹

Suppose a benevolent colonial regime were successful in living up to its "civilizing" ideology: it protected its subjects' rights and delivered enlightened governance to them. In that case, on either variant of functionalism, no claim to self-governance could be pressed against it. *Ex hypothesi*, this regime meets the minimal justice threshold, and it may do better at securing justice than its rivals (also satisfying the maximizing criterion). Still, many people believe that a population subjected to benign colonial administration would have a morally significant complaint: while not subject to grave injustice, they are denied self-rule. I will argue that this violation of self-rule is itself a wrong, even when not accompanied by further rights violations.¹⁰ A key aim of this chapter is to understand the nature of the *pro tanto* wrong involved in the denial of political self-determination.

Violations of self-determination can occur in other cases. Consider:

Military Occupation.¹¹ In 1945, the Allies occupied Germany through a just use of force. Suppose that instead of restoring the territory to the German people, the United States had annexed their zone of occupation, turning it into an additional state of the union. After annexation, the United States governed reasonably justly, protecting the Germans' human rights and granting them rights of democratic participation in the unified polity. Would the Germans have had a claim to political independence?

Humanitarian Intervention. Proponents of humanitarian intervention argue that it is permissible to intervene militarily in another state in cases of genocide, mass expulsions, or gross violations of basic human rights.¹² They believe temporary foreign rule can be acceptable in the aftermath of a justified intervention. Yet most people think occupiers are obliged to restore the country to independence once a decent domestic government can be established. Why do they have this responsibility?

The best way to characterize our intuitions about these cases, I believe, is to hold that annexed, colonized, or occupied populations have a claim to govern themselves independently, and to order their political institutions as they choose. Their claim to self-determination is defeasible, and it may sometimes be outweighed by competing concerns, as in a justified humanitarian intervention. But where

⁹ Neta Crawford, *Argument and Change in World Politics: Ethics, Decolonization, and Humanitarian Intervention* (Cambridge: Cambridge University Press, 1996), 236–9.
¹⁰ For a similar view, see Ypi, "What's Wrong with Colonialism," 161. For skepticism, see Laura Valentini, "On the Distinctive Procedural Wrong of Colonialism," *Philosophy & Public Affairs* 43, no. 4 (2015): 327. See also Margaret Moore, "Justice and Colonialism," *Philosophy Compass* 11, no. 8 (2016): 447–61.
¹¹ This example is drawn from an earlier published paper. See Anna Stilz, "Nations, States, and Territory," *Ethics* 121, no. 3 (2011): 590.
¹² See International Commission on Intervention and State Sovereignty, *The Responsibility to Protect* (Ottawa 2001).

weighty countervailing considerations are not at stake, it ought to be respected. Functionalism, however, seems unable to account for self-determination. On its maximizing variant, no political group can ever claim a right—against a more just colonizing power—to govern itself independently. And while its threshold variant allows a political group that achieves decent rule to govern themselves, their right to independence holds only *pro tem*, and may be lost if in the future they become subject to reasonably just foreign rule.

As noted in the introduction, I agree with many aspects of functionalism, particularly the insistence that a legitimate state must do a minimally good job protecting basic rights. Where foreign rule is the only option for securing these rights, it may be temporarily permissible, and I say more about such cases in Chapter 5. Yet even where self-determination is outweighed by other considerations, in my view, it remains important and may ground future claims to political independence. Unlike the functionalist, then, I deny that the minimal provision of justice is *sufficient* to give a state a claim to rule a territory and its population.[13] Instead, we should distinguish between a temporary permission for an effective agent to use force to secure basic rights, and *legitimate territorial jurisdiction*—a claim-right, held by a state against its competitors, to be the permanent ruler of a territory and its population. Legitimate jurisdiction requires a state that reflects the self-determination of its population.

4.2 Two Dimensions of Legitimacy

On my view, then, legitimacy has two dimensions. Functionalism focuses on the "taker dimension": a (reasonably just) state's role in providing justice-related benefits to its members.[14] As institutional "takers," individuals have interests in protection of their rights (including rights to democratic representation), a fair scheme of distributive justice, or public goods that only a state can provide. This "taker" dimension of evaluation focuses on familiar aspects of the basic structure, e.g., "the way in which the major social institutions distribute fundamental rights and duties and determine the division of advantages from social cooperation."[15] It is concerned with the quality of state institutions, independent of anyone's acceptance or endorsement of them.

But I believe legitimacy also has a second, "maker" dimension: people have an interest in seeing themselves as the authors of their political institutions. It is as

---

[13] Buchanan allows that a government of military occupation might satisfy his functionalist criteria for political legitimacy. See *Justice, Legitimacy, and Self-Determination*, 236.
[14] Buchanan, *Justice, Legitimacy, and Self-Determination*, 247.
[15] Rawls, *A Theory of Justice*, 6. In quoting Rawls, I do not mean to imply that he neglects the "maker" dimension of evaluation; see his remarks on the importance of a "well-ordered society." Among recent works on global justice, Rawls's *Law of Peoples* is notable for the weight it places on self-determination. See Rawls, *The Law of Peoples*, 31, 118.

important that their institutions reflect their priorities and values (in their role as "makers") as these institutions be good ones (from their perspective as "takers"). This second dimension of evaluation focuses not on the internal structure of the state itself (its qualities or characteristics), but rather on the relation between that state and those it rules. Collective self-determination is grounded in this "maker" interest in authorship of our institutions.

This chapter develops a specific account of self-determination, which I call the *political autonomy* theory. My account draws in important ways on Kant's argument that the rules governing our collective political life ought not to be enforced *unilaterally*. Kant holds that to have the right to make and enforce law and policy for a population, the state must represent its subjects' *omnilateral will*: "Only the concurring and united will of all, insofar as each decides the same thing for all, and all for each, and so only the general united will of the people, can be legislative" (6:314).

A key question is: what exactly makes for an omnilateral will? I suggest that an omnilateral will is an *actual* popular will. To enforce law and policy legitimately, a state needs to reflect the shared intention of a significant majority of cooperators on its territory to establish justice through specific institutions. Only then is a state authorized by rightful occupants in a way that gives it a right to legitimate jurisdiction over them.

As noted in the introduction, in using the language of "shared will," I do not imply that a group necessarily shares a common commitment to enacting specific laws or promoting shared substantive values. In a modern pluralist society, a shared will is more likely to take the form of a will to associate with one's fellow citizens in one political community and to support certain institutions. Ordinary political disagreement is thus perfectly compatible with the existence of a shared will as I understand it.

I will also argue that a shared will can exist even if not all citizens in a territory unanimously affirm their membership in their society. There are compelling reasons for discounting nonunanimity in certain cases where (i) dissenters are unwilling to cooperate in a legitimate state that can protect essential private rights or (ii) where too few dissenters share alternative commitments for a territorial unit reflecting their commitments to be institutionally feasible. Thus, in practice, a state should reflect the commitment of a *significant majority* of cooperators within its territory to associate together politically and to support specific institutions.

In offering this reading, I hope to complicate our understanding of Kant's political theory. Kant agrees with the functionalist that our obligation to a legitimate state is rooted in a natural duty of justice. But Kant holds that our natural duty of justice requires us not only to set up a minimally just state, but also to impose that state's political order in a manner that is sufficiently respectful of people's capacity for rational autonomy, including their capacity to make judgments about how, and by whom, they should be ruled. Once the conditions of an omnilateral will are unpacked, we will see that it is permissible to impose a political order on unwilling participants only in a narrow range of cases, and that the Kantian view does not sanction colonial annexation. Understanding the problem of unilateralism, in my view, also allows us to explain why a Kantian should prefer a system of states to a single world state.

4.3 Justice in the State of Nature

I begin by briefly recapitulating some main elements of Kant's theory of legitimate state authority. I will pass over this quickly, since Kant's political philosophy is by now relatively familiar, simply isolating the main claims that are of interest for my argument.

(1) *Natural Duty*: We have a natural duty of justice to respect others' innate right to freedom as independence.

(2) *State*: We cannot fulfill this natural duty without coordinating in a state that can define and enforce one unitary scheme of substantive rights (especially property and contract rights) that binds us all amid disagreement. Our duties to do justice to others are therefore mediated by the state.

(3) *Omnilateralism*: This public scheme of rights ought not to be imposed *unilaterally*. That is, it ought not to be coercively implemented by an agent who demands that everyone else conform to her own judgment of what justice requires, and who privately enforces this demand. Instead, for its imposition to be legitimate, a public scheme of rights must reflect an *omnilateral will*, that is, a set of judgments about the enforcement of justice that are shared.

Kant begins from the idea that everyone has an innate right to independence. A necessary condition for autonomous, self-directed action is being free from the will of others, who might otherwise interfere with one's capacity to set and pursue one's goals. Everyone has a fundamental, coercible natural duty of justice to respect others' independence (*Natural Duty*).

Kant further argues that we cannot fulfill our natural duty of justice without entering a civil condition (*State*). At least some of our general, coercible duties of justice (particularly the duty to respect other people's property and contractual rights) are mediated by legitimate state institutions. We have a duty to comply with and support a legitimate state's system of law because this is necessary to treat other people justly.

Why might duties of justice be institutionally mediated in the way Kant suggests? The main problem is that people disagree about which scheme of rules ought to guide their attempts to do justice to one another, and these disagreements require legitimate authority for their resolution:

> [B]efore a public lawful condition is established, individual human beings, peoples and states can never be secure against violence from one another, since each has

its own right to do *what seems right and good to it* and not to be dependent upon another's opinion about this. (6:312)

Kant argues that these problems of disagreement mean that rights (including the occupancy rights explored in Part I) are not legitimately *enforceable* outside the state. When two individuals, each acting to implement a set of rights that they believe, in good faith, protects the independence of all, disagree in their interpretations of justice, neither is required to submit to the other's judgments. No one can claim the *exclusive* standing to interpret and enforce justice for others, in a way that would put those others under an obligation not to interfere with, compete with, or resist his efforts.[16] As Kant puts it, "rights are *in dispute (ius controversum)*" in the state of nature, since in cases of conflict, there is "no judge competent to render a verdict having rightful force" (6:312). As I argued in Chapter 3, we should not take this to mean that there are no valid *moral* claims (including rights to noninterference with the use of land) in the state of nature. But it does mean that in the absence of a state, each individual is the sole judge of what these moral claims are. Where individuals' interpretations diverge, no single person has the standing to resolve the conflict by using force to overrule others' judgments.

Kant's reflections on private right in the state of nature lead him to two conclusions. First, he argues that people living side-by-side have a derivative duty grounded in their more fundamental natural duty of justice to *coordinate* under public authority (*State*). If they are to discharge their duty to treat others justly, they need to settle on some common public interpretation of rights, because without clearly shared rules, their independence will become precarious indeed. A world in which there is no commonly accepted scheme of rights but only a set of competing and conflicting private interpretations is a world in which no one's independence is fully secure. The natural duty of justice therefore grounds a derivative duty to coordinate, through the state, on a scheme of rights that can be enforced in a unitary way amid disagreement.[17]

Much more could be said about Kant's argument for the duty to enter the state. But I propose to take this background argument largely for granted here and instead to focus on a less-noticed aspect of his view: Kant holds not only that we ought to coordinate in a state, but also that we ought to coordinate in a particular way: omnilaterally, not unilaterally. The required common scheme of rights ought not to be imposed *unilaterally*, since "a unilateral will cannot serve as a coercive law for everyone" (6:356).

To bring out Kant's position, imagine a private individual whose interpretation of justice is substantively correct (i.e., she holds justified, true beliefs about everyone's moral rights) and who is endowed with sufficient power to successfully

---

[16] See Louis-Philippe Hodgson, "Kant on Property Rights and the State," *Kantian Review* 15, no. 1 (2010): 57–87.

[17] For an account of legitimacy that emphasizes the need to coordinate amid disagreement, see Jeremy Waldron, *Law and Disagreement* (Oxford: Oxford University Press, 1999).

bring other people to coordinate around her view. Perhaps she has access to a new weapon no one else possesses. Though she could successfully impose a perfectly just scheme by acting unilaterally, Kant claims that she has some reason not to do that. The fact that her judgment is correct is not sufficient to give her the right to force others to comply with her decisions. The question of legitimacy, in other words, is not settled by the truth of her views about justice: it requires an independent justification.

Kant's basic complaint about unilateralism can be expressed by analogy to international relations. Suppose Country A proposes to undertake a war that, objectively speaking, is perfectly justified: Country A has a just cause, the war has a reasonable prospect of success, it is a last resort (Country A has already tried all other methods to resolve the injustice), and the means it proposes to use to prosecute the war are proportionate to the wrong. Still, many people believe that this war is defective unless it receives *multilateral authorization*: it is not Country A's right to make this decision all on its own and without submitting to an appropriate procedure, such as perhaps (though this is controversial) seeking authorization from the United Nations.[18] Kant holds that the enforcement of rules about private rights is subject to a multilateral authorization requirement of a broadly similar kind.

To understand this account fully, we need to understand the *pro tanto* wrong involved in unilateral enforcement. We also need to understand how this wrong might be overcome, that is, how an agent could be in a position to enforce a scheme of rules about rights *omnilaterally*. Here Kant argues that:

> The legislative authority can belong only to the united will of the people. For since all right is to proceed from it, it *cannot* do anyone wrong by its law. Now when someone makes arrangements about *another*, it is always possible for him to do the other wrong; but he can never do wrong in what he decides upon with regard to himself (for *volenti non fit inuria*). Therefore only the concurring and united will of all, insofar as each decides the same thing for all and all for each, and so only the general united will of the people, can be legislative. (6:314)

What would it mean to form a "concurring and united will of all" under conditions where individuals have differing views about what justice requires? Individuals who are committed to respecting one another's independence, while at the same time differing about which specific rights and duties this entails, may come to a second-order agreement to associate together in institutions that they collectively accept as a legitimate way to specify and enforce their rights. A state will thus represent the "general united will of the people" insofar as it is authorized by a

---

[18] In conditions where multilateral authorization is impossible, it may be permissible for Country A to go ahead and fight: yet we might still think this course of action is less than ideal. If *there had been* a legitimate multilateral body in place, Country A ought to have submitted to its decisions. Further, the international order is defective to the extent that it allows such decisions to be made unilaterally.

significant majority of *cooperators* on a territory who form a joint intention to act together to establish justice through specific institutions. *Cooperators* are those individuals who are willing to acknowledge the basic natural duty of justice, respecting one another as bearers of a claim to freedom as independence (*Natural Duty*), and who adhere to the requirement of political coordination under law that flows from this commitment (*State*). Cooperators who share a will constitute a collectively self-determining people.

4.4 Two Accounts of the Wrong of Unilateralism

A shared will thus helps to overcome the wrong of unilateral enforcement. But what exactly is wrong with unilateral enforcement? I believe there are two problems, both usually present, but one more fundamental than the other. The first—in my view less fundamental—problem concerns inequality: unilateral enforcement sets up a *hierarchical relationship* between the parties involved. Suppose your state-of-nature neighbor goes ahead and uses her powerful weapon to enforce her objectively correct interpretation of private rights. Even though she implements a substantively just scheme, she wields unequal power over us. This might lead the rest of us to see and treat her as our superior. If so, then our social relations might fail to exhibit certain intrinsically valuable features, such as parity of respect and status, that relations among equals ought to have. The basic thought is that unilateral enforcement sets up two classes of people: the powerful rulers, on the one hand, and the others, who must obey the decisions that the rulers make.

If equal social relations are of intrinsic value, then your neighbor has some reason to refrain from acting unilaterally: i.e., to refrain from using her superior private power to implement the substantively correct decision. Recent arguments for the authority of democracy have appealed to this *inequality worry* about unilateralism, and to the role that democratic procedures play in overcoming it.[19] On these accounts, since social equality is intrinsically important, we have reason to make decisions democratically and to treat those decisions as authoritative, even if, in doing so, we settle on a distribution of rights, opportunities, and resources that is less substantively just than we might have achieved through the imposition of one particular agent's view. This *pro tanto* reason in favor of egalitarian authority might sometimes be outweighed by countervailing concerns (e.g., for the quality of political decisions), but it is an important reason nonetheless.

This offers an account of the wrong of unilateralism (i.e., it threatens social equality) and an accompanying interpretation of how a decision-maker might

---

[19] Niko Kolodny, "Rule over None II: Social Equality and the Justification of Democracy," *Philosophy & Public Affairs* 42, no. 4 (2014): 287–336; Daniel Viehoff, "Democratic Equality and Political Authority," *Philosophy & Public Affairs* 42, no. 4 (2014): 337–75.

enforce a scheme of rights *omnilaterally*: such an agent must be authorized through an egalitarian political procedure in which each person subject to the scheme has equal opportunity for influence.

Though social equality is important, I doubt it is our most fundamental worry about unilateralism. Note too that when our state-of-nature neighbor enforces her interpretation of justice, she does so in a way that ignores and supplants everyone else's rational autonomy. An important part of treating others as independent persons involves respecting them as autonomous deliberators, who can reason for themselves how to act.[20] Yet our imagined neighbor is insensitive to the need to engage her fellows in this way. She does not offer them any reasons that might lead them to share her point of view about what justice requires, nor does she inquire into, or respond to, their reasons for not sharing it. Instead, she imposes her judgments by force, leaving others powerless to do anything but go along. This seems a disrespectful method for organizing a society. It also fails to acknowledge others' claim to live in a social world that makes sense to them, that in some way reflects their own convictions about how society should be arranged.[21]

Of course, before coercing her fellows, the neighbor could offer them reasons, hoping to bring them to endorse her rule. Still, this may not suffice to respect their rational autonomy. Consider three scenarios. In the first case, reflecting on her reasons, her fellows come to see her rule as justified, and they form the intention to cooperate in carrying out her directives. Here, there is no disrespect to their autonomy. In the second case, while her fellows see the substance of her decisions as justified, they do not see it as equally justified that *she* be the one to make and impose these decisions. Why not instead act together to establish a just scheme of rights, rather than being subjected to their neighbor's self-appointed rule? In the third scenario, her fellows do not come to endorse the substance of her decisions: their moral judgments are too far removed from hers. Whatever justification there may be for the scheme she imposes, it is not one they can appreciate.

Faced with either of these latter two scenarios, suppose that the neighbor goes ahead and coerces her fellows anyhow. If she does, they will suffer three related harms. First, they are unable to act independently, on the basis of their own sense of justice, to establish and comply with a political order they can affirm. Instead,

---

[20] Famously, Kant's Formula of Humanity, which enjoins us to "so act that you use humanity, whether in your own person, or in the person of any other, always at the same time as an end, never merely as a means" (*Groundwork*, 4:429), constrains how we are to interact with others' rational nature, their capacity to set and pursue ends. See Christine Korsgaard, "The Right to Lie: Kant on Dealing with Evil," in *The Kingdom of Ends* (Cambridge: Cambridge University Press, 1996), 142.

[21] For a similar argument, see Jake Zuehl, *Collective Self-Determination*, PhD dissertation (Princeton University, 2016). Zuehl offers the case of a "robot legislator" that rules a socially equal society in which no one holds *any* political power. While the robot's subjects are socially equal, they lack political autonomy. As Kolodny concedes, the interest in social equality "would be satisfied equally well by one's having no influence at all—so long as no one else had any influence either" ("Rule over None II," 325). Viehoff also suggests that "the authority of democratic decisions rests on the egalitarian fact that none of us have more of a say than any others, not on the further fact . . . that each of us has a positive say." ("Democratic Equality and Political Authority," 340). But this does not suffice for political autonomy.

they see their activities coordinated by external threats they do not endorse (or—in the third scenario—even comprehend). Because of this, they are likely to find life under their powerful neighbor's rule significantly *alienating*. Subject to the neighbor, I imagine I would feel as though a hostile force exercised near-complete control over my life. Further, participants will not experience their political and social world as a cooperative enterprise, in which they have valuable relationships with other participants, or where they can feel at home.

Because it involves these important harms, I believe unilateral coercion is normally *pro tanto* wrong. There is an important class of exceptions: the requirement to refrain from unilateral coercion is restricted to *cooperators* who are willing to recognize and respect others as possessing an equal moral right to independence, and to coordinate in establishing a public authority to specify and enforce this right. Some people—think of murderers or rapists—refuse to recognize others' independence, even in a minimal way. Suppose I hold you back while you are trying to stab me, thus thwarting your unjust attempt to kill me. It is not reasonable for you to press as an objection to my coercion that you find it alienating. By attempting to murder me, you have denied me any sphere of autonomy independent from your will. When someone refuses to acknowledge very basic elements of personal autonomy and independence, his denial of my moral status releases me, in turn, from any requirement to respect his, by refraining from unilaterally coercing him. Of course, more needs to be said about how to define the basic elements of autonomy that condition the requirement to refrain from unilateral coercion, and I will argue later that this condition requires a willingness to respect a scheme of essential private rights. But in cases where people simply refuse to acknowledge others' autonomy and independence, there is no moral loss in coercing them in ways that do not reflect their judgments.

So long as people *are* willing to recognize others' basic claim to personal autonomy and independence, however, I believe it is *pro tanto* wrong to coerce them unilaterally. This is so even when their interpretation of the precise demands of mutual independence is mistaken. When other people attempt, in good faith, to respect the claims that, by their lights, I have—even when their interpretation of my claims is incorrect—I respond to them very differently than I do to people who fail to acknowledge that I have any claim to independence at all. Though they are mistaken, they do not treat me with contempt. For that reason, their capacity for making their own political judgments places demands on me, and I owe them some respect for that capacity. I have *pro tanto* reason to interact with them using persuasive means, rather than coercively.

I should note that even in cases where unilateral coercion is wrong (i.e., in the case of *cooperators* who respect others' independence and who are willing to act together to establish a common public authority) sometimes this wrong can be morally outweighed by other important social values. Perhaps a functioning legal system cannot be achieved unless we subject some dissenters to unilateral coercion.

If there is no other way to secure the essentials of justice, security, and public order, the wrong of unilateral coercion—though important—may be trumped by its strongly beneficial effects. So the constraint on unilateral coercion can be lifted where its recognition would threaten decent governance or entail grave social harms. While self-determination is of very great weight, it is not the only value, and the requirement to respect it is not absolute. I return to this issue below.

In sum, on my view, there is a distinct *autonomy* worry about unilateral coercion. The principle of individual self-determination holds that, as rational agents, we ought to be able to direct our lives, to a significant degree, according to our own judgments. This idea grounds important basic liberties, like freedom of speech, conscience, association, privacy, and the freedom to form valuable intimate relationships. These private liberties enable us to carry out our own values in areas central to our personal identity and self-conception, granting us a protected sphere of individual freedom. But I believe the autonomy principle also has implications for the making and enforcement of political decisions. A scheme of rules about rights might be imposed in a manner that manifests proper respect for the autonomy of its subjects, or it might not. If a set of rules is forced onto a population of cooperators over their explicit objections, and against their will, then the process of its imposition fails to respect their autonomy adequately. This is so, I believe, even if that scheme of rules sets up an otherwise just distribution of rights, duties, and material advantages. Surely, it would be better to decide and carry out the rules governing our common life through the deliberative agency of those subject to them, rather than via a process that circumvents subjects' agential capacities.

Although I have suggested that a legitimate procedure for imposing rules about rights must manifest appropriate respect for each person's rational autonomy, this idea is still vague. There are many problems about how exactly to understand this requirement, especially when there is internal disagreement among members of a group about collective decisions. I will return to these problems later: for now, I note that if political autonomy is an important value, then unilateral enforcement fails to respect it.

4.5 Autonomy and Colonialism

I also think failure of respect for political autonomy is at the core of our complaints about colonialism. Of course, colonialism was wrong for many reasons, including human rights abuses, economic exploitation, and racism. But unilateral coercion was one of its key wrong-making features. A particularly destructive effect of "civilizing" colonialism was the forcible imposition onto a subject population of a social order that bore no relation to their own judgments about how, and by whom, they should be governed. Those who lived through this experience tell of a sense of powerlessness and a loss of orientation and control.[22] This produced lasting alienation among these peoples, a problem distinct from other abuses perpetrated by colonial institutions, and one that persists today in the form of great bitterness and resentment. Even in the best imaginable scenario, where colonial institutions are substantively just, still they deny the autonomy of colonized subjects, disregarding their claim to shape their common life on the basis of their own judgments.

Of course, most historical cases of colonialism also raise concerns about social equality, since colonial rulers typically stood in relations of political superiority to those they ruled. Subject peoples were often denied input into political decisions, which were made by a separate class of rulers. One might therefore object that I have misidentified the wrong in colonialism. Perhaps what makes colonialism *pro tanto* wrong is not a violation of autonomy, but rather a violation of the subject people's democratic rights to exercise a fair share of political power. Yet while important, I doubt that political inequality is truly the fundamental concern here. One way to see this is to ask whether our objection to colonialism would be neutralized if the colonizers treated their subjects as political equals.

Consider the following case:

> *Democratic Incorporation.*[23] Suppose that instead of extending support to the 2011 Libyan revolutionary movement, France had overthrown Qaddafi's regime, occupied the country, and annexed Libya's territory, much as it annexed Algeria in 1830. Further, suppose that after annexation, France governed Libya reasonably justly and extended its inhabitants democratic participation rights within a wider French republic. Imagine that there were no distinctions between French citizens and "the former Libyans" in terms of their democratic or other rights. Would the former Libyans have had a complaint?

If the imagined incorporation is objectionably unilateral—as I believe it is—then it is hard to see how the democratic equality argument explains this. Because Qaddafi's regime threatened grave humanitarian abuses, there was arguably a right to intervene in Libya in 2011.[24] Since Libya was a nondemocracy prior to the intervention, on the democratic argument, each Libyan had an outstanding individual claim to be enfranchised in the political decisions governing him.[25] But France responded to these claims by granting the Libyans democratic rights

---

[22] For powerful accounts, see Luther Standing Bear, *My People, the Sioux*, new ed. (Lincoln: Bison Books, 2006); Jonathan Lear, *Radical Hope* (Cambridge, MA: Harvard University Press, 2006).

[23] I introduced this case in my "Decolonization and Self-Determination," *Social Philosophy and Policy* 32, no.1 (2015): 10–11, and the next three paragraphs follow the discussion there.

[24] I recognize that this controversial judgment could be challenged. But my argument does not hang on whether the intervention in Libya was justified. So long as the reader agrees that intervention in a nondemocratic country can *sometimes* be justified, she should feel free to substitute a case she regards as meeting the appropriate criteria of justification.

[25] Libya did have an organ of political representation under Qaddafi: the General People's Congress. However, real power remained with Qaddafi himself: there was no right to form political parties or contest elections.

after the annexation. Indeed, there are real colonial cases that followed this model, cases in which colonizers democratically enfranchised their subjects. In the 1950s, for instance, France granted full citizenship—with suffrage rights—to all adult men and women in its former Algerian colony.[26] A second case is the United Kingdom of Great Britain and Ireland: from the Act of Union in 1801 until its independence in 1922, Ireland formed an integral part of a wider Britain, electing their own MPs to the British House of Commons.[27]

One might object here that an imposed regime, like the one envisaged above, cannot be democratically legitimate. The thought is that the *incorporation itself* was not authorized through an egalitarian procedure, even if later decisions were. But suppose that just prior to incorporation, a referendum had been held in the combined Franco-Libyan territory, and that a majority (composed almost entirely of metropolitan French) had voted in favor. Would the annexation then be legitimate? If legitimacy simply requires that all involved individuals have equal influence over the decision, it seems it would: no individual has been disenfranchised here. Yet intuitively, the annexation still seems objectionable.[28]

It might be further objected that a combined referendum does not represent a fair distribution of political power. But what—in addition to equal influence over the decision—is required for a fair distribution of political power? Presumably, the idea is that granting citizens from larger countries the power to vote on decisions about whether to incorporate smaller countries has the de facto effect of disenfranchising them, preventing them from exercising any effective say in this matter.

One might therefore supplement the equal influence criterion with some "boundary-drawing" principle. One possible suggestion is that those people who are primarily affected by a political decision are entitled to exercise a greater share of political authority about that decision. Applied to cases of annexation, this might imply that people who reside in a territory are presumptively entitled to exercise greater influence over decisions about that territory's annexation. After all, these people are most strongly affected by proposals to depart sharply from existing political arrangements.[29]

I am skeptical that affectedness will justify our intuitions about democratic incorporation. Intuitively, a fair merger requires two separate referenda: one within French territory and one in Libya (indeed, nothing in my political autonomy account rejects mergers if they are approved by a majority of both populations). But the affectedness criterion simply tells us that since both French and Libyan residents are affected, both should have a say. It cannot tell us why that process should take the form of two separate votes, rather than a single one (at least not

---

[26] See Todd Shepherd, *The Invention of Decolonization* (Ithaca: Cornell University Press, 2006), 19–54.
[27] See John Ranlegh, *A Short History of Ireland* (Cambridge: Cambridge University Press, 1983).
[28] For related discussion of the democratic "boundary problem," see Abizadeh, "On the Demos and its Kin"; Goodin, "Enfranchising All Affected Interests, and Its Alternatives"; David Miller, "Democracy's Domain," *Philosophy & Public Affairs* 37, no. 3 (2009): 201–28.
[29] I thank Jonathan Quong for suggesting this argument to me.

without importing prior assumptions, beyond affectedness, about normatively appropriate boundaries between groups). Further, affectedness produces counterintuitive conclusions when applied to cases of decolonization. While annexation is a sharp departure from the status quo, so too was decolonization. Should French citizens, for that reason, have been allowed to vote in a referendum on whether Algeria should remain within their Empire? While French imperialists were affected, I do not think they were entitled to a say. Finally, as already discussed in the introduction, affectedness tells in favor of far-reaching revisions to existing boundaries. Advocates of global democracy commonly appeal to the fact that our decisions affect people beyond our borders. Given the economic and political power of the United States, many proponents of affectedness support extending everyone a vote in US elections. For this reason, affectedness seems unlikely to support claims to collective self-determination.

The objector might finally reply that a fair distribution of political power requires some other boundary-drawing principle. Perhaps boundaries should be demarcated, so far as possible, to align with people's shared preferences, so as not to create permanent minorities. I am sympathetic to this proposal. Relatedly, the existence of majority voting procedures strikes me as insufficient to realize self-determination in the absence of further conditions on the group constituted by those procedures, including whether it contains subordinated minorities. But this view seems to me indistinguishable from my own: to be legitimate, a state needs to reflect the shared will of a significant majority of the cooperators within a territory as to how they ought to be governed. If this view is correct, however, it has implications beyond political annexation and decolonization. Groups that persistently find themselves in the minority when it comes to fundamental issues about how to organize political life, and who seek a sphere in which to shape their institutions in accordance with their distinctive shared goals, will also have *pro tanto* claims to political autonomy.

In sum, I believe the *autonomy* worry about unilateralism—the worry that unilateral enforcement fails to respect adequately subjects' claim to guide their collective life by their own rational judgments—is best positioned to explain our concerns about colonialism. Individuals have an interest in political autonomy: in being subject to political institutions that in some way reflect their judgments and priorities. In the next section, I try to say more about what political autonomy is. While autonomy is familiar in the personal context, it is unclear how it might be extended to the context of collective decision-making.

4.6 What Is Political Autonomy?

To move forward, it may help to say more about the nature of autonomy in general. In the broadest sense, "autonomy" describes a person's ability to freely conduct her life on the basis of her own judgments and values. But this capacity can be broken down into two distinct components.

The first component is *self-directed agency*. We act in a self-directed way when we act on motives that are in some appropriate sense "our own." On prominent "hierarchical" accounts of autonomy, a desire counts as the agent's "own" when that agent endorses its functioning from the perspective of a higher-order attitude that has the authority to "speak for" the agent. This higher-order attitude reflects her practical judgment, her capacity to weigh and engage with reasons.[30] The self-directed person, in other words, has her own evaluative and moral judgments, and she identifies with some of her occurrent desires, and rejects others, on the basis of these values.

We can define "self-directed agency," then, as action that is reflectively endorsed by the agent based on her judgments. Self-directed action, on this view, is not the same thing as doing what the agent wants, since not everything we desire accords with our practical judgments. An "unwilling" addict who acts on his desire for a drug he prefers not to take, is moved by a desire that does not reflect his values.[31] In taking the drug, he is not self-directed. It is only when I act on desires endorsed by my practical judgments that I act in a self-directed way.

Yet self-directed agency is not sufficient for autonomy. Autonomy also has a second, *thinking* component. An autonomous agent holds her judgments in a way that is responsive to her own independent reasoning processes. Of course, many of our values are acquired as a byproduct of socialization, not necessarily through conscious reflection. But normally, an autonomous agent is able to critically reflect on her values, and freely to endorse or discard them. We hold our values because we see their objects as good, and we can raise the question of whether or not they truly *are* good, by deliberating. If, upon deliberation, we no longer see our evaluative and moral commitments as supported by reasons, then we can modify them. So an autonomous agent's practical judgments are undergirded by, and responsive to, her own authentic reasoning. One way of interfering with an agent's autonomy is to interfere with the authenticity of that agent's reasoning processes, through methods like manipulation, deception, brainwashing, or mind control.[32] The neuroscientist who implants new values into a subject, preventing him from calling those implanted values into question, makes him the instrument of *her* judgments, not his own.[33]

---

[30] See Michael Bratman, *Structures of Agency* (Oxford: Oxford University Press, 2007), 101. See also Gary Watson, "Free Agency," in *The Inner Citadel*, edited by John Christman (Brattleboro: Echo Point, 1989), 109–21; Alfred Mele, *Autonomous Agents: From Self-Control to Autonomy* (Oxford: Oxford University Press, 1995).

[31] For this example, see Harry Frankfurt, "Freedom of the Will and the Concept of a Person," in *The Importance of What We Care About* (Cambridge: Cambridge University Press, 1988), 17.

[32] Mele, *Autonomous Agents*, ch. 9.

[33] Consider Michael Walzer's worry about a Swedish government that introduces a wondrous chemical into Algeria's water supply, turning the Algerians into Swedish style social democrats. Surely, the objection to this intervention is an objection to manipulation: it circumvents the Algerians' ability to

So autonomy has two components: (i) self-directed action that reflects the agent's evaluative and moral judgments, where those judgments are (ii) supported by her authentic reasoning.

The importance of autonomy tells in favor of granting individuals a considerable degree of control over their personal lives, especially when it comes to core identity-related features of that life, such as one's choice of religion, associates, sexual partners, occupation, whether to start a family, and so on. The value of autonomy is less commonly thought to bear on the choice or enforcement of other-regarding social rules. Yet there is a classic line of argument—dating to Rousseau—that holds that personal autonomy has an important political analogue. The basic idea is that just as our central life commitments express our own judgments, so too should our political institutions. Rousseau held political autonomy to be a key element in the justification of democratic procedures, subjection to which, he argued, enabled the subject to obey laws she prescribed to herself. I propose that Rousseau was right to hold that there is a political analogue to personal autonomy, though I will conceive it rather differently than he did.

A familiar rejoinder to this Rousseauian argument points out that democratic voting procedures are insufficient to render obedience to law compatible with individual autonomy. Citizens have only a tiny, negligible influence over political decisions, and this influence rarely if ever affords them the power to ensure that these decisions reflect their own judgments. Since other people always share in political power, whether decisions reflect *my* judgments is always partly up to *them*. Indeed, they may impose their alien views on me, as happens whenever I am in the dissenting minority on some serious political question. Here, it seems, we are ruled by the majority, we do not rule ourselves. I agree with the rejoinder's proponents that democratic voting procedures are neither necessary nor sufficient to realize self-determination, and I will say more about this in the next chapter. Still, I think political autonomy remains an important value even if Rousseau misconceived its connection to democratic procedures.

Why might autonomy be an important value in the political context? Consider that the characteristic *means* by which political rules are imposed and implemented is via coercion or force. Like others, I think the use of this type of means poses a special threat to autonomy.[34] The problem is not simply that coercion limits my options or deprives me of freedom. Many permissible acts of others—and even acts of nature—can limit my options and deprive me of freedom. Yet even when deprived of the specific options I might have preferred, I am usually still able to make self-directed choices, setting and pursuing my own ends among the options

rationally form and implement their own political judgments. Michael Walzer, "The Moral Standing of States," in *Thinking Politically*, edited by David Miller (New Haven: Yale University Press, 2007), 231.

[34] Many other thinkers have suggested this. See Frankfurt, *The Importance of What We Care About*, 42; Raz, *The Morality of Freedom*, 154; Pettit, *On the People's Terms*, 147; Blake, *Justice and Foreign Policy*, 84; Rawls, *Political Liberalism*, expanded ed. (New York: Columbia University Press, 2005), 137.

that remain. But most cases of coercion or force go beyond this, subjecting the coercee to the will of the coercer. A coercer intends for his target to perform a relatively specific course of action, and he deliberately changes the circumstances of her choice so that she has no reasonable alternative to doing this. He "makes her" do what he wishes. Normally, this deprives the coercee of self-directed agency, substituting the coercer's judgments for her own. Thus, coercion presumptively threatens autonomy.

Note, however, that the state is a comprehensively coercive institution. States impose a whole web of threats upon their subjects, which structure the social world in which those subjects live and operate. Moreover, political coercion is inescapable: individuals cannot generally leave their state or take refuge in other social associations to get away from it. So it is natural to think that subjection to such a comprehensively coercive institution raises a concern about its subjects' ability to live their lives according to their own judgments. This is particularly true of *alien* political coercion, that is, political coercion that bears no relation to the priorities, values, and beliefs of those subjected to it. When one is pervasively subject to alien coercion, substantial aspects of one's life can come to seem hostile and threatening. In such a scenario, it can become difficult to maintain any sense of oneself as an agent who charts her life in accordance with her own purposes. Indeed, this worry seems to be what motivates many voluntarists, who hold that it is an impermissible infringement of our freedom to subject us to state power without our consent.[35]

The importance of the political analogue to personal autonomy, I believe, lies in mitigating this threat of alien state coercion. Where the state's use of coercion reflects subjects' own judgments as to how, and by whom, they should be governed, they are enabled to relate in a distinctive way to their state and to the constraints it imposes on them. Because the subject can see the point of these coercive demands—in terms of judgments she is herself committed to—she also sees reason to hold herself to such demands (though she may not always desire to do so). Here, the state is no longer an overwhelming, alien power, but rather a tool that allows her more effectively to carry out commitments that are her own.

I suggest, then, that there is an important autonomy interest in enjoying what Niko Kolodny has termed "correspondence." Someone enjoys correspondence when her political institutions match her judgments in some way.[36] She lives under an institution that she endorses, accepts, or believes to be justified or appropriate. The importance of correspondence is not that congruence between subjects' attitudes and their institutions is intrinsically valuable, but that where it exists, it allows for individuals to experience autonomy, even while subject to political power.

---

[35] Simmons, "Justification and Legitimacy," 136.
[36] Niko Kolodny, "Rule Over None I: What Justifies Democracy?" *Philosophy & Public Affairs* 42, no. 3 (2014): 199.

To be sure, in a diverse political community, no individual's personal judgments can be mirrored by each-and-every political decision. Yet diversity of political opinions does not make correspondence impossible. There is a second-order sense in which an individual's judgments *are* often reflected in her governing institutions: namely, when she shares a commitment to a political enterprise and to certain values and procedures by which she believes that enterprise should be structured. Participants can freely accept their group's policies, and the outcomes that result from them, even when those outcomes diverge from their first-order judgments, so long as they share these second-order commitments. A commitment to participating in cooperative political action is therefore important in enabling correspondence.[37]

Consider a partnership undertaking a joint venture, say, running a coffee shop together. Several philosophers have offered theories of the agency involved in such cases, arguing that it is undergirded by a structure of joint intentions. As they cooperate over time, this coffee shop group will likely develop some shared commitments about how their enterprise should run. This does not mean that the partners will converge in all their first-order judgments. More probably, they will divide on some issues. Yet even when they do not converge, partners are often able to generate second-order shared commitments—not reducible to their own first-order judgments—about how their joint venture should go. Such commitments can unify a group even when they diverge in their views on specific issues. Once such shared commitments have developed, members will generally act on them and feel entitled to expect the others to act on them. Because a group can arrive at shared commitments, they can develop a group standpoint. This standpoint consists of a set of core values and priorities about how to organize more specific plans of action. The group standpoint will probably not fully correspond to any one person's first-order views. Still, each member can accept the group's standpoint and share in it, if she values the joint venture and intends to participate in it.

I believe there is a perfectly straightforward sense in which we can speak of this small-scale partnership as sharing a will. Their shared will is to cooperate in running their coffee shop, and to license the values and priorities that make up their group standpoint. A shared will, then, is nothing more than an interlocking structure of cooperative intentions on the part of each participant, amid common knowledge on the part of all that those intentions obtain. Moreover, the object of a group's shared will need not be first-order policy decisions: it can be abstract ideals and decision procedures. As I have emphasized throughout, the common priorities reflected in our institutions need not be shared substantive values (and in modern states, typically will not be). Instead, it is enough that each member of the group values the common political *endeavor* and accepts some procedural commitments about how this endeavor should be constituted. Typically, this involves a shared

---

[37] For a similar view, see Ronald Dworkin, *Freedom's Law* (Cambridge, MA: Harvard University Press, 1996).

intention to associate together politically and to support certain institutions, including a commitment to the higher-order values that structure these institutions.

Further, if they value their enterprise, members may feel slighted when their group's standpoint is not respected by others. While I often disagree with my colleagues about whom to hire, I prefer that we make our own hiring decisions together—through our accepted consultation processes—even though that means recognizing some decisions with which I disagree. Indeed, I would consider myself disrespected if the dean overruled our collective decision, even if the result was to impose my preferred candidate. Though our hiring decisions do not always correspond to my first-order preferences, there is still an important, second-order sense in which *my* priorities are reflected in these decisions. I share a commitment to a valued cooperative enterprise together with these colleagues, and to certain shared policies by which I believe that enterprise should be governed.

Though there is more to be said about the notion of a shared will (and I will return to this idea in the next chapter), for now, let me stress the important role that a group's shared political will plays in ensuring correspondence for its members. In the ideal case, when each member participates in a group's shared will, and government imposes laws and policies on the basis of that shared will, then this use of political coercion will not be *alien* to the members. Though she does not personally endorse every outcome, each member is governed by political institutions that she views as appropriate, since she endorses the cooperative political project and the values and procedures by which it is guided.

Omnilateral coercion differs from *unilateral* coercion, then, because it is based on a joint intention—in which each cooperator shares—to act together to establish justice through specific institutions. Though correspondence is ultimately an interest of individuals, it can be furthered by an individual's membership in a self-determining group, if she affirms her participation in the group and accepts the higher-order values and procedures that structure it. In the ideal case, rule by the group's institutions will be in the service of each individual's interests in self-directed agency and in nonalienation.

To be valuable, however, correspondence must meet three additional conditions. First, correspondence only serves autonomy under conditions where the subjects' shared political will is freely formed in a manner that is accountable to their own deliberative processes. If rulers instead "implant" their subjects' political judgments—through manipulation, deception, brainwashing, or the like—then correspondence will not promote their autonomy. In this scenario, subjects will be instruments of their rulers' judgments, not their own.

Second, correspondence between a group's shared political will and their institutions must come about through some *causal process*. A group might enjoy correspondence merely because of the goodwill of a benevolent absolutist who happens to give the people what they think right. But to ensure political self-determination, a government must *be constrained* to reflect the citizens' shared will, even should the benevolent ruler change his mind, or should the citizens shift their shared commitments as to how they wish to be governed. Thus, a group must not only enjoy correspondence now, but their enjoyment of correspondence must be temporally robust across changes in their government and in the nature of their shared commitments. This requires some channel by which the people might revoke authorization of their government if it were to cease to reflect their shared will, and I say more about this in the next chapter.

Third, correspondence is valuable only for a restricted domain of constituents. The reason correspondence is valuable is that it promotes autonomy. But autonomy has a private and a public dimension, and political autonomy has moral weight only where it is consistent with basic elements of personal autonomy. The popular will that a state ought to represent is, therefore, a will that is shared among a significant majority of *cooperators*, those individuals who are willing to recognize and respect others as bearers of a claim to private independence and to coordinate in political institutions that will protect this claim. Again, there is no requirement to refrain from unilaterally coercing noncooperators. Further, some people may count as cooperators, in the sense that they are willing to acknowledge others' basic moral claims, and are willing to coordinate under *some* minimally just public authority, yet the particular government they would prefer is simply infeasible, given other people's commitments. I explain below why their claims to political autonomy, though important, are outweighed. Since self-determination is limited by other values, most real-world cases will fall short of the ideal case described above, in which all citizens' interests in correspondence are fully realized.

Why care about correspondence, even for this restricted domain of agents? Unless we suppose that the legitimate state reflects the shared will of its people, it is difficult to see how it could ever solve the problem of unilateral coercion characteristic of the state of nature. The problem of unilateral coercion is a problem of deciding for others what justice requires and compelling them to submit to one's judgments. This is supposed to be a problem even where the coercer's view of justice is *correct*. But if unilateralism is a problem for private individuals in a state of nature, then it is also a problem for the state. What makes the state's enforcement of a system of rights—even an objectively correct system of rights—any less unilateral than the powerful neighbor's enforcement of justice in the state of nature? Only, I submit, the fact that the cooperators among its population affirm its procedures and institutions, judging this an appropriate way to enforce justice among themselves. In that way, they grant their legitimate state the standing to decide on their behalf.

My political autonomy account overlaps in some ways with Michael Walzer's views, so it may help to discuss his account briefly here. Walzer argues that "a state is legitimate or not depending upon the 'fit' of government and community, that is, the degree to which the government actually represents the political life of its people."[38] He holds that this explains why it is wrong to coercively interfere with another political community: such interference forces its people to be governed by "someone else's conceptions of political justice and political prudence."[39] Instead, he maintains that "people should be treated in accordance with their own ideas about how people should be treated."[40]

I agree with Walzer that there is an important value for people in being governed in a way that reflects their shared judgments, so long as these judgments are consistent with basic claims to personal autonomy and independence. Like him, I have argued that state legitimacy requires a certain "fit" between government and its people's shared political will. Yet Walzer characterizes self-determination much more broadly, as the right of a community to be "governed in accordance with its own traditions" and links this to the existence of an "inherited culture."[41] Unlike Walzer, I believe the state need not strive for "fit" with majority cultural or religious values. As I noted in Chapter 2, most territories are inhabited by culturally and religiously diverse populations. Under these conditions, for the state to seek "fit" with the majority religion or culture—by, say, establishing a church or an official national language—sends the message that those who do not share this religion or culture are second-class citizens. This violates an important expressive duty to treat citizens as civic equals. I will return to my differences with this liberal nationalist view in the next chapter.

My political autonomy account also overlaps in some ways with Rawls's "liberal principle of legitimacy." I share with Rawls the concern that it is wrong to exercise coercive power over someone where they cannot accept the moral basis for that power.[42] Unlike Rawls, however, I appeal to morally controversial values of independence and autonomy to explain why this is so. I also differ from Rawls about what exactly is required to render political power legitimate. Rawls holds that it is sufficient that political power be exercised on the basis of a constitution that could be *hypothetically* accepted by adherents of diverse reasonable comprehensive doctrines. But I hold instead that for a state to be legitimate, an *actual* shared commitment to a collective political venture and its structuring ideals is required—a commitment to pursuing these ideals *together*, through particular institutions.

To pull these threads together, then, let me define "political autonomy" as (i) a causal relation of correspondence (ii) between the shared political will of a significant majority of *cooperators* and their institutions, (iii) when that relation is achieved under conditions that enable their free deliberative reasoning.

---

[38] Walzer, "The Moral Standing of States," 223.
[39] Walzer, "The Moral Standing of States," 224.
[40] Walzer, "Nation and Universe," in *Thinking Politically*, edited by David Miller (New Haven: Yale University Press, 2007), 198.
[41] Walzer, "The Moral Standing of States," 220–1.   [42] Rawls, *Political Liberalism*, 217.

4.7 Is Political Autonomy Possible?

It is natural to object that however desirable this ideal of political autonomy might be, it is unachievable. As Michael Blake notes, "we should take care before we insist that a given attitude or political conception simply *is* that which is held by the country in question." Instead, as he emphasizes, states "are composed of persons, who disagree and quarrel and find their own answers to a variety of disputed questions."[43]

A good account of political autonomy must be compatible with these facts. Even if it is conceptually possible for a group to share a will, as I suggested in the last section it is, one might still object that it is extremely unlikely that an entire territorially defined population will achieve unanimity of this kind. There is a wide range of values and attitudes among us. Must a legitimate state be responsive to all these values and attitudes?

No. As I have emphasized, there is reason to ensure "fit" between state institutions and the shared intentions only of a restricted domain of *cooperators*, those who are committed to showing respect for the independence of others and to establishing institutions that reflect this commitment. Essential elements of such a commitment are: (i) a willingness to define a scheme of private rights that meets the conditions of what I shall call *basic justice*, and (ii) an acknowledgment that this requires coordinating in a territorially defined state, which can enforce a unitary interpretation of the contours of those rights. Claims to political autonomy, then, are *necessarily moralized claims*.

I also hold that even when unilateral coercion is wrong, because it disrespects a cooperator's autonomy, sometimes this wrong can be outweighed. The requirement to respect self-determination is not absolute: it is sometimes permissible to subject people to alien coercion if this is the only way to achieve social goals of truly overriding importance.

I unpack these ideas by briefly outlining three paradigm cases of dissent, where there is some lack of "fit" between state institutions and the shared priorities of a subpopulation of the state's constituents. In the first two cases, I believe it is permissible to subject dissenters to alien coercion, either because they fall outside the domain of cooperators or because their claims to political autonomy, though important, are outweighed. In the third kind of case, however, I believe dissenters have a claim to an institutional means that would afford them greater political independence. For this reason, my political autonomy account will sometimes support claims on the part of persistently alienated minorities to internal autonomy, or even to secession, and I say more about these implications in the next chapter.

In my first paradigm case, dissenters lack the "fit" constitutive of political autonomy only because they refuse to acknowledge any duty to cooperate on

---

[43] Blake, *Justice and Foreign Policy*, 32.

minimally just terms. Where dissenters' priorities are incompatible with the foundational duty to respect others' independence, as I have argued, there is no moral loss in overriding their judgments. I believe there is some essential minimal content as to what could count as a reasonable interpretation of mutual private independence. Where dissenters are unwilling to cooperate in a state that meets these minimal requirements, their claims to political autonomy have no weight because they are inconsistent with *basic justice* for others.

Basic justice, as I define it, is a condition on political legitimacy, a condition for a group to have the right to make and enforce its own laws and policies. As I stressed at the outset, legitimacy and justice are distinct values. Sometimes it is impermissible, because illegitimate, to enforce even ideally just laws and policies (e.g., where their enforcement would involve colonial rule). (I concede that even illegitimate enforcement may sometimes become *temporarily* permissible, if in particular time and place there is no other way to secure basic justice, and I will say more about these cases in Chapter 5.)

Sometimes it is permissible for a state to enforce laws and policies that are not ideally just, so long as those laws are enacted in accordance with collectively authorized procedures. Still, the failure to acknowledge very basic elements of personal independence may undercut a group's claim to decide collectively, by demonstrating that they lack a commitment to the fundamental requirement from which political autonomy's value is derived.

A community respects basic justice, on my view, when it aims at securing private autonomy and independence for its members, and respecting the autonomy and independence of outsiders, on a reasonable (though possibly mistaken) understanding of what that value means.[44] Even where a community makes mistakes about justice, its laws and policies may be legitimate, so long as they reflect a good-faith attempt to define a scheme of rights that secures private autonomy and independence for all. But some acts cannot be reconciled with even a minimal commitment to these values. Basic justice sets that threshold. A minimally just state, on my view, must protect (for insiders) and respect (for outsiders) at least:

(1) *Security rights*: to freedom from torture, slavery, arbitrary imprisonment, and severe threats to personal integrity;

(2) *Subsistence rights*: to an economic minimum capable of meeting basic needs;

(3) *Core personal autonomy rights*: to freedom of conscience and thought, to personal property, and the freedom to form family relationships; and

(4) *The preconditions of collective self-determination*: to free expression, free association, and public political dissent.

---

[44] For a similar view, see Ronald Dworkin, *Justice for Hedgehogs* (Cambridge, MA: Belknap Press, 2011), 322.

Security and subsistence rights are prerequisites for autonomous agency of any kind. They define a minimum level of control necessary to lead a life of our own. To some extent, these rights could be recognized—if imperfectly—even in a pre-institutional state of nature. Even in that scenario, others would have a duty to refrain from deliberately harming us in ways that infringe our bodily integrity or threaten our subsistence.

Personal autonomy rights reflect the principle that each person should be free from the will of others when forming her own values and expressing these in the conduct of her life. Personal autonomy is especially important when it comes to judgments about fundamental ethical obligations, in matters of religion and intimate relationships. Personal autonomy is a scalar value, and protections for it can be more or less robust. But no society that failed to protect religious freedom, freedom of thought, the right to family, and personal property could be said to have even a minimal commitment to it.

Finally, the *preconditions of collective self-determination* are meant to ensure that individuals have an opportunity to form their own autonomous political judgments. These rights ensure that citizens can develop their own political views and make informed assessments of their institutions. If members of a society are coerced or manipulated into their political values, then outsiders have less reason to respect or defer to these commitments. Like personal autonomy, protections for collective self-determination can be more and less robust, but no society that controls its citizens' access to information, prohibits free discussion and free association, or denies its citizens the right to publicly express political dissent safeguards these preconditions.[45]

On this interpretation, the Kantian view is committed to certain basic rights as threshold criteria for state legitimacy.[46] Of course, most well-ordered states will implement substantive rights that go beyond these minimal conditions, and outsiders and the international community may wish to promote and incentivize respect for a longer list of rights than this. But the idea is that a state must grant its members at least these minimal guarantees to have legitimate jurisdiction over its population and territory. It is crucial to keep this distinction between basic justice and other aspirations in view.[47]

---

[45] For similar criteria, see Wenar, *Blood Oil*, 227–9, 235–8.

[46] For another Kantian argument for human rights, see Valentini, "Human Rights, Freedom, and Political Authority," *Political Theory* 40, no. 5 (2012): 573–601.

[47] As others have suggested, this may ground reasons for foreign states and other agents in the international community to act to secure these basic rights. For the idea that the function of human rights is to set bounds to states' external legitimacy and can trigger duties of international assistance, interference, or intervention, see Rawls, *The Law of Peoples*, 79–80; Beitz, *The Idea of Human Rights*, 116; Joseph Raz, "Human Rights without Foundations," in *The Philosophy of International Law*, edited by John Tasioulas and Samantha Besson (Oxford: Oxford University Press, 2010), 321–38. I particularly emphasize the role of basic justice as setting a threshold for *coercive intervention*.

For their claims to political autonomy to carry moral weight, then, claimants must be willing to cooperate in a legitimate state that can secure basic justice. We are not required, out of respect for their judgments and values, to allow dissenters to act in ways that clearly violate this moral requirement. To such dissenters (including fascists, racists, theocrats, and so on) we can only say: your alienation must be discounted, because greater recognition for your values is not compatible with upholding basic justice for others.

More difficult, perhaps, is the case of dissenters (e.g., anarchists) who may acknowledge duties of basic justice in principle but refuse to accept the derivative duty to support a political state. If Kant's argument for the injustice of anarchism is correct, however, we also have a reply to these dissenters: a territorial authority is necessary to specify, interpret, and enforce a common, public interpretation of rights. If a state is necessary to secure basic justice, then those who live alongside the anarchist have a claim against him to support and comply with that state.[48]

Finally, some dissenters are alienated because their values are incompatible with acknowledging others' equal claims to political autonomy. At the moment of decolonization, for example, many British imperialists were disaffected at the thought that they could no longer continue living in the glorious British Empire. Should their disaffection count as a reason to coerce Indians to continue to be ruled by the Raj? No. While dissenters can permissibly be forced to cooperate against their will when their cooperation is essential to sustaining basic justice for others, that is the *only* reason they can permissibly be forced to cooperate. Since basic justice for the British could perfectly well be guaranteed within "little" Britain, imperialists had no right to coerce the alienated Indians to uphold their imperial identity. Using coercion to force a dissenter to uphold someone else's identity, without any further justice-based rationale, is wrong. So if greater recognition for one person's values would involve forcing the unwilling cooperation of another—under conditions where the latter's cooperation is not *required* to sustain minimally just institutions—then the former's dissent must be discounted.

These three scenarios together make up our first paradigm: cases where dissenters in some way refuse to recognize the equal autonomy of others. Our discussion illustrates that claims to self-determination must be understood as *moralized claims*: not everyone has a claim to be coerced by a state that reflects their judgments, because not everyone's judgments are worthy of respect. Where dissenters refuse to acknowledge the requirements of basic justice, to recognize a duty to cooperate in a legitimate state, or to respect others' equivalent claims to self-determination, then their values and priorities can be overridden without any moral loss.

Let me comment briefly on a second paradigm case where dissent should be discounted. These are cases where dissenters' priorities are compatible with others'

---

[48] For a similar line of thought, see Jonathan Quong, *Liberalism without Perfection* (Oxford: Oxford University Press, 2011), 128.

rights in *principle* but not in *practice*, because of institutional infeasibility constraints. Here I appeal to the importantly *territorial* nature of our natural duties of justice: we cannot establish a unitary interpretation of property and contractual rights, enforce those rights, and punish violators, unless people who live in proximity and interact regularly are subject to the same institution. If each person signed up for the jurisdictional organization of his choice, then interactions between persons in the same contiguous space would continue to generate conflicts and disputes.[49] If disaffected individuals refuse participation in *any* feasible institutional configuration, then their alienation should be overridden. It may be possible to exercise jurisdictional authority over certain matters (e.g., education or cultural policy) on a nonterritorial basis, and I am open to the thought that dispersed minorities may sometimes have a claim to nonterritorial self-governance in these areas.[50] But most dimensions of state authority, such as the prevention of violence, the establishment of property rights, environmental policy, and so on, must be performed on a territorial basis. Since dispersed minorities are unable feasibly to organize a territorially based unit, they cannot claim political autonomy in these areas.

To explain why these individuals' dissent should be discounted, I stress once again that self-determination is not absolute: when respecting it would entail very grave social costs, it can be outweighed. In this case, there is indeed a *pro tanto* wrong in coercing dissenters who fail to participate in a group's shared political will. But this wrong is outweighed by the fact that there may be no other feasible way to secure the essentials of justice, security, and public order. Where very weighty social goods cannot otherwise be achieved, it is permissible, all things considered, to subject some dissenters to illegitimate coercion, despite the *pro tanto* wrong to them. I will say more about such cases in the next chapter.

Finally, there are some scenarios where I believe we have a duty to allow for the self-determination of those whose shared will does not "fit" with their institutions. This brings us to the third paradigm case, where alienated groups have a claim to institutional reconfiguration. Here I have in mind groups who have shared political commitments that are (i) consistent with the provision of basic justice for others, (ii) who possess or can create a territorially organized structure of representation, and (iii) whose dissent can be feasibly addressed, at reasonable cost, by granting them separate political institutions. In cases of this kind, I believe we compromise the political autonomy of dissenters by coercing them within alien institutions that they reject.

---

[49] For similar points, see Wellman in Wellman and Simmons, *Is There a Duty to Obey the Law* (Cambridge: Cambridge University Press, 2005), 14–16; Quong, *Liberalism without Perfection*, 129.

[50] See Helder de Schutter, "Non-Territorial Jurisdictional Authority," in *Recognition and Redistribution in Multinational Federalism*, edited by J. F. Grégoire and M. Jewkes (Leuven: Leuven University Press, 2015), 35–56.

Because a variety of institutional configurations is consistent with our natural duty of justice, it is often not true that *coercion by the current coercer* is necessary for basic justice to be realized. The innate Kantian right to independence (i.e., the right to determine our lives in accordance with our own judgments) gives people standing to reject alien state coercion whenever that coercion is not *necessary* to securing basic justice for others. This means that people's shared political will as to how they ought to be governed should be extended some respect, so long as that is consistent with fulfilling basic duties of justice. As I develop further in the next chapter, this account will often give reason to support claims on the part of persistently alienated minorities to internal autonomy and sometimes to secession.

Let me now sum up this account. To have an exclusive moral right to make and enforce law and policy within a territory, on my view, a state must show:

(1) That it meets the requirements of basic justice, by enacting a scheme of private rights that guarantees security, subsistence, a minimum of personal autonomy, and the preconditions for collective self-determination for all its subjects, and respecting the basic rights of outsiders.

(2) That its population has a right to occupy their territory, i.e., that the area is fundamental to their located life plans, which were not unjustly established (i.e., no expulsion of prior occupants or violation of others' claims to an equitable distribution of space).

(3) That its institutions reflect the shared political will of a significant majority of cooperators among these occupants—i.e., their actual joint commitment to a political endeavor, and to a set of procedures as to how that endeavor should be governed.

(4) That those who dissent from this shared will lack any right to an institutional alternative because (i) their claims are inconsistent with respecting others' independence or (ii) their priorities cannot currently be accommodated by a feasible alternative institution, and so are outweighed.

I believe this account provides a convincing, and broadly Kantian, response to the worries about colonialism and involuntary annexation with which we began. The essential thought is that our natural duty of justice has two dimensions: on the one hand, we are bound to respect others' *personal autonomy*, which requires us to cooperate together in a legitimate state that can enforce private rights, but on the other, we are also bound to respect their *political autonomy*—the moralized claim, held by cooperators, to be ruled in a way that reflects their shared judgments about how, and by whom, they should be governed.

This value of political autonomy, in my view, provides us moral reason to favor a system of separate states to a single world state. While coercion by *some* minimally just state is necessary for securing private autonomy, by itself, this is insufficient to decide how many states we should have, or which particular people should be subject to which ones.[51] Should we institute a unitary world state, or a plurality of states? A federal system? Internal autonomy for indigenous peoples or other minorities? The view I have developed suggests we should adopt the feasible, minimally just institutional configuration that will ensure the greatest "fit" between people's convictions regarding how and by whom they should be governed, on the one hand, and the institutions that rule them, on the other. So long as they are willing to respect others as independent equals, people have a *pro tanto* claim to be ruled in a way they endorse. If basic justice can be provided within a plurality of distinct states, then those who prefer separate institutions will have a prima facie claim to establish them. Further, it is the violation of political autonomy that explains what is wrong with colonialism and involuntary annexation. Securing basic justice for people in the metropole almost never requires coercively imposing a political order on unwilling subject peoples. In the next chapter, I turn to a closer examination of political autonomy's institutional implications.

---

[51] Kant does suggest that for right to be fully realized, a global juridical framework is required. But which units should exist within that framework is indeterminate.

5
Refining the Political Autonomy Account

Chapter 4 laid the groundwork for a political autonomy account of self-determination, drawing in part on Kant's argument that a legitimate state should represent its people's *omnilateral will*. I interpreted an omnilateral will as an *actual* popular will. To avoid alien coercion, a legitimate state should reflect the shared commitment of a significant majority of cooperators within its territory to associate politically and to support specific institutions. I held that this Kantian theory of self-determination provides a justification for favoring a system of states to a world state, and for opposing colonialism and involuntary annexation.

This chapter extends the political autonomy theory by responding to a variety of challenges. Self-determination is already recognized as a cardinal principle of international law: Article 1 of both 1966 international human rights covenants declares that "all peoples have the right of self-determination," by virtue of which "they freely determine their political status and freely pursue their economic, social, and cultural development."[1] Article 1(2) of the UN Charter, the 1960 General Assembly Resolution Granting Independence to Colonial Peoples, and the 1970 Declaration on Friendly Relations also give prominent place to self-determination.

But self-determination has proved enduringly difficult to theorize. Among the many questions it faces are: Is collective self-determination possible in a modern mass society, where citizens have (and can only have) a negligible influence over political decisions? How do we define the "self" in self-determination? Does self-determination require democratic governance or is it compatible with nondemocratic arrangements? Does self-determination apply only to overseas dependencies or also to internal minorities? How does it cohere with other international principles, such as territorial integrity?

Here, I attempt to answer these questions. Section 5.1 asks whether, even if self-determination is possible in small, face-to-face groups, it could be realized in a large, complex, hierarchical modern state? To answer, I draw on recent theories of shared agency, beginning with small groups and then "scaling up" to the state. Section 5.2 takes up the question of who "the people" are and outlines my "endogenous" approach to peoplehood. Section 5.3 argues that democracy is not

---

[1] See UN General Assembly, *International Covenant on Civil and Political Rights*, Resolution 2200A (XXI) (December 1966); *International Covenant on Economic, Social, and Cultural Rights*, Resolution 2200A (XXI) (December 1966).

required for self-determination, Section 5.4 considers objections, and Section 5.5 outlines the implications of my view for secession and internal autonomy. I conclude the chapter by contrasting my political autonomy theory with two alternatives: the liberal nationalist theory and the peoplehood theory. Against liberal nationalists, I argue that in pluralist societies, collective self-determination should be based on neutral political values, not on national culture. And while my account overlaps with the peoplehood approach, I argue that I improve upon it by offering a clearer explanation of self-determination's *value*.

5.1 Self-Determination as Collective Agency

In explaining how people might share a will, Chapter 4 introduced the example of a partnership undertaking a joint venture—running a coffee shop together. I argued that there is a straightforward sense in which we can speak of this small-scale partnership as sharing a will. Their shared will is to cooperate in running the shop, and to license the priorities and procedures that make up their group standpoint. Yet while business partners can share a will, many would object that the citizens of a modern state cannot. The worry is that the model of self-determination is appropriate only to small, face-to-face groups, and thus does not scale up to an organization of the size and complexity of the modern state.

However, sustaining the state seems to have features in common with the joint intentional activity of smaller-scale groups. Ordinary citizens coordinate their behavior in many ways that support their government's rule. They cooperate with officials, judges, and the police; they comply with the law. They respect one another's legal rights: what it means for something to be my property, for example, is that my possession of it is generally recognized by my fellow citizens. By paying taxes, the people contribute to the institutions that enforce their laws and policies. Finally, when their state affords them representation, citizens offer input into the shape of their political activity, voicing opinions about how their enterprise should go. So it does not seem wrong to interpret political activity as jointly intentional—on a grand scale—among the citizenry. Though they do not know each other personally, citizens still participate in a shared activity together: they uphold, reproduce, and sometimes direct, a common scheme of law. Indeed, many civic acts, such as voting, or paying taxes, would make little sense if we did not expect our fellow citizens to play their parts alongside us.[2]

---

[2] See Christopher Kutz, *Complicity* (Cambridge: Cambridge University Press, 2000). One might object here that I require overly demanding levels of participatory commitment. What about the millions of "checked-out" citizens who are not politically active, knowledgeable, or patriotic? I deny that citizens must be highly participatory in order to share in a group's political will. Some evidence for this is given by other joint endeavors. While I value my university, I do not attend college-wide faculty meetings or wear the university logo, and I cannot name all the deans. Still, I "play my part" willingly, and I would be upset if my university was destroyed or merged without our consent, even if my own interests went unaffected (e.g., if I easily found another job with a higher salary). Likewise, the importance

Still, there are differences between the citizenry of a modern state and partners in a coffee shop. One might object that these differences are so great as to undercut any assertion that a people's shared activity could be a form of self-determination. Consider:

(1) A modern state is *hierarchical*: it is made up of leaders who direct and followers who comply.

(2) A modern state is *coercive*: it can punish people who refuse to "play their parts."

(3) A modern state is *impersonal*: no member can know or interact with all the other members.

(4) A modern state is *involuntary*: while the coffee shop partners freely joined their association and can easily leave, most citizens are born into their state and may not be able to exit.

These four features do differentiate modern states from small-scale partnerships. Still, I do not think they show that cooperation on the basis of a shared will is an inappropriate model for the state. Indeed, I think many modern states are at least partially self-determining enterprises, despite the four features listed above. Let me begin by discussing hierarchy and coercion.

While all states are reproduced through their citizens' shared activity, that activity is not always a form of free cooperation. While the citizens of North Korea intentionally support their government's rule, they likely do so because they would suffer grave harms if they did not. Sometimes, however, official coercion serves only to stabilize citizens' cooperation—facilitating the achievement of their genuinely shared commitments—rather than imposing a project on them from outside. Here, governing officials are a tool for a self-organizing citizenry to carry out their joint purposes more effectively.

Since one may doubt that hierarchy and coercion can be so lightly dismissed, let me explain how our coffee shop could evolve hierarchy and coercion while remaining a self-determining enterprise.[3] The thought is that if a hierarchical and coercive coffee shop can remain self-determining, then a hierarchical and coercive state might be self-determining too.

Suppose the partners get busier. Because of their business's increased complexity, it is now harder to figure out who should do which tasks at what time. So the partners decide to appoint a manager. She begins making most of the decisions day to day, and she may even be issuing directives to the partners about how to divide their labor or what prices to set. The fact that the partners have introduced

---

of citizens' shared will may be quite apparent in exceptional scenarios like foreign occupation, even if it is not apparent in everyday political life.

[3] For a similar attempt to "scale up" from small-scale groups, see Scott Shapiro, *Legality* (Cambridge, MA: Harvard University Press, 2011), 156–70.

hierarchy into their enterprise does not necessarily mean they are dominated by the manager. Even if she is largely running the show, it is possible that the manager furthers the shared aims of the partners.

When would that be the case? One criterion is *procedural*: the partners hired her, and if they become dissatisfied enough with her performance, they could fire her. On a "minimalist" interpretation, the manager's acts reflect the shared aims of the partners so long as they have not dismissed her yet. (One worry is that the manager, once installed, might be able to manipulate the partners to prevent her own dismissal, e.g., by hiding relevant information.)

We should therefore add a *substantive* criterion: what the manager does must be a reasonable pursuit of the joint venture's aims, as these were worked out among the participants. The manager has certain "constitutional" purposes to pursue: these are defined by the commitments that constitute the group standpoint. As I said, these commitments may be abstract, and they may conflict in concrete cases. Part of the manager's role is to fill them out with plans that are more specific. But to meet our substantive criterion, these plans must be "reasonable" elaborations of the group standpoint. And there will be some acts the manager could undertake that could not be plausibly interpreted that way. A manager who embezzled the coffee shop's funds would not count as pursuing the purposes of the partners, under any reasonable description of those purposes. Even if she successfully hid the evidence or blackmailed the partners and prevented herself being fired, we would not want to say that she furthers the partnership's aims.[4]

Now let me add in coercion: in addition to the organizational problems, suppose some partners are concerned that members are shirking their duties. Perhaps they have added new partners, so the group has gotten large. It is becoming hard to rely on everyone showing up for scheduled shifts. This threatens to create a culture of "slacking": since Amy knows that Bob is often late, she feels she can be late too. Still, the partners value their enterprise, and they do not want to see it unravel. So they devise a solution: from now on, the manager will have the power to fine anyone who does not show up for work on time. This will give everyone incentive to comply, and return the partnership to a culture of efficiency, or so they hope.

Even though the coffee shop now features both hierarchy and coercion, I submit that the partners are still *self-determining* through their manager. They can be self-determining despite hierarchy so long as the manager's decisions qualify as reasonable elaborations of their shared commitments, and so long as there is some way of dismissing her if she begins to abuse her powers. And they can be self-determining despite coercion, so long as they see independent reason—apart from the manager's threat to fine—for playing their part in the shared plan that she now coordinates. I believe the partners do see such an independent reason. Because they value their venture, they have reason to show up for work, so long as

[4] Pettit, "Rawls's Political Ontology," and *On the People's Terms*, ch. 5.

the others do, and the manager's coercion assures everyone that this will occur, thus stabilizing their enterprise.

What about the last two features of the modern state—the fact that it is both *impersonal* and *involuntary*? Do they undermine the possibility of genuine self-determination? I doubt it. Even when an institution is too large for all members to know one another, it can still feature significant levels of cooperation. Though I do not know most of the other students and employees at my university, still I "play my part" in it willingly. Many large groups—think of megachurches, or trade unions—do not exhibit close personal ties among the participants, yet still they cooperate on the basis of shared commitments.

Finally, what about the fact that the state is *involuntary*? This is the most compelling of the disanalogies between the state and the coffee shop. Most citizens were born into their state, and they may have no reasonable opportunity to leave. Still, I doubt that involuntariness undermines the state's claim to be a self-determining organization. Some theorists argue that respect for the self-determination of a group cannot rest on respect for the judgments and priorities of its members, unless individuals have consented to membership.[5] I reject that view. In the social contract tradition, consent was valued as a way of ensuring that political institutions reflected individuals' judgments and priorities. But consent is a red herring here. For a group to reflect the priorities of its members, its aims must be *freely shared* by constituents, but membership need not be consensual for this to be the case. We do not consent to our families, but not having chosen one's family does not mean that one's family is an alien constraint on one's life. In good families, children have a valuable relationship with their parents, which they care about and endorse. In this situation, though members did not join the family, it *reflects their goals and purposes much as if they had*. Many other social groups, like workplace and school associations, are only quasi-voluntary, since our options to join and leave them are constrained. Still, these groups can (and often do) instantiate members' shared aims. So the fact that a relationship is not consented to does not show that the relation is not one of collective self-determination, in which members freely cooperate on the basis of shared commitments.

5.2 The Endogenous Approach to Peoplehood

Our discussion in the last section showed that it is not impossible for the citizenry of a modern state to be self-determining. But how do we define the "self" that has a claim to self-determination? Often existing institutions fall short of guaranteeing self-determination for all or part of their constituencies, especially when they contain alienated subpopulations. Which, if any, of these groups count as

---

[5] See Beitz, *Political Theory and International Relations*, 78.

"peoples" that should enjoy self-determination? While most theories begin by defining "peoples" with reference to characteristics like language, culture, or interlinked interests, I will argue instead that the constitution of the people is *endogenous* to existing institutions. A people is born only when its members engage in institutionalized political cooperation and come to endorse that cooperation. To introduce this endogenous approach, I briefly contrast it with two other views.

On a *nonpolitical* view of peoplehood, some social process independent of political institutions creates a self-determining people. For Locke, this is an act of consent by which individuals agree to form one commonwealth, a bond that persists even when their legislative power is overthrown or dissolved.[6] For nationalist theories, this is a cultural socialization process that creates a group with a common language or traditions. Of course, as a matter of history, states have often played a significant role in facilitating such socialization processes, adopting "nation-building policies" to diffuse a common culture throughout their territories. Yet both of these accounts hold that even if states were to be removed from the map, the world would remain carved into peoples, identifiable by shared features that objectively unite them. There is some Archimedean point of view, independent of political institutions, from which to delineate peoples.

On the *institutionalist* view of peoplehood—endorsed most prominently by Hobbes—a "people" is created only through representation by a state.[7] By unifying individuals through a structure of institutional roles and decision-procedures, the state brings into being a corporate body, distinct from its members, to which the acts of this institutional structure can be attributed.[8] This view sees the state as a corporate agent: a "fictive" person in its own right, which forms and executes its own intentions. The state is similar in this respect to other incorporated groups, like churches and business corporations. Like these other corporate groups, the state's internal decision-making structure (or "constitution") gives its attitudes a certain independence from the attitudes of the individuals who make it up.

My *endogenous* view of the people sits between the nonpolitical and the institutionalist conceptions. I agree with the institutionalist that some structure of representation is necessary to create groups with the corporate agency to act as peoples. I also think that peoples typically have an institutionalist genealogy: they emerge because groups have shared a history of acting together in political institutions (or sometimes, reacted against that history). But the institutionalist view faces a question: are the state's individual members implicated in any way in their institutions? Do those institutions reflect *their* judgments and priorities?

---

[6] Locke, *Second Treatise of Government*, ch. 8.
[7] For an account of institutional representation, see Hobbes, *Leviathan*, ch. 16, though Hobbes also adds the condition that a state must be *authorized* by its individual members, which brings him closer to the position argued for here.
[8] Peter French, *Collective and Corporate Responsibility* (New York: Columbia University Press, 1984); Philip Pettit, "Responsibility Incorporated," *Ethics* 117, no. 2 (2007): 171–201; Pettit and Christian List, *Group Agency* (Oxford: Oxford University Press, 2011).

After all, North Korea too has a decision-making structure by which it forms intentions and acts in the name of its people. But we would be hard-pressed to say that the North Korean state "represents" those it rules, or that the state's acts can be imputed to them as the results of their own agency. Instead, they are forced against their will to go along. For the state to represent its population, then, it must meet a further condition: it must receive "uptake" from its people, who support its institutions in the appropriate way. There must be a connection, in other words, between the collective agency of the state and the agency of its individual members.[9] In my view this agency connection obtains when individuals *willingly participate* in their state.

A member willingly participates when, upon reflection, she *endorses* her intention to "play her part" in a political institution.[10] To "play one's part" is to carry out the tasks associated with one's role: obeying the law, paying taxes, voting, cooperating with officials, and contributing to the formation of public opinion. It is important that a citizen's participation be the product of her own judgments, not of coercion or manipulation by external agents. This requires some appreciation of the purpose behind the institution, and an awareness of how one's own contributions further its achievement. When individuals willingly participate in this way, their state partly reflects their own self-directed agency.

Some may wonder whether willing participation is a type of consent. The two ideas are not the same. To transform rights and obligations between people, consent is generally thought to require communicative expression: it is not just a state of mind. Coercion or lack of decent alternatives may also invalidate consent.[11] Yet willing participation need not satisfy these conditions: it may not be not publicly communicated, and it can occur against a coercive background where alternatives are lacking. Like consent, willing participation is concerned with an individual's attitudes: there is to that extent a similarity between the concepts. But willing participation is a weaker condition than consent. It also matters whether willing participation is *reasonable*. If it is inappropriate for the individual to see herself as a participant in a shared enterprise, for example, because the political venture is thoroughly unjust, then her participation may show only that she is dominated or manipulated. So unlike consent, which can make a moral difference even when it is unreasonably given, participation lacks normative significance under these conditions.

---

[9] For a similar view, see Lucia Rafanelli, "A Defense of Individualism in an Age of Corporate Rights," *Journal of Political Philosophy* 25, no.3 (2017): esp. 290–2.
[10] Stefan Sciaraffa, "Identification, Meaning, and the Normativity of Social Roles," *European Journal of Philosophy* 19, no. 1 (2009): 107–28.
[11] See Nir Eyal, "Informed Consent," in *The Stanford Encyclopedia of Philosophy* (Fall 2012 edition), edited by Edward N. Zalta. https://plato.stanford.edu/entries/informed-consent/; John Kleinig, "The Nature of Consent," in *The Ethics of Consent*, edited by Franklin Miller and Alan Wertheimer (Oxford: Oxford University Press, 2010), 3–24.

My endogenous view of the people reflects this additional willing-participation condition: a "people" is constituted when a state is upheld through the willing participation of its members. State institutions mark out individuals as potential members of a self-determining community. Still, there are further "success conditions"—beyond state structures—for the achievement of collective self-determination. If members willingly participate in their institutions, acting together to implement their decisions, then a self-determining people is born. If members do not willingly participate, while a state may exist, there is no "people" that this institution could be said to represent. On the endogenous view, there is no independent criterion for delineating "peoples" beyond the fact that political institutions either succeed or fail at eliciting willing participation from the populations they rule.

Unlike in the coffee shop case, often citizens' shared intentions do not pre-exist the establishment of their state. Instead, the state attempts to *create* shared intentions by facilitating institutionalized joint activity among its constituents. Yet I do not think it matters morally whether authority structures or willing participation comes first, so long as a group exhibits cooperative attitudes. As a historical matter, shared political wills are often the product of prior acts of illegitimate political coercion. But this genesis does not necessarily render a shared will illegitimate. A state that was started in an initially illegitimate way, over time, might generate acceptance for its constitutional structures among those it rules. If willing participation emerges under authentic deliberative conditions, then I believe this people will be self-determining, even though their shared intentions were in part brought into being by previously illegitimate institutions.

Willing participation matters because it helps to guarantee *correspondence* for individuals. As I argued in Chapter 4, when each member participates in a group's shared will and the state's use of coercion reflects that will, political coercion will not be *alien* to participants. Instead, participants will be ruled by institutions they regard as appropriate, and they will act freely in complying with their institutions. However, it is important to note that willing participation is often *partial*: sometimes much of the population "signs on" to a particular state, but some subgroups fail to support it willingly. When this happens, I believe the state's coercion of those alienated subgroups may be illegitimate (though as I note below, the state may have a temporary enforcement *permission* until a more legitimate arrangement can be agreed). For this reason, the ideal of self-determination may sometimes call on us to reconfigure political boundaries, enabling alienated groups to be governed by institutions that better reflect their shared commitments, and I come back to this point in Section 5.5.

What makes the constitution of the people endogenous on this approach? In defining the people, we look to the patterns of affirmation and alienation that emerge as artifacts of existing states. We then ask: are there feasible institutional alternatives—consistent with the provision of basic justice—that would afford alienated groups greater political autonomy? We delineate a new "proto-people"—when we do—not because we are recognizing something that already exists, but because we have some reason to hope that a new institutional configuration will lessen alienation, facilitating willing participation at reasonable cost. "Proto-peoples" are institutional structures that seem likely to generate greater "uptake" from alienated constituents and that could provide a basis for minimally just rule. Typically, this will involve a group whose members (i) desire to cooperate together politically, and (ii) seem capable of sustaining institutions that could meet the conditions of basic justice, though (iii) they currently lack their own state or substate political institutions and so do not have the corporate structure to act as peoples. Often, this will mean looking to political parties, liberation movements, and other organized bodies that have representative institutions and a reserve of political support. But whether these organizations succeed in forging a new people will depend on whether they are able to elicit sufficient willing participation in future political arrangements. Of course, in speaking of such groups, founders or political leaders might refer to "We the People," but we should see this language as aspirational or performative, as aiding the group in constituting itself as a people.[12]

Thus, the value of political autonomy—the importance, to the individual, of participating in a shared political will—should play a continuing role in the boundary-drawing process. On this approach, the process of constituting the people is never finished, once and for all. The "people" is a mutable entity and negotiating and renegotiating our institutional arrangements is a process that we can expect to be ongoing.

I have already stressed that self-determination is one value among others—it is not an absolute right—and it can sometimes be outweighed by competing concerns. If an existing regime is the only means for providing decent rule, if reconfiguring it would jeopardize urgent interests, or would entail unreasonably high costs, then that regime may have permission to govern alienated constituents, on a *pro tem* basis. But regimes that do not realize self-determination are not fully legitimate, and they may be displaced if alternatives become feasible in the future. So while there is no prepolitical answer to Who are the people?, the ideal of self-determination gives us guidance about how to (re)negotiate political boundaries.

5.3 Is This Democracy?

What institutional arrangements might afford us reasonable confidence that a government reflects the shared will of its people?[13] As mentioned in Chapter 4, some thinkers—including Rousseau—have seen self-determination as closely connected with democracy. Does the people's shared will require democracy?

---

[12] I thank Alan Patten for comments on this issue.
[13] Charles Beitz, "The Moral Standing of States Revisited," *Ethics and International Affairs* 23, no. 4 (2009): 336–8, usefully discusses these complexities.

In my view, no. Collective self-determination has three institutional preconditions: (i) the protection of basic security, subsistence and personal autonomy rights, (ii) the formation of deliberative public opinion, and (iii) the existence of a channel for revoking government authorization. These conditions fall short of modern democracy, which requires additional institutions like the equal right to vote for representatives, to associate in political parties, and to compete for office.

Let me begin with basic rights protection. As I outlined in Chapter 4, basic justice is a threshold criterion for state legitimacy. Fulfillment of these rights is necessary to show that the state is a reasonable interpreter of citizens' duty to respect freedom-as-independence. Further, basic rights protection is also a precondition for any process of free political cooperation.[14] Where citizens' joint activity is carried on solely out of fear, it carries no moral weight. A minimal scheme of rights—including protections for personal inviolability, the essentials of private autonomy, and subsistence—is a background condition of a self-determining community, since it is possible to cooperate with others freely only where one is not unduly vulnerable with respect to one's essential needs and interests.

A second condition is the presence of mechanisms for the formation of deliberative public opinion: in Chapter 4, I called these *preconditions for collective self-determination*. Citizens must be able to discuss the shared priorities that make up their group standpoint and provide orientation to their government. They must be free to form their own views, to declare them, and to listen others' views. Here my view overlaps somewhat with theories of democracy. On a broad definition, "democracy" refers to any system that ties the state's authorization to exercise political power to a process of shared deliberation among citizens.[15] My account of self-determination has much in common with this broad ideal. Because correspondence between subjects' shared will and their political institutions only serves autonomy under conditions where their judgments are freely formed, arenas for the formation of deliberative opinion, including protections for free expression, conscience, and association, are essential preconditions for collective self-determination. These rights ensure that citizens can develop their own views and make informed judgments about their institutions. They also help safeguard people against manipulation by external agents, including their own government. Thus, collective self-determination reflects some of the values underlying democracy, including autonomy, deliberative communication, and popular control.

Yet there is also a narrower definition of "democracy" that associates it closely with elections and voting. On this view, "democracy" refers to a procedure for group decision-making that grants each person subject to it equal opportunity for

---

[14] Rawls similarly argues that the protection of human rights is a precondition for "a decent scheme of political and social cooperation" (*Law of Peoples*, 65).

[15] The *locus classicus* for this view is Joshua Cohen, "Deliberation and Democratic Legitimacy," in *Philosophy, Politics, Democracy* (Cambridge, MA: Harvard University Press, 2009).

influence: a procedure such as majority rule.[16] I do not see a procedure of equal influence as necessary for collective self-determination. Equal votes are not necessary because a group, under authentic deliberative conditions, and against a background of basic rights protection, might commit to being governed nondemocratically. If this seems far-fetched, consider that many smaller-scale ventures do just this. In a small-scale setting, everyone might simply agree that an individual is wise and virtuous and shares the community priorities, and defer to her judgments day to day.

> "Which business site should we purchase?"
> "Amy used to be a real estate agent, so I'm sure she knows best."
> "Well, let's do whatever she says."

In a small tribe, collective self-rule might function much like this: indeed, such groups often feature informal decision-making by respected elders. Many nonpolitical associations, including churches, schools, businesses, and so on, are governed by nondemocratic norms that their participants genuinely accept and that protect their fundamental interests.

Analogously, a political group's shared policy for governance might involve equal opportunity for influence, but it also might not. Participants may instead agree that a particular individual—say, their *monarch*—is especially good at interpreting the group's shared commitments and defer to her political judgments day to day. So long as these participants share commitments about how their joint venture should go, and so long as the monarch's decisions respect basic rights and count as reasonable elaborations of those commitments, participants will be as self-determining under their monarch as they would be in a democracy. After all, even in a democracy, it is the majority—not the whole people—who make ordinary decisions. So long as the cooperators, by and large, affirm group norms that grant the majority a right to decide, its decisions are legitimate. But these same conditions can also legitimate a nondemocratic procedure.

Of course, it is true that an agreement on delegation to a monarch is unlikely in any modern pluralistic society. Yet I wish to leave open the possibility that societies that are not fully modern or pluralistic can also be self-determining. To impose elections, political parties, and competition for office on these societies—where they endorse alternative institutions that could protect basic rights and ensure deliberative freedom—would violate their right to collective self-determination. One might further object that in the real world, it is unlikely that any nondemocracy will meet the conditions for rights protection I have laid out. That may be true: my aim is not to show that existing nondemocracies are collectively self-determining.

---

[16] For "narrow" definitions, see Kolodny, "Rule Over None I and II"; Thomas Christiano, "Self-Determination and the Human Right to Democracy," in *The Philosophical Foundations of Human Rights*, edited by Rowan Cruft, S. Matthew Liao, and Massimo Renzo (Oxford: Oxford University Press, 1995).

I argue only that it is conceptually possible that a nondemocracy *could be* self-determining.

Granting for the sake of argument that a population could commit to a nondemocratic form of government, what if they change their minds as to how they wish to be governed? My final condition is that there must be some channel for the people to revoke authorization of their government. As I indicated in Chapter 4, to ensure self-determination, there must be some causal connection between the shared will of the group and their institutions. A group should not enjoy correspondence merely because of the goodwill of a benevolent absolutist who gives the people what they think right. One might think that only democratic procedures could serve this causal function. To be self-determining, one might argue, a group must have the ability to *control* their institutions to serve their shared commitments, whatever those commitments might be. Voting procedures provide a necessary causal mechanism to ensure this.[17]

I think one can imagine a range of mechanisms that could afford the requisite control. Lockean popular rebellion seems antiquated and unreliable, but it might be sufficient in a premodern society where the power of leaders depends heavily on the cooperation of the people and technologies of social coercion are undeveloped. Mass protests and noncooperation movements are a modern version of the same idea. Of course, these methods may be insufficient in states that possess armies and secret police. Yet I believe that even under contemporary conditions, it is possible for citizens to authorize a government that is not democratic—say, a constitutional monarchy—so long as there is some mechanism by which they could initiate a process of constitutional reform, for example, an amendment procedure.[18]

One might finally object that a society can be legitimately governed nondemocratically only if all members unanimously accept the regime. As soon as there is one dissenter to the popular will, on this view, a community must be democratically ruled.[19] But I do not see why this should be so. Were we to require democracy, the dissenter would be afforded the right to impose his political judgments on everyone else. Moreover, it seems we have a good rationale for discounting this dissenter's objections. So long as a nondemocratic state protects its population's basic rights, and satisfies the other deliberative and control conditions for collective self-determination, this dissenter has a natural duty of justice to coordinate with others under a common territorial authority. In my view, this means that even internal dissenters must persuade a sufficient number of their fellows to support democracy; they lack standing to impose it on an unwilling population.

To conclude, then, while democratic rights provide robust institutional guarantees that citizens authorize their regime, the institutional forms that safeguard

---

[17] I owe this objection to Zuehl, *Collective Self-Determination*. A similar objection is also considered in Beitz, *The Idea of Human Rights*, 182–4.
[18] For a similar argument, see Altman and Wellman, *A Liberal Theory of International Justice*, 27–9.
[19] Christiano, "Self-Determination and the Human Right to Democracy." For a similar requirement of "near unanimity" in the case of Rawls's "decent societies," see Beitz, *The Idea of Human Rights*, 156–7.

collective self-determination can vary depending on the historical and social context.[20] In particular, one should be wary of dismissing non-Western forms of government in favor of electoral democracy. Of course, it will be more difficult to *know* in a nondemocratic context whether the citizenry *does* authorize its government, and in disputed cases, this may tell in favor of conducting supervised plebiscites to allow people to express their views about whether to continue with a monarchy, say, or a tribal regime. But while electoral democracy is one way of realizing collective self-determination, it may not be appropriate in all times and places.

5.4 Objections and Replies

Having now laid out my political autonomy theory, let me consider two important objections to it. The first objection takes issue with *basic justice* as a condition on collective self-determination. As we have seen, basic justice includes the fulfillment of security, subsistence, and essential personal autonomy rights, as well as the deliberative freedoms of speech, conscience, and association. This is a robust set of liberal rights. One might therefore worry that the political autonomy view is unable to account for historical wrongs of colonialism since most precolonial regimes would have failed to meet these justice conditions. Can the political autonomy view explain why colonizing these peoples was wrong?

It is important to stress that it is not necessary that a people exhibit a Weberian state, formal legal rights, or a Kantian understanding of justice to claim self-determination. What is necessary is that their institutions protect certain fundamental interests: but these protections can take many different forms, compatibly with different political traditions. Further, when a group falls short of the basic justice threshold, this fact by itself is not sufficient to show that they can permissibly be subjected to military occupation by foreigners. For an invasion and occupation to be just, it must demonstrate a just cause (such as national self-defense or *in extremis* humanitarian intervention) and meet associated conditions of necessity and proportionality.

Still, if a group whose institutions do not satisfy the basic justice threshold is justly subjected to foreign occupation—perhaps in the aftermath of a defensive war or a justified humanitarian intervention—then I believe it is permissible for occupiers to rule this group until they become capable of establishing a decent domestic regime. As I argued in Chapter 4, illegitimate coercion, while *pro tanto*

---

[20] For a view that states should be democratic to be members in good standing in international society, see Buchanan, *Justice, Legitimacy, and Self-Determination*, 146–7. Compare Rawls's discussion of decent hierarchical peoples in *The Law of Peoples*, 62–78. Rawls stops short of saying, as I do, that the people must be able to revoke their authorization of government. Joshua Cohen also argues that collective self-determination does not require full democracy, in "Is There a Human Right to Democracy," in *The Arc of the Moral Universe* (Cambridge, MA: Harvard University Press, 2010), 357–8.

wrong, can be permissible if it is the only way to secure essential rights and public order. So long as the aim of an occupying force is to prepare the people for eventual self-government, they have a temporary *enforcement permission*. This enforcement permission depends on its being exercised in accordance with the aim of facilitating the people's future self-determination, not on the basis of other, more nefarious aims, like exploitation, resource-extraction, or the permanent acquisition of their territory.

Further, an enforcement permission is not the same thing as a right to legitimate jurisdiction over the subject people and their territory. For that, a state that enables the self-determination of the population is required. It is possible, of course, that institutions of temporary occupation might generate support for a more permanent integration into the occupying state. But that is a choice for the subject population to make. Thus, even where self-determination is temporarily overridden by the need to protect basic justice, it remains important. It gives foreign rulers reason to work toward a situation in which self-determination can be re-established, and it requires them to be willing to redraw political boundaries. Only a state that enables its population's self-determination has *full legitimacy*: a claim-right, against rivals, to be the preferred ruler of the territory and its population. So while my account does allow that self-determination can sometimes be outweighed, it can explain why benign foreign rule is something we should work to overcome.

A second objection is that my political autonomy view cannot account for the wrong of annexation by a state with similar political values. Suppose that Denmark is annexed by Sweden. Although not identical, the two countries' political values are very similar. Perhaps the laws posttakeover would even be largely the same as they would have been had Denmark remained independent. Would Swedish rule, then, realize correspondence between the Danes' shared political will and the institutions that govern them?[21]

I reply that correspondence with shared political values is not sufficient for political autonomy. A participant in a group's shared will does not simply intend that values X, Y, and Z be realized. Instead, she intends that *we* pursue values X, Y, and Z *together*. In addition to shared values, then, a shared will includes a reference to a group engaged in institutionalized political cooperation. Sweden's takeover of Denmark fails to reflect this "we" dimension of a people's shared will, which involves being governed by *Danish* institutions. As I have stressed throughout, normally a shared political will involves not only a commitment to support certain institutions, but also a commitment to associate politically with a group of fellow citizens.

A good theory of the *we* involved in self-determination, however, must be compatible with the fact that no member can know all of the other members and that the group's membership is constantly changing. Political groups are large: individual members of a citizenry cannot be personally acquainted with all the

---

[21] Thanks to Laura Valentini for this objection.

other members. And since minors (and immigrants) are gaining the vote every day, this constantly changes the membership of the group that controls governing institutions. Membership in a citizenry is thus much like membership in other large, institutionalized groups, such as a university, a union, or a large corporation. In these cases, what makes the group *the same group* over time is a continuity of institutional structure, not a continuity of participants. Princeton University is the same university it was in 2000 not because its membership is the same but because the institutions that currently govern it stand in a lineal relation to the institutions of that time, and they have been shaped throughout the intervening period by the members of the university. While Princeton University pursues much the same values as Yale or Harvard does, it pursues them through a distinctive institutional structure that its members value and endorse.

This "we" component of a people's shared will raises questions about the relation between my view and the liberal nationalist approach, about which I say more in Section 5.6. For now, I simply note that while a sense of collective cooperation is an important part of a people's shared will, I doubt this must be rooted in prior commonalities like a shared language or national culture. The endogenous account instead suggests that sharing political institutions is often sufficient, even in the absence of further ties.

5.5 Secession and Internal Autonomy

What are the implications of my political autonomy theory for secession or internal autonomy for minorities? Under current international law, these subgroups are not thought to possess claims to self-determination. Instead, the right of self-determination has been limited to overseas colonies and populations under foreign military occupation or apartheid government.[22] Some commentators invoke a "saltwater test," which holds that peoples with a right of self-determination must be separated from the larger state by an ocean.[23] It is unclear whether there is any sound moral case for the "saltwater test," since territorially contiguous populations, like overseas groups, can be subjected to alien domination. Though there is some movement to widen the scope of the legal right—especially by applying it to indigenous peoples—this is not yet binding.[24]

Contrary to the international legal consensus, I believe that self-determination is not a *sui generis* value that applies to overseas decolonization, occupation, and

---

[22] See Antonio Cassese, *Self-Determination of Peoples: A Legal Reappraisal* (Cambridge: Cambridge University Press, 1995), 126–40.

[23] Daniel Philpott, *Revolutions in Sovereignty* (Princeton: Princeton University Press, 2010), 156.

[24] The UN Declaration on the Rights of Indigenous Peoples adopted by the General Assembly in 2007 attributes the right of self-determination to indigenous peoples (Art. 3), but it is not a binding legal instrument. See James Anaya, *Indigenous Peoples in International Law* (Oxford: Oxford University Press, 2004).

apartheid cases alone. Instead, I think our intuitions about these "focal" cases can be justified only by invoking an interest on the part of persistently alienated groups in redrawing political boundaries. This same interest may justify self-determination in additional cases, such as autonomy for indigenous peoples, or greater independence for Scotland or Quebec. I believe that those who strongly support decolonization have reason to endorse self-determination for these minorities as well. As outlined in the introduction, a key reform proposal of this book is that the value of self-determination requires states to move away from a unitary legal order, toward a more pluralistic constitution that can accommodate internal autonomy for their minorities.

Why might internal minorities have a moral claim to collective self-governance? Recall that when an individual willingly participates in the shared will of a self-determining group, rule by that group's institutions will further her interests in nonalienation and self-direction. But we must recognize that these correspondence interests are not fulfilled for persistently alienated internal minorities. Their basic rights may be protected, but they do not endorse their participation in the political enterprise. Instead, they reject their inclusion in the state.[25] Where minorities' political priorities are (i) consistent with the provision of basic justice and (ii) can be feasibly addressed through institutional reconfiguration, I believe the persistent alienation of these subgroups deserves an institutional response. In some cases, we may be morally required to redraw political boundaries to afford internal minorities greater self-determination.

Before proceeding, I recall a point already stressed in Chapter 4: not every dissenting minority has a claim to self-determination. Claims to self-determination are *moralized* claims. This means the complaints of some alienated groups should be dismissed, where they refuse to recognize the equal independence of others. Groups that are alienated because they hold aims at odds with basic justice—fascists, racists, theocrats, and so on—are not wronged when their self-determination is denied. We should also dismiss the complaints of groups who are alienated simply because they refuse to acknowledge others' equivalent claims to political autonomy. Nostalgists for empire have no right to institutions that would uphold their imperial self-image.

Finally, a feasible institutional response to the alienation of dispersed and disaffected ideological minorities (such as socialists) is sometimes lacking. Recall from Chapter 4 that while alien coercion is *pro tanto* wrong, this wrong can sometimes be outweighed by other social values, particularly by the need to achieve a stable and functioning legal system. Since, on a Kantian view, the state plays an essential role in establishing and enforcing property and other rights, jurisdiction

---

[25] I am not suggesting that alienated dissenters should not be fully included or should lack civil, political, or social rights. I simply highlight that the self-determination of this *particular* people does not further their interest in political autonomy.

over most matters needs to be territorially defined if states are to carry out morally mandatory tasks. Groups claiming self-determination must therefore be capable of territorial organization in representative institutions. Since dispersed minorities are unable to fulfill this condition, they cannot claim territorial self-determination since that would be inconsistent with upholding basic justice for others. (I allowed in Chapter 4, however, that dispersed minorities may be able to claim self-governance over issues that can feasibly be organized on a nonterritorial basis.)

So there is a variety of moral limits to self-determination. Some of these limits are *principled*: in cases where dissenters' priorities are incompatible with others' freedom-as-independence, there is no moral loss in denying them self-determination. Other limits are *practical*: where dissenters' priorities are sufficiently just but cannot be feasibly institutionally addressed, there is some moral loss in denying them self-determination, but this loss is strongly outweighed by countervailing reasons.

Still, there are cases where greater political autonomy for persistently alienated minorities is feasible compatibly with protecting others' basic rights, and in these cases, I believe we are required to institute it. If another institution would be equally consistent with others' independence, and more reflective of the priorities of alienated subgroups, why can't they institute it instead?

Consider, then, the situation of dissenters who are persistently alienated, not because they deny a duty to cooperate in a minimally just state, nor because they deny the basic rights or political autonomy of others, but because they seek an alternative configuration of political units. These people do not see why this *particular* government should be the one ruling their lives. They might be persistently alienated because their subgroup has a legacy of conflict or oppression at their current state's hands—many colonized or indigenous peoples fall into this category. Or they might be persistently alienated because, though they have no significant history of oppression, they share distinctive political priorities on many issues, priorities that are not shared by the majority. Scotland and Quebec are persistent minorities of this kind. On my view, a group has a *pro tanto* claim to enjoy greater self-determination if the group:

(1) finds itself unable, over a significant period, to affirm political participation in their current state;

(2) possesses representative, territorially based practices of political cooperation that can be more willingly affirmed (perhaps through a substate political unit or organized national liberation movement); and

(3) has the political capacity to construct minimally just institutions on the basis of those practices.

Unlike Allen Buchanan, who argues that self-determination is only a *remedial* right against a government that persists in serious injustices, I hold that an alienated group can have a claim to self-determination even where they have not been unjustly treated.[26] But unlike plebiscitary theorists of secession such as Andrew Altman and Christopher Wellman, on my view, self-determination does not necessarily imply a right to secede unilaterally.[27] Instead, I believe self-determination is a weighty moral claim that must be applied with due regard for circumstance: it does not necessarily generate a right to secede, and it may sometimes be permissibly overridden.

First, the claim to self-determination is not always best satisfied through an independent state. Other arrangements (like confederal institutions, internal autonomy, or devolution) can be appropriate vehicles for self-determination in many circumstances. The fact that a persistent minority lacks correspondence gives them a *pro tanto* claim to greater self-determination, but their claim must be weighed against a variety of competing concerns. Such an assessment is necessary to determine (i) whether they have an all-things-considered right, and (ii) which institutional vehicle is most appropriate for fulfilling that right.

In some scenarios, a self-determination claim is outweighed by urgent competing reasons, generating no all-things-considered right. As I have emphasized, there are good reasons for overriding self-determination in cases where recognizing it would entail grave risks to just institutions, such as a threat of civil or international war or ethnic conflict; a high probability of human rights violations; or where the costs of institutional reform are so great as to jeopardize the performance of essential state functions. The moral reasons in favor of self-determination are defeasible: in any concrete case, we will need to balance the claims of minorities against a range of countervailing concerns.[28]

If a minority's claim is not outweighed by competing reasons, then we must decide which institutional vehicle should be adopted to respond to it. This depends on an assessment of the political context, including whether there are significant dissenting groups on the territory claimed by the alienated minority, the cost of a potential secession to others' expectations, and the weight of an alienated group's grievances. Often a bare majority within a territory supports independence, but there is a substantial subgroup that wishes to remain within the overarching state. In situations like this, a fair treatment of both groups' correspondence interests will usually tell in favor of federalism or internal autonomy, rather than secession. A federal solution allows for some measure of fulfillment of the self-determination claims of both groups, enabling those who identify with the overarching state to

---

[26] On my view, while potential injustice is a constraint on self-determination, it is not a necessary condition for it. See Buchanan, *Justice, Legitimacy, and Self-Determination*, 351–7.
[27] Altman and Wellman, *A Liberal Theory*, 46.
[28] Compare David Miller, "Secession and the Principle of Nationality," *Canadian Journal of Philosophy* 26, Supplementary Volume (1997): 261–82. Miller does not insist that each nation should have its own state; instead, he says only that nations "have a good claim to political self-determination" (265). He also remains agnostic about which institutional forms would best guarantee self-determination.

be governed by it in some areas, while still granting the alienated minority a forum for collective decision-making in areas of concern to them.[29]

A minority's claim will be of greater weight—and may tell in favor of secession over internal autonomy or federalism—where that group has grievances in addition to persistent alienation, i.e. they are victims of a current or historical injustice or denial of political representation. Here the minority may have a moral claim to secede, even at significant cost to the remainder state, and even if there are other minorities on their territory who wish to remain. One must still assess their claim against the possibility that a secession would lead to a civil or international war or render the remainder state unable to perform morally mandatory functions for its population. If a secession would result in a rump state unable to provide for its own national defense or to sustain a viable economy, then that may tell in favor of federalism or internal autonomy even when the minority has significant justice-based grievances.

In yet further scenarios, such as the division of Czechoslovakia or the secession of Norway from Sweden, nearly everyone within a territory supports political independence, there is no real prospect of civil or international war or human rights violations, and both resulting states will be perfectly viable and able to perform essential legitimating functions. Here, the alienated group may have a moral right to secede, and the overarching state may be obliged to recognize that right, entering negotiations to arrange for legal separation.

As this discussion illustrates, the institutional implications of any given self-determination claim depend on a complex balance of competing moral reasons, and require careful contextual judgments. Because of this complexity, I agree with Allen Buchanan that the legal right to *secede* unilaterally is best seen as a remedy against serious injustices. A principle of unilateral plebiscitary secession is unsuitable for incorporation into international law. It would likely prove destabilizing in terms of peace and respect for human rights, and it disregards the careful contextual assessments that are necessary in these matters.

Still, on my view, states containing persistently alienated subgroups have a moral obligation to negotiate greater political autonomy for those groups in cases where (i) this is consistent with sustaining minimally just institutions, and (ii) there is a feasible institutional alternative that can be implemented at reasonable cost. There are many circumstances where it is quite feasible to allow for greater self-determination at relatively low institutional risk, as in 1934, when the US Congress passed the Indian Reorganization Act, ending 50 years of federal control over Native American affairs; after World War II, when decolonization dismantled the colonial empires; and in 1999, when Canada created the province of Nunavut to guarantee self-determination to its Inuit minority.[30]

---

[29] Alan Patten, *Equal Recognition* (Princeton: Princeton University Press, 2014), 237–47.
[30] Compare the discussion of "context-dependent" moral requirements in Patten, *Equal Recognition*, 24–7.

So while a legal right to secession seems inappropriate, internal autonomy is a fitting institutional response to minority self-determination claims in a wide range of circumstances. For this reason, I believe we should work to institutionalize a qualified right to internal autonomy for minorities as a matter of international law. This right should be restricted by an exception clause for serious threats to public order, which would allow it to be overridden in circumstances of political instability. But it would place states under a legal obligation to accommodate the self-determination claims of their minorities in most ordinary circumstances. As I allowed above, there are some cases in which there is a moral claim to secession, not just to internal autonomy, and where the overarching state is obliged to negotiate political independence. But since this claim is dependent on favorable contextual assessment, it is difficult to institutionalize as a legal matter.

The UN Declaration on the Rights of Indigenous Peoples, which affords indigenous peoples "the right to autonomy or self-government in matters relating to their internal and local affairs," therefore provides a model that should be applied to other minorities.[31] My political autonomy view supports efforts to extend the legal right of self-determination to new contexts, including self-determination for indigenous peoples and autonomy arrangements for regional or substate minorities.[32] International law ought to be reformed to recognize a more robust right to self-determination than it now does.

I also believe that when a government persistently fails to respond to a minority's qualified demands for self-determination—without being able to point to valid countervailing considerations, such as the threat of conflict—this should provoke some international concern. It is not a matter of internal discretion whether a state should grant autonomy to its indigenous peoples or other minorities. Many theorists already take the view that a state's persistent violation of human rights is a matter of international concern, grounding secondary responsibilities on the international community to act to secure these rights.[33] I believe the persistent denial of political self-determination should provoke some international concern as well. The means used to express this concern, however, should be proportionate to the weight of the interest at stake and the institutional risks involved. Highly coercive means like military interventions or economic sanctions should be reserved for violations of human rights. But other, less coercive approaches (like "naming and shaming" or imposing conditions on membership or the receipt of benefits

---

[31] UN General Assembly, *UN Declaration on the Rights of Indigenous Peoples*, (September 2007), Article 4.

[32] See Buchanan, *Justice, Legitimacy, and Self-Determination*, 26–7, for an argument that a principle of secession is inappropriate for inclusion in international law. The *UN Declaration on the Rights of Indigenous Peoples* has been interpreted by some as broadening the right of self-determination. While Buchanan favors intrastate autonomy arrangements, he argues that there is a *right* to these arrangements only in cases of human rights violations (405).

[33] See the discussions in Beitz, *The Idea of Human Rights*, 128–31; Miller, *National Responsibility and Global Justice*, ch. 7, and "Grounding Human Rights," *Critical Review of International Social and Political Philosophy* 15, no. 4 (2015): 407–27.

from international organizations) can be proportionate and effective means to induce states to grant self-determination to their internal minorities.[34] Minority groups who find their peaceful demands for self-determination continually refused by their state have a claim to some proportionate remedy from the international community.

5.6 Nationalist Theories

Perhaps the most prominent alternative to my political autonomy theory sees self-determination as rooted in the significance of national culture. One great strength of this liberal nationalist position is its clear account of self-determination's *value*. Liberal nationalists argue that it is important to individual well-being to be able to live within the framework of one's own culture, and to transmit one's culture to one's children, if one chooses. Political self-determination rights over territory, in their view, help to guarantee this.[35] When cultural nations are granted a territorial unit of their own, their members can speak their language in public life; honor their traditions through public symbols, the educational curriculum, museums, and holidays; and format that territory's political and civil institutions in ways that reflect their cultural preferences. All this helps to ensure that they can lead substantial parts of their lives within their culture and transmit it to future generations.

Liberal nationalists typically argue that cultural groups sharing a sufficiently wide range of institutions and practices are good candidates for political self-determination: these include nations, indigenous peoples, and other large, territorially concentrated cultures.[36] Margalit and Raz refer to "encompassing groups," with "a common character and a common culture," including "styles of life, types of activities, occupations, pursuits, and relationships."[37] Will Kymlicka describes "an intergenerational community, more or less institutionally complete, occupying a given territory or homeland, sharing a distinct language and culture."[38] Miller lists similar characteristics, including language, religion, shared history, and connection to an ancestral territory.[39] For these thinkers, it is important that members of a culture share—or believe themselves to share—certain objective common features. A nation is more than a group of people who find themselves thrown together in one political institution, or have a common aspiration to constitute a state.

---

[34] For this argument, see Alan Patten, "Self-Determination for National Minorities," in *The Theory of Self-Determination*, edited by Fernando Teson (Cambridge: Cambridge University Press, 2016), 120–44.
[35] Avishai Margalit and Joseph Raz, "National Self-Determination," *Journal of Philosophy* 87, no. 9 (1990): 449. Gans, *The Limits of Nationalism*, 7.
[36] Margalit and Raz, "National Self-Determination," 448.
[37] Margalit and Raz, "National Self-Determination," 443.
[38] Kymlicka, *Multicultural Citizenship*, 18.
[39] Miller, *National Responsibility and Global Justice*, 124.

Liberal nationalists argue that national cultures are important to their members for two reasons: first, they provide key life options, including occupational, religious, and associational goals and pursuits, and second, members of a nation typically identify with their culture. While not all members of the group share in its cultural patterns, the frequency with which certain traits are shared is usually higher within the group than outside it.[40] Many of members' important life goals will be influenced by their participation in the national culture. Further, most members will identify with their nation. Nationhood has a high social profile: people are treated by others as belonging to their nation, and that affects how they define themselves. Membership of a national culture will frequently—though not invariably—be a deep constitutive feature of an individual's self-identity.

How might the value of national culture support political self-determination rights? The standard liberal nationalist argument holds that political self-determination provides a vehicle for preserving national cultures. National groups, on this view, have legitimate claims to use the state to advance their languages, cultures, and identities, and to govern particular homelands. Raz and Margalit mention concerns about persecution, and the likelihood of a broader majority neglecting, ignoring, or simply being indifferent to a minority nation's cultural prosperity. Kymlicka argues that territorial autonomy provides cultural groups with valuable "external protections," preventing them from being outvoted by the larger society when it comes to issues like education and language policy.[41] Granting nations political self-determination rights, on this view, is necessary to enable these groups to protect their culture from the potentially harmful decisions of outsiders.

Many nationalists further emphasize the benefits for liberal institutions of promoting a common public culture shared by all citizens. A shared sense of nationality generates the solidarity and trust necessary to sustain an effective welfare state and to practice deliberative democracy. Nationality motivates people to make sacrifices for anonymous compatriots they have never met, and to trust that these sacrifices will be reciprocated. A shared national culture also facilitates the sense that one's co-citizens will genuinely consider one's interests and opinions in their democratic deliberations, and it provides a common language in which to conduct these deliberations.[42] For this reason, Miller argues that "states may legitimately take steps to ensure that members of different ethnic groups are inducted into national traditions and ways of thinking."[43] Such "nation building" is an effective way to encourage social integration and to facilitate the democratic state's provision of public goods.

Unlike liberal nationalists, I have argued that self-determination is rooted in the value of political autonomy, not cultural protection or promotion. While I agree

---

[40] Patten, *Equal Recognition*, 67.   [41] Kymlicka, *Multicultural Citizenship*, 28.
[42] Kymlicka, *Politics in the Vernacular* (Oxford: Oxford University Press, 2001), 225–6.
[43] Miller, *On Nationality*, 142.

with nationalists that collective self-determination is an important value—one which plays a key role in justifying the pluralistic, decentralized structure of our international system—I do not see its value as deriving from the importance of national culture. Instead, self-determination is important because it enables individuals to relate in a distinctive way to coercive state institutions. When an individual is ruled by institutions that are shaped through a cooperative endeavor she affirms, the potentially "alien" quality of state coercion is mitigated. Politically autonomous individuals can avoid alienation and experience self-directed agency even while subject to coercive power.

There are several differences between my political autonomy view and liberal nationalism. First, there is an important conceptual distinction: the political autonomy theorist is concerned with persistent alienation from the state, but some cases of persistent alienation have nothing to do with cultural protection, and there may be failures of cultural protection that do not lead to alienation. Second, I have emphasized that "peoples" are not defined by cultural characteristics, but rather by their willingness to engage in political cooperation together. Groups who cooperate to sustain a multinational state (like Belgium, India, or Canada) will count as self-determining "peoples," on my view, through they would not qualify as national cultures. On my endogenous theory, "peoples" are not created through a process of cultural socialization. Finally, on my view, we allow for the political independence of new "proto-peoples"—when we do—not to preserve a culture but to lessen alienation from our political institutions. On my approach, the "people" is a mutable entity, and negotiating our institutional arrangements is an ongoing process.

Though there are differences between my political autonomy view and liberal nationalism, there is also overlap between them. Following Michael Walzer, I have held that people have an important interest in enjoying "fit" between their judgments and their political institutions, which I have called a relation of *correspondence*.[44] To know whether a particular state's rule over a particular population and territory is legitimate, I hold that we must make some (normatively constrained) reference to the population's *actual attitudes*. There must be a sufficient level of willing participation in a state's institutional structure for it to represent a self-determining people. While "nationhood" can describe a shared culture, it is also used to describe a common sense of civic participation, and my view comes close to this sense of the term. Finally, since persistently alienated groups can qualify for self-determination rights, my account might be invoked to support cultural nationalist movements. Members of minority cultures often feel alienated from institutions dominated by a national majority. It may seem rather likely that the result of applying my view would be a significant reconfiguration of territorial boundaries along national lines. For this reason, it is important to say more about the precise relationship between cultural nationalism and political autonomy.

[44] Walzer, "The Moral Standing of States," 223.

Unlike liberal nationalists, I believe that in modern pluralist societies, political self-determination should not be used as an instrument for cultural protection or promotion. Neither majority nor minority nations should attempt to use public institutions to preferentially express and reproduce their values, traditions, and identity to the exclusion of other cultures. I grant the main premise of the liberal nationalist argument: individuals *do* have an important interest in living within the framework of their language and culture, if they choose, and in passing these traditions to their children. While important, in my view, this interest is not sufficient to ground a right to the preservation of one's culture. But it does ground a claim on the state to maintain a fair framework within which individuals can pursue culturally diverse ways of life.[45] While liberal nationalists hold that a fair framework requires that national groups be granted a homeland territory in which to secure the preservation of their cultures, though controlling the choice of official language(s), the public school curriculum, state symbols, and so on, I believe important liberal values stand against this.

It is a familiar fact that whether as a result of immigration or past conquest, cultural groups do not typically stand in neat, one-to-one relationships with political territories. Walzer acknowledges this:

> Most of the states that make up international society are nation-states. To call them that doesn't mean that they have nationally (or ethnically or religiously) homogeneous populations. Homogeneity is rare, if not non-existent, in the world today. It means only that a single dominant group organizes the common life in a way that reflects its own history and culture and, if things go as intended, carries the history forward and sustains the culture. It is these intentions that determine the character of public education, the symbols and ceremonies of public life, the state calendar and the holidays it enjoins. Among histories and cultures, the nation-state is not neutral; its state apparatus is an engine for national reproduction.[46]

Under pluralistic social conditions, however, I believe it is objectionable for a dominant national group to organize political institutions in ways that preferentially reflect its own history and culture. Such nation building expresses the view that the state (or territorial subunit) specially belongs to that preferred national group, implicitly devaluing minorities.[47] Certain sociological features of culture are important here: people are often categorized or "pigeonholed" on the basis of their culture, making culture an especially salient marker of social division. Given this, when the state specially identifies itself with a particular culture, it sends a message

---

[45] For this "proceduralist" view, see Patten, *Equal Recognition*, ch. 5.
[46] Walzer, *On Toleration* (New Haven: Yale University Press, 2008), 25.
[47] For similar arguments about the establishment of religion, see Christopher Eisgruber and Lawrence Sager, *Religious Freedom and the Constitution* (Cambridge, MA: Harvard University Press, 2007), 121–58; Cécile Laborde, *Liberalism's Religion* (Cambridge, MA: Harvard University Press, 2017), 82–91.

to cultural minorities that they are "outsiders," not "real" or "full" members of the political community, while at the same time expressing to the cultural majority that they are "insiders": they belong in a more robust sense than others.[48] By symbolically establishing a particular cultural identity as defining the core of the political community and treating major institutions as instruments for the expression and reproduction of that identity, the state communicates to those who do not share this identity that they have a lower rank in the political community. This violates an important obligation of justice: the state should treat all its citizens as civic equals, adapting and formatting its institutions in ways that express their equal status. For this reason, at least in pluralistic societies, I believe that the state ought not to privilege or promote one component group's culture above others, using its public institutions as privileged vehicles for that culture's reproduction. To do so would undermine the equal civic status of citizens on the territory who do not share that culture.

To be sure, liberal nationalist views come on a spectrum, from those who advocate a unitary nation-state to those who allow for greater pluralism. Many liberal nationalists support extending some degree of recognition to minorities. At the very least, toleration and equal rights should be afforded to persons who acknowledge a nationality different from the territorial majority.[49] Miller also argues that the content of the public culture promoted by a nation-state should be *inclusive*: it should be "as far as possible independent of group-specific cultural values"[50] and "compatible with people belonging to a diversity of ethnic groups."[51] Other liberal nationalists go even farther, arguing that the state should recognize or promote *multiple* national cultures. Some, like Gans and Kymlicka, favor multination states in which national minorities are granted their own territorial subunits, with "nation-building" rights equivalent to the statewide majority's. Kymlicka also argues for "polyethnic rights" for immigrants to help them integrate into the dominant national culture (including transitional bilingual education, and some recognition for their heritage and practices).[52]

Typically, however, these *liberal multinationalists* distinguish between the package of rights that should be afforded to *minority nations* (i.e., nations that have historically been associated with a territory) and the rights of other groups, such as immigrants and refugees. The latter lack any claims to use their language in public life, to enjoy self-government, or to share in state symbols: instead, they must accept integration into one of the historic nations. Because of the preferences afforded to minority nations, the distance between liberal nationalism and liberal multinationalism is not as great as it might at first appear. Even those (like Kymlicka and Gans) who favor a pluralized, multinational state generally support allowing

---

[48] For similar worries, see Gans, *The Limits of Nationalism*, 71; Patten, *Equal Recognition*, 32.
[49] Miller, *On Nationality*, 72.   [50] Miller, *On Nationality*, 137.
[51] Miller, *On Nationality*, 22.
[52] Kymlicka, *Multicultural Citizenship*, 30–1. See also Gans, *The Limits of Nationalism*, 83.

nations to use public institutions as a vehicle to establish their cultural dominance, even when there are dissenting groups within their territory.[53] So both liberal nationalists and multinationalists ultimately argue that it is permissible to use state power to promote preferred national cultures and to ensure that immigrants and small or territorially dispersed minorities integrate into those cultures. The only difference is that, for liberal multinationalists, these nation-building powers should be afforded to both substate nations and to majority ones.

Unlike liberal nationalists and multinationalists, I regard nation building as *prima facie* objectionable. Unless a sufficiently compelling justice-based rationale can be provided for it, nation building fails to respect citizens' interests in equal civic status and in a fair opportunity to pursue their preferred cultural identity. Indeed, the very reasons why minority nations are justified in objecting to a statewide majority's attempts to establish its culture strike me as equally good reasons for dissenting groups to oppose a minority nation's use of substate institutions to establish its cultural dominance in areas where it forms a local majority. Both these efforts send the message that political institutions (statewide or substate) "belong" in a special way to a preferred national group, devaluing citizens who do not share that identity.

Like liberal multinationalists, then, I think a just state should recognize a variety of cultures. But I see no reason why the state should confer special privileges on minority nations, rather than extending equivalent rights to all cultures on its territory, including immigrant and refugee cultures. Further, this requirement to recognize multiple cultures, it seems to me, is best grounded in the state's obligation to treat its citizens equally, by remaining neutral among their competing ways of life.[54] After all, most liberals would object to a group's using the tools of state power to establish a particular religion, specially identifying the state with a given sect's beliefs and commitments. So why shouldn't liberals equally object to a group's using the lever of the state to privilege a particular national culture?

On my alternative "neutralist" view, then, the state ought *not* to promote certain national cultures over others.[55] Instead, a liberal state ought to see itself as the state of all its citizens, who share a common commitment to a political project, despite their diverse cultural backgrounds. Such a civic state should place special value on publicly acknowledging the equal status of its diverse members. This public acknowledgment ought to be reflected in the expressive qualities of the state's institutions, in the way citizens treat one another, and in the attitudes and expectations they have of those who do not belong to the majority culture. Under pluralistic social conditions, this gives the liberal state a strong reason not to

---

[53] Patten, *Equal Recognition*, 5, also makes this point.
[54] For an argument for minority rights rooted in the liberal state's obligation to remain neutral, see Patten, *Equal Recognition*.
[55] Jürgen Habermas, "Struggles for Recognition in the Democratic State," in *Inclusion of the Other*, edited by Ciraran Cronin and Pablo de Greiff (Cambridge, MA: MIT Press, 1998), 228; Brian Barry, *Culture and Equality* (Cambridge, MA: Harvard University Press, 2001), 27–33. See also Patten, *Equal Recognition*, 27.

publicly privilege a particular national culture if it is to treat citizens of other nationalities with equal respect. And while liberal nationalists often argue that promoting a single national culture is the best way to generate the solidarity and social cohesion necessary to support redistribution and democracy, we might dispute this claim. Cultural minorities often feel alienated from institutions preferentially organized around the culture of the majority. A better basis for social solidarity might instead be a common political identity, which recognizes and affirms the distinctiveness of various minorities.

There will no doubt be many objections to this ideal of a culturally neutral state. Some argue that the very notion reflects a misleading view of the relationship between culture and politics. Surely, politics cannot be stripped of all cultural content: politics always operates in particular language(s), and within institutions that are "culturally formatted." Indeed, one of the most commonly cited conclusions of recent work on multiculturalism is that the liberal state simply cannot attain cultural neutrality of sort I argue for. Kymlicka holds, for example, that the "idea that the government could be neutral with respect to ethnic and national groups is patently false."[56] While it is possible to separate the state from religion, Kymlicka stresses that it is not equally possible to separate the state from culture. Since the state must take decisions about languages, holidays, symbols, school curriculums, and so on, some cultural features will necessarily be inscribed into its public institutions and spaces.

This objection assumes that the neutralist ideal must imply a *strict separation* between culture and the state. But cultural neutrality, as I understand it, is not an ideal of strict separation. Rather, it is an ideal of *equal treatment*: under conditions of pluralism, the state has a weighty reason not to favor, promote, or privilege one of its component cultures over others. "Separation" is one derivative policy or strategy for approximating this goal. But separating state and culture is not the only or always the best way to treat diverse citizens equally: as Alan Patten puts it, "a state that is neutral towards culture is not one that takes no notice of culture, or disentangles itself from culture."[57] Securing civic equality may require separation in some scenarios, but in other cases, state policies supporting or promoting culture are perfectly compatible with equal treatment.

Consider four cases where securing equal civic status does not require strict separation. First, the weighty reason against privileging a specific culture arises only under conditions of cultural *pluralism*. It is therefore more acceptable for states to use political power to protect a culture in those (few) territories that are inhabited by homogeneous populations, perhaps Japan, Iceland, or some indigenous territories. Where all or nearly all citizens share the same culture, using state policy to support this culture does not send an invidious or exclusionary message. The closer we get to cultural homogeneity, then, the greater justification there will be for state policies to reflect widely shared cultural preferences. As we move

---

[56] Kymlicka, *Multicultural Citizenship*, 111.   [57] Patten *Equal Recognition*, 27.

away from homogeneity, however, there will be strong reason to adopt policies that treat the state's component cultures equally.

Second, sometimes the reason against privileging a particular culture is *decisively outweighed*. In certain cases, requiring a degree of cultural uniformity in public institutions is an essential means for the state to carry out its morally mandatory functions. Insofar as a particular cultural requirement is necessary for the state to provide public services, protections, or benefits that are required by justice, it is permissible to impose this requirement, so long as it is narrowly tailored to achieve these justice-related goals in a manner that places the least burden on citizens' competing cultural interests. For example, since the range of jobs open to citizens not fluent in a language of broad use is likely to be small, it is acceptable for a liberal state to educate the children of a tiny cultural minority in a language of wide social mobility; this is justified by the state's mandate to protect their right to economic opportunity. So long as the state adopts a language policy, from among a menu of possible policies, that pursues these important public purposes in a way that is not unduly burdensome to the minority's other language interests (by, say, allowing for bilingual schooling in their mother tongue alongside the language of wider use), this decision is permissible. Because the decision is justified with reference to the state's morally mandatory aims, and because state policies are narrowly tailored to impose minimal restrictions on citizens' competing cultural interests, the state is not privileging a national culture in a way that would send an invidious message to those who are disfavored. Any disadvantages to cultural minorities are instead an unavoidable byproduct of the state's morally essential aims. Yet where no compelling justice-based rationale can be provided for it, discretionary "nation building" does express an invidious message, one at odds with the state's obligation to treat its citizens as civic equals.

Third, even a state that contains a number of different component cultures may find that these cultures contain partial areas of "overlap" in their values and practices. This may give rise to a thinner "political culture," composed of those symbols, values, and norms shared in common by all the state's component cultures. For example, a state may contain several different linguistic communities, each of which would have an important objection to the state's privileging one of their languages as its official language. But these linguistic communities may all value the protection of open space for aesthetic and recreational purposes. When the state sets aside land for these purposes, then, it can appeal to widely shared values, which belong to what we might call the "public political culture." In formulating policies that reflect these specific values, the state does not privilege one cultural group at the expense of others or imply that some citizens are less preferred members of the political community.

Finally, rather than attempting to "strip" its political institutions of all cultural values, the state may instead extend each component culture roughly equivalent public support and assistance. Instead of doing without official symbols, or recognizing only majority cultural symbols, the state might adopt "composite" symbols, representing the variety of distinct cultures that make up the state. Rather than having no official language or establishing the language of the national majority, the state might instead adopt several official languages. Instead of forgoing public holidays or recognizing only one culture's holidays, the state might establish a variety of holidays or enable people to designate their preferred days off. Such a state attempts to provide cultural recognition in an "evenhanded" manner, offering each component culture roughly equivalent opportunities (perhaps in proportion to their number of adherents) to pursue their preferred practices and traditions in the public sphere.[58] Though such a state remains "entangled" with culture, it satisfies cultural neutrality in the sense that it treats all its component cultures equally—it does not privilege one subgroup at the expense of others.

So while neutralists have sometimes taken the view that the state should relegate culture entirely to the private sphere, cultural neutrality does not require this. A government may provide cultural goods that are valued by its citizens, or support culture in various ways, as long as it does so in a manner that does not unequally privilege one component culture in society over others. There is a variety of different strategies of cultural provision that a state might pursue compatibly with respecting the equal civic status of citizens with diverse cultural commitments. In Chapters 6 through 8, I will offer specific examples of environmental and resource policies, some of which reflect particular cultural values. In each case, I will explain why this form of cultural promotion is compatible with the "equal civic status" constraint I set out above.

It is beyond the scope of this book to develop a full theory of cultural neutrality. But using the example of language policy, I briefly argue that the idea is not implausible or incoherent. In my view, multiculturalists have been overly hasty in concluding that the state necessarily acts nonneutrally in matters of language and culture. Instead, I believe a state's language policy will satisfy cultural neutrality if it meets three criteria:

(1) as a moral baseline, the state should strive to offer all cultural groups comparable opportunities to use their languages in schools and public institutions;

(2) the state may depart from this baseline—imposing linguistic rationalization in a common language—when it serves truly important public purposes (such as securing adequate economic opportunity, democratic participation, sufficient solidarity to sustain liberal institutions, or to prevent the state's resources from being dissipated at the expense of other justice-related public

---

[58] Patten, *Equal Recognition*, 162, defends "prorating," which requires the state to devote the same per capita level of resources, facilities and in-kind goods to different cultures. On this proposal, cultures with fewer adherents might receive less assistance.

goods), but it may not do so for merely trivial reasons (like slightly improved social solidarity, or lower administrative costs); and

(3) if the state departs from the equal baseline and imposes some linguistic rationalization, it should adopt that language policy, from among a menu of possible policies, that achieves these important public purposes at least cost to the competing interests of citizens who would like to invest in other languages.[59]

Why should a liberal state embrace these restrictions on its public promotion of language? A liberal state should place special value on publicly acknowledging the equal standing and diverse cultural ties of its citizens of different nationalities. This gives the liberal state a weighty reason to take steps to ensure that its institutions are not "tilted" against minorities' cultural preferences, including their language preferences, unless it can offer a sufficiently compelling reason why institutions must be structured this way. By refusing to narrowly tailor its language policy, the state would send the message that the majority nation "owns" the state.

5.7 Neutrality and Legitimacy

To avoid misunderstanding, I clarify the status of the cultural-neutrality requirement within my overall view. One might worry that if neutrality is a requirement of Kantian justice, then my account is unable to explain the wrongness of annexation where local political institutions are nonneutral.[60] Many citizens currently value their states as a vehicle for preserving and promoting their unique cultural or religious heritage. But if my account is correct, then these citizens are doing an important injustice to minority groups, by establishing their culture without a compelling reason. Could a society with neutral political institutions permissibly annex a group whose political institutions grant special privileges to, say, a shared Catholic identity?

In reply, recall from Chapter 4 that legitimacy and justice are distinct values. I have argued that the best account of justice requires a culturally neutral state. But the fact that someone's view of justice is correct does not mean that this person has the right to impose it on others, as our discussion in Chapter 4 stressed. Instead, only collectively authorized agents may legitimately use force to implement their decisions. This means that legitimacy and justice often pull in different directions. A legitimate state can have the right to make and enforce laws even when those laws fall short of the full demands of justice. Thus, while a culturally neutral state is in my view a requirement of justice, this does not entail that foreigners

---

[59] These requirements are similar to those recommended in Patten, *Equal Recognition*, ch 6. They also draw on an earlier paper of mine. See Anna Stilz, "Civic Nationalism and Language Policy," *Philosophy & Public Affairs* 37, no. 3 (2009): 257–92.
[60] I thank Jonathan Quong for this objection.

have permission to intervene coercively in another society's nonneutral political order. Their nonneutral polity may be legitimate, and therefore worthy of respect, even though it is not fully just. It is crucial to keep this distinction between legitimacy and justice in mind.

As I emphasized in Chapter 4, on my view, a state will be legitimate if it: (i) protects certain essentials of *basic justice* and (ii) facilitates the self-determination of its population. So long as the Catholic society's promotion of its identity takes a "mild" or "moderate" form (i.e., it does not infringe minorities' basic rights and liberties, including respecting their freedom of conscience) then their institutions are not so unjust as to void their right to decide for themselves. If the Catholic society meets these requirements, it will be impermissible for outsiders to annex its territory or interfere with its institutions, even if its laws and policies fall short of justice in important ways. Foreigners should instead *persuade* the Catholic society to change their cultural policies; they may not impose neutral institutions by force.

On my view, even this Catholic society's right to collective self-determination is grounded in its members' interests in *political autonomy*, i.e., their interests in being ruled by a state that reflects their shared political will, not in their interest in promoting their preferred culture or religion. But there is no guarantee that groups possessing the right—on political autonomy grounds—will not use it for other purposes, including protecting their cultural or religious heritage. Respect for their political autonomy requires respecting their "right to do wrong" in this case.

Given that majority groups may use their self-determination rights to promote their national cultures, the practical implications of applying my political autonomy account may turn out to look rather similar to liberal nationalism. For it is perhaps empirically predictable that many people will feel alienated from a state that adopts a policy of neutrality rather than privileging their culture in the public sphere. If such groups can claim self-determination on political autonomy grounds and then use it for cultural promotion or preservation, then the results of the political autonomy view and those of liberal nationalism may approximate one another.

Still, there is an important difference between the two views. While liberal nationalists hold that the protection or promotion of specific national cultures is a justified aim of the state, I have argued that these policies are morally objectionable. One's willingness to affirm one's state should not be conditioned on that state's commitment to injustice. While this duty of cultural neutrality is *unenforceable* by external agents and must be recognized and adopted by citizens themselves, it remains a morally binding duty of justice. The attitudes that support privileging the majority culture are attitudes we should criticize, and should work to change over time, by convincing people to adopt a more egalitarian conception of their civic identity. Though political autonomy does give citizens a license to enact cultural promotion policies immune from external interference, my theory does not consider those policies just, as the liberal nationalist does. To the extent people in a pluralist society feel alienated solely because their state does not preferentially promote their culture, their alienation is unreasonable, because it is at odds with an important duty to treat fellow citizens as moral equals. We ought to criticize such alienation, and to persuade people to revise their attitudes.

To sum up, in most modern societies, I believe the popular will reflected by a state's institutions ought to center on inclusive political values that do not privilege one cultural strand in society over others. A "people," on my view, is a group that shares a commitment to collective cooperation and are willing to "sign on" to a common scheme of constitutional procedures and values. Membership in a "people" ought not to be conditioned on integration into more particularistic cultural practices and traditions. The more self-determining groups define their identity around shared political values, the more likely they are to bring culturally diverse citizenries to affirm their cooperation together. I do not deny that some alienated cultural minorities could currently claim self-determination rights on my account, or that applying my view might involve reorganizing some territorial units along national lines. But to the extent that cultural minorities are presently alienated, I believe this often has its roots in the fact that many states have adopted an unjust "nation-state" ideal that privileges certain cultures over others. Were a "cultural-neutrality" requirement widely implemented, I believe the practical implications of the political autonomy view would diverge markedly from the nationalist one. Though current patterns of political alienation may reflect patterns of cultural distinctiveness, they need not do so, and we should work toward a world in which the two are increasingly disentangled.

5.8 Peoplehood Theories

Unlike liberal nationalists, *peoplehood* theorists attribute the right of self-determination to a collective that does not necessarily possess shared cultural characteristics. Rawls defines "peoples" partly with reference to their "common sympathies," which (quoting Mill) he describes as making "them cooperate with each other more willingly than with other people, desire to be under the same government, and desire that it should be government by themselves, or a portion of themselves, exclusively."[61] These sympathies need not be based on objectively shared cultural features: indeed, Rawls notes that if common sympathies "were entirely dependent upon a common language, history, and political culture, with a shared historical consciousness, this feature would rarely, if ever, be satisfied," since different cultural groups are frequently intermingled on the same territory.[62]

---

[61] Rawls, *The Law of Peoples*, 23. Rawls defines "peoples" as having three features: (i) a government that serves their fundamental interests, (ii) citizens united by common sympathies, and (iii) a moral nature. See also Mill, "Considerations on Representative Government," ch. 16, in *On Liberty and Other Essays*, edited by John Gray (Oxford: Oxford University Press, 1998), 427.

[62] Rawls, *The Law of Peoples*, 24.

Peoplehood theorists generally appeal, as I have done, to ideas of cooperation or collective agency.⁶³ My account shares significant overlap with this approach.

Yet, to date, I believe that peoplehood theorists have not articulated a sufficiently compelling explanation of *why* the self-determination of peoples, so defined, is *valuable*. While collective agency is a metaphysically coherent idea, the thought that "peoples" have an independent, irreducible moral status is less attractive. On plausible accounts of value individualism, the importance of collective self-determination should somehow derive from its contribution to individuals' autonomy and well-being. Extant peoplehood theories, however, fall on the horns of a dilemma: *either* they fail to identify clearly an individual interest that is served by rights of collective self-determination *or* they identify such an interest, but not one that seems morally weighty enough to justify imposing costly correlative duties to respect collective self-determination over territory.

For the first horn, consider the account offered by Andrew Altman and Christopher Wellman. They argue that self-determination is a distinctively *collective* value: on their view, "We the People"—as a group agent—has an interest in controlling significant aspects of its political life.⁶⁴ Altman and Wellman hold that the right to self-determination cannot be reduced to a bundle of individual claims, since "the individual does not choose the laws; the group does."⁶⁵ Further, Altman and Wellman argue that since states are nonconsensual associations, the autonomy of a self-determining people cannot plausibly be seen as an extension of the autonomy of its members. Still, they hold that group self-determination is morally important. We must presuppose self-determination's importance, they maintain, if we are to account for our pretheoretical intuitions about colonialism and annexation. But, surely, one might reply: why not instead give up our intuitions about annexation, if we cannot ground them in any plausible individualistic rationale? If no one's interests or autonomy would be set back, why *not* disrespect a group's political independence?⁶⁶

For the second horn, consider the account offered by Margaret Moore, who points out that "peoples" differ from other identity groups because they strongly aspire to self-government.⁶⁷ Racial, religious, class, and other identity groups do

---

⁶³ See also Allen Buchanan, "Self-Determination, Revolution, and Intervention," *Ethics* 126, no. 2 (2016): 447–73.

⁶⁴ Altman and Wellman, *A Liberal Theory of International Justice*, 11. See also Wellman, *A Theory of Secession* (Oxford: Oxford University Press, 2005).

⁶⁵ Altman and Wellman, *A Liberal Theory of International Justice*, 19.

⁶⁶ Though self-determination is an irreducibly collective right, Altman and Wellman hold that individual members are wronged when their group's self-determination is violated or denied. Individuals can be owed respect in virtue of their role in contributing to the political capacities of the collective: "the group is entitled to dominion over its self-regarding affairs only because it has achieved a certain status, a status achieved by the joint activities of individual group members" (*A Liberal Theory of International Justice*, 39). But since individuals can participate in the same joint political activities if they are annexed—only by supporting a larger, rather than a smaller state—it is unclear why exactly their abilities are disrespected by annexation.

⁶⁷ Moore, *A Political Theory of Territory*, 54–6.

not similarly demand reconfiguration of political boundaries. Members of a "people," on the other hand, typically hold an intense preference for a political sphere in which to make their own decisions. Yet while this approach isolates an individual interest served by collective self-determination, it does not seem to have significant moral weight. If the desire for self-determination is just a *desire*, then it is not clear why its denial generates any strong moral complaint. Does frustration of our preferences, on its own, show that an injustice has occurred?[68] Only sometimes—and usually in the presence of further moral considerations—do strongly held preferences ground claims of justice on our social institutions. So it seems necessary to offer a further explanation of why it is of *particular* moral significance to satisfy people's preferences regarding *political governance*. If the value of collective self-determination is just the value of giving people what they want, then it is hard to see it as something we have deep reason to care about.

My political autonomy account avoids the first horn of the dilemma by offering an individualist explanation of self-determination's value. I believe that the self-determination of a political collective is valuable because, and to the extent that, it serves its members' interests in political autonomy: their interest in being ruled by a state that reflects their judgments about how they should be governed. Members' political autonomy will be served when they share a political will with others, and their state reflects that shared will. Unlike Altman and Wellman, I believe that the autonomy of a self-determining group is indeed an extension of the autonomy of individuals. A self-determining group can serve its members' interests in political autonomy even where that group is not consensually formed, provided they reasonably affirm their cooperation together. And though not everyone on a political territory will find their political autonomy interests served by the people's self-determination, I have argued that this is not problematic, since (i) political autonomy is a *moralized* interest—it has weight only for cooperators—and (ii) it is limited by other values, including the requirement to participate in a feasible territorial configuration that can provide basic justice, and so it can permissibly be outweighed. In some cases, then, we have a good rationale for subjecting people to alien political coercion.

My political autonomy account avoids the second horn of the dilemma by explaining why self-determination is more than a mere preference. A "people's" common sympathies, on my view, are significant because they constitute a *free basis for political cooperation*. Individuals who share a political will can establish and enforce justice through a joint exercise of self-directed agency, rather than being subjected to external commands by force. When a state reflects the shared will of a significant majority of cooperators on its territory, its use of coercive power is not hostile and dominating to them, because they affirm its standing to decide and enforce justice on their behalf. This enables willing political cooperators to

---

[68] Patten, *Equal Recognition*, 97–9, discusses similar worries.

relate to their state institutions in a valuable way. Because the subject can see the point of the state's coercive demands—in terms of commitments she endorses—she also sees reason to hold herself to these demands. She relates to the state not as an alien power, but as an instrument for carrying out judgments that she, in part, shares.

Because of this connection with rational autonomy, the desire not to be alienated from a political enterprise is more than a mere preference. Rather, it is connected to a significant human interest in self-direction, in setting one's own purposes for oneself. The importance of common sympathies, in my view, lies precisely here: in recognizing such sympathies, we allow for the possibility of willing subjection to political power, which mitigates the threat of domination by the state. I believe this explains why self-determination is a weighty value that should be prioritized in the design of our international order.

As cosmopolitan theorists often point out, however, "common sympathies" are significantly malleable. My endogenous approach to peoplehood recognizes this: I hold that political boundaries may need to be reconfigured in an ongoing way. This opens the hope that global social entrepreneurs may one day persuade us all to come together to cooperate freely in a world state. Were that to happen, humanity itself might share an omnilateral will that could legitimate political coercion on a global scale. Following Kant and Rawls, however, I hold that until such a will arises, we must preserve "significant room for the idea of a people's self-determination and for some kind of loose or confederative form of a Society of Peoples."[69] I return to the legitimacy of a world state and how we might attempt cosmopolitan reforms without it in the conclusion to this book.

---

[69] Rawls, *The Law of Peoples*, 61.

PART III
EXCLUSION

6
Territorial Distribution

To this point I have argued that a state has a right to *jurisdiction* over its territory if (i) its population has a right to occupy the area governed by their state; (ii) the state implements a system of law that secures basic justice for insiders and respects it for outsiders; (iii) the state represents the shared will of a significant majority of cooperators in its population; and (iv) those who dissent from this shared will lack any right to an institutional alternative.

But states also claim *exclusionary* sovereignty rights that extend beyond territorial jurisdiction. Often these claims involve denying outsiders access to both their territories and the natural resources situated there. As Simmons highlights, these exclusionary rights resemble the claims made by landowners to exclude others from their property.[1] In Parts III and IV of the book, I investigate which, if any, exclusionary sovereignty rights can be justified on the basis of the core values of occupancy, basic justice, and collective self-determination theorized thus far. Do the core values ground only the state's *jurisdiction*, its right to make and enforce law within its territory, immune from outside interference? Or can the core values also be extended to justify some or all of states' *exclusionary claims*?

One significant exclusionary claim is the right to establish the terms on which people may enter and settle on a territory. Often, this claim threatens serious harm to outsiders. Consider the photograph—shown around the world in September 2015—of three-year-old Aylan Kurdi, whose lifeless body washed up on a beach in Turkey after he and his family fled civil war in Syria. Kurdi lost his life because of a state's putative right to regulate the admission of foreigners to its territory.

This chapter argues that the core values of the territorial states system imply a strong moral right to relocate for migrants in Kurdi's situation and others like it. Recall from Part I that appropriation of territory must comply with a fair-use proviso to be respectful of others. I argued there that any act of legitimate appropriation for one's own use must be consistent with a rule that would allow others a similar use. Space over and above that fair share can permissibly be settled and used by other people.

This chapter attempts to more precisely specify this fair-use proviso. I argue that to live up to its own legitimating ideals, the states system must afford people access to space in cases where their *fundamental territorial interests*—connected to the three core values—are threatened. This may sometimes require *redistributing*

---

[1] Simmons, *Boundaries of Authority*, 187.

territory away from historic homeland groups: in the case of future refugees displaced by climate change, we may have reason to afford political autonomy and cultural rights to groups that have not been previously associated with a particular space. Taking this condition seriously, I argue, requires revisions to our refugee and asylum practices. In the next chapter, I take up the question of whether exclusion can be justified in the case of would-be migrants whose fundamental territorial interests are not at stake.

In developing the fair-use proviso, I am looking for a principle that applies to the earth considered primarily as living space and territory, not as a commodity for economic exchange. In my view, the use value of land is "special" from the point of view of justice, i.e., distinct distributive constraints apply to it.[2] Recall from Chapter 3 that rights to occupy the earth's spaces are *primitive rights*, grounded in basic moral requirements to respect other persons' self-preservation and autonomy. Primitive rights do not extend to full liberal property ownership, including claims to alienate and derive income from the earth. This gives us a principled basis for distinguishing the fair-use proviso as it applies to occupancy from other distributive principles that might apply to the earth as an exchangeable commodity. I see no reason why inhabitants' rights over land must extend to the full economic value of the area's natural resources, and I say more about this in Chapter 8.

For now, however, I set aside questions about the distribution of benefits from commodified natural resources. This is because my main concern is with the distribution of the earth's living spaces, which I see as a *sui generis* problem. So the chapter's aim is relatively narrow: to develop a special principle governing the distribution of occupancy rights. I accept that additional distributive principles will be necessary alongside this one, though I do not attempt to specify them here.

The chapter unfolds as follows: in Section 6.1, I examine and reject an ambitious argument that as human beings, we are entitled to equal shares of the earth. In Section 6.2, I dismiss the converse view that the earth is not subject to any distributional criteria. Both of these positions fail to provide a way of comparing competing claims to space that is suitably fair to different political communities. Section 6.3 then proposes a criterion for comparing landholdings based on their usefulness for satisfying fundamental territorial interests. I argue that a "fair share" of territory must be defined with reference to these interests. I identify two categories of territorial interests: first, *basic* interests in access to a territory that can afford us a minimally decent life, and second, *practice-based* interests in the free pursuit of our place-related plans and projects. Section 6.5 argues for a *full proviso* that grants weight to both types of interests, and Section 6.6 argues that implementing this proviso may sometimes require redistributing territory away from historic homeland groups. Section 6.7 considers some objections to my full proviso, and Section 6.8 concludes.

---

[2] See the discussion of this issue in Christopher Armstrong, *Justice and Natural Resources* (Oxford: Oxford University Press, 2017), 10; though he rejects the position I take here.

6.1 An Egalitarian Theory of Fair Shares?

It might seem easy to define fair shares of the earth: we take existing theories of distributive justice and apply them to this good. For many cosmopolitans, it is misguided to think that delineating fair shares of territory requires *sui generis* principles. Instead, we can extend an egalitarian theory of justice to deal with this problem. This section examines two attempts of this kind, both of which apply a theory of *equal resources* to the division of the globe. The first holds that each individual ought to possess the same *quantity* of geographical space; the second, that each ought to possess a share of equal *market value*. I argue that both attempts fail because they impose a way of valuing land that cannot be reasonably endorsed across different political communities.

The cosmopolitan egalitarian approach has been explored by Charles Beitz, Thomas Pogge, Hillel Steiner, and Brian Barry, and it is canvassed in Mathias Risse's recent work.[3] The view's attraction stems in part from the fact that the earth is an *uncreated* resource. Because no one produced the earth, considerations of desert or responsibility that might otherwise be invoked in favor of unequal shares have no place here. Given that no one labored the earth's spaces, no one is responsible for their existence, and no one morally deserves them, what else ought we to do but share them out equally?

If all human beings are entitled to an equal share of the earth, this has important implications for the right to exclude.[4] Risse offers an arresting example in which the population of the United States shrinks to two people who remain able, through electronic means, to control access to US territory. He argues that it would be unreasonable of these two to exclude outsiders from this space since these outsiders have symmetrical claims to the earth. (While Risse holds that it would be unreasonable for the two to exclude outsiders, he does not think it would be unjust, so long as their basic needs could be fulfilled elsewhere. I say more about Risse's account of justice proper in the next section.) Drawing on these intuitions, Risse proposes that for outsiders to be reasonably expected to accept exclusion, a state's territory must be *proportionately used*. The proportionate-use criterion ties a state's right to exclude to an assessment of whether its inhabitants control more than their equal per capita share of land. If they control more, their state has no right to exclude, but if they control their per capita share or less, it does.

What might it mean for an area to be used proportionately? Risse imagines a hypothetical measure that "evaluates a region's overall usefulness for human

---

[3] See Beitz, *Political Theory and International Relations*, 141; Barry "Humanity and Justice in Global Perspective," *Nomos* 24 (1982): 219–52; Steiner, "Territorial Justice and Global Redistribution," in *The Political Philosophy of Cosmopolitanism*, edited by Gillian Brock and Harry Brighouse (Cambridge: Cambridge University Press, 2005), 28–38; Joseph Mazor, "Liberal Justice, Future People, and Natural Resource Conservation," *Philosophy & Public Affairs* 38, no. 4 (2010): 380–408, for similar arguments, and the useful discussion in Armstrong, *Justice and Natural Resources*, ch. 1.

[4] See Oberman, "Immigration and Equal Ownership of the Earth."

activities,"[5] in terms of the size of the territory, its climate, minerals, oil, water, location on the globe, vegetation, topography, and so on. The proposed measure assesses the *unimproved* value of the earth's biophysical space. These different dimensions of a territory's usefulness could be summed up into an overall figure denoting that space's value. Then one could divide the value of the space by the number of people living there. A territory is relatively underused if the average person in it has access to a bundle of the earth's resources more valuable than the global average. States with relatively underused land, according to Risse, have an obligation to permit immigration until "individuals... populate the earth in proportion to the overall usefulness of its regions for human purposes."[6]

Unfortunately, we lack this hypothetical measure of the earth's value. (Risse also expresses some uncertainty as to how, as a practical matter, one should operationalize it.) One possibility would be to use population density as a proxy: as Risse puts it, the proposal would be "to allocate regions to groups in proportion to their size."[7] On this view, each person is owed access to a $1/n$-sized amount of the earth's surface, where n refers to the total number of the globe's inhabitants. Larger territories should have correspondingly larger populations.

Yet this proposal lacks intuitive appeal. Consider two representative individuals, one a member of a nomadic hill tribe in Burma, the other a resident of modern-day Tokyo. The hill tribesman disposes of more space than the Tokyo dweller does and depends on that larger space to sustain his way of life. If we operationalize proportionate use by population density, it seems the nomads are wronging the Tokyo dwellers by taking up too much space, so they must allow Tokyo dwellers to migrate into tribal territory. Yet imagine informing the Tokyo inhabitant of her new right to move to mountainous Burma to claim her fair share of the earth. It seems unlikely that she would care: nothing about her projects depends on accessing such a large quantity of space. She can live a flourishing life where she now is, in Tokyo.

The population-density interpretation does not take sufficient note of the diversity of people's lives, and their distinctive relationships to space. Tokyo dwellers require less land because they have grown up in a dense urban environment, adopting pursuits suited to that environment, whereas the Burmese nomads' lives reflect cultural practices—formed amid a very different geography and ecology—that require the use of much more space.[8] As Avery Kolers puts it:

> land shapes the character of the people... their dwellings, cuisine, and eventually social relations and kinship patterns develop over time due to features of their environment such as climate, soil, and so on; and the people in turn shape the

---

[5] Risse, *On Global Justice*, 154. [6] Risse, *On Global Justice*, 154.
[7] Risse, "Taking Up Space on Earth," *Global Constitutionalism* 4, no.1 (2015): 81–113.
[8] Kolers, *Land, Conflict, and Justice* (Cambridge: Cambridge University Press, 2009), 53, also stresses the way in which people's conceptions of the good "co-evolve" with land.

character of the land, for instance, causing forests and grasslands to grow or shrink—undertaking significant urbanization, etc.[9]

Allocating each person a $1/n$-sized amount of the earth's surface runs roughshod over this diversity. An equal per capita quantity of land will favor those ways of life that happen to require less space (where the surplus can potentially be traded at a profit), while grossly disadvantaging others.

The fact that redistribution of the earth might make some ways of life impossible is not a sufficient argument against Risse's proposal if there is an otherwise compelling reason for redistributing this way.[10] Yet is there such a reason? It does not seem important that we all have access to an equally sized region of the earth, so long as we can otherwise live a valuable life.[11] Of course, having a reasonable place to live is an important background condition for leading a flourishing life. But this does not require disposing of an equal *quantity* of land. So long as the Tokyo dweller is content with her life, why should we care—from a moral point of view—about how the amount of space available to her compares with the amount available to others? Faced with real people and their projects, an abstract commitment to an equal per capita distribution of biophysical space seems like a strange crusade, rooted in fascination with a pattern.

A second interpretation of equal per capita shares tries to overcome these problems, in part, by better incorporating a concern for land's *usefulness*. It seems unfair for one group to have access to an infertile, landlocked, disease-ridden space, while others enjoy a fertile, resource-rich, disease-free area, even if the two spaces are equally large. This approach holds that we can use the hypothetical *market value* of an area's land as a way of operationalizing equal shares.[12] Ronald Dworkin famously proposed using a hypothetical auction to generate an equal distribution of resources. Dworkin argued that the auction device was especially fair, because it measures a person's share of resources in terms of the costs it imposes on others: bidders should be charged the amount that others would have been willing to pay for the resources to be put to their purposes instead.[13] On Dworkin's "envy test," shares count as equal if they are such that no one would prefer to trade her bundle of resources with anybody else.

Though Dworkin envisioned applying his auction device to a single society, we could extend it globally.[14] Hillel Steiner imagines societies bidding competitively for the land they occupy, paying others for the opportunity cost of foregoing their preferred uses of the area.[15] This would require countries whose land is of

---

[9] Kolers, *Land, Conflict, and Justice*, 99.   [10] Dworkin, *Sovereign Virtue*, 75.
[11] My critique of Risse is in some ways similar to Amartya Sen's critique of Rawls and other resourcist theorists of justice for "fetishizing" goods. See Sen, "Equality of What?" *The Tanner Lectures on Human Values* (Stanford University 22 May 1979), 216.
[12] Risse, "Taking Up Space on Earth," 14.   [13] Dworkin, *Sovereign Virtue*, 84.
[14] As Kolers canvasses: see *Land, Conflict, and Justice*, 53.
[15] Steiner, *An Essay on Rights* (Oxford: Wiley-Blackwell, 1994), 236; "Territorial justice and global redistribution," *Philosophy & Public Affairs* 37, no. 4 (2010): 35.

above-average market value to pay higher taxes (to compensate those living in less valuable places, as Steiner argues) or to accept more migrants (on Risse's account), whereas countries whose land is of average or below-average market value might be exempt from taxation, or exclude migrants.

As both Miller and Kolers have pointed out, however, there are important worries about the global auction proposal.[16] One problem, which Dworkin acknowledges, is that any auction device needs some prior definition of property rights in order to be carried out.[17] The market value of a particular piece of land depends substantially on the background rules that specify what can be done with it. A piece of land containing gold deposits, but subject to environmental restrictions that make mining impossible, will not fetch the same price that a biophysically identical piece of land not subject to these rules would. Steiner's global auction proposal adopts full liberal ownership as the background against which hypothetical market values are to be assessed. For Steiner, societies need not *convert* to a liberal property regime, but they must pay the value that their land *would have had* were it held under such a regime.

But why is full liberal ownership the privileged background here? Different countries have different property rules: some hold goods in common ownership or impose significant restrictions on private ownership. Some countries set aside areas for historic or environmental preservation. The choice of a liberal property regime imposes contested property concepts on those who do not share them and suggests that alternative property definitions—allowing for common ownership, or restrictions on environmentally damaging or culturally or ecologically disvalued exploitation—are "improper" ways of relating to land. As Kolers stresses, this approach is imperialist: "it takes a set of social, political, and economic institutions from one place and drops them into another place, ostensibly for the benefit of the recipients, but without input from the putative beneficiaries."[18]

Steiner's "global auction" proposal also disadvantages poor societies that happen to occupy territories with economically valuable land, particularly if they do not wish to exploit their natural resources. On Steiner's view, since the Navajo reservation sits atop uranium deposits, the value of Navajo land is to be determined by the amount that mining companies would be willing to pay to exploit these deposits.[19] This is so even if the Navajos themselves consider the land sacred and have no interest in exploiting it. Because their land has above-average market value, the Navajos will have to pay very high taxes (on Steiner's view) or accept very large numbers of immigrants (on Risse's). So the Navajos are unlikely to be

---

[16] See Miller, *National Responsibility and Global Justice*, ch. 3; Kolers, "Justice, Territory, and Natural Resources," *Political Studies* 60, no. 2 (2012): 272; Kolers, *Land, Conflict, and Justice*, 53–8.

[17] Dworkin, *Sovereign Virtue*, 65–6.

[18] Kolers, *Land, Conflict, and Justice*, 55. See also Moore's critique of global egalitarianism's "non-neutral assumptions," in *A Political Theory of Territory*, 180.

[19] Note that Pogge's approach avoids this objection insofar as it taxes only the stream of benefits deriving from exploitation of a resource.

able to use their land to lead the kind of lives they see as valuable. To support their increased population (or pay the taxes), the Navajos will likely have to exploit the uranium anyway, even though the reason they bid on the territory was to be able to live there in accordance with a different (noncapitalist) set of priorities. So the market value metric forces certain societies to live in a manner their members reject.

Yet, surely, the pursuit of global equality ought not to force the Navajos to forego a way of life that has significance for them. A key purpose of a just global system is to establish fair background conditions that allow different political communities to freely pursue and maintain *different* ways of life. If it is to fulfill this purpose, a fair-use proviso for territory should not rest on nonneutral modes of valuing land that cannot be shared across (otherwise morally legitimate) political communities.[20]

6.2 Territory as a Nondistributable Good?

In response to these problems with global resource egalitarianism, some theorists argue that the use of land is not subject to any distributive constraints. Kolers holds that "uniform theories of global distributive justice are inapplicable to territory."[21] Margaret Moore also dismisses "the idea of territory as a distributable good."[22] These theorists often stress that geographical space is very different from fungible goods like money. People have special place-based attachments that are not substitutable by a generalized share of other goods.

When it comes to land, Kolers proposes a relativist distributive criterion. Kolers allows that outsiders could sometimes make claims to settle another community's territory. But in assessing whether the claim is valid, he argues that we must ask whether the territory is "full," relative to the current occupants' own conception of land use (Kolers calls this criterion "plenitude"). A place could be "full," on this view, even where it is uninhabited—think, for example, of a wilderness preserve that was valued for aesthetic reasons. If part of the current occupants' territory is "empty," by their own lights, then outsiders could permissibly settle

---

[20] Suppose I am correct that we ought not to impose a level of taxation on the Navajos that required them to mine the land that they regard as sacred. Does this provide a decisive objection against imposing on them a much lower level of taxation, one that they could pay only by bearing some additional costs not as extreme as having to mine the land? I believe we ought not to impose any level of tax on the occupancy of land (though I will argue in Chapter 8 in favor of taxes on natural resources used as commodities for exchange). I argued in Chapter 2 that stable territorial occupancy is a necessary background condition for well-being and personal autonomy. In my view, we should not have to pay taxes on goods to which we are entitled as basic preconditions of our autonomy and flourishing. These are goods we have a duty to provide one another *gratis*. The fact that the Navajos have basic claims to their territory thus grants them immunity from taxation on it, in much the same way that my basic claims to my organs and my talents grant me immunity from taxation on them.

[21] Kolers, *Land, Conflict, and Justice*, 107.   [22] Moore, *A Political Theory of Territory*, 7.

there. But if the current occupants *appropriately see the area as full*, based on their intentional projects involving that space, then would-be settlers can permissibly be excluded, so long as they have a territorial base somewhere else.[23] Kolers holds that his *plenitude* criterion is superior to other distributional criteria because "it has the particularity to connect specific groups to land, but also the universality to be compelling across cultural lines."[24]

The intuitive problem with Kolers's approach, however, is it accords dispositive authority to the viewpoint of the local society, regardless of that viewpoint's impact on others.[25] Consider a society that finds its home territory "full" because it values preserving vast uninhabited spaces for aesthetic reasons.[26] Think of what such a society, on Kolers's theory, might be permitted to say to migrants fleeing their countries for urgent reasons, such as famine, civil war, or natural disaster. Kolers's view implies that these migrants could permissibly be denied resettlement by a society of aesthetes who wish to preserve their mountain landscapes uninhabited so as not to ruin the view. To be sure, Kolers allows that if a group comprises "refugees" who lack a "base territory," they may press revisionist territorial claims. He holds that "whether they are genuinely refugees must…be determinable by a body such as the United Nations High Commissioner for Refugees, which would assess the claim to refugee status based on familiar standards."[27] Under current international law, people suffering from famine, civil war, or natural disaster do not count as refugees, though perhaps Kolers could offer a revisionist definition. The deeper problem, however, is that since Kolers denies that there is any culturally universal criterion by which to compare competing interests in land, it is hard to see why the interests of "refugees"—however defined—should trump. On what basis can we say that these interests are of morally greater urgency?

Though the earth's living space is not a tradable commodity, it is plausible to think that the interests of outsiders in settling an area must be weighed against the intentional projects of the locals, by some objective (not relativist) criterion, and could sometimes override them. Such conflicts are likely to become increasingly salient over the coming decades, as the frequency and severity of climate change–related disasters like hurricanes and cyclones increases and as territory becomes less habitable in the face of desertification, sea level rise, and salination.[28] Large numbers of people may in the future be forced to leave their homes. Since 1990, the Intergovernmental Panel on Climate Change has observed that

[23] Kolers, *Land, Conflict, and Justice*, 118.   [24] Kolers, *Land, Conflict, and Justice*, 126.
[25] For a similar worry, see Armstrong, "Resources, Rights, and Global Justice: A Response to Kolers," *Political Studies* 62, no.1 (2014): 216–22.
[26] A more obvious problem for a relativist distribution of land would be a society that endorses a wasteful high-consumption lifestyle. But since Kolers imposes a sustainability criterion on territorial rights, his view avoids this objection, albeit at the expense of implying that most modern industrialized societies, with their "Anglo-American" ethnogeographies, lack rights in their territories.
[27] Kolers, *Land, Conflict, and Justice*, 150.
[28] See Jane McAdam, "Introduction," in *Climate Change and Displacement: Multidisciplinary Perspectives*, edited by Jane McAdam (Oxford and Portland: Hart Publishing, 2010), 1.

"millions of people would likely be uprooted by shoreline erosion, coastal flooding, and agricultural disruption, and that climate change might necessitate"... "migration and resettlement outside of national boundaries."[29] Not only individuals, but entire political communities are threatened. Rising sea levels attributable to climate change are poised to swallow several countries—including Kiribati, the Maldives, Micronesia, and Tuvalu.

No right to exclude outsiders can be made compatible with each person's status as a common owner of the earth unless it rests on some comparative assessment of the urgency and weight of competing claims to space. In certain instances, current occupants must *reshape* their projects involving land: they cannot evade a requirement to accommodate outsiders by claiming that the land is "full" by their own lights.

What we need to develop this proposal is some way of comparing landholdings that is suitably fair to different cultures and ways of life. Such a metric should not involve imperialist imposition of unshared values on otherwise morally legitimate communities who reasonably reject them, nor should it require people to assimilate to a liberal property regime, or pay higher costs for not doing so, as the *equal quantity* and the *equal market value* approaches did. But it should still allow us to assess conflicting interests in land, without granting dispositive authority to the projects of the current inhabitants. What distributive principle might serve this function?

6.3 A Shareable-Interest Approach

In a liberal society, we are familiar enough with the problem of constructing a scale according to which to compare the benefits and sacrifices of people who do not share a common way of life. To arrive at a public scale for interpersonal comparisons, we abstract away from citizens' determinate conceptions of the good, relying instead on the structure a variety of such conceptions have in common. Though reasonable citizens pursue different life plans, there are certain broad similarities among these plans. As a Presbyterian—not a Catholic, Muslim, or an atheist—I can appreciate that the pursuit of beliefs about ultimate value has a central place in the lives of those who do not share my specific doctrines, just as it does in mine. This allows us to share the conclusion that certain rights, liberties, and opportunities will help to advance our plans, whatever they are.[30]

We can take an analogous approach to comparing benefits and burdens across societies with different conceptions of land use. We do not have to share another

---

[29] McAdam, *Climate Change, Forced Migration, and International Law* (Oxford: Oxford University Press, 2012), 2.
[30] Here I draw on John Rawls, "Social Unity and Primary Goods," in *John Rawls: Collected Papers*, edited by Samuel Freeman (Cambridge, MA: Harvard University Press, 1999), 350–87; Scanlon, "Preference and Urgency," in *The Difficulty of Tolerance*, 70–83.

group's idiosyncratic way of relating to land, so long as we can bring it under a more general structure that is common to many spatial ways of life. We abstract away from the peculiarities of any given society's "ethnogeography" and try to isolate features that various conceptions of land share. This approach can provide a basis for consensus among different (morally legitimate) political communities, yet still allow for variation in their ways of life. Call these the "fundamental territorial interests." As I noted at the beginning of the chapter, these interests are connected to the three core values that ground territorial sovereignty.

Consider the following fundamental territorial interests:

(1) *Material Interests*: everyone has an interest in using the earth as a *material resource* to meet their needs. The earth is valuable as a livable environment, a sustainable ecosystem, and a source of nonsubstitutable goods like clean air, fresh water, and resources necessary to produce essential medicines. The earth also serves as a location for developing an infrastructure for subsistence and economic production. People's interests in the earth as a material resource are usually particularized, in the sense that they have a greater prima facie interest in some spaces than in others. Many subsistence practices depend on territory with certain geological or ecological characteristics.

(2) *Located Life Plans*: geographical space also plays an important role in individuals' personal projects and relationships. Most complex goals and relationships require us to form expectations about our continued use of, and secure access to, a place of residence. Refugees consigned to temporary camps find it difficult to marry, start a family, or invest in education because they do not know whether, when, and where they might be uprooted.[31] The earth also serves as a stable location for the communal practices that generally feature in our activities and attachments. As inhabitants of the earth, we have an interest in others not undermining our shared practices, or preventing their establishment, at least where there are no urgent competing concerns at stake. Many communal practices depend on particular infrastructures found in some places and not others, giving people who participate in these practices a greater prima facie interest in inhabiting a particular area.

(3) *Basic Justice*: everyone has an interest in access to a jurisdictional space that is governed by minimally just political institutions. Since states are territorially defined, accessing these institutions can sometimes require settling in another territory. I assume that a minimally just state must protect at least: (i) *security rights*, such as freedom from torture, slavery, arbitrary imprisonment, or threats to personal safety; (ii) *subsistence rights*,

---

[31] Laura Ferracioli, "The Appeal and Danger of a New Refugee Convention," *Social Theory and Practice* 40, no. 1 (2014): 130, has a nice discussion of these issues.

to an economic minimum capable of meeting basic needs; (iii) *core personal autonomy rights*, to freedom of conscience and thought, personal property, and the freedom to form long-term family relationships; and (iv) the *preconditions of collective self-determination*, including the deliberative freedoms of speech, association, and public political dissent. Oppressive governance or lack of state capacity often leaves people without sufficient institutional protection for their basic human rights.

(4) *Political Self-Determination*: territory serves as an important resource for the construction of self-determining political communities. When individuals together control the coercive structures that govern their lives, political power is less likely to be hostile and dominating, and more likely to reflect constituents' values and priorities. Territory provides a site within which such self-determining communities can be stably organized.

These fundamental territorial interests can be subdivided along an axis, reflecting the fact that, in Kolers's words, "territory is both a highly particular good and a universal good."[32] Many of our territorial interests are *basic interests*. These are generic interests that nearly everyone has, regardless of the shape of their more particular life commitments. Some of these reflect biological needs, such as adequate food, water, clean air, shelter, health, and a livable environment. Others reflect generally shared social needs, such as access to a permanent legal residence somewhere on earth, and to governance by minimally just institutions. (Social needs, unlike biological ones, can change over time, and are not defined in naturalistic terms.) *Basic territorial interests* are interests in living in some reasonable territory or other that affords us a life of a decent standard (where "decency" is relative to the prevailing level of historical and cultural development). This includes the fulfillment of core human rights, as well as the guarantee of essential material and ecological interests.

Yet we also have important *practice-based interests* in territory. These are particularized interests that reflect priorities only some people value and care about. Often, practice-based interests are (second-order) interests in satisfying our basic territorial interests *in a specific way*. Consider nomadic Bedouin tribes in the Middle East, who maintain a pastoral economy herding sheep, goats, and camels. The Bedouins do not just have an interest in living in some decent place or other: they have an interest in living in Arabia, where they can carry on their valued way of life. As Kolers puts it, to require these Bedouins:

> to settle and take up sedentary occupations such as manufacturing, oil-drilling, or, just as likely, servicing tourists—even if they were provided with a community of fellow Bedouin transplants and given decent wages and benefits—would be a great imposition and assault of their ability to get by in the world.[33]

---

[32] Kolers, *Land, Conflict, and Justice*, 10. See also Moore, *A Political Theory of Territory*, 6.
[33] Kolers, *Land, Conflict, and Justice*, 93.

While the Bedouins might be able to procure their subsistence by moving somewhere else, this would be highly disruptive to the lives they value. Practice-based interests reflect the aspects of our well-being that depend upon the goals and projects that we endorse.

Practice-based interests in territory have three features. First, they are not universally shared; they are interests only for some specific people, who possess particular values, attachments, and commitments. Second, they are interests in identifiable places, not simply in having some sufficiently decent place to live. The Bedouins would not be equally well-satisfied with life in Alaska as they are with life in Arabia. Third, they are usually interests in sustaining a specific mode of life, which often involves satisfying basic territorial interests, but is usually not the *only* way of satisfying those interests.

These features of practice-based interests may seem too idiosyncratic to play any role in a scheme of public rules governing territorial distribution. Yet while the substance of practice-based interests differs widely across people, the interest in pursuing *some* place-based projects is not idiosyncratic. It is a common feature of nearly everyone's otherwise different life plans that they wish to use a space on earth for the economic, social, cultural, and political practices that they value. As Scanlon suggests, "even if the goods [valued by someone] are quite foreign to us and of no value in our society, we can understand why they are of value to someone else if we can bring the reasons for their desirability under familiar general categories."[34] While urban dwellers in industrialized societies do not share the Bedouins' highly specific practices, they too have an important interest in the place that is central to their lives.

The role of practice-based interests in territory can be illuminated by analogy to religion and intimate relationships, other elements of people's conceptions of the good that are widely thought to deserve some political protection. While the content of people's beliefs differs across religions, we appreciate that commitments involving the meaning of life are central elements of a broad range of typical lives. Similarly, while the nature of intimate relationships differs across different social structures, we recognize that close family and personal ties are centrally important for many people. Were we to deny all institutional accommodation to these commitments, many people's comprehensive life plans would suffer. *Mutatis mutandis*, the same reflections apply to practice-based interests in territory: the opportunity to use land for valued economic, social, cultural, and political practices is a good that can be recognized cross-culturally, since commitments with a similar abstract structure play a role in most people's lives.

The core idea, then, is that our territorial interests can be divided into two categories: first, some interests in territory are grounded in biological and social needs, the satisfaction of which is essential for living a decent life. These are our

---

[34] Scanlon, "Preference and Urgency," 75.

basic territorial interests. Second, there is a more abstract common interest in the free pursuit of our place-based plans and projects, *whatever they are*, grounded in the fact that commitments of this shape play a role in the (otherwise morally acceptable) lives of most people, making it possible to achieve wide consensus on their importance. These are our *practice-based interests* in territory.[35] I will argue that a "fair share" of territory should be defined with reference to these two categories of interests. While it is fairly uncontroversial that people are owed access to a space that can satisfy their *basic* territorial interests, I argue that a proviso on the just appropriation of territory ought to give weight to practice-based interests as well. This may require changes to our refugee and asylum practices, as I discuss in Section 6.6 with reference to the case of future climate change refugees.

6.4 A Minimalist Proviso?

Surely, a fair distribution of the earth should grant everyone equal opportunity to satisfy basic territorial interests. As common owners, human beings are entitled to use the earth's spaces to fulfill their material needs and to secure their rights. The fact that the earth happens to be divided among territorial states is not sufficient to override this claim. A *minimalist proviso* would require that the global pattern of territorial holdings be consistent with everyone's access to a living space that can afford him a decent life. This will sometimes require positive action to provide outsiders with access to territory. It might also require the redistribution of certain nonsubstitutable resources—e.g., fresh water, or resources crucial to the production of essential medicines. But once everyone's basic territorial interests were satisfied, the minimalist proviso would place no further constraints on the pattern of holdings.

Some version of a minimalist proviso is widely endorsed. Risse argues that as a matter of justice (unlike reasonable conduct, which requires proportionate use) all common owners of the earth have a right to "an equal opportunity to satisfy basic needs to the extent that this turns on collectively owned resources."[36] He concludes that co-owners of the earth "have claims to relocation in the event their existence becomes impossible where they presently live."[37] Moore similarly holds that there is "a basic right to subsistence" that sometimes justifies facilitating outsiders' "access to resources."[38] David Miller argues that human rights create fallback responsibilities on the international community when a domestic state

---

[35] For a similar distinction between "universal value" and "culturally specific value," see Miller, "Territorial Rights: Concept and Justification."
[36] Risse, *On Global Justice*, 111.
[37] Mathias Risse, "The Right to Relocation: Disappearing Island Nations and Common Ownership of the Earth," *Ethics and International Affairs* 23, no. 3 (2009): 282.
[38] Moore, *A Political Theory of Territory*, 181.

fails to protect them, including a duty to admit people whose human rights cannot be protected where they are currently located.[39]

The minimalist proviso is progressive: it goes beyond the limits to territorial sovereignty currently acknowledged as a matter of international law. While states are generally granted a right to exclude foreigners from their territory, refugees are considered an important exception to this rule. A "refugee," as defined by the 1951 UN Convention Relating to the Status of Refugees, and its 1967 Protocol, is a person who:

> owing to a well-founded fear of being persecuted for reasons of race, religion, nationality, membership of a particular social group or political opinion, is outside the country of his nationality and is unable or, owing to such fear, is unwilling to avail himself of the protection of that country.[40]

The Refugee Convention delineates a narrow class of exceptions to a state's right to control its borders. "Convention refugees" are defined by four key characteristics:

(1) they are outside their country of origin;
(2) they are unable or unwilling to seek or take advantage of the protection of that country, or to return there;
(3) that inability or unwillingness is based on a well-founded fear of being persecuted; and
(4) the persecution feared is based on reasons of race, religion, nationality, membership of a particular social group, or political opinion.[41]

International law places states under an obligation of *non-refoulement*, prohibiting them from returning asylum seekers to places where they might face persecution.

Three points about the Refugee Convention are worth noting. First, the Convention excludes would-be migrants who face threats to their basic territorial interests that are just as severe as persecution—threats like famine, civil war, natural disasters, and ecological devastation. Since these people do not suffer *persecution* on the basis of one of the so-called "protected grounds," the Convention does not apply to them.[42] Second, the *non-refoulement* obligation applies only to people who are physically located within the borders of a particular country. Individuals who are displaced inside their own country and people in distant refugee camps fall outside the Convention's scope. (Though some countries operate refugee

---

[39] Miller, *Strangers in our Midst* (Cambridge, MA: Harvard University Press, 2016), 34.
[40] See UN General Assembly, *Convention Relating to the Status of Refugees* (28 July 1951), and *Protocol Relating to the Status of Refugees* (31 January 1967).
[41] Guy S. Goodwin-Gill and McAdam, *The Refugee in International Law*, 3rd ed. (Oxford: Oxford University Press, 2007), 37.
[42] Matthew Lister, "Who Are Refugees?" *Law and Philosophy* 32, no. 5 (2013): 650, has a nice discussion of this issue.

resettlement programs to assist these people, there is no international legal obligation to do so.) Finally, while the Convention allows a would-be refugee to *seek* asylum in a particular host country, it does not impose any obligation to grant it. A state may remove an asylum seeker to a third country, provided there is sufficient protection against *refoulement* there.[43] Thus, while the international community has a legal obligation to ensure refugees some general safe haven, no country is assigned a specific duty to admit anyone. Increasingly, rich states have taken measures (including visa requirements and airline carrier restrictions) to prevent potential asylum seekers from reaching their borders in the first place. For example, they fine airlines that allow people to board without the proper documents, require preinspection, or turn back potential asylum seekers outside their territorial waters. For those who do make it to the territory, states often offer only "temporary protection," requiring refugees to recertify their need for sanctuary after a period or face deportation.[44]

Compared with the current Refugee Convention, then, the minimalist proviso would require radical reforms: first, with respect to the question of who counts as a refugee, and second, with respect to the specific remedies refugees are owed. The minimalist proviso envisions a regime that affords people whose basic territorial interests are persistently unfulfilled in their country of origin secure access to their fulfillment somewhere else.[45] This includes people whose human rights are violated for reasons other than persecution, such as famine, civil war, or severe economic deprivation, and people whose territory is unlivable for reasons that have little to do with human rights violations, such as ecological devastation or natural disaster.

Second, the minimalist proviso holds that these people are owed not just temporary protection, but *a new territory of permanent residence*. While the 1951 Convention permits refugees to be afforded protection in temporary camps, or through short-term protected status in host states, these remedies do not suffice to satisfy the minimalist proviso. So long as the threat to their basic territorial interests in their home country is a long-term one, the minimalist proviso would justify granting them occupancy rights. The duty to grant occupancy to outsiders would extend up to the point where further admission would jeopardize local inhabitants' *similarly basic territorial interests*.

---

[43] James Hathaway and Michelle Foster, *The Law of Refugee Status*, 2nd ed. (Cambridge: Cambridge University Press, 2014), 90.
[44] Matthew Price, *Rethinking Asylum: Its History, Purpose, and Limits* (Cambridge: Cambridge University Press, 2009), 9.
[45] Many scholars argue that the purpose of the international refugee regime should be to ensure that people whose basic needs are unfulfilled in their country of origin can seek access to their fulfillment somewhere else. "A refugee," argues Andrew Shacknove, is "a person whose government fails to protect his basic needs, who has no remaining recourse than to seek international restitution of these needs, and who is so situated that international assistance is possible." Shacknove, "Who is a Refugee?" *Ethics* 95, no. 2 (1985): 281.

Finally, according to the minimalist proviso, it is not morally significant that people are already located within the boundaries of the state where they wish to claim a right to settle. Even those who might still be in their home state or in a refugee camp have a claim to a new permanent residence, and the international community has a duty to respond to this claim, either through a resettlement program or through assistance to a third-party state that might integrate them permanently.

It might be objected that those who suffer from civil war, rights violations, or severe economic deprivation could address their plight where they now are, by participating in processes of self-determination to create better domestic institutions. Maybe they can be held politically responsible for their failure to use their current territory to protect their own basic territorial interests, and so have no claim to be provided with additional space. In response, I grant that where people's basic territorial interests go persistently unfulfilled in their home state, other states have a disjunctive duty: either (i) to assist them in securing these interests where they now are or (ii) to allow them to relocate. But where the international community *fails* to provide the necessary assistance, then it cannot appeal to the fact that migrants' basic territorial interests *could* be satisfied in situ to justify preventing their relocation. If the victims are not assisted at home, they have a strong claim for admission elsewhere.[46] Nor can people whose basic rights are persistently violated be held responsible for their failure to participate in processes of collective self-determination. As I argued in Chapter 4, the provision of basic justice is an important precondition for self-determination: some scheme of basic guarantees is necessary to ensure that citizens can exercise political agency, rather than simply being subject to naked domination by others.

In our current world, taking the minimalist proviso seriously would mean that a significant proportion of the global population counts as refugees.[47] In 2013, for example, 10.7 percent of the world's population fell below the World Bank's $1.90/day poverty line, which we might take as a measure of subsistence rights.[48] Much like ordinary refugees, these people face a life-threatening situation. About half of these extremely poor people live in sub-Saharan Africa. On the minimalist proviso, these people have just as strong a claim to relocate as do Convention refugees who suffer from persecution.

Of course, only a small proportion of those whose subsistence rights are threatened in their home countries will be able to move. People tend to migrate from middle-income countries that are undergoing industrialization and development and experiencing rapid social and economic change. Moreover, migrants also tend

---

[46] Kieran Oberman, "Reality for Realists: Why Economic Migrants Should not Just 'Go Home and Wait for Assistance,'" *European Political Science* (2017): 1–18.

[47] See Ryan Pevnick, *Immigration and the Constraints of Justice* (Cambridge: Cambridge University Press, 2011), 86–103.

[48] The World Bank, "Understanding Poverty" (11 April 2018).

to be "self-selected" from the population within these countries: they are not the poorest people from their home areas. So one might object that relocation is unlikely to be a good remedy for extreme poverty.[49]

Even if development is in principle a better strategy for addressing extreme poverty, there is still reason to grant the extremely poor a remedial right to migrate. First, denying their claim to enter would make wealthy countries complicit in the violation of their subsistence rights.[50] Second, there is considerable controversy about what alternative strategies might be effective in fostering economic development. Many economists doubt that foreign assistance can transform institutions in the manner required to foster effective growth. So even if migration is a second-best strategy for solving extreme poverty, in some cases, it might be the only one available. Third, granting those whose subsistence rights are jeopardized the remedial right to migrate would also give wealthy countries an incentive to find better ways to assist the extremely poor in situ. Finally, since economic development is a long process, many people will remain in extreme poverty for a long time to come. The importance of ensuring these individuals' subsistence rights within their lifetimes tells in favor of granting them a remedial right to migrate. Even if relatively few people are able to exercise the right, this does not undermine its value for those who can. All these reasons tell in favor of adopting the minimalist proviso, and moving beyond our current Refugee Convention to institutionalize a wider range of limits to states' territorial sovereignty.

6.5 The Full Proviso

While the minimalist proviso is progressive, I think it does not go far enough. To see why, notice that the minimalist proviso could potentially be satisfied by a world state that provided its constituents with minimally just governance and a decent place to live. But, surely, this configuration would fail to afford people a fair chance to pursue their preferred place-based ways of life. As already noted, this was a key complaint about the *equal quantity* and *equal market value* approaches: these proposals denied people an adequate opportunity to lead the place-based lives they saw as valuable. If a global distribution of territory is to set up a fair framework for people to pursue their own ends, it must reference our practice-based interests, as well as our basic territorial interests.

But in what way should practice-based interests be taken to matter? As co-owners of the earth, global inhabitants cannot demand the unconditional satisfaction of

---

[49] Douglas Massey, "Why Does Immigration Occur? A Theoretical Synthesis," in *The Handbook of International Migration: The American Experience*, edited by Charles Hirschman, Philip Kasinitz, and Josh DeWind (New York: Russell Sage, 1999): 34–52.

[50] See Carens, *The Ethics of Immigration*, 202–3; Pevnick, *Immigration and the Constraints of Justice*, 89–91, for similar considerations.

their practice-based interests. The fact that people have a strong attachment to their located practices does not allow them to claim as much territory as they like in which to pursue them. Recall that I argued in Chapter 5 that the interest in living within one's culture, while important, was not strong enough to ground a right to cultural survival. Rather, it grounds a right to a fair institutional framework within which to pursue cultural preferences. Similarly, one's interest in a located way of life, while important, does not ground an unconditional right to continue that way of life, if that would come at the expense of others' reasonable claims. No matter how important unspoiled mountain views are for the community of aesthetes, they cannot keep large swathes of the earth uninhabited when future climate refugees, say, are in urgent need. Instead, they may be required to restrict substantially the scope of their projects or, in severe cases, to give up those projects entirely.

The fact that our practice-based claims are not unlimited, however, does not mean that they have no role to play in a just territorial distribution. A fair division of territory should grant everyone a chance to pursue the place-based projects that matter to them, so long as they do not deny any one else the chance to do the same.[51] To ensure this, territorial occupancy should be distributed in a way that is *responsive* to people's place-based commitments. So far as is consistent with constraints of fairness toward others, individuals should be afforded the chance to lead the place-based lives they value.

I therefore propose what I call a *full proviso*. The full proviso holds that a just distribution of the earth's spaces must (i) satisfy everyone's basic territorial interests and (ii) grant groups with shared practice-based interests the right to use geographical space in ways that reflect these interests, so long as the groups are of sufficient size, and so far as this is institutionally feasible.

The size restriction is necessary because territorial (sub)units and land-use rights are scarce and expensive public goods. One person's or a very small group's place-based interests are not sufficient to ground a claim to a territory. But the aggregated interest of a sufficiently large group of people can be sufficient. Where many people together have an interest in a public good, the case for that good's provision becomes much stronger. The institutional feasibility qualification is also important, because practice-based interests suffice to ground a right to territory only in cases where the costs to other people, and to liberal political values, are not too high. Political institutions must perform a number of important functions, including providing personal security; defining property; providing essential public goods like roads, education, public health; and so on. If a claim to use territory conflicts with these essential public purposes, it may permissibly be overridden.

---

[51] See Patten's conception of a "fair opportunity for self-determination," developed in *Equal Recognition*, from which I have learned.

Since the full proviso references both basic and practice-based interests in territory, applying it requires us to weigh these categories of interest against each other. How are we to perform this weighing? I suggest a two-part proposal:

First, basic territorial interests always trump practice-based interests. Suppose Group A currently controls a space that is essential to their unique way of life. Any loss or downsizing of their land, or admission of new members to their community, would make it impossible to sustain their place-based projects. But Group B's *basic* territorial interests are unsatisfied, perhaps because they are suffering from ecological devastation or human rights violations where they now are, and Group A is best situated to fulfill their claim, for example because they have the easiest access to Group B or the greatest capacity to take Group B in. Then Group A has a stringent duty to grant territorial occupancy to Group B, at whatever cost to their preferred way of life, up to the point where their own basic territorial interests are threatened. Current occupants' interests in maintaining their economic, social, cultural, and political practices cannot trump outsiders' *basic* territorial interests.

Second, conflicting practice-based interests in territory must be *balanced*. Suppose again that Group A controls a space that is essential to their unique way of life, and that any loss or downsizing of this space, or admission of new members, would set back their projects significantly. B is a group with shared mode of land use and/or an aspiration to political self-determination. But members of Group B lack any opportunity to pursue these practice-based territorial interests in their current location, perhaps because of cultural oppression or political domination, or because their territory has become uninhabitable through no fault of their own.

In this case, members of Group B have an outstanding *pro tanto* claim to a territorial base in which they can freely pursue the lives that matter to them. Group A has a *pro tanto* duty to Group B to either (i) take effective action to secure Group B's opportunity to pursue their practice-based interests where they are now located or (ii) to provide Group B with a territorial base out of its current holdings, so long as its own members' basic territorial interests will not thereby be jeopardized. In some cases, this will require not only redistributing territorial occupancy, but also granting land-use or cultural-autonomy rights, or redrawing political boundaries.

The proposed full proviso has two aims: first, to extend some *recognition* to our practice-based interests in territory, and second, to *limit* their claims. To see why recognition is necessary, consider the implications of adopting a policy of non-recognition, as the minimalist proviso does. So long as the settlement of outsiders does not jeopardize locals' ability to satisfy their basic territorial interests, on this view, it is permissible, no matter what its effects on local social, economic, cultural, or political practices. But this minimalist proviso would license migration flows that could have devastating effects on local inhabitants. Think of the white settlers moving West across the Plains in the nineteenth century. Driving away the buffalo, they destroyed the hunting patterns of the Plains tribes, causing them to face economic and cultural collapse. A minimalist proviso would permit this migration, so long as some dispensation was available that would allow the Plains Indians to satisfy their basic territorial interests, even if that involved (as, historically, it did) feeding them rations on a small reservation. Surely, however, a fair distribution of territory ought not to allow outsiders to undermine locals' territorially based practices, at least in the absence of a compelling justice-based reason why outsiders must access the area.

Why might local inhabitants have a good justification for excluding would-be migrants in cases like these? The local inhabitants have special claims to live in this region, and to use the area for practices they value, and the settlement of these new people would undermine their ability to do that. So long as would-be migrants enjoy a territorial base where their basic territorial interests are protected and they can pursue the practices that matter to them, allowing them to use *this* space too—under conditions that would impair current occupants' flourishing—would grant them more than their fair share. Thus, the full proviso aims to ensure that people's practice-based territorial interests are *recognized*: the distribution of the globe should grant people a special claim to use a place on earth for the located practices that they value. As I explore in the next chapter, such practice-based harms may sometimes provide a good justification for excluding would-be migrants. (As I will stress, this does not extend to a claim to exclude outsiders *at discretion*, but it may ground a claim to exclude settlers who would cause harm to important social practices.)

Yet local practices, while significant, matter only within certain bounds of fair distribution: locals' claims must also be *limited*. To see this, consider the following case. Suppose, contrary to fact, that the white settlers had been forced to return to Europe in the mid-nineteenth century, because the Eastern United States was suddenly rendered uninhabitable in a natural disaster. The effects on those in the Old Country would no doubt have borne some similarity to the effects of white settlement on the Plains Indians. Traditional ways of life might have been significantly disrupted, and the prior inhabitants forced to give up much of their land. But we would judge the case quite differently. Under such circumstances, the prior occupants would have been *obliged* to "downsize" their way of life, accepting even drastic changes to their practices, so that other inhabitants of the earth could be accommodated using the available resources.[52] The full proviso also aims to reflect this intuition: it requires that territorial occupancy be redistributed in cases where outsiders' basic territorial interests are unsatisfied or where they lack

---

[52] For discussion of "downsizing," see A. John Simmons, "Historical Rights and Fair Shares," in *Justification and Legitimacy*: ch. 11.

a territorial base in which to pursue the social, cultural, economic, and political practices that matter to them.

In sum, where settlers already possess a territorial base that (i) protects their basic territorial interests and (ii) allows them to pursue their preferred practices, they can be excluded if their settlement would threaten significant harms to current occupants. But where they lack a reasonable territorial base, current inhabitants cannot refuse them entry. As I will now argue, locals may also be required to afford such would-be settlers territorial autonomy and cultural recognition.

6.6 Redistributing Occupancy and Territory

Many liberal nationalists hold that groups historically associated with a territory *take priority* when it comes to that territory. For example, Will Kymlicka and Alan Patten argue that migrants can reasonably be expected to waive their linguistic, cultural, and political self-determination rights as a condition of entry into a new country.[53] Miller agrees: because immigrants join a society "with an existing public culture," he argues, "they must acknowledge its precedence in some domains."[54] On this view, the historic nations in a locality have a right to ensure the paramount status of their culture(s), language(s), and political institutions in that space, making the acceptance of their practices a condition of entry. I believe that if we endorse the full proviso, we must abandon this thesis about the priority of historic homeland groups. Instead, the constraints of common ownership may sometimes require the redistribution of territory away from these groups. Unpacking this argument will allow me to elaborate further some implications of the cultural neutrality requirement I argued for in Chapter 5, especially with respect to language rights and the use of public space.

Often, the full proviso can be satisfied without any territorial redistribution. The primary responsibility for securing people's basic territorial interests, and for providing them an opportunity to pursue their preferred social, cultural, and political practices, falls on their current government. I argued in Chapter 5 that states should respond in good faith to their minorities' qualified demands for internal autonomy, renegotiating political boundaries with dissenting groups. I also argued that states should recognize their minorities' cultural rights, enacting a multilingual and multicultural regime. The state should depart from this regime only when necessary to achieve essential justice-based purposes and, even then, at the least possible cost to the interests of cultural minorities.

So long as people's practice-based territorial interests can be satisfied in their homeland, the international community should work to guarantee them in situ.

---

[53] Kymlicka, *Multicultural Citizenship,* 78–9, 96–7; Patten, *Equal Recognition,* ch. 8.
[54] Miller, "Majorities and Minarets: Religious Freedom and Public Space," *British Journal of Political Science* 46, no. 2 (2016): 449.

This requires incentivizing states to grant internal autonomy to their minorities and providing international aid to allow groups with an existing territorial base to continue to maintain it. Think of the displacement pressures induced by climate change, which may require building dam walls, upgrading drainage, constructing desalination plants, and so on, to afford people the opportunity to stay in their territory. But sometimes people's territorial interests cannot be secured without relocation. Communities may be expelled from their territory without any realistic prospect of return, like the Crimean Tatars under Stalin, or communities may face the loss of their territory altogether, such as sinking Pacific Island states, currently at risk of disappearance in the face of flooding and land salination.

I take it as uncontroversial that people whose territory is disappearing, like the I-Kiribati, have individual relocation rights, since their basic territorial interests are under threat where they now are. Realistic options would likely involve their relocation to another Pacific Island country or to New Zealand, Australia, or the United States, the non–Pacific Island countries to which they have the strongest links.[55] While I do not develop a theory of responsibility for redistributing territorial occupancy in this chapter, I believe the latter three states are plausible candidates to bear these burdens, both because they have historically contributed to carbon emissions and because their national wealth gives them more capacity than other countries to integrate those who might be resettled.[56]

For the sake of argument, suppose that the I-Kiribati will in the future be admitted to Australia. Would it be sufficient to grant them residence and citizenship within Australian territory, thereby protecting their basic territorial interests? Though individual relocation rights are important, in my view, they are not enough to ensure that the I-Kiribatis are treated as equal co-owners of the earth. The I-Kiribatis—and more broadly, anyone who relocates out of necessity—have as much claim as anyone else to a share of geographic space in which they can pursue their distinctive values and priorities. The fact that they have lost their territory is just bad luck, or worse, an injustice that has been inflicted upon them by carbon-emitting nations: it does not deprive them of this claim.

Were they to be admitted, then, the I-Kiribatis will have *practice-based* interests in using Australian territory for the located social, cultural, and economic practices they value, and as a site in which to exercise political self-determination. I believe this interest can ground a *pro tanto* claim to be afforded the institutional means to pursue these aims. Of course, this conflicts with the Australians' interest in using the land they have hitherto historically possessed. On the standard view, as I noted, historic homeland groups *take priority*: the Australians are considered

---

[55] See John Campbell, "Climate-Induced Community Relocation in the Pacific," in *Climate Change and Displacement: Multidisciplinary Perspectives*, edited by McAdam (Oxford: Hart, 2010), 67.

[56] Historic responsibility and capacity are often invoked as criteria for liability in work on climate justice. See Steve Vanderheiden, *Atmospheric Justice: A Political Theory of Climate Change* (Oxford: Oxford University Press, 2008), 73–9.

to have a special right to use "their" geographic space to pursue their preferred practices and to engage in political self-governance. Immigrants and refugees are expected to integrate into the already established society, adopting its language and political culture.

I am not convinced that historic homeland groups take priority because they were there first. Instead, I think that when a refugee group is sufficiently large and politically organized, it has a *pro tanto* claim to settle together and to exercise cultural and political autonomy in the new territory. The inhabitants of Kiribati and Tuvalu, in interviews, express considerable anxiety relating to the loss of their "identity, culture, and self-determination, and the loss of 'home.'"[57] Most of them reject the label of "refugee," in part, because they view refugees as people who desire to escape their state. Yet people from Kiribati and Tuvalu have no such desire: they view their country's political institutions and its culture and traditions as something of which they are justifiably proud, something they are losing against their will.[58] They do not wish to be deprived of these goods. So why should they? Their claim to sustain their social, cultural, economic, and political practices does not disappear just because they have had the misfortune to lose their home territory.

In addition to protecting the *basic interests* of climate change migrants, then, I believe we also have moral reason to recognize their *practice-based interests* in territory. There are different ways this might be done. In some cases, granting climate change refugees territorial autonomy within a political subunit will be the best way to accommodate these practice-based interests. Cara Nine has argued that we ought to redraw political boundaries to construct a New Kiribati or New Tuvalu.[59] One way of operationalizing this idea might be to settle climate change refugees in sparsely inhabited areas, granting them partial sovereignty over these areas, on the model of Native American tribal governments in the United States.[60] Many countries, including Australia, contain large swathes of uninhabited space: in Australia, for example, 23 percent of land is "Crown land," neither publicly owned nor held in freehold title, but either vacant or used for conservation purposes.

On this approach, we should attempt to re-establish the community's cultural and political institutions on a new territorial base. We have reason to relocate ecological refugee communities together, so that family and social ties are not disrupted. As far as possible, we should also relocate them to a territory that allows

---

[57] McAdam, *Climate Change, Forced Migration, and International Law* (Oxford: Oxford University Press, 2012), 36.
[58] See McAdam and Maryanne Loughry, "We Aren't Refugees" *Inside Story* (30 June 2009) http://insidestory.org.au/we-arent-refugees.
[59] Cara Nine, "Ecological Refugees, States Borders, and the Lockean Proviso," *Journal of Applied Philosophy* 27, no. 4 (2010): 359.
[60] Why not grant them full sovereignty? Where refugees can be compactly settled on unoccupied territory and can form a viable state without risk of conflict or political instability, they may have a moral claim to secede. But, as I argued in Chapter 5, this claim depends on a complex balance of factors and will not apply in many cases.

them to maintain core aspects of their way of life. Geographical, infrastructural, and economic features of the territory will likely matter to this resettlement process. In Kiribati, there is no agriculture to speak of: fish and coconuts are mainstays of the Kiribati diet, and major elements in the economy. Another concern is whether the I-Kiribatis could maintain their language in the new place, using it as a medium of instruction in schools and receiving government services in it.

Redistributing unoccupied or sparsely inhabited land is especially easy to justify since it involves minimal disruption of the locals' projects. Where groups can be compactly settled in a sparsely inhabited area, we might also draw territorial or subunit boundaries to grant them a political majority, so long as they agree to refrain from imposing their culture on prior inhabitants of the area (who have now become a local minority). Such resettled groups might be required to designate the minority's language as an official language in which government services, education, and signage must be provided, and to accommodate their most important cultural practices. In exchange, the resettled group should be allowed to organize their territorial unit in ways that partially reflect their linguistic and cultural preferences. So long as state-subsidized education and public services are provided in the local minority language, for example, a "New Kiribati" should feel free to determine to also provide instruction in the I-Kiribati language in local schools, and to use that language in local government, if it wishes to do so. As I argued in Chapter 5, satisfying cultural neutrality does not require strict "separation" between state and culture. Public institutions may provide goods that are distinctively valued by the component cultures in the society they govern, so long as they do so in an evenhanded fashion, providing roughly equivalent per capita assistance to each group. If the I-Kiribati's language policy supports the use of English in public schools and the provision of public services to cater to the Australian minority, then using public institutions to support I-Kiribati, as well, does not communicate a message of inferiority.

No doubt this would greatly reshape the Australians' relationship to the region on which—in the future—the I-Kiribati might be resettled. The Pacific Islanders have a different political economy and relationship to land than do the Australians: by and large, their land is held under customary forms of land tenure, not in fee simple, and cannot be alienated except through traditional arrangements.[61] Their use of that space will likely reflect different priorities than the Australians'. This raises the question of whether a historic nation has a right to ensure that its territory continues to reflect its culture. Many liberal nationalists argue that it does. For example, Miller argues that the "state is not required to remain neutral when what is at issue is the culture of the indigenous majority."[62] Instead, the historically dominant nation is entitled to ensure that its territory continues to reflect its cultural

---

[61] Campbell, "Climate-Induced Community Relocation in the Pacific," 60.
[62] Miller, "Majorities and Minarets," 448.

priorities, by regulating land use, passing building codes, and so on, in order to preserve traditional architecture and other culturally valued characteristics.[63] In building their new life, Miller argues, incoming minority groups must accommodate to the historic nation's hegemony: this is part of their more general obligation to "acknowledge and adapt to the public culture of the receiving society."[64]

In my view, a historic nation may not claim cultural dominance over its territory when faced with the competing claims of refugee or minority communities. Just as the state ought to offer its minority citizens comparable opportunities to use their languages in public institutions, so, too, it ought to offer them a presence in shaping the look and feel of its territory. Thus, while the I-Kiribati should recognize the private property of the local Australian minority, and maintain some public spaces that continue to reflect the Australians' values, they should also feel free to pass laws that would recognize their preferred forms of collective land tenure, and to shape other public spaces in accordance with their own traditions. In this way, each group is afforded equivalent opportunities to pursue their distinctive place-based priorities. Even though these activities will alter the character and physical appearance of the Australian countryside, locals are required to accept these alterations for the sake of responding to others' reasonable claims to use the earth. We should therefore think of the I-Kiribati's *pro tanto* claim to maintain their territorially based practices—if they wish to do so—as being *just as* weighty as the Australians' to maintain theirs. The Australians have as much reason to "downsize" their place-based aims in response to the I-Kiribati's loss of their historic territory as the I-Kiribati themselves do. The territory does not "belong" to the Australians in the strong sense that would entitle their land-use preferences to take precedence over those of others who lack a fair share.

Note that I have not argued that refugee groups *always* have a moral right to territorially based autonomy, much less that they should have an internationally recognized legal right. Rather, I have argued that when these groups are large and well-organized enough to support distinctive institutions, there is an important moral reason to afford them territorial autonomy. This, of course, must be weighed against countervailing concerns, including other people's interests in the territory, the ability of public institutions to continue performing essential legitimating functions, and the risk of undesirable consequences, like war, instability, ethnic or social conflict, and so on. When strong countervailing reasons exist, the refugee community's *pro tanto* claim to territorial autonomy may be justifiably overridden. But there are other scenarios in which territorial autonomy can be granted at relatively low institutional cost. Here it is important to note that Kiribati and Tuvalu are small communities: there are about 100,000 I-Kiribatis and about 10,000 Tuvalans. A territorial autonomy arrangement might be quite feasible for them, even if it would not be for much larger groups. So practice-based territorial

---

[63] Miller, "Majorities and Minarets," 439.   [64] Miller, "Majorities and Minarets," 450.

interests suffice to ground a right only where they are strong enough to outweigh various conflicting reasons, especially interests in the maintenance of a stable, minimally just structure of political authority.

Of course, there is no guarantee that there will always be uninhabited or sparsely populated areas in which future climate change refugees could be resettled. Much depends on the scale of future displacement, about which we cannot be certain. In cases that are more difficult, climate change migrants might have to be resettled in ways that are largely territorially intermixed with previous inhabitants. Here it may not be possible to grant them political autonomy over a territorial subunit. Even in this case, however, I believe they are still owed cultural recognition, in matters of language policy and in the use of public space. For example, institutions that govern intermixed areas should be required to recognize the I-Kiribati language, and to provide public services in it. They may also be owed nonterritorial forms of political autonomy, for example, the right to collective decision-making on education, cultural affairs, and other matters that can feasibly be administered on a nonterritorial basis, or special group representation rights.[65]

If the analysis I have offered is correct, historic nations do not necessarily take priority when it comes to their homelands. The strongest argument in favor of the traditional prerogatives of homeland groups is that people are permitted to use their own resources to show some partiality to their own attachments and projects.[66] Yet this assumes that homeland groups are *entitled* to the areas they now control. It is permissible to show partiality toward my projects only within the bounds of my fair share of resources. With respect to territorial holdings to which I am not entitled, I cannot argue that it is permissible to devote them to my attachments and projects. However, the full proviso suggests that the territorial entitlements of historic homeland groups can be called into question as circumstances change. In such cases, homeland groups may no longer retain a claim to (parts of) their historical territories, in the face of revisionist pressures from other groups.

6.7 Objections

Many will object that my full proviso does not go far enough. Consider the following case:

Resettlement. Two groups, A and B, each with a population of 10,000, both lose their territories because of climate change. They are resettled to an uninhabited island. Group A is given 70 percent of the island, while Group B is given 30 percent. Basic territorial interests are protected for the members of both groups, and

---

[65] See de Schutter, "Non-Territorial Jurisdictional Authority."
[66] See Patten, *Equal Recognition*, ch. 8.

each group has a territory in which to pursue their practice-based interests. Under the full proviso, then, this allocation seems acceptable. But is it fair to allocate the territory in this way?[67]

It seems to me that there are plausible scenarios on which this 70/30 split could represent a fair distribution. For example, if one group is composed of city dwellers, like the inhabitants of Tokyo in our earlier example, and the other is composed of nomads, then the envisioned distribution might be perfectly fair. Given the nomads' subsistence practices, they require a larger geographical space to secure their basic territorial interests than the Tokyo dwellers do. Enforcing a 50/50 split of the island, on the other hand, would mean the hill tribesmen would have to pay extra to buy land that Tokyo dwellers do not need.

The objector might continue, however, that the nomads' attachment to a mode of procuring their subsistence is an expensive taste that deserves no special recognition. There is no reason why institutional norms regulating the distribution of territory should try to be responsive to people's patterns of place-based attachment. So long as a global distribution grants everyone a fair bundle of *generic* goods, resources, and opportunities, and so long as that distribution is imposed through fair political processes, then people have no complaint when institutional norms make their preferred ways of life impossible.[68]

This objection holds that a distribution of the earth's spaces would be fair, even if, without any justice-based rationale, it required people to assimilate to one common mode of life. I reject this view: people have a morally significant complaint when institutions are biased or "tilted" against their cultural preferences—including their land-use preferences—in ways that make it difficult to maintain their practices, unless a sufficiently compelling reason can be offered to explain why institutions must be structured this way. The aim of a fair distribution of the earth's spaces, I have argued, should be to set up a framework in which people can freely pursue *different* ways of life. If that aim is to be realized, then the metric we use to compare people's holdings must be *responsive* to the fact that people have different (morally legitimate) social, economic, and political practices. This was an important reason for rejecting the thought that people have claims to equal shares of the earth, since equal shares cannot be defined without imposing a unitary set of property rules, based on liberal ownership, a framework which can be reasonably rejected by diverse (morally legitimate) political communities.

Perhaps, though, the objection could be reformulated in a more sophisticated way. The objector might say it is true that we should not care as a matter of principle *how much* land each group has, but we should care that each group's use of land affords them an equivalent quality of life. Along these lines, Chris

---

[67] I thank Minh Ly for the objection.
[68] See Lea Ypi, "Structural Injustice and the Place of Attachment," *Journal of Practical Ethics* 5, no. 1 (2017): 1–21.

Armstrong argues that land should be distributed to equalize opportunities for well-being. This might allow some people to appropriate more than an equal share of space, so long as their appropriation contributes to an overall equality in access to well-being.[69] And it might seem that the plausibility of the above example trades on the idea that while the nomads possess more land than the Tokyo dwellers, both groups enjoy a roughly equivalent quality of life (indeed, one might think that Tokyo dwellers are better off overall). Should we not then try to formulate a distributive criterion that ensures people's lives are equally enhanced, so far as possible, as a result of their appropriation of the earth?

There is some plausibility to the thought. But views like these often do not clarify exactly what is meant by "well-being." Consider a view that supposes people can "convert" land into pleasurable mental experience. If Group A gets the same enjoyment from 70 percent of the island as Group B gets from 30 percent of the island, then we might hold that this distribution is in fact an equal one, on the proposed metric. Or consider another view, which holds that people use land to satisfy their preferences. On this view, so long as both group's preferences are equally well-satisfied by their holdings, the 70/30 distribution of the island counts as fair.

Yet I reject the underlying accounts of welfare on which these views depend. Beyond the satisfaction of basic biological and social needs, people's well-being depends on projects and relationships that they freely endorse. Well-being, for the most part, derives from a person's active engagement in valued pursuits: it is not—as the first view supposes—derived from the conversion of goods into pleasurable mental experiences. Often people pursue activities that they consider valuable (such as creative work) even though those activities cause them much pain and suffering. These people are not made better off if we prevent them from pursuing the challenges they care about, and instead provide them with a bundle of consumption goods calculated to produce greater enjoyment.

The idea that we should distribute goods to satisfy people's preferences equally is also problematic. Some preferences are important from the perspective of a public distribution, whereas others are not. A fair distribution requires us to provide those goods that are publicly deemed important, not the goods that are most highly valued according to a person's idiosyncratic preference scheme. While a disabled individual might prefer a mink coat to a wheelchair, we are required to afford him mobility, not to satisfy his tastes and preferences.[70] The fundamental interests a public distribution ought to secure are not defined by the subjective weight individuals attribute to them, but by an objective, public criterion of importance.

Since the goals, projects, and relationships upon which various people's well-being depends are incommensurable in value, I believe that beyond fundamental

---

[69] Armstrong, *Justice and Natural Resources*, 71–6.
[70] See Scanlon, "Preference and Urgency."

territorial interests, this fact makes it difficult to *compare* people's well-being directly. A Tokyo dweller may value his rich, cosmopolitan life as a graphic designer, whereas the nomad may care equally about his deep bonds to his extended family and natural environment. So long as both are content with their pursuits, I do not think we can say that the well-being of one is less than, greater than, or equal to that of the other. Their lives are simply very different, and the goals and projects they contain are not commensurable.[71]

The full proviso reflects this incommensurability: its aim is to ensure that everyone's basic biological and social needs are provided for and that they are in a position to use the earth's spaces for the place-based projects they endorse, *whatever those projects are*. It does not go further to hold that there is some additional underlying currency of value to which very different people's well-being could be reduced, compared, and judged to be equal in quantity. All we can say is that the goals and projects they pursue matter to them.

6.8 Conclusion

This chapter began to address whether the core values that justify a system of territorial states can ground exclusionary sovereignty rights. I argued that if it is to be justified, the states system must impose a *fair-use proviso* on the distribution of territory. This means a state may not exclude outsiders in cases (i) where their basic territorial interests are persistently unfulfilled where they now are or (ii) where they lack a territorial base in which to pursue the social, cultural, economic, and political practices that matter to them. I held that this fair-use proviso imposes a disjunctive duty on states, either to take effective action to guarantee others' territorial interests in situ or to provide these outsiders with territory out of their current holdings. Considering the case of future climate migrants, I suggested that fulfilling this duty requires not only guaranteeing individual relocation rights, but also extending cultural and political autonomy to refugees.

The arguments of this chapter raise important further questions, however. First, can states exclude migrants whose fundamental territorial interests are *not* at stake? What about travelers, students, economic migrants, and so on? I address the exclusion of these people in the next chapter.

Second, is the fair-use proviso *enforceable*? I believe the duty to secure fundamental territorial interests is an enforceable duty, the recognition of which is an essential condition for the moral legitimacy of the international states system. As common owners of the earth, everyone is entitled to a place on the globe where he can lead a reasonable life. Constituent states in the international system lack the authority to exclude migrants when these fundamental territorial interests are

---

[71] For similar reflections, see Raz, *The Morality of Freedom*, 343.

at stake. Indeed, other states will have the license to interfere, in proportionate ways, with a state's illegitimate decision to exclude necessitous migrants, acting collectively to defend refugees' right to a reasonable place to live. Given this, what kinds of international institutions might be required in order to limit states' territorial sovereignty to conform to the fair-use proviso? How might these institutions be established? I will offer some thoughts on this issue in Chapter 8 and the conclusion.

7
Is There a Right to Exclude?

As Joseph Carens notes, the refusal of admission to a country is a "gateway decision" that has "enormous implications for all the subsequent life choices a person can make."[1] In Chapter 6, I argued that states have no right to exclude persons whose *fundamental territorial interests* are pervasively threatened. But do states ever have *any* right to exclude? A state's territorial jurisdiction need not imply exclusion rights. Within the EU, for example, member states make and enforce law inside their territories, but they have no right to keep EU citizens from moving in or out. Perhaps the whole world should be organized like the EU.[2]

This chapter focuses on what we might call *opportunity migrants*, those who are not suffering from persecution, persistent violations of their basic human rights (including subsistence rights), environmental devastation, or cultural or political oppression. Instead, opportunity migrants seek better job opportunities, reunification with their families, association with friends or organizations, education or training, or a more congenial political and cultural environment. I argue that the state has a *conditional* right to exclude migrants of this sort, if their settlement would significantly harm its inhabitants.[3]

A different view argues for a *discretionary* exclusion right: the view that the state has a moral right to exclude migrants at will, for any reason (or even for no reason). This discretionary right may sometimes be overridden by foreigners' urgent competing interests (e.g., in the case of refugees), but it allows for the exclusion of many people. Some theorists hold that the discretion to exclude is justified on grounds of collective self-determination. Others hold that it derives from the citizenry's right to avoid unwanted obligations.

Instead, my conditional model suggests that a state may exclude would-be migrants only where it can offer a plausible case that their entry would cause harm. Developing this view requires answering two questions: first, what counts as a relevant harm? I should specify at the outset that I am not using the term "harm" to refer to any lowering of a person's welfare from the status quo. Rather a "significant harm," as I use the term, describes setbacks to certain legitimate moral interests

---

[1] Carens, *The Ethics of Immigration*, 257. [2] Carens, *The Ethics of Immigration*, 271–2.
[3] I set aside the case of *compensatory* migrants. A state that has contributed to colonialism, for example, has a stringent responsibility to rectify its wrongs, and one policy that might be considered is allowing preferential immigration status to former colonies. But I assume here that the state is considering would-be migrants to whom it has no special duties of rectification.

that, as a matter of justice, ought to be protected. I will develop an account of these legitimate interests as the chapter unfolds.

Second, how high is the burden of justification for restricting migration? If there is a human right to immigrate—as some have argued—threatened harms to inhabitants must be grave to justify restricting entry. But if migration is not the subject of a human right, then restrictions might be justifiable in a broader range of scenarios.

On the conditional model, states have a standing duty to accept migrants if their entry would not set back locals' legitimate interests. I call this the *duty to allow harmless migration*. Much cross-border movement is harmless, so this standing duty is not trivial. States have duties to allow outsiders to enter for travel, study, business, and visits to friends, relatives, and associates, for example. This extends to a duty to permit permanent settlement, if the numbers and consequences are manageable. Significant harms generally derive from the dislocations caused by a high *rate* of migration over a short period of time.[4]

In cases that are more complex, where there is some threat of harm, the conditional model requires the state to balance the interests of would-be migrants against the costs to its members. These competing interests should be assessed according to the urgency of the objective human needs they serve, not according to the strength of either migrants' or locals' preferences. An important question is whether the claims of would-be migrants and locals must be balanced impartially or whether government is permitted to attribute greater weight to its own members' claims. If would-be migrants' fundamental territorial interests are satisfied in their home country, then I argue that a government can grant priority to its constituents. This priority is not infinite: where harms to locals are relatively minor, and the benefits to would-be migrants very great, states should accept increased migration.

Before expounding my argument, I clarify its status. The conditional model addresses the *substance* of a morally acceptable immigration policy. It is not an argument about who has the *legitimate authority* to decide the policy. I believe that a self-governing people has the right to set its own immigration policy, free from external interference. I am not suggesting that peoples should be forced (e.g., by a foreign power or international body) to accept harmless migrants. As I noted in Chapters 4 and 5, we should be careful to keep questions of substantive justice distinct from questions of legitimacy. I grant that citizens have the authority to decide their migration policy, and that if they decide wrongly (i.e., on my view, to exclude harmless migrants), this is a decision that outsiders are obliged to respect.

Still, even if the choice is up to them, citizens must ask themselves: what policy do we have most reason to adopt? Reflecting on this question, they must consider whether there are moral reasons to allow would-be migrants to enter. My argument

[4] Pevnick, *Immigration and the Constraints of Justice*, 145.

addresses a citizen who is considering this question. She does not doubt that she and her co-citizens have the authority to decide. She is wondering what they *should* decide. An important task of the political philosopher is to provide her with the theoretical tools to arrive at an answer. I argue that she and her co-citizens should decide to exclude migrants from their territory only where their settlement would significantly harm current inhabitants.

This conditional model of exclusion is relatively neglected in the philosophical literature, currently the site of a debate between those who defend the state's discretionary right to exclude and those who defend a human right to immigrate.[5] I begin in Sections 7.1 and 7.2 by examining these views. My strategy here is a dialectical one: it is by showing the limits of these other arguments that I hope to make space for my own view. The most plausible arguments for the state's right to exclude ground only a *conditional* right to exclude in cases where harm is likely. Similarly, the most plausible account of the right to immigrate (examined in Section 7.3) shows that in cases where cross-border movement implicates fundamental personal autonomy interests, migrants have a strong claim to settle. Yet this tells in favor of a claim to relocate only where these fundamental interests are at stake, not a right to relocate at will. Seeing the limits of these alternatives paves the way to the conditional model sketched in Sections 7.4 and 7.5.

7.1 Collective Self-Determination

Two prominent arguments for the state's discretionary right to exclude (considered here and in Section 7.2) are:

(1) the argument from *collective self-determination*, and
(2) the argument from the *right to avoid unwanted obligations*.[6]

I share with proponents of the first argument the view that collective self-determination is an important value. On my political autonomy account, self-determination requires correspondence between the shared will of a significant majority of political cooperators and their governing institutions. Though no individual's personal priorities can be mirrored in every political decision, I argued in Chapter 4 that there is an important, second-order sense in which individuals' judgments and priorities can be instantiated in their political institutions. This is so when they are committed to a joint political venture, and to certain values and procedures that structure this venture, and their institutions reflect these shared

---

[5] For an excellent recent defense of the conditional model, see Bas Schotel, *On the Right of Exclusion: Law, Ethics, and Immigration Policy* (London: Routledge, 2012).

[6] Another argument holds that the discretion to exclude is part of citizens' ownership of their political institutions. See Pevnick, *Immigration and the Constraints of Justice*, ch. 2. I set aside this argument because it invokes strong natural property rights, including rights of bequest and inheritance, which were rejected in Chapter 3.

commitments. Correspondence, I argued, is in the service of individuals' interests in *self-direction* (i.e., in establishing social order through their own free agency) and *non-alienation* (i.e., in being ruled in a way that reflects their convictions about how society should be arranged). Where the state reflects its subjects' shared values and priorities, they can relate in a distinctive fashion to their state and to the constraints it imposes.

Other proponents of collective self-determination, however, have argued that self-determination also tells in favor of a discretionary right to exclude migrants. This argument comes in both a liberal nationalist and a democratic variant. Michael Walzer connects the right to exclude to the preservation of cultural and national identity: he holds that "the distinctiveness of cultures and groups depends upon closure and, without it, cannot be conceived as a stable feature of human life."[7] Without the right to exclude, Walzer claims:

> there could not be *communities of character*, historically stable, ongoing associations of men and women with some special commitment to one another and some special sense of their common life.[8]

Walzer argues that, in most situations, there are no norms for immigrant admissions beyond the democratically specified understandings of the political community. As he puts it, "the distribution of membership is not pervasively subject to the constraints of justice. Across a considerable range of the decisions that are made, states are simply free to take in strangers (or not)."[9]

Walzer does acknowledge two limits to a political community's right to shape its own membership. One derives from the external principle of *mutual aid*. States' control over territory subjects them to the demand either to admit necessitous strangers or to cede them land, where this can be done at sufficiently low cost. A second limit comes from the internal principle of *political justice*: "the processes of self-determination through which a democratic state shapes its internal life, must be open, and equally open, to all those men and women who live within its territory, work in the local economy, and are subject to local law."[10] But within these limits, "the members of a political community have a collective right to shape the resident population."[11]

David Miller likewise argues that collective self-determination grounds a discretionary right to exclude. He contends that because "immigrants will differ in their beliefs, values, interests and cultural preferences" from native inhabitants in a way that might change a community's political decisions and culture, citizens have a right to limit immigration.[12] Since "the public culture of the country is something people have an interest in controlling," citizens have a right to decide

---

[7] Walzer, *Spheres of Justice*, (New York: Basic Books, 1983), 39.
[8] Walzer, *Spheres of Justice*, 62. [9] Walzer, *Spheres of Justice*, 61.
[10] Walzer, *Spheres of Justice*, 60. [11] Walzer, *Spheres of Justice*, 52.
[12] Miller, *Strangers in Our Midst*, 63.

whether to admit immigrants and, if so, how many.[13] One of Miller's important assumptions is that a society has a legitimate interest in promoting and protecting its existing national culture, including "recognizing and embracing national symbols, speaking the national language, accepting some version of the 'national story,' and acknowledging the preeminent position of certain cultural features, including possibly a particular religion, within the national consciousness."[14] This public culture is valuable, in part, because it provides the trust and solidarity necessary to sustain a redistributive welfare state.

A more democratic variant of the argument links exclusion to the state's right to freedom of association. Most people believe that an individual's claim to personal autonomy grants her an important domain of discretionary choice about the shape of her life, including her choice of associates. Christopher Wellman holds that collective self-determination grants states a similar freedom to choose their associates. "Just as an individual has a right to determine whom (if anyone) he or she would like to marry," Wellman argues that "a group of fellow-citizens has a right to determine whom (if anyone) it would like to invite into its political community."[15] Like Walzer and Miller, Wellman suggests that control over membership is especially central to self-determination. Because people rightly care about how their political communities evolve, it matters to them who will have a say in controlling the country's future.[16] Nothing in Wellman's argument, however, turns on a commitment to cultural homogeneity. On his view, a diverse group is just as entitled to shape its future as a homogeneous one.

Central to all these views is the idea that a group cannot count as self-determining unless it has control over its own membership. As van der Vossen puts it, "self-determination ... includes not only determination by the self *of its actions* but also determination by the self *of the self.*"[17] Should we endorse this view?

First, consider the liberal nationalist variant, on which control over membership is required to protect a group's national culture. I granted in Chapter 5 that individuals have an important interest in living within their language and national culture. But I argued that a state should respect this interest by providing a neutral framework within which citizens can pursue their diverse cultural aims. This means that when the state provides valued cultural goods, it should do so evenhandedly, catering to the preferences of different groups on its territory, unless there is some overriding reason to impose (limited) cultural or linguistic

---

[13] Miller, "Immigration: the Case for Limits," 200. See also Miller, *Strangers in Our Midst*, 154.
[14] Miller, *Strangers in Our Midst*, 8; see also 26–9.
[15] Wellman, "Immigration and Freedom of Association," 116. Wellman concedes that this presumptive right not to associate with immigrants must be assessed against competing considerations—specifically egalitarian and libertarian arguments in favor of free migration—but he argues that it is not outweighed by them.
[16] Wellman, "Immigration and Freedom of Association," 115.
[17] Bas van der Vossen, "Immigration and Self-Determination," *Politics, Philosophy and Economics* 14, no. 3 (2014): 278.

requirements to achieve a compelling justice-related purpose. Even here, the state should impose these requirements at least cost to citizens' competing cultural interests.

What does the neutralist model imply for immigration policy? Distinguish two paradigm cases: in the first case, the state is inhabited by a largely culturally homogeneous population (imagine Iceland or an indigenous people's territory). In the second, the state is inhabited by a pluralistic population, including previous cohorts of immigrants and their descendants, as well as historic national minorities.

In the first case, it may be acceptable to use immigration policy to protect the national culture, if immigrants' interests in settling are not urgent. Since almost all constituents share this culture, the state's institutional framework is not "biased" in favor of some people's cultural preferences over others, and it does not send the message that anyone is a second-class citizen. In crafting its immigration policies, it seems permissible for this state to consider the costs of the changes that would be required were it to become a culturally heterogeneous state. On the neutralist model, it would then have to provide recognition and public support to immigrant languages, to rework state symbols and holidays, to accept changes in the look and character of public space, and so on. These costs ought to be weighed against the benefits to incomers and might sometimes tell in favor of restricting immigration.

But matters are different in the case where an already pluralistic society limits immigration in order to promote cultural homogeneity. Absent some special justification, the promotion of a national culture is not a justified state aim in this context. Consider Israel's Law of Return, which grants every Jew a right to immigrate to Israel. Other important groups in Israeli society, including the Israeli Arabs, the Druze, the Bedouins, or more recent immigrants and refugees, are not extended this status. This immigration policy sends the message that the Israeli state prefers new Jewish members to new members from these minority groups.[18] As Michael Blake emphasizes, "to restrict immigration for national or ethnic reasons is to make some citizens politically inferior to others."[19] Even if a collectively self-determining *demos* has the authority to set its own migration policy, this is an unjust decision for it to make.

My argument does not entail that in a culturally pluralistic state, citizens have *no* legitimate interests in controlling the character of their society, only that such interests should not involve the privileging of one cultural group at the expense of

---

[18] One important justification for Israel's Law of Return is as a warranted *exception* to neutral immigration policies, since Jews are a historically persecuted and vulnerable minority. On this view, redress for past injustice could justify at least temporary deviations from equal treatment. But absent such a justification, such privileging is prima facie objectionable.

[19] Michael Blake, "Immigration," in *The Blackwell Companion to Applied Ethics*, edited by Christopher Wellman and R. G. Frey (Oxford: Blackwell, 2003), 224–37.

others. Since Wellman's democratic argument references citizens' interests in shaping their society's future, it avoids the objection from sectarianism pressed above. But a worry about Wellman's position is that it does little to explain the basis for the state's supposed right to free association. In arguing for the state's freedom of association, Wellman invokes an *analogy* with the rights of self-determining individuals. He contends that "like autonomous individuals, legitimate political regimes are entitled to... self-determination, one important component of which is freedom of association."[20]

But do self-determining states have the same rights as self-determining individuals? Not obviously. While I agree that both legitimate states and individuals have rights to self-determination, I do not think we can infer the shape and scope of a state's self-determination rights by analogy to the rights of individuals. Instead, the state's claim to autonomy rests on the personal and political autonomy interests of those it governs. It therefore must be shown that the state's freedom of association is somehow necessary to serve or protect its members' interests, especially their interest in being ruled by an institution that reflects their own (morally acceptable) values and priorities. While the state is a legal person, capable of rights and duties, which specific rights and duties it has should be determined with reference to its legitimate purposes, which are in turn justified by the contribution the state makes to the autonomy and well-being of its members.

Is a right to exclude migrants necessary for the state to protect its members' personal and political autonomy? In some cases, yes. It does seem warranted to exclude migrants who pose a threat of institutional usurpation. To threaten usurpation, (i) migrants must differ sharply from locals in their political values; (ii) they must come in numbers large enough to bring about a significant transformation of a society's institutions; and (iii) that change must be produced, not through *persuasion* of prior inhabitants, but by coercive imposition. Political autonomy would be jeopardized by a large influx of theocrats, say, who rejected liberal values and intended to use their majority in the political process to impose illiberal policies.[21] Institutional usurpation is analogous to colonial annexation: it destroys a social order that reflects a population's shared commitments and replaces it with one that does not. Such usurpation might occur if newcomers rendered prior inhabitants a permanent minority in their country.

Settler colonialism differs from ordinary migration because settlers typically threaten the political autonomy of locals. Settlement projects usually transfer migrants onto a territory with the aim of establishing political control of the area. Consider the ongoing settlement of Israelis in the West Bank or the Han Chinese

---

[20] Wellman, "Immigration and Freedom of Association," *Ethics* 119, no.1 (2008): 116.
[21] I recognize that similar arguments have been invoked to justify keeping Muslims out of Europe. For a summary, see Liav Orgad, *The Cultural Defense of Nations* (Oxford: Oxford University Press, 2015), 34–8. But there is no imminent risk of a Muslim political takeover, so, in my view, these arguments are inapt in that case.

in Tibet. To forestall Tibetan and Palestinian self-determination, the Chinese and Israeli governments are subsidizing the massive influx of their nationals into these areas. These projects aim to establish a majority large enough to control the local political process. If newcomers are party to a project of political usurpation, it seems permissible to exclude them even where their reasons for entry would otherwise be compelling.

Citizens also have an interest in protecting their political institutions against changes that fall short of usurpation. Sometimes political concerns are more widely shared within a constituency than they are in the world at large. When a group can control migration into their unit, they have a greater ability to ensure that their institutions reflect their (morally acceptable) shared preferences. For example, I believe Norwegians would have a legitimate grievance at being "swamped" by an influx of libertarians who so outnumbered them that they were required to give up their welfare state, even if other features of their institutions were not threatened. It is true that not *every* Norwegian values the welfare state. Still, even those who dissent from this specific decision may value the Norwegians' ability to shape their own policies. Thus, limits on immigration could sometimes be necessary to protect political programs, so long as the process of self-determination that led to these programs is widely valued.

None of this, however, entails that a self-determining state should have the same free association rights a self-determining individual has. If the state's rights are justified by the role they play in securing the personal and political autonomy of its members, then the state's moral prerogative to exclude migrants is limited to those scenarios where migrants *actually do threaten* members' political autonomy. But this is very rarely the case. Most of the time, the admission of new migrants has no effect on members' ability to continue to be governed by institutions that reflect their shared commitments. For that reason, in most scenarios, I believe the state has no right—on self-determination grounds—to exclude migrants.

Is this consistent with a state's right to refuse a political merger, for which I argued in Chapters 4 and 5? I held there that Libya could decline democratic incorporation into France, and Denmark might refuse to fuse with Sweden. I believe these positions are consistent. Note that a forced political merger *necessarily* imposes new political institutions on people, in a way that undermines their political autonomy. If, as I argued in Chapters 4 and 5, a people has a claim to be ruled by institutions that reflect their shared political will, then they must have the right to reject forced political mergers. Yet immigration, unlike a political merger, almost never threatens to impose unwanted institutions on people. In normal cases, immigrants are unlikely to destroy, take over, or significantly transform the state's institutions and policies. So there is no inconsistency in treating the two cases differently.[22] If the shape and scope of a state's associative prerogative is determined

---

[22] For a similar view, see Schotel, *On the Right of Exclusion*, 39.

by the political autonomy interests of its members, then a state should always have the right to reject unwanted mergers (since they always undermine members' political autonomy), but rarely have the right to reject unwanted migrants (since they almost never do). Of course, as I have argued, a legitimate state's right to decide its immigration policy may give it the "right to do wrong," refusing entry to migrants who ought morally to be admitted. But still, that would be an unjust decision for it to make, outside the scope of their justified exclusionary prerogative.

Can migration be resisted, on political autonomy grounds, simply because it changes the demographic composition of society? An influx of migrants might cause some citizens to become alienated from their state because they are unwilling to cooperate with newcomers perceived as different. Those who value living in a whites-only environment, say, might become disaffected through migration of Hispanic residents to their neighborhood. Many scholars, in this vein, express concern that increased diversity erodes social trust and solidarity.[23] Can a political community reject unwanted migrants out of prejudice or dislike, claiming that its citizens will become less likely to support their institutions if they have to cooperate alongside them?

I believe we should discount alienation that derives from prejudicial attitudes, rather than from the imposition of unwanted political institutions. Recall from Chapter 4 that claims to self-determination are *moralized* claims. I argued there that we have an important reason to respect the political autonomy of *cooperators* who acknowledge certain basic moral duties, especially the duty to respect others as independent equals. Those who exclude migrants out of prejudice typically deny these basic moral duties, treating certain classes of people as inferior. For this reason, I argued earlier that no wrong is done when we deny self-determination to fascists, racists, theocrats, or imperialists, since they reject the fundamental moral requirement from which self-determination's value is derived. On my political autonomy account, people's *actual* preferences about how, and by whom, they wish to be governed have moral significance, but only where those preferences are consistent with a basic commitment to respect for others' equal moral worth. Where dissenters clearly fail to acknowledge this requirement, there is no loss in overriding their viewpoints.[24]

This may seem ad hoc; but I do not think it is. In many contexts, it is permissible to exclude people from organizations on some grounds, but not others. An employer can refuse to hire an applicant because she failed a skills test, but not

---

[23] Robert D. Putnam, "*E Pluribus Unum:* Diversity and Community in the Twenty-First Century," *Scandinavian Political Studies* 30, no. 2 (2007): 137–74; Paul Collier, *Exodus: Immigration and Multiculturalism in the 21st Century* (Oxford: Oxford University Press, 2013), ch. 2.

[24] Miller also argues that discriminatory selection criteria show disrespect for the equal status of the would-be entrant, treating "her as though she were of no moral significance." Miller, *Strangers in Our Midst*, 105.

because of her race. A professional board can deny someone a medical license because he lacks appropriate training, but not on the grounds of his sexual orientation. Similarly, a state might exclude a would-be migrant to preserve its citizens' valued political institutions, but not out of animus to her ethnicity. Restrictions on permissible exclusion are common to many areas of our social life.

It might further be argued that in the shifting demographics case, alienated individuals do not necessarily hold racist or fascist beliefs: perhaps they respond reflexively to increased diversity in their social environment, gradually becoming less willing to support their political institutions. Still, at best, these attitudes provide only a *nonideal reason* for restricting immigration. By a "nonideal reason," I mean a moral reason for immigration restriction that we have in virtue of the fact that other agents are poorly motivated, and their unwillingness to comply with their moral duties threatens significantly harmful social consequences. By contrast, an *ideal reason* for restricting immigration is one that we would have even when dealing with well-motivated agents under conditions of full compliance.

Much evidence shows that unconscious bias is a significant factor driving these attitudes of discomfort or aversion.[25] Prejudice, implicit bias, or dislike may provide nonideal reasons to limit immigration if these attitudes prove to be unchangeable in the short term, and if disregarding them would lead to seriously harmful consequences. But nonideal reasons also call on us to *reshape* attitudinal constraints over the longer term, so that it eventually becomes feasible to act on our ideal reasons. People's attitudes are not a brute sociological fact: they are subject to rational control, and where those attitudes are intrinsically morally objectionable, we should try to alter them.[26] Public policy may foster increased social interaction in diverse contexts, or institute civic education programs to combat prejudice against migrants, for example.

So far, we have an argument for limiting migration, on self-determination grounds, only in cases where immigrants' settlement would (i) threaten institutional usurpation or (ii) undermine widely valued political policies or programs. Culturally homogeneous societies may also have an interest in (iii) limiting migration to protect a shared national culture, but this will not typically apply in pluralistic societies, where such policies would send the message that the state favors certain groups over others.

However, none of our cases (i)–(iii) tells in favor of a discretionary right to exclude. Admitting moderate numbers of migrants is unlikely to have discernible influence on a group's policies or the character of its political institutions. Most immigrants are in fact eager to embrace prevailing political values and institutions. These considerations provide reason for excluding migrants only where the flow of incomers threatens substantial institutional change. And there may be

---

[25] See John Jost et al., "The Existence of Implicit Bias," *Research in Organizational Behavior* 29 (2009): 39–69.
[26] Pevnick, "Social Trust and the Ethics of Immigration Policy," *Journal of Political Philosophy* 17, no. 2 (2009): 146–67, 151.

other ways to prevent that institutional change: e.g., by requiring migrants to undergo citizenship education or seeking to inculcate a respect for civic values.

Let me consider two objections to the idea that collective self-determination can justify even a qualified claim to exclude. First, one might object that political autonomy cannot support excluding migrants from settling within the state's *territory*, only their exclusion from *citizenship*.[27] The state might control the composition of its citizenry without controlling its territorial boundaries.[28] By allowing foreigners to take up long-term residence without the right to naturalize, we could reconcile open borders with self-determination.

I agree that outsiders cannot usually be barred from entering a state's territory temporarily. On the conditional model, as I already emphasized, the state has a standing duty to allow *harmless migration*. But I believe democratic states have an important interest in avoiding the creation of a class of permanent "denizens" within their borders. For this reason, if political autonomy can sometimes justify conditional exclusion from citizenship, I believe it can also justify exclusion from territory. A social ethos characterized by an absence of caste distinctions is a fundamental democratic achievement. A permanent class of "denizens" would undermine this achievement, by undermining the political equality that plays a key role in sustaining it.[29] When some people are marked out as "rulers," while others are publicly known to be "ruled," that power hierarchy will structure their ongoing relations, leading them to regard and treat one another in ways that entrench differences in social status. For this reason, if migrants intend to take up long-term residence within the state, they ought to be placed on a path to citizenship.[30]

A second objection is that the self-determination argument could apply to citizens, as well as to immigrants. Some citizens, like some would-be immigrants, hold political views that are illiberal or at odds with existing political structures. If a citizenry has a right to shape its membership to preserve shared political values, then might it disenfranchise or deport current citizens who are not committed to these values?[31] In my view, political autonomy does ground an interest in shaping future citizens' political attitudes. But this interest is constrained by other principles. This includes respect for occupancy rights, democratic equality, and the requirements of basic justice. As I argued in Chapter 2, if occupancy of a particular place is fundamental to a person's located life plans, and she has formed these plans

---

[27] See Sarah Fine, "Freedom of Association Is Not the Answer," *Ethics* 120, no. 2 (2010): 338–56.
[28] Fine, "Freedom of Association Is Not the Answer."
[29] Kolodny, "Rule over None II"; Viehoff, "Democratic Equality and Political Authority."
[30] For an argument that citizenship should be legally mandatory for long-term immigrants, see Helder De Schutter and Lea Ypi, "Mandatory Citizenship for Immigrants," *British Journal of Political Science* 45, no. 2 (2015): 235–51.
[31] See Cole, *Philosophies of Exclusion*, 142–3; Javier Hidalgo, "Self-Determination, Immigration Restrictions, and the Problem of Compatriot Deportation," *Journal of International Political Theory* 10, no. 3 (2014): 261–82; Jan Brezger and Andreas Cassese, "Debate: Immigrants and Newcomers by Birth: Do Statist Arguments Imply a Right to Exclude Both?" *Journal of Political Philosophy* 24, no. 3 (2016): 367–78.

without wrongdoing, then she cannot permissibly be removed or deported. Political autonomy must also be compatible with fulfillment of citizens' human rights, and their democratic enfranchisement. Still, current citizens shape "newcomers by birth" through social formation and civic education in ways that they are less able to shape immigrants, and I believe such shaping is permissible. Given their political socialization, it is predictable that most members of the new generation will accept their society's core political values.

In sum, the argument from collective self-determination to a discretionary right to exclude seems dubious. In pluralistic societies, self-determination can only justify *conditional* limits on migration in cases where support for a country's political institutions or valued programs or policies is seriously threatened.

7.2 Harm and Unwanted Obligations

Let me now turn to a different defense of the discretionary right to exclude. Michael Blake derives the state's right to exclude from a more general right to *avoid unwanted obligations* where there is no reason in place to show why *we*, specifically, should be obliged.[32] His argument begins from the state's *jurisdictional* nature: the state controls a distinct territory within which it has special obligations to *protect* and *fulfill* human rights. While the obligation to respect human rights is global in scope, the obligation to protect and fulfill is specifically local: it binds within a restricted space. When a would-be migrant whose human rights were already protected and fulfilled in her home state enters another state's territory, she imposes an obligation on its inhabitants to contribute to guaranteeing her rights. This limits the freedom of those inhabitants, and Blake holds that people have a presumptive right to be free from the imposition of unwanted obligations without their consent. This gives locals a right to reject would-be immigrants whose human rights are already protected and fulfilled elsewhere.

Yet on Blake's account, the precise sense in which immigrants constrain the freedom of a state's prior inhabitants is somewhat murky. Normally, we would say that a person's freedom was constrained if important options were no longer available to her, or if her life plans and projects were impaired or damaged. But the entry of a migrant does not necessarily have such effects. Prior inhabitants already have a duty to support legitimate institutions—to pay taxes, comply with the law, and so on—and the burdens of their support may not be appreciably increased by migration (if there are only a few migrants, or if they also contribute, through their taxes and compliance, to sustaining domestic political institutions). As Michael Kates and Ryan Pevnick point out, the "primary way that immigration affects the freedom of a state's current inhabitants is by increasing the *costs* (financial

---

[32] Blake, "Immigration, Jurisdiction, and Exclusion," *Philosophy & Public Affairs* 41, no. 2 (2013): 103–30.

and otherwise) of upholding certain existing institutions."[33] But if this is correct, it tells only in favor of a conditional right to exclude where migration is costly.

Blake might reply that the mere triggering of a duty to a person constrains my freedom, even if that duty is not costly or burdensome to me. But do we have a weighty objection to others' triggering nononerous duties for us? When I cross the street, I trigger duties on drivers to slow down; when I sit down in a chair in the lecture hall, I trigger duties on others not to sit there; when I take a shopping cart at the store, I trigger a duty on you not to take it for yourself, and so on. These duties do limit your moral freedom in trivial ways, but their imposition seems perfectly permissible. Everyday life would be impossible if we were obliged to seek others' consent every time we imposed a duty on them. Construed as a general objection to triggering moral duties for others, Blake's argument seems too broad. If Blake's argument is instead more narrowly construed, in a way that brings in considerations of cost, then it supports only conditional exclusion.

What costs to receiving societies might tell in favor of limiting migration? Consider the following ideal reasons for limiting migration (in roughly decreasing order of urgency). An "ideal reason," again, is a reason for limiting migration that might exist even where all citizens are well-motivated and in full compliance with their moral duties:

(1) *National Security*: Cross-border movement can sometimes produce serious threats to constituents' safety. I assume there is a justification for excluding terrorists, invading armies, and others who threaten the security of a state's inhabitants.

(2) *Institutional Subversion*: As I argued above, inhabitants of the host society have an interest in maintaining their political institutions, as well as specific programs or policies that reflect widely shared priorities. This can justify limiting entry of migrants with sharply different commitments, if they come in large enough numbers.

(3) *Public Services*: Migrants typically make demands on public services, including healthcare, housing, schools, and law-enforcement. Given the immense demand to migrate, if a wealthy country were to cease controlling its borders, a sudden influx of people could overwhelm these services. The cost of integrating migrants is also a concern, since there are prerequisites for successful functioning in a wealthy, industrialized host society. Unskilled immigrants, especially those from societies with peasant economies, are unlikely to have the education or skills to integrate without considerable social support. This integration process demands resources and planning, and could justify limiting migration flows to allow the state to keep up.

---

[33] Pevnick and Kates, "Immigration, Jurisdiction, and History," *Philosophy & Public Affairs* 42, no. 2 (2013): 10.

(4) *Welfare State*: Average welfare benefits in developed countries are many times the per capita income of some countries, and under an open-borders scheme, this might attract those seeking to live off public benefits. If subjected to such high demand, a welfare state may become unsustainable, undermining the availability of these benefits, and exacerbating inequality. One option here is to place waiting periods on eligibility for public assistance and social insurance programs. But some public benefits, like emergency healthcare, may be difficult to regulate in this way.

(5) *Protection of Inhabitants' Ways of Life*: Very high rates of migration might undermine prior inhabitants' social and cultural practices. I argued in Chapter 2 that our interest in the stability of our located life plans justifies a right to occupancy. This does not extend to a right to exclude outsiders from the territory if their entry is not disruptive to the inhabitants' residence and social practices. Still, population flows that damage or destroy inhabitants' social practices do infringe local occupancy rights. This is especially true for indigenous communities, whose traditional ways of life would be threatened by a mass influx of settlers onto their land. But it is likely true to a lesser extent of other local communities. A plausible version of this concern will limit it to *significant* harms to social and cultural practices that are not unjust or sustained by prejudicial attitudes. Still, sometimes large influxes of newcomers can have deleterious impacts on prior inhabitants, by limiting their ability to live in their area (since they are priced out), or by undermining their capacity to continue using their language in public life, to work in their jobs, or to practice their religion or crucial elements of their culture. Such serious impacts might provide a reason to limit migration. A general immigration target could work to protect social, cultural, and economic practices already established on the territory from impacts that might undermine them. Such a general target would not necessarily involve the privileging of the majority culture at the expense of minorities.

(6) *Special Obligations to the Domestic Poor*: Some theorists argue that an open immigration policy, especially for low-skilled migrants, can suppress the wages of the domestic poor, cause job losses, and increase inequality in the receiving state.[34] Economists debate the impact of current levels of migration on the domestic labor market, though the consensus is that the effects are small. Some argue that low-skilled immigration has had a slightly negative impact on the distribution of income in the United States, exacerbating wage stagnation among unskilled workers, prominent since

---

[34] See Stephen Macedo, "The Moral Dilemma of US Immigration Policy: Open Borders versus Social Justice?" in *Debating Immigration*, edited by Carol M. Swain (New York: Cambridge University Press, 2007), 63–81.

the 1970s.[35] Others hold that low-skilled migration has no effect on the wages of the unskilled because immigrants tend not to compete directly with native-born workers, whose better communication skills afford them different types of jobs.[36] New immigrants instead tend to compete with previous cohorts of immigrants.

I will not try to adjudicate this dispute here: since current levels of migration are restricted, it is in any case difficult to extrapolate from this evidence to what would happen if border controls were relaxed or removed. I simply suggest that if admitting more migrants *would* suppress the wages of the domestic poor, cause job losses, and increase inequality, this might be a good reason to restrict admissions. Of course, to some extent, the domestic poor can be compensated through welfare benefits, improved education, or retraining. Still, not all losses may be compensable, given the role that productive work plays in a person's sense of self-respect and status in society. So there may be circumstances in which immigrant admissions could compete with the state's special obligations to its own worst-off.

There are also nonideal reasons for limiting migration in some circumstances. A "nonideal reason," recall, is a reason that exists in virtue of the fact that some citizens are poorly motivated and unwilling to comply with their moral duties, and this threatens harmful social consequences.

(7) *Backlash*: A society's political institutions may be challenged from migration *backlash* among its own constituents. Citizens upset by large numbers of newcomers might vote for illiberal political parties, threatening a liberal polity's stability.[37] If backlash is sufficiently widespread, this may provide a nonideal reason to limit migration, at least temporarily, while also giving the state and its citizens reason to work to transform these political attitudes.

(8) *Social Cohesion*: As noted above, many scholars express concern that increased diversity erodes the social trust and solidarity necessary to maintain a welfare state.[38] These findings are disputed: dissenting scholars argue that social solidarity depends more on features of institutions than

---

[35] See George J. Borjas, "The Labor Demand Curve is Downward Sloping: Re-examining the Impact of Immigration on the Labor Market," *Quarterly Journal of Economics* 118, no. 4 (2003): 1335–74. For a contrasting view, see David Card, "Is the New Immigration Really So Bad?" *Economic Journal* 115, no. 507 (2005): 300–23, and "Immigration and Inequality," *American Economic Review* 99, no. 2 (2009): 1–21.

[36] See Gianmarco Ottaviano and Giovanni Peri, "Rethinking the Effects of Immigration on Wages," National Bureau of Economic Research. Working Paper 12497, revised version (May 2008); Arash Abizadeh, Manish Pandey, and Sohrab Abizadeh, "Wage Competition and the Special Obligations Challenge to More Open Borders," *Politics, Philosophy, Economics* 14, no. 3 (2015): 255–69.

[37] Carens allows that backlash worries may provide grounds for limited restrictions on migration in "Migration and Morality: A Liberal Egalitarian Perspective," in *Free Movement*, edited by Brian Barry and Robert E. Goodin (University Park: Pennsylvania State University Press, 1992), 32.

[38] Putnam, "*E Pluribus Unum*," 137–74.

on the characteristics of the populations they govern.[39] If the threat to social cohesion is so grave as to undermine the liberal state's ability to provide important goods, it might provide a nonideal reason to limit migration, at least temporarily, while also working to reshape citizens' attitudes.

So there are several reasons a state might have for wishing to limit cross-border migration flows when they would impose significant costs on its inhabitants or its own institutional functioning. The conditional model suggests that these costs would provide at least *pro tanto* reasons for exclusion. Still, we must also weigh these costs against the claims of the migrants themselves. An important question is what level of social cost would establish a conclusory case in favor of limiting migration. That depends in part on the strength of the migrants' claims, to which I now turn.

7.3 A Human Right to Immigrate?

Several theorists argue that the freedom to enter foreign states, and to settle there permanently if one wishes, is a human right, and that immigration restrictions are generally unjust because they interfere with this right.[40] While these theorists often reference the case of poor migrants seeking to move to wealthy countries, their view is broader: everyone—including the highly advantaged—has a right to move wherever they wish.[41] If it existed, a human right to immigrate would have dramatic implications for border control, since rights are typically thought to have priority over other social values. If global freedom of movement is a basic human right, then laws restricting it will be very difficult to justify.

To establish a human right to immigrate, Carens relies on a "cantilever" argument, which starts from the observation that domestic freedom of movement is already widely recognized to be a human right.[42] If restrictions on domestic movement are unjust, then why not also international border controls, which have similar effects on our ability to live, work, and travel? The cantilever argument commits itself to no particular account of the rationale for domestic freedom of movement: it holds that whatever that rationale is, it also applies to cross-border movement.

---

[39] See Will Kymlicka and Keith Banting, "Immigration, Multiculturalism, and the Welfare State," *Ethics and International Affairs* 20, no. 3 (2006): 281–304.

[40] Kieran Oberman, "Immigration as a Human Right," in *Migration in Political Theory: The Ethics of Movement and Membership*, edited by Sarah Fine and Lea Ypi (Oxford: Oxford University Press, 2016), 34; Carens, *The Ethics of Immigration*, 225; Philip Cole in Cole and Wellman, *Debating the Ethics of Immigration*, (Oxford: Oxford University Press, 2011), 160.

[41] Carens, *The Ethics of Immigration*, 278.

[42] I take this term from Miller, "Is There a Human Right to Immigrate?" in *Migration in Political Theory*, edited by Sarah Fine and Lea Ypi (Oxford: Oxford University Press, 2016), 15. See Article 12 of the *Universal Declaration of Human Rights*, and Article 13 of *the International Covenant on Civil and Political Rights*.

By itself, the cantilever argument fails to convince. In drawing the contours of a right, we need to go beyond merely noting a similarity between one protected class of actions (moving domestically) and another (moving across borders). The shape and scope of a right depend upon the underlying interests that ground our recognition of it. Consider freedom of expression. Many people believe that stringent protections should be afforded to political speech because it is essential to the healthy functioning of a democracy, and to scientific, informational, and creative speech because of its importance for people's ability to seek truth. Yet most societies also limit certain categories of speech.[43] Laws regulating deceptive and false advertising, libel and slander, and campaign contributions are compatible with freedom of expression. Though they limit speech, these regulations do not jeopardize the fundamental interests that free expression is designed to protect, and they safeguard other important interests against threats that unrestricted speech might pose. So in deciding whether border controls violate the right to freedom of movement, we must give an account of the interests served by that right, and assess whether limits on international movement threaten these interests.

Here, many proponents of the human right to immigrate invoke an unsatisfyingly broad interest in freedom. As Carens puts it, "the vital interest at stake [is]…freedom itself. You have a vital interest in being free, and being free to move where you want is an important aspect of being free."[44] Kieran Oberman argues that the human right to immigrate is rooted in a basic human interest in being free to access the full range of "life options," including friends, family, associations, expressive opportunities, religions, jobs, and marriage partners.[45] Finally, Javier Hidalgo and Chris Freiman argue that there is a presumption against the state coercively restricting our liberty unless such restrictions are necessary to protect liberty itself.[46]

These arguments raise three concerns. First, they are wholly beneficiary-centered. Oberman, for example, stresses how immigration controls hamper would-be migrants' ability to access life options but says little about the impacts that migration flows may have on the life plans of those who are already settled. But, surely, the justification of a right must take account not only of the beneficiary's interests, but also of the consequences for other people of the general recognition of that proposed right. For example, if domestic freedom of movement would serve the right-holder's fundamental interests nearly as well, while imposing many fewer costs on others than global freedom of movement, this may tell in favor of border controls.

---

[43] Scanlon, "Freedom of Expression and Categories of Expression," in *The Difficulty of Tolerance*, 85.
[44] Carens, *The Ethics of Immigration*, 249.
[45] Oberman, "Immigration as a Human Right," 35.
[46] Christopher Freiman and Javier Hidalgo, "Liberalism or Immigration Restrictions, But Not Both," *Journal of Ethics and Social Philosophy* 10, no. 2 (2016), 3–4.

Second, the liberty interest cited is implausibly broad. It seems to rest on a libertarian conception of freedom, according to which any state restriction on our options is presumptively wrong.[47] Such a broad view of freedom would render much ordinary state action (e.g., minimum wage or maximum working-hours limits, professional licensure requirements, and environmental or historic preservation laws) illegitimate. Many of these state actions also coercively restrict our options, but it is not obvious that they are unjustified.

Finally, our general interest in freedom from restriction seems insufficiently weighty to support the argument. As Joseph Raz emphasizes, this broad conception of negative liberty "does not tell us anything about which freedoms are important, which are not, and why."[48] A prohibition on jaywalking, or on driving the wrong way down a one-way street, restricts my freedom, as does a prohibition on my entering my house of worship.[49] But the latter prohibition is of greater concern, and not because it leaves me with a smaller number of options from which to choose. We care, not just about quantity of options but also about the *quality* of our reasons for wanting control over certain options.[50] To determine *which* choices people should control, we must bring in an account of their fundamental interests. What makes the difference between a nonbasic liberty that can be restricted for trivial reasons and a basic liberty that cannot?

Rawls defines a "basic liberty" as "an essential social condition for the adequate development and full exercise of the two powers of moral personality" that political citizens possess.[51] These two moral powers are the capacity to form, revise, and pursue a conception of the good, and to access sufficient means for pursuing one's determinate conception thereof (*personal autonomy*), and the capacity for a sense of justice in applying principles of justice to the basic structure of society (*political participation*). Personal autonomy, in the former sense, is especially tightly linked to our fundamental convictions about what has value and our need to live out these convictions.[52] Such convictions often present themselves as imposing nonnegotiable obligations, in matters of religion, intimate personal relationships, and central ethical and moral ideals, and they structure many of our most important decisions about how to live.

---

[47] In this vein, advocates of the right to immigrate often voice complaints about the state "blocking interactions between consenting adults." Oberman, "Immigration as a Human Right," 41. See also Freiman and Hidalgo, "Liberalism or Immigration Restrictions," 5; and Michael Huemer, "Is There a Right to Immigrate," *Social Philosophy and Policy* 36, no. 3 (2010), 435.

[48] Raz, *The Morality of Freedom*, 6–12. Even Carens admits freedom of movement can be restricted in some cases, though he sees these restrictions as an enhancement of "overall freedom." *The Ethics of Immigration*, 248.

[49] Ronald Dworkin, *Taking Rights Seriously* (Cambridge, MA: Harvard University Press, 1978), 268–9; Charles Taylor, "What's Wrong with Negative Liberty?," *Philosophy and the Human Sciences* 2, no. 8 (1985): 217–19.

[50] Miller draws a similar distinction between *basic* freedoms and *bare* freedoms in "Immigration: The Case for Limits," in *Contemporary Debates in Applied Ethics*, edited by Andrew Cohen, Christopher Wellman (Malden: Blackwell, 2004), 193–206.

[51] Rawls, *Political Liberalism*, 291–324.

[52] Ronald Dworkin, *Life's Dominion* (New York: Vintage Books, 1994), 157.

Rawls further clarifies the *significance* of a basic liberty: "a liberty is more or less significant depending on whether it is more or less essentially involved in, or is a more or less necessary institutional means to protect, the full and informed and effective exercise of the moral powers."[53] The more a freedom can be argued to be an essential institutional means to protect personal autonomy or political participation, the weightier the claim to that freedom will be. But since some freedoms, like the freedom to defame others, or to drive the wrong way down a one-way street, are not connected to the two moral powers, there is no presumption against restricting them.

What about the freedom to migrate? Is it plausibly connected to personal autonomy, and if so, is this freedom *significant*? I believe that relocation abroad can sometimes be a means of pursuing central personal autonomy interests. Consider Carens's examples:

> One might want a job; one might fall in love with someone from another country; one might want to belong to a religion that has few adherents in one's native state and many in another; one might want to pursue cultural opportunities that are only available in another land.[54]

Relocation to join loved ones may be an important guarantee for intimate family relationships. Travel abroad may be a means of practicing my religion, to make a special pilgrimage or simply to find other adherents with whom to practice (suppose I am a Mormon stranded in Japan). Relocation can also serve occupational freedom: suppose it is my aspiration to become an aeronautical engineer, but I live in Sierra Leone, and the only suitable degree programs are in the United States and Europe.[55]

Yet not every desire to relocate rests on a fundamental personal autonomy interest. Migrants' reasons for settling elsewhere have different levels of urgency. Consider the following spectrum:

a. a desire to move to enjoy nicer weather (roughly 1 million American expats have flocked to Mexico seeking a low-cost beach lifestyle);

b. a desire to move to access higher wages (a skilled professional receives a lucrative job offer elsewhere);

c. a desire to move to access educational, career, or religious opportunities that one could also pursue at home, though less successfully (a Canadian is accepted to a PhD program at Toronto, but wishes to attend Harvard's higher-ranked program);

d. a desire to move to access a society or culture more congenial to one's temperament or aspirations (one is an atheist in a strongly religious society);

---

[53] Rawls, *Political Liberalism*, 335.   [54] Carens, *The Ethics of Immigration*, 239.
[55] Carens, "Migration and Morality: A Liberal Egalitarian Perspective"; Oberman, "Immigration as a Human Right."

e. a desire to move to access decent wages (a low-skilled worker enjoys a minimal standard of living at home and could earn more abroad);
f. a desire to move to pursue educational, career, or religious opportunities that do not exist at all at home (the would-be aeronautical engineer in Sierra Leone must leave to pursue her chosen career);
g. a desire to move to join one's spouse or children;
h. a desire to move to secure one's subsistence, a livable environment, the protection of one's basic human rights, or to avoid cultural or political oppression. (This category was discussed in the last chapter, where I argued that states have no right to exclude migrants whose fundamental territorial interests are threatened).

I believe these reasons for moving are roughly in increasing order of urgency. Some of these reasons (f–h) reference interests that, in part, ground domestic basic liberties, while others (arguably, a–c) do not. Reasons (d) and (e) are difficult intermediate cases, to which I shall return. But, still, this list illustrates that some reasons for migrating are grounded in high-value interests, of the sort protected by fundamental freedoms domestically, while others are not. Reasons for migrating rooted in core personal autonomy interests may give rise to a strong claim to relocate.

Miller has criticized this argument, holding that:

> what a person can legitimately demand access to is an *adequate* range of options to choose between—a reasonable choice of occupation, religion, cultural activities, marriage partners, and so forth. Adequacy here is defined in terms of generic human interests rather than in terms of the interests of any one person in particular—so, for example, a would-be opera singer living in a society which provides for various forms of musical expression, but not for opera, can have an adequate range of options in this area even though the option she most prefers is not available.[56]

I agree with Miller that no wrong is necessarily done to a person if not every valuable option is available in her society, so long as the options at her disposal safeguard certain generic human interests. The fact that my choice of marriage partners here in the United States does not run to North Koreans does not mean that I do not have a perfectly adequate choice of partners. While I chose my husband from a less-than-global range of options, my choice was not less authentic because of that fact.

Unlike Miller, however, I think that, sometimes, domestic states are not capable of providing an adequate range of options internally. This is especially true, I believe, when (i) people are *committed* to a conception of the good that comprehensively

---

[56] Miller, "Immigration: The Case for Limits." See also Pevnick, *Immigration and the Constraints of Justice*, 85.

structures their life, and (ii) a proposed border restriction would deprive them of access to an option that is fundamental to their pursuit of that conception, in a way that makes it very difficult for them to adjust. Suppose I went abroad on a school trip, met a North Korean, and fell in love with him. It is much more harmful to deny me the ability to marry and live with this North Korean than it is to restrict my opportunities to meet and fall in love with North Koreans in the first place.[57]

In a world of extensive cross-border interaction, many people are committed to projects and relationships involving individuals and opportunities in other countries. Frequently, this is because people have lived, for a time, in another country and developed attachments there. As Joseph Raz notes:

> denying a person the possibility of carrying on with his projects, commitments and relationships is preventing him from having the life he has chosen. A person who may but has not yet chosen the eliminated option is much less seriously affected. Since all he is entitled to is an adequate range of options the eliminated option can, from his point of view, be replaced by another without loss of autonomy.[58]

While frustrated in their desires, would-be migrants can often seek out other options, much as I can apply for other jobs when I do not receive a coveted new position. But sometimes migration is the *only* option for pursuing an important autonomy interest, as when there are no opportunities in one's home country to receive a particular education or to practice a chosen career. These autonomy-interests ground a weighty *pro tanto* claim to enter. This claim must still be assessed against possible countervailing considerations, including costs to those in the receiving society. But this *pro tanto* claim is a good first step in an argument for a right to migrate.[59]

It might be objected here that would-be migrants should be held responsible for shaping their aspirations to suit their circumstances. Rawls argues, in this vein, that individuals are responsible for forming their life plans in accordance with the share of resources they can expect to have in a just distribution. But much

---

[57] Matthew Lister, "Immigration, Association, and the Family," *Law and Philosophy* 29, no. 6 (2010): 717–45.
[58] Raz, *The Morality of Freedom*, 411.
[59] The proponent of a human right to immigrate might object that we do not require a person to demonstrate a personal autonomy interest in order to travel or relocate domestically—so long as he obeys applicable traffic and property rules, he is free to move as he chooses. Why not treat international movement similarly? Because the underlying balance of interests is not the same. Two additional interests in part ground domestic freedom of movement: (i) our interest in generic options, and (ii) our interest in self-protection against government power. Beyond the options to which she is currently committed, a person has an interest in access to some range of *possibilities*, options she might be interested in pursuing at some point, now or in the future. A suitable range of generic possibilities need not contain *every* option, however. Second, we also have a *self-protection* interest against the potentially arbitrary use of political power. Lawmakers' decisions have a pervasive impact on citizens' conditions of life, and if badly made, they can inflict serious harms. Freedom of movement is a condition for the moral acceptability of an institution that allows officials to control and intervene in subjects' lives in these ways.

depends here on whether a just distribution of territory should extend to the right to impose discretionary constraints on outsiders' geographic mobility. I have argued that territorial occupancy rights do not include a moral claim to exclude outsiders from an area purely at will, in cases where their settlement will not jeopardize prior inhabitants' legitimate interests. Given this, these outsiders do no wrong in forming projects that involve people and opportunities in other countries. If there is no discretionary right to exclude, then this constraint is not one they can be reasonably expected to take into account.

Let me sum up this discussion. I believe proponents of the human right to immigrate are correct to highlight that relocation abroad can sometimes be an important institutional means to pursue personal autonomy interests that also ground our domestic basic liberties. In part, this is due to current patterns of global interconnectedness, which encourage people to commit to goals, projects, and relationships involving foreign people and places. Though personal autonomy could be guaranteed in a more autarkic world, its implications are different in the interconnected world we live in. People whose reasons for moving across borders reference fundamental autonomy interests have a strong *pro tanto* claim to relocate to a new country, even if they have not yet lived there. While this argument does not support a general human right to migrate, it may support a right to migrate for specific protected reasons. Presumably, though, the immigrants' claims would need to be weighed against the claims of local inhabitants. I now turn to how we should balance these competing interests.

7.4 Balancing Conflicting Claims

How might the conditional model of exclusion work? Here it is worth making two assumptions explicit. First, unlike proponents of open borders, who generally hold that only *catastrophic* social costs can justify exclusion, I believe that migrants' interests in settling must be balanced against the interests of the receiving society's inhabitants without a strong presumption in favor of the would-be migrant.[60] While I reject the human right to immigrate, I do not believe that states should regulate immigration solely in the interests of their own members, e.g., to promote national economic well-being. Instead, in crafting immigration policy, citizens and officials have a moral duty to take the interests of would-be migrants into account. But I deny that we should begin with a strong *presumption* that migrants' interests will be dispositive.

Second, I believe that a government may show some partiality to the interests of its own constituents, so long as would-be migrants' fundamental territorial

---

[60] Carens argued in an early article that immigration could permissibly be restricted only if it would lead to a complete breakdown in social order. Oberman argues that the human right to migrate may not be restricted unless host country citizens are threatened with deprivation of basic goods like food and shelter. Oberman, "Immigration as a Human Right," 47.

interests are protected in their home society. Here again I differ from Carens, who argues that "we have to weigh the claims of those trying to get in equally with those who are already inside."[61] Open-borders theorists typically reject or problematize the assumption that the state has special duties to its own members, invoking the moral arbitrariness of state boundaries. If migrants have strong interests in settling, why shouldn't the state treat those interests impartially with the interests of its constituents? Doesn't this rest on an arbitrary distinction among morally equal persons?

In my view, a justified division of responsibility among states grounds special duties to constituents. A legitimate state has special responsibilities to the population it rules: it ought to provide them justice-related benefits, protect and fulfill their rights, and generally show concern for their fates. The state ought to preferentially specify and enforce rights, provide public goods, and apprehend and punish criminals on behalf of its own inhabitants. This does not mean that states should pay no regard to the interests of outsiders, but they should not view themselves as having equally strong obligations to provide these benefits to them.

Why is this division of responsibility justified? Recall from Chapter 4 that the value of self-determination provides us moral reason to favor a system of separate states.[62] A system of separate states is justified, on my view, because it allows for political order to be imposed in a manner that shows proper respect for people's judgments as to how, and by whom, they should be ruled. I argued there that individuals have an important interest in avoiding subjection to *alien coercion* that in no way reflects their values and priorities. Though this is an interest of individuals, it can be furthered through an individual's membership in a self-determining group.

Consider, then, a representative individual, not knowing her citizenship, tasked with choosing principles to structure the international system. Alongside a strong interest in seeing her basic rights protected, this individual would recognize a strong interest in avoiding alien coercion. For this reason, in the normal case, she would prefer a rule permitting institutions to take responsibility for a territorially based population only when those institutions reflect their shared political will. She would allow for certain exceptions to this rule in the case of serious human rights violations or grave threats to a livable environment. But outside these exceptional cases, I believe she would see the interest in collective self-determination as taking priority over less-urgent interests like increased income and access to desirable options and opportunities. She would not be willing to endorse benevolent colonial rule, for example, because it brought benefits of this less-urgent kind.

If this is right, then the value of collective self-determination grounds a territorial division of responsibility among states. The state has, and *ought to have*,

---

[61] Carens, "Migration and Morality," 37.
[62] A division of responsibility among states is invoked by Miller, *National Responsibility and Global Justice*, 249–61; Beitz, *The Idea of Human Rights*, 128–31.

special duties toward its own constituents that it does not have toward outsiders. To maintain otherwise would allow that a state should *rule* these outsiders—delivering justice-related benefits to them and taking responsibility for their fates—even when it does not reflect the collective will of the cooperators in that population. But if there is good reason to disallow benevolent colonial rule, then there is also good reason to endorse a territorial division of responsibility. States *should* take greater responsibility for the fates of people within their boundaries, and less responsibility for the fates of people elsewhere. Otherwise, they would disregard weighty claims to collective self-determination. Since the division of responsibility among states can be justified, the institution of jurisdictional boundaries—involving, as it does, differential claims to government concern—is not morally arbitrary.

It might be objected that while this argument plausibly explains why the state should not take responsibility for outsiders in general, it is less plausible with respect to would-be migrants. While there is a weighty reason to avoid ruling foreign populations against their will, would-be migrants are eager to be governed by the host state. Indeed, these people often find their birth state significantly alienating and see foreign institutions as better expressing their values. Why, then, should the state not consider itself equally responsible for them?

There is considerable weight to this objection, and I believe that migrants' self-determination interests help to explain why states do not have a discretionary right to closure. But the state should consider itself responsible for these migrants only if it should allow them to settle on its territory. In deciding whether or not to allow migrants to settle, I think it is permissible for the state to consider the effects of their settlement on its prior inhabitants—to whom it has prior special duties—and on its own institutional functioning. In the same way, I am entitled to consider the effects on my existing advisees when deciding whether to take on several new students, or the effects upon my existing children of adopting four more.

This calculus assumes that the background territorial division of responsibility among states is a justified institutional rule. In this, it is akin to other institutional rules, as, for example, a department's system of allocating thesis advisees to thesis advisors. Various higher-order considerations tell in favor of establishing a system that allocates special responsibilities in a certain way (in the case of the system of states, these are the higher-order values of self-determination and basic justice; in the case of thesis advising, these might be the values of recognizing mutual academic interests and allowing for roughly equal advising burdens among faculty). Once a justified system allocating these special responsibilities has been set up, I might be faced with a request, say, from one of my colleague's advisees who would like to switch to be advised by me. In deciding whether to grant this request, I may consider the effects of taking on a new student on my existing advisees, and my ability to fulfill my responsibilities to them. The student who would like to switch certainly has a claim: I should give weight to her interests in my deliberations. But it is also permissible for me to balance that claim against the interests of my existing advisees with some priority for the latter, on grounds that I already have justified special duties to them.

Similarly, a territorial division of responsibility involves a justified special duty, on the part of each state, to provide justice-related benefits preferentially to its own population. The state is entitled to consider this responsibility when deciding whether to acquire additional duties to new people. This argument does not establish a discretionary right to exclude: I doubt there is such a right. But it does explain why, faced with would-be migrants, a state might permissibly appeal to its special responsibilities to existing constituents as a good reason for prioritizing the claims of the latter over the former. In doing so, the state is not appealing to a morally arbitrary fact. In general, if that state were to take equal responsibility for foreigners outside its territory, it would have to unilaterally coerce unwilling people, and benevolent colonial relations are something nonmembers themselves have reason to reject. The essential strategy for developing the conditional model, then, is to begin with a state that has (justified) special responsibilities to its own population, but also reason to give weight to the claims of migrants to enter. In what scenarios might such a state reasonably exclude outsiders in fulfillment of its responsibilities, and when might it be obliged to accept them?

Recall that on the conditional model, states have a standing duty to accept would-be migrants in cases where they threaten no significant harms. This *duty to allow harmless migration* limits how a state ought to control the land it governs: it cannot simply ignore migrants' interests in settling. Because outsiders have significant interests in relocation, when their movement is not harmful to inhabitants, states have a duty to allow it. One necessary condition for a state's moral claim to exclude is that the migrant's proposed entry must threaten some significant harm to its inhabitants. In the absence of any such threat, borders ought to remain open: states have no general right to closure.

What about the more complex cases, where harm is threatened? Here I have argued that the state must balance the interests of would-be migrants against the costs to its members, though it is permitted to give greater weight to members' claims. The priority for constituents is not infinite: where harms to constituents are relatively minor and the benefits to would-be migrants very great, the state has a moral duty to admit the migrants.[63]

Recall the cost-based reasons a state might have for restricting migration:

Ideal Reasons:

1. National Security
2. Institutional Threat
3. Public Services

---

[63] James Woodward, "Commentary: Liberalism and Migration," in *Free Movement*, edited by Brian Barry and Robert Goodin (Oxford: Oxford University Press, 2016), 59–84, proposes a similar approach.

4. Welfare State
5. Protection of Inhabitants' Ways of Life
6. Special Obligations to the Domestic Poor

Nonideal Reasons:

7. Backlash
8. Social Cohesion

Like migrants' interests in moving, these costs vary in their urgency. Let me start with the most serious ones. Reasons 1–4, and sometimes 7, reference significant threats to the stability of liberal political institutions. If a liberal state were to become unable to deliver important social services, to sustain its welfare state, or if its central political institutions were threatened, this would provide a strong case for restricting entry. These considerations provide reason for placing a ceiling on overall numbers of migrants at the limit of a state's "absorptive capacity." This limit is likely to be quite high, much higher than current rates of immigration to industrialized societies. Still, it may be lower than the overall demand to migrate under an open-borders regime. Given projections about future climate change and mass migration, it is worth thinking about the ethics of scenarios in which the demand to migrate could outstrip a state's absorptive capacity.

Of course, it is hard to know *ex ante* exactly what the limits of a state's absorptive capacity are. All we can say is that significant threats to national security, public order, the welfare state, or a nation's core values and institutions—were they to emerge—would constitute good reasons to restrict migration. Significant threats of this sort are, I believe, weighty enough to trump migrants' interests in moving in all but the most severe cases—i.e., where people seek to move to secure fundamental territorial interests, such as protection of their human rights and a livable environment. Even here, these migrants might be justifiably excluded from a particular state if there are other potential host states whose institutional functioning is not so gravely threatened. It is true that migrants' interests in subsistence or basic rights protection are more urgent than inhabitants' interests in sustaining their liberal constitutional order or preserving their welfare state. But I have argued that that state is not required to weigh the interests of would-be migrants strictly impartially.

A familiar worry is that the remotest possibility of a threat to these values can be exploited as a reason to close borders. A mere subjective perception of threat is not sufficient to restrict migration. Nor is it sufficient for authorities simply to claim that they have considered migrants' interests. Instead, government must be required to publicly justify its exclusionary policies before an impartial forum. One way of institutionalizing this may be to give domestic courts a greater role in reviewing immigration policy.[64] Excluded migrants might be given legal standing

---

[64] Schotel, *On the Right to Exclusion*, 170–9.

to challenge the state's migration policies in its own courts. To defend exclusion, government would need to make a reasonable showing of harm—drawing on the objective methods of social science, and publicly available evidence—and to demonstrate that migration limits have a realistic prospect of averting this harm. For example, if threats to the welfare state are at issue, authorities must demonstrate that large percentages of migrants are dependent on public benefits, and that the programs' fiscal stability is threatened. A court that was not convinced that the restrictions served a legitimate objective might be empowered to strike them down. I recognize that this justificatory model still leaves much room for debate over when evidence is "clear" and when threats become "significant," but it would be a significant advance over the status quo.

Consider now three less-urgent reasons for restricting migration: 5, defense of prior occupants' ways of life; 6, special obligations to the domestic poor; and 7, concerns about social cohesion and integration. I assume a scenario where the demand to migrate does not threaten to overwhelm the state's absorptive capacity and destabilize its political institutions. Nevertheless, the flow of migrants would likely cause other nontrivial harms, by exacerbating domestic inequality, lowering wages, decreasing social trust, or undermining important social and cultural practices.

These less-urgent costs, in my view, are weighty enough to justify excluding some categories of migrants. Consider again:

a. a desire to move to enjoy nicer weather;

b. a desire to move to access higher wages above an already decent level; and

c. a desire to move to access educational, career, or religious opportunities that one could also pursue at home, though less successfully;

These are cases where would-be migrants have an attractive "territorial base" somewhere else and they lack any urgent interest in moving. Where their entry would threaten significant harms to the locals' economic prospects, social cohesion, or valued social and cultural practices, then I believe that the locals have a sufficient justification for excluding them. Local inhabitants have special claims to live in this region, and to use the area for the practices that they value, and the settlement of these people would threaten that. Governments may consider such harms to their inhabitants when deciding whether to grant would-be migrants the right to settle on their territory.

Most difficult are cases where migrants have interests in relocation that are plausibly more urgent than the costs to locals. Consider (in increasing order of urgency):

a. a desire to move to access a society or culture more congenial to one's temperament or aspirations;

b. a desire to move to access decent wages;

c. a desire to move to pursue educational, career, or religious opportunities that do not exist at all at home; and

d. a desire to move to join one's spouse or children.

Even if locals are threatened with minor harms to their less-urgent interests, sometimes a government ought to allow increased migration, if it would confer much greater benefits on incomers. Though government can grant some priority to its inhabitants' interests, this priority is not infinite. Trivial harms to constituents do not trump weighty benefits to outsiders. For example, even if allowing family reunification for immigrants would decrease social trust and cohesion, receiving societies still ought to facilitate it because of the very great goods intimate association brings to people's lives. If the locals can provide this weighty benefit while suffering only minor harms to themselves, they should do so, though this comes at some cost to them.

While locals should be prepared to accept some costs to benefit migrants whose fundamental territorial interests are not at stake, I do not think that they are obliged to bear great burdens. The most difficult case is that of low-skilled migrants whose basic subsistence is not threatened at home, but who could greatly benefit from the preferable job opportunities available in wealthy countries. This case is difficult because there are very large numbers of such migrants, and if all of them came, significant harms to the domestic poor, to cohesion and integration, and to social and cultural practices would likely result. I think the best that can be said is that states should be as open to these migrants as they can be without suffering significant setbacks to the legitimate interests outlined above. The most important conflict, in my view, is with obligations to the domestic poor. To the extent that states can remain open to low-skilled immigration while discharging its obligations to its own worse-off (perhaps through compensation or retraining programs), it ought to do so. But there are limits to this approach: a wealthy state cannot take in all the economic migrants who would like to come. Since a state has special duties to its own constituents, harms of this kind can provide reason to limit migration, even when—impartially considered—the economic benefit to would-be immigrants would outweigh losses to the domestic worse-off.

7.5 Conclusion

This chapter continued to investigate whether the three core values defended in this book can justify states' exclusionary claims to territory. I held that states have only a *conditional* right to exclude migrants whose fundamental territorial interests are not at stake. While citizens have the authority to decide their immigration policy, they ought morally to adopt a policy that excludes migrants only when they threaten some significant harm. Where migrants' entry is harmless, locals are obliged to allow it—and this means allowing a significant degree of permanent settlement by outsiders who desire to move to their land. States also ought to facilitate labor migration to the extent that is consistent with their special obligations to their domestic poor. When migration flows must be restricted to prevent significant social harms, states should prioritize—within the queue—those would-be migrants who have fundamental personal autonomy interests in relocating to their territory. As noted in the introduction, however, the right to control borders is not the only exclusionary right states currently claim: they also claim sovereignty over their natural resources. Chapter 8 turns to the grounds and limits of these resource rights.

PART IV
LOOKING FORWARD

8
Resource Sovereignty and International Responsibilities

Among the territorial rights states claim is the exclusive right to control, regulate, and manage the natural resources found within their territories, and sometimes to profit from their sale or taxation. In international law, this prerogative is enshrined in the doctrine of Permanent Sovereignty over Natural Resources, proclaimed in 1962 by UN General Assembly Resolution 1803 (XII). This doctrine recognizes the "inalienable right of all states to freely dispose of their natural wealth and resources...in the interest of their national development and of the well-being of the people of the State concerned."[1] As Chris Armstrong notes, permanent sovereignty constitutes "the status quo of the contemporary world order," granting individual nation-states "an extensive and often exclusive set of rights over the resources within their territories."[2]

If construed as an unqualified right, however, permanent sovereignty seems implausible. All inhabitants of the globe depend upon its atmosphere, water systems, and central climate-regulating functions. A principle that would allow states to exploit their natural resources without any regard for outsiders' interests in these areas might jeopardize urgent needs. Moved by such concerns, many cosmopolitans criticize permanent sovereignty as insufficient to cope with the ecological challenges facing the world today. On their view, the idea that any country could have unfettered rights to control, use, and manage "its" natural resources is at odds with the long-term sustainability of the planet. Cosmopolitans increasingly argue that important resources like forest carbon sinks, biodiversity

---

[1] UN General Assembly, "Permanent Sovereignty over Natural Resources," UN Resolution 1803 (XVII) (14 December 1962). Though General Assembly resolutions do not constitute binding law, the permanent sovereignty principle has been incorporated into treaties, including in the 1966 human rights covenants, Article 1(2) of which proclaims that "all peoples may, for their own ends, freely dispose of their natural wealth and resources without prejudice to any obligations arising out of international economic co-operation, based upon the principle of mutual benefit, and international law. In no case may a people be deprived of its own means of subsistence." In 2005, the International Court of Justice in the case *Armed Activities on the Territory of the Congo* (*Democratic Republic of the Congo v. Uganda*) also declared permanent sovereignty a "principle of customary international law." See para. 244.

[2] Armstrong, *Justice and Natural Resources*, 133.

"hotspots," watercourses, glaciers, and fisheries should be managed through supranational arrangements.³

Following Nico Schrijver, I will understand the legal doctrine of permanent sovereignty to entail the state's possession of the following rights:

(1) a right to possess, use, and "freely dispose" of the natural resources within its territory;

(2) a right to freely determine and control the exploration, development, and disposition of these resources;

(3) a right to manage natural resources in accordance with national developmental and environmental policies;

(4) a right to regulate foreign corporations and investors in their activities regarding these resources; and

(5) a right to nationalize or expropriate property in resources, subject to the requirement to pay appropriate compensation.⁴

This chapter investigates the plausibility of the permanent sovereignty principle, with specific reference to the case of forest carbon sinks. A sustainable solution to climate change will likely require countries with large forests to conserve these areas, facilitating their use for global carbon sequestration. Can countries appeal to the doctrine of permanent sovereignty to insist on exploiting their forests as they like, even if that exposes people in other regions of the globe to grave harms?⁵ As the world moves toward commodifying carbon, rights over these sinks become increasingly important.⁶ But strong permanent sovereignty rights over forests appear to conflict with the demands of climate justice. Can we define a more qualified resource-sovereignty principle that would be compatible with the protection of the environment? Or should the very idea of resource sovereignty be discarded altogether?

This chapter argues against discarding resource sovereignty. Instead, I defend a limited resource-sovereignty principle, different from the permanent sovereignty doctrine as it exists in international law. This alternative principle is narrowly tailored to protect morally important interests in occupancy and self-determination. I argue that resource sovereignty (i) should be interpreted primarily as a principle

---

³ Christopher Armstrong, "Against 'Permanent Sovereignty' over Natural Resources," *Politics, Philosophy & Economics* 14, no. 2 (2015): 129–51; Alejandra Mancilla, "Shared Sovereignty over Migratory Natural Resources," *Res Publica* 22, no. 1 (2016): 21–35.

⁴ Schrijver, *Sovereignty over Natural Resources: Balancing Rights and Duties* (Cambridge: Cambridge University Press, 1997), 391. Schrijver argues that permanent sovereignty entails duties, and not just rights. I return to this later in the chapter.

⁵ For discussion of this issue, see Megan Blomfield, "Global Common Resources and the Just Distribution of Emission Shares," *Journal of Political Philosophy* 21, no. 3 (2013): 283–304; Mancilla, "Rethinking Land and Natural Resources, and Rights over Them," *Philosophy and Public Issues* 6, no. 2 (2016): 125–41.

⁶ Steve Vanderheiden, "Territorial Rights and Carbon Sinks," *Science and Engineering Ethics* 23, no. 5 (2017): 1273–87.

of jurisdiction rather than ownership (in particular, it does not extend to a discretionary right to exclude outsiders from the economic benefits derived from exploiting these resources) and (ii) resource sovereignty should be constrained by duties of environmental justice that require cooperation in international institutions. Forests are one example of a broader category of transboundary problems that require policy coordination at the global level to address. Considering this example thus allows me to engage the debate about how authoritative global institutions managing these problems should be designed. Though I develop my argument primarily with reference to forests, I believe the core ideas could be applied to other problems, including the more robust international refugee regime that is plausibly required to discharge the duties argued for in Chapter 6.

8.1 Permanent Sovereignty

To begin, I say more about the history of the permanent sovereignty principle in international law, which evolved as part of the decolonization movement. Anticolonial leaders saw permanent sovereignty over natural resources as a corollary of their political self-determination. As Chile, which introduced the UN Resolution establishing the principle, argued, "Self-determination would be an illusion in a country whose natural resources were controlled by another State, and it would be farcical to give a country political freedom while leaving the ownership of its resources in foreign hands."[7]

Anticolonial leaders sought control over their natural resources as part of a more general program of economic independence. A key concern was the ability of postcolonial countries to cancel or alter exploitative concession agreements, dating from the colonial period, under which Western corporations had won rights to develop those resources.[8] As Kamal Hossain puts it, "the principle was originally articulated in response to the perception that during the colonial period inequitable and onerous arrangements...had been imposed upon unwary and vulnerable governments."[9] These arrangements gave foreign corporations and investors (for example, the so-called "Seven Sisters" group of oil companies) extraordinary control over a host state's resources, conferring on it the right to receive only modest royalties and taxes. Anticolonial leaders saw permanent sovereignty over their resources as a way to "end the systematic plundering that had characterized their economic life since the age of empire."[10] Permanent

---

[7] Schrijver, *Sovereignty over Natural Resources*, 52.
[8] Schrijver, *Sovereignty over Natural Resources*, 20–4.
[9] Hossain and Subrata Roy Chowdhury, *Permanent Sovereignty over Natural Resources in International Law* (New York: Saint Martin's, 1984), ix.
[10] Christopher Dietrich, *Oil Revolution: Anticolonial Elites, Sovereign Rights, and the Economic Culture of Decolonization* (Cambridge: Cambridge University Press, 2017), 3.

sovereignty would give them the right to nationalize enterprises and/or renegotiate concession agreements on more favorable terms.[11] The permanent sovereignty doctrine was linked, in their eyes, to the overcoming of structural hierarchies in the global economy, granting developing countries more control in their relations with foreign corporations and investors.

Concerned about their access to oil and other important resources, Western states generally opposed permanent sovereignty. They argued that postcolonial states' control over their resources should be restricted by duties to respect other states' need to access raw materials and to contribute to an expanding world economy.[12] Western states also worried that permanent sovereignty might expose their corporations to uncompensated expropriation of assets. They were concerned to ensure the payment of "adequate, prompt, and effective compensation" in response to any nationalization.[13] Postcolonial states generally regarded these arguments as a shield for continued neocolonial domination.

After the UN General Assembly's adoption of the permanent sovereignty principle in 1962, it was increasingly appealed to as part of a broader program to transform the international economy through a New International Economic Order (NIEO), a call for which was inaugurated in 1974 at a Special Session of the General Assembly. The NIEO Declaration called for eliminating "the remaining vestiges of alien and colonial domination, foreign occupation, racial discrimination, *apartheid* and neo-colonialism" in the global economy, addressing international inequalities with deep roots in the colonial past. The NIEO was predicated on the values of self-determination and sovereign equality, and it proclaimed "the right of every country to adopt the economic and social system that it deems most appropriate for its own development" and to enjoy "full permanent sovereignty...over its natural resources and all economic activities."[14]

Since their economies generally relied on the sale of raw materials, by leveraging their permanent sovereignty to form cartels among primary product producing states, the developing countries hoped to negotiate durably higher prices for their exports. This project was encouraged by the success of the oil-producing nations of OPEC in raising the price of oil following the Yom Kippur War in 1973. Yet the NIEO failed. The high oil prices demanded by the OPEC countries had a severe impact on the economies of non–oil developing countries. Eventually, the debts

---

[11] Though developing countries pressed for the right to expropriate without compensation, this was not included in the final text of the resolution, which required "appropriate" compensation, though not the "adequate, prompt and effective" compensation advocated by Western countries.

[12] Schrijver, *Sovereignty over Natural Resources*, 39–41.

[13] Schrijver, *Sovereignty over Natural Resources*, 23.

[14] UN General Assembly, *Declaration on the Establishment of a New International Economic Order*, Resolution 3201 (S-VI) (1 May 1974). An important difference between the NIEO and cosmopolitan programs for global distributive justice was the central place the former gave to the claims of self-determining peoples. Their program was one of equality of peoples, not equality between individuals. For this point, see Samuel Moyn, *Not Enough: Human Rights in an Unequal World* (Cambridge, MA: Harvard University Press, 2018), 90, 158.

these states contracted to pay for oil imports caused a sovereign debt crisis that required significant economic restructuring, giving Western lenders and the International Monetary Fund power over postcolonial countries' economic policies, and paving the way to the "Washington Consensus" era of late-twentieth-century globalization.[15]

Despite the NIEO's failure, the doctrine of permanent sovereignty persists in international law. In recent years, it has been broadened to include new claims to maritime and seabed resources. Under the 1982 UN Convention on the Law of the Sea (UNCLOS), countries have extended their territorial waters to 12 miles offshore, created new "Exclusive Economic Zones" in which they enjoy fishing and mineral rights, and established a mechanism for claiming exclusive rights over extended "continental shelves."[16] At the same time, UNCLOS also established a competing principle of the "common heritage of mankind" to govern the high seas. It envisaged the establishment of an International Seabed Authority that could regulate deep seabed mining in these areas, and which would share the benefits of these resources globally.

Several questions arise in interpreting permanent sovereignty, both as the doctrine is understood in international law and in theorizing an alternative resource-sovereignty principle, as I will below. First, what counts as a "natural resource" for purposes of the principle? Here I define "natural resources" as raw materials, not manufactured by humans and available from the natural environment, that are now useful or could become useful under conceivable technological, economic, or social circumstances in satisfying human wants and needs.[17] On this definition, what counts as a resource is to a certain degree historically variable: it depends on the state of technology at a given time, which allows natural goods to be employed in specific ways. Thus, not every naturally occurring object (e.g., blades of grass) counts as a resource, only those that given current levels of technology might plausibly be instrumentally exploited to meet human needs.[18]

Often, certain individuals or groups will conceive a particular good as a "resource," while others will not. For example, mining companies may view the Black Hills as a resource because of the mineral wealth found there, whereas the Lakota Sioux—who see it as sacred—may disagree. On the view I adopt here, a good counts as a "resource" if *someone* views that object as instrumentally valuable, even if others dissent (though whose view about the disposition of the resource should prevail is a further question).[19]

Second, who are the holders of permanent sovereignty rights—are they states or peoples? This has been a subject of debate in the relevant international resolutions,

---

[15] Dietrich, *Oil Revolution*, 303. [16] Schrijver, *Sovereignty over Resources*, ch. 7.
[17] For similar definitions, see Armstrong, *Justice and Natural Resources*, 11; Moore, *A Political Theory of Territory*, 163; Schrijver, *Sovereignty over Natural Resources*, 11–19; Leif Wenar, *Blood Oil*, 202.
[18] Moore, *A Political Theory of Territory*, 163. [19] Moore, *A Political Theory of Territory*, 164.

which speak interchangeably of both agents.[20] In international law, the holders of permanent sovereignty are generally held to be states, and perhaps territories under occupation or foreign administration.[21] I will argue instead that a justified alternative principle should attribute resource sovereignty to any group with a valid claim to self-determination, including indigenous peoples and other qualified minorities. Substate groups that express their self-determination through internal autonomy rather than sovereign statehood should also be granted sovereignty over their natural resources.

Third, what is resource sovereignty exactly? The core claim, as articulated in the international law documents, is the right of a self-determining people "to freely dispose of its natural wealth and resources."[22] But what does "freely dispose" mean? Is this best construed as a principle of national *ownership*? Or something weaker?

As a matter of international law, permanent sovereignty has been interpreted to include the right to nationalize oil, gas, minerals, and other resources. As Cara Nine notes, however, "resource rights inhabit two different and sometimes clashing spheres of thought."[23] On the one hand, they are claims to *jurisdiction* over the resources situated within a state's territory. But, on the other hand, they are often thought to extend to *ownership* of those resources. Yet, as Nine correctly insists, jurisdiction and ownership are theoretically distinct rights. A collective may have the right to "articulate and adjudicate rights over goods within its domain" (*jurisdiction*) without necessarily also having a "claim to control the access to and benefits from natural resources within its domain" (*ownership*).[24] This is clear enough in the case of private property: the state of New Jersey exercises jurisdiction over my house, adjudicating and enforcing my property rights in it, but it does not *own* my house.

Which, if any, construal of resource sovereignty we should favor depends on the normative grounds for it. The next two sections investigate four arguments for resource sovereignty, based on (i) natural property rights, (ii) international conventions, (iii) occupancy rights, and (iv) respect for collective self-determination. I conclude that occupancy and self-determination provide the most promising supports for a resource-sovereignty principle, but these arguments do not justify national ownership. Instead, I defend a more limited resource-sovereignty principle: a *presumption* that groups who occupy a territory should have rights of *jurisdiction* over its natural resources, including the right to decide how they are to be managed and used. This presumptive right, however, may be subject to exceptions, explored in Section 4.

---

[20] The 1962 Declaration refers to both "states" and "peoples"; the 1966 human rights covenants attribute permanent sovereignty to "peoples"; and the 1974 NIEO Declaration speaks of "states."
[21] For this reading, see Schrijver, *Sovereignty over Natural Resources*, 143–60.
[22] Article 1(2), *International Covenant on Civil and Political Rights*.
[23] Nine, *Global Justice and Territory*, 116.   [24] Nine, *Global Justice and Territory*, 9.

8.2 Against National Ownership

The permanent sovereignty principle in international law is often appealed to in support of the claim that "France belongs to the French; America's natural resources belong to the American people; the resources of Nigeria belong to the Nigerian people; and so on."[25] But national ownership has weak normative foundations. Consider two unconvincing arguments for it.

First, classical natural law thinkers (including Grotius, Pufendorf, and Vattel) held that occupants could acquire full property in their country's resources.[26] In occupying an area, Grotius argued that the people could acquire two distinct rights: "Jurisdiction and the Right of Property, as distinguished from jurisdiction."[27] The right of *jurisdiction*, according to Hugo Grotius, was a right to make and enforce laws (including property laws) within an area, whereas the right of *property* was a kind of supreme ownership over that space. Broadly following Grotius, Vattel coined the term *domain* (a term related to eminent domain), to refer to the supreme ownership that a nation held over its territory. It was by virtue of the domain, Vattel argued, that "the nation alone may use this country for the supply of its necessities, may dispose of it as it thinks proper, and derive from it every advantage it is capable of yielding."[28] According to Vattel, the domain also allowed the nation to exclude foreigners from appropriating anything in the area: "No one can form any pretensions to the country which belongs to the nation, nor ought to dispose of it, without her consent, any more than of the things contained in the country."[29]

To substantiate national ownership, however, natural lawyers invoked a primordial agreement in favor of first occupancy as a rule for creating property in the earth's resources. As Grotius puts it:

> [T]he Original of Property...resulted from a certain Compact and Agreement, either expressly, as by a Division; or else tacitly, as by Seizure. For as soon as living in common was no longer approved of, all Men were supposed, and ought to be supposed to have consented, that each should appropriate to himself, by Right of first Possession, what could not have been divided.[30]

---

[25] Wenar, *Blood Oil*, 193.

[26] While Locke's first labor account is the most well-known theory of natural property rights, I set it aside here since it does not seem very plausible as a basis for natural resource ownership. Many resources, such as oil and mineral deposits, are the result of naturally occurring processes for which the people living on the territory are not responsible.

[27] Grotius, *DJBP*, II. 3. iv. Grotius's views are complex: he held that in some countries, only the right of jurisdiction has been occupied, leaving foreigners free to come and take, e.g., unused land, while in other countries both the rights of jurisdiction and property have been occupied, prohibiting any outside appropriation of land or goods in the area. Pufendorf was less qualified: for him, occupancy "establishes dominion for the whole group, as such, over all things in that district... Therefore, if anything be discovered in such an area that is still without a private owner, it should not at once be regarded as unoccupied, and free to be taken by any man as his own, but it will be understood to belong to the whole people." Samuel Pufendorf, *Of the Law of Nature and Nations*, Bk. 4, ch. 6, §4.

[28] Vattel, *Law of Nations*, 213.   [29] Vattel, *Law of Nations*, 302.

[30] Grotius, *Rights of War and Peace*, edited by Richard Tuck (Indianapolis: Liberty Fund, 2005), 426–7.

As outlined in Chapter 3, Grotius maintains that certain rights over material goods, including land, could arise in virtue of our moral duties to respect the self-preservation and autonomy of other people. But these are primitive use-rights, not full property claims. At some point, Grotius holds that humans decided to move beyond primitive rights, introducing claims of full property. No longer content to live on what each person could produce independently, they decided to divide their labor and specialize economically, to facilitate the creation of a social surplus. A division of labor, however, requires some system of exchange, and to work well, exchange requires people to have more extensive claims to goods than the primitive right allows. If people are allowed to benefit from a good only insofar as they personally use it, they have no incentive to produce beyond what they need for their own use. Incentives for greater productivity therefore tell in favor of instituting more robust and permanent rights to goods. These conventional property rules, however, require more than the will of a single individual or group to be legitimately established. An agreement among humankind is necessary to ensure everyone consents to the new dispensation.

So while natural rights theory might at first seem to support national resource ownership, absent the background assumption of a global agreement, that theory is unable to bear much normative weight. While it may be legitimate to occupy a country, the people's more exclusionary claims to resources require global consent.

Perhaps, though, there is a global agreement (of sorts) on the principle that peoples own the resources situated in their territories. International conventions (including the principle of permanent sovereignty) might provide an alternative ground for national ownership rights. This follows a standard view of property, which sees it as a conventional right conferred by background legal institutions or social practices. Hume argues that property is determined by conventions that assign ownership of objects and define the conditions for valid contracts and transfers. The existence of clear principles allocating property serves the general interest of society, by making peace, stability, and prosperity possible. While Hume was primarily concerned with domestic property rules, we might offer a similar account of the international rules regarding territory. Perhaps permanent sovereignty over natural resources is justified because allocating territorial ownership to peoples serves peace, stability, and prosperity in our international system.[31] On this view, states are bound to respect natural resources as the people's property because a convention to that effect has been established *among states themselves.*

---

[31] Thomas Baldwin, "The Territorial State," in *Jurisprudence: Cambridge Essays*, edited by Hyman Gross and Ross Harrison (Oxford: Clarendon, 1992), 207–30. For similar arguments, see Rawls, *Law of Peoples*, 38–9; Wenar, *Blood Oil*, 190–207.

To be convincing, however, this account requires a further assessment of the *moral validity* of existing conventions. It is not only important that we have *some* scheme of rules defining territorial rights, it is also important that these rules be morally acceptable. Until the early twentieth century, for example, international conventions held that it was permissible to acquire territory by conquest.[32] This repugnant rule created no binding moral entitlements. Though this rule may have given rise to expectations for those who lived under it, those expectations were not legitimate. So the existence of a convention of permanent sovereignty does not settle the matter: we need a further evaluation of this convention's moral validity, by comparing it to feasible alternatives. Is permanent sovereignty a morally acceptable rule, or—like the rule of conquest—should it be rejected?

Construed as a strong ownership right, it is not obvious permanent sovereignty is morally acceptable. Following Armstrong, we can separate out various standard incidents of resource sovereignty.[33] Some of these incidents are characteristic of *property*. The right of *access* is a right to interact with resources in a group's territory and to draw non-subtractive benefits from them. "*Withdrawal*" is the right to enjoy subtractive benefits from these resources, using them in a way that diminishes their value for others, e.g. by consuming a nonrenewable resource. "*Exclusion*" is the right to determine who can access the resource or withdraw benefits from it, including the right to forbid others from doing so. "*Alienation*" is the right to sell a resource, and the "*right to derive income*" is the right to enjoy the proceeds of that sale. Other incidents of resource rights are more characteristic of *jurisdiction*. "*Management*" is the right to set rules for how the resource can be used, and whether it should be conserved or protected. The "*right to regulate alienation*" is a right to set the terms on which resources can be sold or transferred. The "*right to regulate income*" is the right to set rules about who can derive income from the resource and to levy taxes on these benefits.

A strong permanent sovereignty principle allocates all these incidents to a single agent, the people who govern the territory. But concentrating control over resources in this way may jeopardize urgent interests. To return to our central case of forest carbon sinks, under an unqualified permanent sovereignty principle, peoples have a right to refuse to conserve their forests—for trivial or even for no reasons—forcing those in other regions of the globe to lose their lands to desertification and flooding. They can also claim full property in their forests' carbon-sequestration capacity, excluding others from ecosystem services at will. At the very least, these troubling implications make it worth investigating whether there are feasible alternative conventions that might better protect our shared interests in the sustainability of the earth.

---

[32] Korman, *The Right of Conquest*.   [33] Armstrong, *Justice and Natural Resources*, 22–3.

8.3 A Limited Resource-Sovereignty Principle

What alternatives might there be? A radical view, supported by some cosmopolitan theorists, would eliminate resource sovereignty altogether. Such a proposal might be defended on the basis that the distribution of natural resources across the earth is "morally arbitrary." As Charles Beitz argues, "The fact that someone happens to be located advantageously with respect to natural resources does not provide a reason why he or she should be entitled to exclude others from the benefits that might be derived from them."[34] To be sure, forests and other natural resources have been shaped by historical patterns of human settlement and land use, and they have to be maintained in the present. Those involved in these activities have a claim to be compensated for their efforts, insofar as these efforts conserve the forest and make it useful for others. But the improvement-based claims of contemporary agents will typically fall short of anything like full property in the forest or its carbon-sequestration capacity.[35] So—once relevant compensation claims are deducted—why not instead hold that each inhabitant of the earth has an equal claim to a say in how forests are managed, and a right to benefit equally from their ecosystem services? Why should we think that local peoples, or the states in which they reside, have any special priority? Perhaps forests should be administered in the interests of humankind, not in the interests of those people who are arbitrarily located where the forests happen to be.

Resource cosmopolitans would therefore treat the world's forests as a global commons with respect to which every human being is symmetrically situated, reallocating their control and benefits in line with fair distributive principles. Beitz defends a "resource redistribution principle which would give each national society a fair chance to develop just political institutions and an economy capable of satisfying its members' basic needs."[36] Paula Casal proposes progressive taxes on both the use and ownership of natural resources, and argues for redrawing boundaries to afford landlocked nations equal access to the sea.[37] Tim Hayward argues that justice requires the enforcement of an equal per capita allocation of access to ecological space.[38]

In perhaps the fullest resource cosmopolitan account to date, Chris Armstrong argues for shifting the benefits of natural resources to equalize individuals'

---

[34] Beitz, *Political Theory and International Relations*, 138.
[35] As Armstrong puts it, improvement-based claims are "best responded to by granting not full and exclusive rights over all the natural resources in a territory, but an appropriate share of the income from the relevant resources." See Armstrong, *Justice and Natural Resources*, 133.
[36] Beitz, *Political Theory and International Relations*, 141. Beitz allowed, however, that permanent sovereignty might be defended as a remedial right, since "resource-consuming nations have taken more than their fair share." See 142, note 31.
[37] Casal, "Global Taxes on Natural Resources," *Journal of Moral Philosophy* 8, no. 3 (2011): 307–27.
[38] Hayward, "Global Justice and the Distribution of Natural Resources," *Political Studies* 54, no. 2 (2006): 349–69.

opportunities for well-being across the globe.[39] Armstrong holds that we should abandon the doctrine of permanent sovereignty since "there are compelling reasons to favor a dispersal of management rights over a variety of resources to the transnational and even global level, rather than accepting a regime under which decisions whether and how to exploit resources are vested with nations or states."[40] Some resources—usually those beyond occupied territories, such as the high seas and seabed, Antarctica, and the moon—are already considered "to fall outside the jurisdiction of any state," as part of the "common heritage of mankind."[41] Armstrong advocates extending such regimes, over time and as circumstances allow, to include other natural resources.[42] For the most part, however, he focuses on feasible incremental proposals (like taxes on carbon use and sovereign wealth funds) that might move the world gradually in the direction of greater equality.

Unlike resource cosmopolitans, I believe the idea of resource sovereignty should be retained, not abandoned. I propose, however, that resource sovereignty should be understood in a more limited way than it often is, primarily as a principle of jurisdiction (which confers only a conditional right to exclude outsiders from resources on the territory) rather than property (which would confer on the state a discretionary right to exclude outsiders from these resources, and to enjoy the full stream of income from exploiting them).

Why not eliminate resource sovereignty completely? Resource cosmopolitans typically fail to notice that people are *not* symmetrically situated with regard to many natural resources, including forests.[43] Instead, some people have morally significant interests in specific resources—especially the interests in *occupancy* and in *collective self-determination*. A limited resource-sovereignty principle would protect these important interests: it is not, as some resource cosmopolitans hold, a mere ideological justification for safeguarding the unjust advantages of the lucky.

First, consider the interest in occupancy. As I argued in Chapters 2 and 3, it is plausible that a country "belongs" to its people in the weak sense that they have occupancy rights in it. This gives them a claim to use that area as a permanent residence and as a site for the economic, social, and cultural practices they value. Our moral duties to respect others' self-preservation and autonomy ground duties not to remove people from the places they (not unjustly) occupy, and not to interfere with their use of space in ways that would undermine their located relationships, goals, and pursuits. As I suggested earlier, this reason for respecting someone's existing projects is especially weighty in cases where that life project is an *essential*

---

[39] Armstrong, *Justice and Natural Resources*, ch. 3.
[40] Armstrong, *Justice and Natural Resources*, 145.
[41] Armstrong, *Justice and Natural Resources*, 205.
[42] Armstrong, *Justice and Natural Resources*, 214–5.
[43] Armstrong is to some extent an exception: he argues that resource egalitarians can integrate some claims of attachment to specific resources while still equalizing people's shares overall. But he attributes no validity to claims of self-determination and argues against any presumption that peoples should control the resources on their territories.

means to carrying out a person's *comprehensive aims*. These are aims that structure many choices and activities and are closely related to a person's sense of her life as her own. International conventions defining resource rights should be compatible with occupants' continued pursuit of their comprehensive aims.

Located life plans may give occupants a claim to some of the incidents of resource control listed above. Armstrong highlights the case of the Saami people of Scandinavia, whose way of life depends on herding reindeer. Since the Saami's central economic and cultural practices require access to the reindeer, this gives them a prima facie right to use and manage reindeer herds. But, as I elaborate below, the located-life-plans argument will typically not extend, e.g., to undiscovered oil and mineral deposits, which are not incorporated into anyone's life projects. There is no natural duty to respect plans formed for the sole purpose of excluding others from a good to profit through exchange. I also emphasized that the interest involved in a primitive occupancy right does not extend to rights to exclude apart from use, to alienate, bequeath, or derive income.

So while occupancy is a moral interest that any system of conventional resource rights should respect, it does not determine all aspects of resource regulation. The core claim involved in occupancy is that others not interfere with our use of resources in ways that undermine the located practices central to our lives, so long as these practices are compatible with the fair-use proviso defended in Chapter 6. As I suggested, a plausible version of this concern will limit it to *significant* harms to social and cultural practices that are not unjust. Still, if international conventions regulating resources forced the Saami to move from their homeland out of necessity (e.g., because they could no longer maintain their subsistence practices there), or—without any compelling justice-based rationale—made it impossible for them to continue to practice their religion or central elements of their culture, I believe they would have a legitimate complaint.

Collective self-determination, on my view, grounds a second morally significant interest in natural resource control. The anticolonial leaders who supported permanent sovereignty thought control over resources was necessary for a people to choose freely its own political and economic system. Since rules around the extraction and use of resources "impinge on many different aspects of the collective life of the community," no community can effectively shape its own society if it lacks any right to decide how the resources in its territory are managed and used.[44] Laws defining property rights and regulating public space are an important part of self-determination. As Nine argues, this reflects "the importance that a group's geographical surroundings have for most aspects of members' lives."[45] A socialist society, for example, might want to place its natural resources under collective control, establishing agricultural cooperatives or nationalizing extractive industries. Many indigenous peoples prohibit the alienation of tribal lands, or view

---

[44] Moore, *A Political Theory of Territory*, 166.   [45] Nine, *Global Justice and Territory*, 119.

particular areas or natural formations as sacred, barring exploitation of these places. To deny political communities authority over the rules governing the use, management, and alienation of the resources in their territory would significantly limit their ability to determine the social world in which they live.

This connection between self-determination and resource control is illustrated by several conflicts involving indigenous groups. In the 1970s Hydro-Quebec, the largest hydroelectric project in the world, began to dam or divert several major rivers, flooding more than 4,000 square miles of forests to generate electric power. This resulted in the significant transformation—indeed, the partial destruction—of the Cree homeland. Cree Grand Chief Matthew Coon-Come described this project, initially authorized without consultation with the tribe, as "a terrible and vast reduction of our entire world."[46] Conflicts have also arisen regarding mineral resources. Some indigenous peoples have allowed mineral extraction, seeing it as a way of generating economic development. But this often involves significant spatial and social transformations. The Laguna Pueblo saw its economy completely transformed from agriculture to wage-based mining, and had to live with total reshaping of their geographical environment, as 400 million tons of earth were removed to create an open-pit uranium mine. Though the area has since been reclaimed, it will never return to its natural state, and no one can enter the land because of the continued danger of radiation poisoning.[47] Conversely, the Northern Cheyenne in Montana, who sit atop coal deposits proposed for the largest strip mine in the United States, have refused mining leases to protect their land and air quality.[48] Because of the transformations often involved in resource extraction, I believe there is a (defeasible) presumption that the local community should have the right to control it. Though a people does not *own* their natural resources, the interests in occupancy and self-determination suffice to ground a presumption that they ought to be able to determine the rules that govern their use, development, and exploitation.

As I argued in Chapter 5, under pluralist social conditions, the state ought not to privilege one component culture in society above others in regulating land use. But the above resource policies need not be at odds with this "equal civic status" constraint. When a state nationalizes extractive industries or imposes environmental regulations, it is acting in accordance with a process of political self-determination that is widely valued. Such policies do not privilege one cultural strand in society above others.

Consider next a prohibition on alienation or exploitation of indigenous lands. If the political unit making this decision governs a territory inhabited by a largely homogeneous population, then it is less objectionable for policies to reflect widely shared cultural values about land use. Where all or nearly all

---

[46] Quoted in Colin Calloway, *First Peoples: A Documentary Survey of American Indian History* (Boston: Bedford/Saint Martins, 2007), 539.
[47] Calloway, *First Peoples*, 472.   [48] Calloway, *First Peoples*, 540.

citizens share the same culture, policies that reflect this culture send no invidious or exclusionary message.

Finally, even where an authority governs a pluralist society whose component cultures have quite different conceptions of land use, it need not "strip" its property and land law of all reference to cultural values. Instead, it may regulate some land in accordance with one component culture's preferred values, while regulating other lands to reflect other groups' favored modes of land use. For example, a state may prohibit alienation of indigenous lands, while allowing other lands to be held in full liberal ownership. This affords each component culture roughly equivalent recognition of their preferred place-based practices. So it is possible for a state to enact environmental and resource policies that reflect particular cultural values while still respecting the equal civic status of diverse citizens.

The limited resource-sovereignty principle defended here departs from the permanent sovereignty doctrine in international law in several ways. First, I limit resource sovereignty to *legitimate* political communities that meet the standards of *basic justice* and *collective self-determination* outlined in Chapters 4 and 5. I argued there that to gain the right to rule (including the right to resource sovereignty) a regime must (i) protect certain essential private rights (including security, subsistence, core elements of personal autonomy, and deliberative freedom) for all its subjects, and respect these rights in outsiders, and (ii) it should reflect the shared will of its population as to how, and by whom, they should be ruled. As Leif Wenar stresses, this involves basic conditions for popular accountability, including citizens' access to information, their ability to freely discuss and deliberate about the regime's resource management, and their right to express dissent publicly.[49] Resource sovereignty should not be attributed to whichever regime is effectively able to control a territory.

Second, I hold that substate minorities, as well as states, are morally entitled to resource sovereignty, since they possess the important interests in occupancy and self-determination that ground the right. The UN Declaration on the Rights of Indigenous Peoples, in this vein, declares that states should give recognition to the rights of indigenous peoples over their traditional lands.[50] As I argued in Chapter 5, persistently alienated internal minorities (including indigenous peoples and other permanent minorities) often have moral claims to self-determination. To the extent that sovereignty over natural resources is a corollary of self-determination, internal minorities may claim it. Thus, on my view, "peoples" are the most appropriate subjects of resource sovereignty, though a people's right may sometimes be exercised (e.g., in international negotiations) by the state that legitimately represents them.

---

[49] Wenar, *Blood Oil*, 227–9, 235–8.
[50] Article 24, *UN Declaration on the Rights of Indigenous Peoples*.

Third, I view resource sovereignty as a presumption in favor of the people's *jurisdiction over resources*, which must be carefully distinguished from a claim to national ownership. As Margaret Moore emphasizes, the above arguments apply only to occupied land (and perhaps to ancillary areas, jurisdiction over which is necessary to serve inhabitants, such as coastal waters). These arguments do not ground sovereign control over unoccupied areas, like uninhabited islands, the atmosphere, the Arctic and Antarctic, or the ocean bed. As Moore stresses, these areas are "not really land that anyone lives on and so cannot be viewed as central to the people's collective self-determination."[51] Rights over the earth's unoccupied areas might instead be established by international conventions, in accordance with fair distributive criteria.

Do the interests in occupancy and self-determination ground a right to exclude outsiders from underground mineral deposits, like oil, gas, or coal? That depends on the extent to which these deposits can be extracted without discernable impact on a society's common life. Certain extractive techniques, like open-pit mining or mountaintop removal, have very significant effects on the community. To the extent that extraction would involve such transformations, the community has a moral claim to control it.

Yet in other cases, it may be possible to extract underground resources without affecting a society's common life. Suppose crude oil deposits under a group's territory can be extracted by rigs located on neighboring lands, using minimally invasive techniques with little risk of environmental damage. The interests in occupancy and self-determination do not ground a right to veto extraction in this case. Note that I do not say that the extraction of these resources *should* be allowed, only that the morally significant interests that ground resource sovereignty are not at stake in this question. The decisions about whether to allow exploitation of such resources, to whom to allocate the exploitation rights, and how to share the economic benefits might be determined by international conventions in accordance with fair principles of distributive and environmental justice.

Next, suppose a local community does engage in the extraction of oil, gas, or minerals located within its occupied territory, accepting the potentially transformative impacts this may have. In such a case, I doubt they have a strong claim to the full value this exploitation might generate. As Moore puts it, the arguments from occupancy and self-determination justify "a limited and defeasible right to *control* the rules governing the acquisition, use, and transfer of natural resources ... [not] a right to the full stream of benefit from the resource."[52] To be sure, resource extraction often involves costs (including environmental costs, opportunity costs, and the costs involved in developing the necessary infrastructure). The community may have a claim to be compensated for bearing these costs. But this may fall short of a claim to the full exchange value of their oil, gas, or minerals. Thus,

---

[51] Moore, *A Political Theory of Territory*, 167.   [52] Moore, *A Political Theory of Territory*, 174.

while the right to *decide the disposition* of the resources within their occupied territory is exclusively held by the local community, the right to those resources' *exchange value* may not be. Once a resource is extracted and sold on international commodity markets, (part of) its economic value may be shared with outsiders under fair international conventions.

This limited resource-sovereignty principle is consonant with the account of the right to exclude defended throughout this book. I held in Chapter 3 that occupancy rights ground only a *conditional* claim to exclude others from a space or good insofar as that space or good (i) serves as an essential material support for people's important life activities, (ii) these activities would be set back by a competing use, and (iii) the fair-use proviso is satisfied. Where a space can be used by others without detriment to inhabitants' life activities, or where the fair-use constraint is not satisfied, there is no moral claim to exclude. Chapter 7 applied this account to argue that states may exclude migrants only in cases when their entry would cause harm to local inhabitants. My account of resource sovereignty builds on this view, holding that peoples can exclude outsiders from natural resources only where their interests in occupancy and collective self-determination would be impaired by a competing use. This limited right to exclude does not extend to the full material value of the resources: the shape and scope of rights to this exchange value depend on justified international conventions.

What distributive criteria might guide the establishment of such conventions? As noted in the introduction, I will not attempt to defend a theory of global distributive justice in this book. While many resource cosmopolitans appeal to the luck egalitarian view that justice requires mitigating undeserved advantages, I note that this is controversial and need not be the only distributive criterion on which fair international conventions could be based. Other theorists defend sufficientarian accounts of justice. Still others embrace instrumental or relational egalitarianism, holding that while distributive inequality is not bad in itself, it should be corrected where it has negative consequences for other important values.

For the moment, I bracket these debates to sketch a distributive proposal broadly in line with the proviso defended in Chapter 6. On this proposal, the economic benefits from natural resources should be distributed so as to (i) satisfy everyone's basic territorial interests and (ii) to ensure that groups with shared place-based aims have a territorial base in which to pursue these aims. Guaranteeing basic territorial interests would mandate the provision of subsistence resources to everyone around the globe. Along these lines, Thomas Pogge proposes a global resource dividend (GRD), which would require countries to pay a surcharge on the extraction and sale of oil or minerals, with the proceeds to be used to finance global poverty relief.[53] Securing groups with shared place-based aims have a territorial

---

[53] Pogge, "An Egalitarian Law of Peoples," *Philosophy & Public Affairs* 23, no. 3 (1994): 195–224; *World Poverty and Human Rights* (Cambridge: Polity, 2008), ch. 8.

base involves duties to help maintain others' territories in the face of threats arising from nature (e.g., volcanoes, earthquakes, or hurricanes) or human actions for which the group is not responsible (such as the displacement pressures on small island nations from climate change). Global resource taxes might therefore finance not only poverty relief, but also the infrastructure (e.g., levees, earthquake resistant buildings, desalination plants, and so on) necessary to afford people an opportunity to stay in their territory and to maintain it.

I will not here attempt to vindicate this distributive proposal against possible alternatives. Instead, I simply highlight the crucial point that limited resource sovereignty is compatible with some global redistribution of the economic value of the world's natural resources. The morally significant interests that ground resource sovereignty are not infringed by international arrangements to more fairly share the value of these resources, so long as these arrangements are established by legitimate means (e.g., through multilateral treaty), and so long as they ensure that the domestic community has the right to make "decisions about whether or how natural resources are to be used."[54] Proposals like Pogge's GRD would tax the proceeds from the exploitation of natural resources without touching jurisdictional control over them, or interfering with decisions concerning their development and use. Since the limited resource-sovereignty principle is a principle of *jurisdiction*, not ownership, it is perfectly compatible with this program of cosmopolitan reform.[55]

Let me now consider two objections. First, in potentially excluding oil, gas, and other underground deposits from resource sovereignty's scope, one might object that I have moved very far from what the anticolonial framers of Resolution 1803 had in mind. They were concerned to ensure that the income streams from their natural resources would be devoted to their own societies' advancement, not siphoned off for the benefit of their former colonizers. As Wenar argues, we might imagine:

> being a citizen inside a former colony such as Algeria or Indonesia or Zimbabwe, where the national identity hardened in bloody struggles to wrestle national territory and its resource wealth away from relentless empires that clothed their exploitation in the colors of morality. Westerners now come to you saying that you do not entirely own your country's resources, because the British and French, the Dutch and the Japanese, and even the Americans partly own them too.[56]

Does the limited resource-sovereignty principle give short shrift to anticolonial claims? In response, I agree that postcolonial states are not morally required to share the economic value of their natural resources with their former colonizers (though they may have a duty to share with other societies disadvantaged by

---

[54] Pogge, *World Poverty and Human Rights*, 197.
[55] For a similar argument, see Moore, *A Political Theory of Territory*, 174.
[56] Wenar, *Blood Oil*, 348.

colonialism). However, this is not because there is a general right to national resource ownership. Instead, I believe there is a remedial right on the part of formerly colonized countries to enjoy the economic benefits from their resources on a *pro tem* basis. This is part of their broader claim to reparation for the exploitation and political domination they have historically suffered.[57] Considerations of corrective justice thus tell in favor of exempting former postcolonial societies from any effort to share the material value of the world's resources, at least for some period of time. Resource sovereignty as jurisdiction, however, is a general right that accrues to all societies, whether or not they have been historically disadvantaged.

A second objection holds that national ownership can be *derived* from resource jurisdiction: one cannot have one without the other. If the people has the authority to create property rights in their resources, then it must be considered the ultimate owner of these resources. Leif Wenar argues for this conclusion as follows:

(1) To have sovereignty is to have jurisdiction: the right to authorize laws within a territory.

(2) One dimension of territorial jurisdiction is the right to authorize property laws.

(3) This includes the right to authorize laws for natural resources, creating a regime of property rights to govern these resources.

(4) If the sovereign has the right to create any property rights it chooses over resources, then ownership of those resources is originally vested in it.[58]

This argument confuses claims of legitimate authority with claims of ownership. It is true that only a self-governing people has the right to set property rules within its territory, including rules governing natural resources. So long as the people meet the criteria for legitimacy outlined above, they cannot be *coerced* (e.g., by a foreign power or international body) to share the value of their resources. The importance of respecting the members of that society as rational deliberators—who can reason for themselves how to govern their common life—gives outsiders a duty to refrain from interfering in their property laws, even when those laws depart to some degree from substantive justice.

Yet, as I have stressed throughout, legitimacy and justice are distinct values. Even if the choice is up to them, citizens should still ask: what resource policy do we have most reason to adopt? In the domestic case, for example, many argue that it would be unjust for a people to adopt a set of property laws that enables substantial inequalities of income, wealth, and opportunity. In so arguing, they are not implying that some other agent besides the people (e.g., a foreign state) has

---

[57] Beitz defends the Permanent Sovereignty principle along similar lines. See *Political Theory and International Relations*, 142, n. 31.
[58] For this argument, see Wenar, *Blood Oil*, 202–3.

the authority to decide their property rules. Instead, they are putting forward a view about what the people *should* decide. Likewise, even if the people may authorize property laws for their natural resources, it may be unjust for them to refuse to share the economic benefits of these resources, if they have no strong moral claim to their full value.

As noted in Chapter 5, this distinction between legitimacy and justice can sometimes give a people "a right to do wrong."[59] Suppose our democratically enacted tax laws charge me more than is just.[60] Still, these tax laws are legitimate and can be permissibly enforced: both the state's members and outsiders have a duty not to interfere with the state's implementation of them. One might object here that "a right to do wrong" may be acceptable with respect to the *members* of a community, but that it cannot justify wrongs to outsiders (as occurs when a legitimate state refuses entry to harmless migrants, for example, or hoards the value of its natural resources). When wrongs to outsiders jeopardize their *fundamental territorial interests*, I agree that this may render external interference permissible, and I say more about this below. But not every departure from ideal justice triggers a permission to interfere. We should refrain from interfering with some wrongful choices to protect the community members' ability to govern their common life in the light of their values.

In sum, I believe a justified system of international conventions should afford local communities the right to control and manage natural resources when those resources are essential to their common life. This limited principle of resource sovereignty is compatible with globally taxing the extraction and sale of resources, so long as the conventions imposing the tax are legitimately established (e.g., through multilateral treaty), and the local community retains the right to set rules governing these extractions and sales. The limited resource-sovereignty principle, however, does not say anything about jurisdiction over unoccupied areas or over underground deposits that can be extracted with no impact on a society's common life. Resource rights in these areas are fully conventional, and might be determined by international agreement, in accordance with fair distributive criteria.

8.4 Duties of Cooperation and Comanagement

Suppose this argument for a presumption of domestic jurisdiction over resources succeeds. Still, resource sovereignty may be subject to further moral constraints. These constraints arise from the claims of outsiders who are especially reliant on

---

[59] See Jeremy Waldron, *Liberal Rights, Collected Papers* 1981–1991 (Cambridge: Cambridge University Press, 1993), ch. 3. For a contrasting view, see Gerhard Overland and Christian Barry, "Do Democratic Societies Have a Right to Do Wrong?" *Journal of Social Philosophy*, 42, no. 2 (2011): 111–31.

[60] Estlund, *Democratic Authority*, 8.

particular resources, and whose fundamental territorial interests could be harmed by certain uses of them. Where there are very strong competing interests with respect to a resource, occupancy and self-determination may not ground an all-things-considered entitlement to manage it domestically. In other words, there may be important *qualifications* even to the limited principle of resource sovereignty. This section argues that in the case of certain *global systemic resources*, resource sovereignty is further constrained by duties of environmental justice that require cooperation in international institutions. Following Mancilla, I define a "global systemic resource" as an area that "provide[s] key water or ecosystem services, or help[s] to regulate the climate system, such that [its] loss would greatly jeopardize the lives of human beings on earth."[61]

We might think of the carbon-assimilation capacity of the earth's forests as such a global systemic resource. All humans depend upon the earth's climate-servicing systems, of which forest carbon sinks are an important part. (It is estimated that forests have taken up about 25 percent of human-produced carbon dioxide in the past 15 years.)[62] If these forests were suddenly depleted or destroyed, many people distant from the resource would be exposed to serious harm, such as the loss of their homes because of sea-level rise, or the loss of their lands or livelihoods owing to desertification.

Yet forest carbon sinks are also situated within the occupied territories of self-determining groups. Many indigenous peoples depend on forests for their residence and livelihood, and their cultures and ways of life have been shaped by the forest's climate and landscape. Some control over forest areas is an enabling condition of their self-determination, and of the self-determination of the larger states of which they are a part. The choice of how to manage and use these forests, whether to allow some development of them, what conservation strategies to pursue (whether to sell them to private land trusts, create national parks, encourage ecotourism, etc.) will have significant effects on these communities' shape and character.

This gives rise to three important questions:

(1) Do peoples whose territories contain forest carbon sinks have a duty to take into account the interests of outsiders (and future generations) when managing their forests?[63]

---

[61] I borrow this term from Mancilla. See Mancilla, "Rethinking Land and Natural Resources, and Rights over Them," 138. Forests are but one of many potential examples of systemic resources. Others include fish stocks, groundwater basins, and migratory species. I focus on forests for simplicity, assuming that the principles that should regulate them could be extended to further cases.

[62] Blomfield, "Global Common Resources and the Just Distribution of Emission Shares," 290–1.

[63] I believe that there are duties to take into account the interests of future generations by conserving resources. However, since there are important philosophical problems in establishing a specific conservation standard, I refrain from more concretely specifying these duties here.

(2) Do these peoples have a duty to cooperate in establishing multilateral or supranational agencies that might impartially interpret, specify, and apply these environmental justice duties with respect to their forests?

(3) Can peoples who do not voluntarily cooperate in establishing such multilateral or supranational agencies be forced by external agents (such as other peoples, or perhaps the agency itself) to comply?

I believe peoples do have duties to take into account the interests of outsiders in managing their forests. To some extent, these duties of environmental justice are already recognized in international law.[64] Notwithstanding its occasional characterization as a state's right to do whatever it wants with its natural resources, permanent sovereignty is constrained by the duty not to cause transboundary harm. This duty was recognized as early as 1941, when an Arbitral Tribunal ruled in the *Trail Smelter* case that "no State has the right to use or permit the use of its territory in such a manner as to cause injury... in or to the territory of another or the properties or persons therein, when the case is of serious consequence and the injury is established by clear and convincing evidence."[65] Principle 21 of the 1972 Stockholm Declaration on the Human Environment reiterates this "responsibility to ensure that activities within their jurisdiction or control do not cause damage to the environment of other States or of areas beyond the limits of national jurisdiction."[66]

One difficulty here is with determining what counts as relevant "harm," "injury," or "damage." If every resource management decision is subject to transnational regulation, then peoples will lack self-determination over their resources, since almost every choice affects outsiders in some way. I argue that there is a duty to consider the interests of outsiders in decisions concerning natural resources only when the use of those specific resources significantly impacts their *fundamental territorial interests*. As outlined in Chapter 6, these are:

(1) *Material Interests*: in using the earth's spaces and resources to procure adequate food, water, clean air, shelter, health, subsistence, and a livable environment;

---

[64] Schrijver also associates permanent sovereignty with duties, including (i) the duty to ensure that the whole population benefits from resource exploitation, (ii) the duty to have due care for the environment, (iii) the duty to recognize the rights of other states to transboundary resources and to consult with them regarding the use of those resources, and (iv) the duty to fulfill international obligations (e.g., through compensation for taking of property). See Schrijver, *Sovereignty over Natural Resources*, 391–2.

[65] "Trail Smelter Arbitration" (*United States v. Canada*). See Franz Perrez, "The Relationship between 'Permanent Sovereignty' and the Obligation not to Cause Transboundary Environmental Damage," *Environmental Law* 26, no.4 (1996): 1189.

[66] *Declaration of the United Nations Conference on the Human Environment*, Report of the United Nations Conference on the Human Environment (June 1972).

(2) *Located Life Plans*: interests in using specific areas as a stable site for personal relationships and valued social, cultural, and economic practices;

(3) *Basic Justice*: interests in minimally just state institutions that can protect basic rights. This includes an interest in protection from actions that might undermine or destabilize state institutions, or erode their capacity.

(4) *Self-Determination*: interests in using territory to shape a political and economic system that reflects a people's shared values and priorities.

Where fundamental territorial interests are *not* significantly impacted, resource management decisions need not be accountable to the interests of outsiders. Why not? An important aim of a just global system, as I argued in Chapter 6, should be to grant different political communities a fair opportunity to freely determine their own political institutions and to pursue the place-based practices that matter to them. This means societies must dispose of some important domain of choice regarding the shape of their common life. Societies will not dispose of this domain of choice if every resource management decision is held accountable to the interests of outsiders.

Suppose the Navajo Nation is considering whether to designate an area of its land as a protected park. Various non-Navajo interests are at stake in this decision: the potential profits of mining companies that might otherwise exploit the uranium deposits located there, and the employment opportunities of local New Mexicans who might be hired by these mining companies. Nevertheless, the Navajo Nation is not required to take into account these particular interests when deciding this question. The Navajos should be free from the duty to consider interests of this kind, because of the importance of preserving a protected space for its members to shape their own political institutions and to pursue the place-based practices that matter to them.

This does not mean the Navajo Nation is *always* free to refrain from considering outsider interests. The Navajos' sphere of discretion is a limited one. There are two kinds of limits to it. One type of limit is a *morally binding*, though *unenforceable* constraint on self-determination. I have argued that peoples have a duty of justice not to favor one cultural strand in society over others, to allow harmless migration, and to fairly share the economic value of their natural resources. Nonetheless, if a people wrongly chooses to privilege the majority culture, to exclude harmless migrants, or to hoard the profits from their resources, they may not be forced by outsiders to refrain. Because of the importance of their members' interests in political autonomy, I believe that self-determining peoples, like self-determining individuals, sometimes have a "right to do wrong." An individual is permitted to make a wide range of decisions regarding the shape of her life, but she has a moral duty not to lie, not to break her promises, and not to be unkind to others. When considering her domain of choice, she ought to view options that involve deception, promise breaking, and spitefulness as morally "off the table."

Yet if an individual *does* lie, act unkindly, or break a promise, her liberty may not be interfered with. We protect her liberty in these wrongful choices because of the importance of allowing her an independent domain in which to shape her life in the light of her values. Similarly, legitimate peoples should be allowed to govern themselves independently—even when the laws they enact depart to some degree from ideal justice—because their members have morally significant *political autonomy* interests in shaping their collective life on the basis of their own sense of justice. Though unjust, a people's decisions may still be legitimate, and so worthy of respect by outsiders. Instead, we should *persuade* self-determining peoples to endorse cultural neutrality, to admit harmless migrants, and to fairly share their resources, rather than imposing these policies coercively.

Finally, there are also *morally binding, enforceable* limits to self-determination. These enforceable limits are grounded in the requirement to respect the equal self-determination of others. The choice to violate another individual's body or property rights, or to deny her a fair share of opportunity to shape her own life, is not one a self-determining individual is permitted to make. If she does make such a choice, other individuals or the state are entitled to uphold others' sphere of self-determination against her, through coercive force if necessary. Likewise, a legitimate people's sphere of discretion is limited by an enforceable duty to respect the personal and political autonomy interests of members of other societies. It is these limits that my account of fundamental territorial interests, outlined in Chapter 6, are meant to specify. These are cases where a people's decisions not only *affect* outsiders, but risk undermining their opportunity to maintain minimally just political institutions, pursue located life plans, and exercise self-determination. In such cases, the former people is (i) accountable to fundamental territorial interests of these outsiders in its decisions, and (ii) may be required to respect those interests, by coercive means if necessary. Where the use and exploitation of a resource within one group's territory poses a significant threat to the fundamental territorial interests of outsiders who live in another part of the world, I believe these outsiders have an enforceable claim that their interests be taken into account in the management of this resource.[67]

In the case of forests, this is not merely a duty to consider outsiders' interests in good faith, but also a duty to cooperate in establishing international institutions that can promulgate specific duties and policies with respect to forest management, and adjudicate conflicts regarding forests. Why are international institutions necessary, not just a good-faith effort to avoid harm? As Cara Nine emphasizes, in complex cases of mutual dependence on a resource—like forest carbon sinks—what exactly the duty not to cause transboundary harm involves will not always be obvious or transparent upon reflection, but instead requires continual institutional

---

[67] For a similar account, see Iris Marion Young, *Global Challenges* (Cambridge: Polity, 2007), 39–57.

specification. Nine gives the example of shared river catchments, where the "natural features of the river create conditions of ongoing, high stakes mutual effects."[68] People disagree about the precise interpretation of fundamental territorial interests and their weight, as well as about which of many possible schemes of rules for protecting them should be preferred. Since outsiders' fundamental territorial interests are dependent in pervasive ways on decisions regarding the resource, and since groups' plans and priorities with respect to the resource shift over time, managing the resource requires a framework for authoritative decision-making.[69] Protecting fundamental territorial interests also requires sufficient assurance that other agents will do their part of complying with whatever management policies are chosen. In these cases, Nine argues, peoples "should form joint political structures to achieve joint self-determination over the resource."[70]

How might joint resource management be constituted in our central case of forest carbon sinks? International cooperation in this central case might take a variety of forms. Here I sketch one approach that I believe may be reasonably accessible from the status quo, and that can be defended against claims that it unreasonably constrains a society's interest in self-determination. On my proposed approach, peoples have a duty to cooperate in establishing, through multilateral treaty, (i) a set of "baseline" international policies regarding forest use and management and (ii) an international comanagement agency with its own organs and structures that can oversee decisions regarding specific forests.

The forest management "baseline" should be determined as part of a broader climate-mitigation treaty that would set out national targets for both forest conservation and carbon emissions, which, taken together, could avoid destabilizing the global climate. While there is some controversy about what constitutes dangerous climate change, for the sake of argument, I adopt the goal laid out in the Paris Climate Change Treaty: avoiding a global temperature rise in excess of 2 degrees Celsius. To achieve this, a mix of national emissions targets and forest conservation policies must be agreed. Since states can increase or decrease the overall global "greenhouse gas budget" through afforestation and forest degradation, emissions targets and forest policies should be negotiated as a package. Once negotiated, the "baseline" would establish a point from which future negotiations with the international comanagement agency regarding specific forests can begin. In the absence of an international management plan, a country should not depart from its target rates of logging, mining, and other forms of forest degradation, since doing so would jeopardize others' fundamental territorial interests.

In determining the baseline, it may be politically expedient for developed countries averse to undertaking emissions reductions to push for very stringent

---

[68] Nine, "When Affected Interests Demand Joint Self-Determination: Learning from Rivers," *International Theory* 6, no. 1 (2014): 162.
[69] Nine, "When Affected Interests Demand Joint Self-Determination," 158.
[70] Nine, "When Affected Interests Demand Joint Self-Determination," 164.

forest conservation standards, especially in the developing world. But I believe developing countries have a right to resist this, since they have a variety of important interests in forest use besides conservation. This includes the use of forests for traditional cultural and recreational practices, the customary land-tenure rights of indigenous and local peoples, and a variety of subsistence practices involving forests, like hunting and fuel harvesting. Developing countries also have an important interest in developing economically to the level at which they can guarantee their citizens a decent life.[71] Allowing timber, agricultural, or mining industries to exploit their forests may be their best strategy for achieving this. Since developing countries have an urgent interest in securing basic justice for their citizens, I believe they could permissibly decline to cooperate in any forest management agreement that jeopardized their right to develop, e.g., by requiring them to refrain from exploiting their forests without sufficient compensation.

For these reasons, a defensible "baseline" arrangement would grant both developed and developing peoples a right to use forests for traditional cultural and religious practices, and to meet the residential and subsistence needs of local inhabitants. But the baseline should refuse *developed* countries any right to engage in the economic exploitation of forests beyond this, unless they can show that they have undertaken other emissions-reduction measures that would offset the carbon released through deforestation. *Developing* countries, on the other hand, should be granted a prima facie right to engage in the exploitation of their forests to the extent necessary for them to develop. (An important caveat here is that there may be better strategies for economic development that would not involve forest degradation, so developing countries may be obliged to show that they cannot pursue these alternatives.) A developing country will have a duty to refrain from exploiting its forests only if it is provided sufficient compensation to cover its opportunity costs in terms of forgone economic development, as well as compensation for the direct costs of forest protection.[72]

Developed countries have a collective duty to compensate developing countries for protecting their forests, sharing the burden of financing forest conservation in the developing world. Though a variety of principles have been advanced within the climate-justice literature as to how these burdens might fairly be allocated, I will not attempt here to set out what a fully just distribution of compensatory burdens would look like.[73] This is because, in my view, it is not appropriate to

---

[71] Henry Shue, "Subsistence Emissions and Luxury Emissions," *Law and Policy*, 15, no. 1 (1993): 39–60.
[72] Armstrong, *Justice and Natural Resources*, ch. 10; "Fairness, Free-riding, and Rainforest Protection," *Political Theory* 44, no. 1 (2016): 106–30.
[73] For relevant discussion, see Simon Caney, "Cosmopolitan Justice, Responsibility, and Global Climate Change," *Leiden Journal of International Law*, 18, no. 4 (2005): 747–75; David Miller, "Global Justice and Climate Change," *The Tanner Lectures on Human Values* (2008); Darrel Moellendorf, *The Moral Challenge of Dangerous Climate Change* (Cambridge: Cambridge University Press, 2014), ch. 6; Vanderheiden, *Atmospheric Justice*.

condition the duty to cooperate in a forest conservation treaty on its setting up a perfectly just arrangement. Consider a domestic analogy: suppose someone thinks that basic health care for all citizens is a demand of justice and that the most just scheme is a single-payer system. Still, I believe she should contribute her tax dollars to Obamacare, even though it is not ideally just by her lights, simply because doing justice to others requires settling on and abiding by a common view of what justice requires amid reasonable disagreement about that ideal.

I suggest we should reason analogously in the international case. The duty to cooperate in transnational forest management is not contingent on the establishment of a perfectly just scheme. Instead, peoples will have a duty to cooperate in a forest conservation treaty (while perhaps also working to change it) so long as it meets a lower standard of *minimal justice*. A minimally just conservation treaty would (i) produce an agreement that avoids catastrophic climate impacts from deforestation, while (ii) securing impoverished countries' right to develop, (iii) not imposing crippling financial burdens on any specific developed country, and (iv) preventing free riding. A treaty may meet these minimal conditions while still not achieving perfect fairness. If it does, I believe countries will have a duty to cooperate in carrying it out, while perhaps also working to replace it with an even fairer scheme.

A forest conservation treaty should also set up an international comanagement agency that could serve as a clearinghouse for channeling compensation funds to developing countries that successfully conserve their forests, for auditing compliance, and for identifying and publicizing defaulters. Once the baseline is agreed, any departures from it with respect to how a given forest is managed would need to be negotiated between the people claiming resource sovereignty over that specific forest and the international comanagement agency. For example, the comanagement agency might offer to compensate a country for undertaking additional conservation measures not included in the baseline, through afforestation or the prohibition of certain previously permitted exploitative activities. The agency could solicit contributions from developed states to compensate the target group for the costs of undertaking these additional changes, further incentivizing it to conserve. A people that wants to exploit its forests in a new or hitherto prohibited manner could negotiate with the comanagement agency for an agreement to do so, e.g., by showing that this use will not lead to degradation, or by making concessions on other forms of exploitation previously allowed. The main idea is that no change in disposition of a specific forest should go forward without the consent of *both* the international comanagement agency and the people claiming permanent sovereignty over that specific forest.

Along with agreeing a "baseline" and constituting a comanagement agency, a forest conservation treaty should set out criteria for the fair distribution of forest sequestration capacity, which would balance the claims of local people with those of foreigners. One way of compensating locals for their opportunity and conservation costs is to afford them significant economic rights in the carbon sink capacity created by their decision to conserve. This may include the right to sell carbon-sequestration rights on global markets and retain the proceeds. (In cases where these rights are not sufficient to cover the costs of forgone economic development, they may have to be supplemented by additional compensation measures, as argued above.)

Yet foreigners also have an interest in equitable access to sink capacity, especially because counties are entitled to sufficient emissions to guarantee a decent life for their citizens, and because some countries lack the appropriate climactic conditions to create forest sinks of their own. A distributive duty that ensures minimum carbon-sequestration entitlements for impoverished countries might be an appropriate way to balance these claims. This would essentially levy a global resource tax on forest carbon-sequestration capacity, redistributing the proceeds to provide a guarantee of subsistence emissions for the globally disadvantaged.

Once a minimally just agreement on forest management is reached, a degree of coercion will likely be required to provide assurance of compliance and to stabilize the transnational cooperative scheme. A people might agree to this scheme at the moment of its creation, but the balance of political forces could change over time, leading it to withdraw cooperation at a later point. States that do not comply with a multilateral forest arrangement should, in my view, be excluded from the advantages of international cooperation. This will involve denying states that defect from the treaty diplomatic recognition or membership in international organizations, imposing tariffs and trade restrictions in response to infractions, freezing assets, reducing foreign aid, and so on. These are all enforcement measures that states can undertake "horizontally," without instituting any central monopoly of force. Similar coercive measures may also be necessary to provide nonparticipating states an incentive to "sign on" to the arrangement. Along these lines, William Nordhaus recommends a set of "climate amendments" to international trade law that would levy a uniform percentage tariff on goods from countries that refuse to participate in a climate treaty. He suggests that even a relatively low tariff rate is likely to induce high participation in a climate regime.[74]

To the extent that such coercive measures are designed to secure fundamental territorial interests, I believe they are appropriate, despite the general presumption against international coercion. Arguably, this kind of horizontal sanctioning can be seen as a form of coordinated self-defense. When the fundamental territorial interests of a state's citizens are threatened through aggressive military force, it is appropriate for that state to retaliate defensively, and to coordinate with other states in repelling an attack. But states may face equivalent threats to its citizens' fundamental territorial interests that proceed through indirect means—such as

---

[74] Nordhaus, "Climate Clubs: Overcoming Free Riding in International Climate Policy," *American Economic Review* 105, no. 4 (2015): 1341.

extensive deforestation in some other part of the world. Here it seems to me equally appropriate for a state to retaliate defensively, and to coordinate proportionate measures with other states.

Thus, if compliance with an international forest management scheme can be made an effective condition of access to the benefits of international cooperation—including trading relations and membership in international organizations—the incentive to "sign on" in the first place, and for signatories not to defect afterward, will be considerable. I believe there are important historical grounds for optimism about the effectiveness of such horizontal sanctioning measures. It is through mechanisms like these that most significant international reforms, including the obligation to respect human rights, the prohibition on aggressive war, the ban on CFCs damaging the ozone layer, and international free trade, have been brought about so far. States have voluntarily imposed these responsibilities on themselves, through acts of multilateral "self-binding." They have also enforced these agreements themselves, through countermeasures to discourage defection. Similar practices of multilateral restraint—in which states come together to jointly determine principles of forest management, and each state contributes to the enforcement of these principles—could address challenges of ecological sustainability and conservation.

8.5 Conclusion

In sum, I have argued that in the case of certain *global systemic resources*—the loss or degradation of which would jeopardize people's fundamental territorial interests—resource sovereignty must be constrained by duties of environmental justice that require cooperation in international institutions. This argument is similar to the one put forward in Chapter 6, where I held that the states system must impose a fair-use proviso on the distribution of territory, which prohibits states from excluding migrants whose fundamental territorial interests are threatened. In each case, respecting others as coowners of the earth grounds enforceable duties to secure their fundamental territorial interests. As with duties of environmental justice, I believe these duties to refugees require institutionalization in the form of a more robust international migratory regime, which might be pursued through means similar to the forest management scheme outlined above.

I also defended an alternative resource-sovereignty principle, different from the permanent sovereignty doctrine as it exists in international law. My alternative principle is primarily about jurisdiction, not ownership: it is a right to control resource management decisions. As such, it confers only a conditional claim to exclude outsiders from natural resources in cases where their use would threaten morally significant interests in occupancy and self-determination. Finally, resource sovereignty, in my view, does not confer a right to the full exchange value of the natural resources situated within a people's territory: the shape and scope of rights to this economic value depend on justified international conventions.

Yet unlike Armstrong and other resource cosmopolitans, I believe it is morally important to retain a limited principle of resource sovereignty, rather than abandoning the idea altogether. A limited resource-sovereignty principle can play a valuable role in safeguarding the distinctive interests of self-determining groups in their land and resources. Indeed, it may prove especially important to retain such a principle as part of new efforts to combat climate change. To see why, consider some problems that have been involved in the UN's Reduced Emissions for Deforestation and Forest Degradation Program (REDD+), established in 2008 as a partnership between developed and developing states to enhance forest sustainability. This program is a carbon-offset initiative in which developed countries and individuals pay to use the carbon-sequestration capacity of forests in the developing world to offset their emissions. Forest carbon credits are traded on carbon markets, either official compliance markets associated with the 2015 Paris Climate Agreement or voluntary private markets for individuals and institutions interested in reducing their emissions for reasons of philanthropy and corporate social responsibility. Sellers of carbon credits acquire land for large-scale forestry projects, often in the developing world: Latin America is currently the largest supplier of carbon credits, with Asia and Africa active as well.[75]

While REDD+ is often marketed as a "win-win" program for climate change mitigation and for impoverished local communities, in practice, critics have challenged the way the program has been implemented. In 2010, the New Forests Company, a UK-based conservation organization, was charged with evicting over 20,000 people from their homes to make way for its carbon forest plantations. The evicted people had lived in the area for decades under various forms of customary land tenure, but they did not have registered individual titles.[76] Other REDD+ projects have drawn hard boundaries around forests that local people have traditionally relied upon for subsistence, jeopardizing their livelihoods. African villagers blockaded access roads to Mt. Kilimanjaro to protest their violent exclusion by armed park rangers protecting one REDD+ project.[77] Finally, many REDD+ projects have been undertaken without deliberation with the local population and without securing their prior free and informed consent to the project. Carbon-offset projects are often complex and difficult to explain to local people unfamiliar with climate change and carbon markets; they sometimes become

[75] Albert Arhin and Joanes Atela, "Forest Carbon Projects and Policies in Africa," in *Carbon Conflicts and Forest Landscapes in Africa*, edited by Melissa Leach and Ian Scoones (Oxford: Routledge, 2015), 43–57.
[76] Matt Grainger and Kate Geary, "The New Forests Company and Its Uganda Plantations," Oxfam International (2011).
[77] Martin Kijazi, "Climate Emergency, Carbon Capture and Coercive Conservation on Mt. Kilimanjaro," in *Carbon Conflicts and Forest Landscapes in Africa*, edited by Melissa Leach and Ian Scoones (Oxford: Routledge, 2015), 58–79.

aware of these projects only when the land around them is suddenly enclosed by an international conservation agency.[78]

Examples like these have led REDD+ to be criticized in some quarters as a form of "green grabbing": the appropriation of land for international environmental ends to the detriment of the local community.[79] Green grabs involve the transfer of resources from the poor and marginalized to the rich and powerful, in ways that re-entrench severe social inequalities. Such land grabs are argued to impose the "top-down" agendas of the affluent residents of the Global North at the expense of the concerns of residents of the Global South, including their land-tenure rights, food security, and cultural traditions.

Not all REDD+ projects constitute "green grabs," nor do I think international forest management must take this form. But where REDD+ projects have been more successful, it is because they build in important forms of recognition for peoples' resource sovereignty, allowing them significant control over conservation decisions. REDD+ projects differ in their design and implementation, and some have given local actors considerable autonomy in rule making and management. Successful programs have worked to strengthen, rather than weaken, community land tenure; involved democratically elected committees that represent the local inhabitants; and implemented mechanisms to share the profits from marketing carbon offsets. According to a local village elder, one REDD+ project in Kenya, so designed, should be seen as "for the people and with the people."[80]

Examples like these, I believe, give us reason to be skeptical of proposals that would eliminate or override peoples' resource sovereignty altogether. A limited resource-sovereignty principle, which grants legitimate peoples the right to decide the disposition of their natural resources, can play an important role in safeguarding many indigenous and postcolonial societies against global power inequalities. For that reason, even in the age of the Anthropocene, the idea of resource sovereignty is not outdated.

---

[78] Mucahid Bayrak and Lawal Marafa, "Ten Years of REDD+: A Critical Review of the Impact of REDD+ on Forest-Dependent Communities," *Sustainability* 8, no. 7 (2016): 620.

[79] James Fairhead, Melissa Leach, and Ian Scoones, "Green Grabbing: A New Appropriation of Nature?" *Journal of Peasant Studies* 39, no. 2 (2012): 237–61.

[80] Joanes Atela, "Carbon in Africa's Agricultural Landscapes: A Kenyan Case," in *Carbon Conflicts and Forest Landscapes in Africa*, edited by Melissa Leach and Ian Scoones (Oxford: Routledge, 2015), 121.

9
Conclusion: Territorial Sovereignty and Global Institutions

This book has offered a qualified defense of a territorial states system. Though I have argued for reforms to our current international order, I also held that important aspects of it—including the central structuring role played by jurisdictional boundaries—can be morally defended. Three core values, in my view, are served by an international system made up of self-governing, spatially defined political units.

The first core value is the *right of occupancy*. I argued that an important aim of a just international system is to protect people's claims to the regions they not unjustly occupy. Occupancy is a right to reside permanently in a particular geographical space and to make use of that area for social, cultural, and economic practices. It also includes a claim-right not to be removed from the area, to be allowed to return if one leaves or is expelled, and not to have one's use of that space interfered with in ways that undermine the located practices in which one is engaged. I argued that occupancy rights are grounded in the role that geographical places often play in individuals' central life plans, and in their interest in controlling and revising their commitments to these plans.

Yet I also held that the right of occupancy is limited. First, I suggested that we should understand occupancy as a primitive use-right, not a full property claim. Occupancy confers a more limited claim to exclude than a full property right, and it does not extend to powers of contractual transfer, like the right to alienate, loan, bequeath, and derive income. Second, I also rejected the view that occupancy can be passed down perpetually through generations. Unlike property rights, I held that occupancy claims do not depend on a "clean" chain of historical title. While wrongdoers will typically lack occupancy rights, their descendants may rightfully occupy the area, though first-generation (and sometimes second- or third-generation) expellees may have claims to return. Present-day occupancy can therefore legitimate states' territorial claims even if it is in part the legacy of historic dispossession.

Part II turned to the question of how a state might acquire legitimate jurisdiction over a population of rightful occupants. I argued that a state will have a right to rule a group and its territory if it satisfies the second and third core values that underpin the states system: *basic justice* and *collective self-determination*. To rightfully wield political power, a state must protect certain essential private rights—including security, subsistence, core elements of personal autonomy, and deliberative freedom—for all its subjects, and respect these rights for outsiders. In addition, a legitimate state's institutions must reflect the shared political will of a significant majority of cooperators on its territory. A group shares a political will when they are jointly committed to a common political enterprise, and to certain values and procedures by which they believe their enterprise should be structured. I argued that collective self-determination is morally important because it serves individuals' interests in *political autonomy*—in being ruled by a state that reflects their judgments and priorities. This includes interests in *nonalienation*, in not relating to the state as a hostile, dominating agency, and in *self-direction*, in acting independently to comply with a political order they can affirm. Though political autonomy is ultimately an interest of individuals, I held that it can be furthered by an individual's membership in a self-determining group, if she affirms her participation in that group and accepts the higher-order values and procedures that structure it.

Because of the importance of self-determination, I argued that groups with common priorities ought to be allowed to govern themselves, insofar as this is consistent with maintaining a stable, minimally just structure of authority. Yet while self-determination plays a crucial role in justifying a decentralized and pluralistic international order, our current states system does not fully realize this ideal. To live up to its legitimating principles, I argued that the states system must do more to recognize the self-determination of persistently alienated internal minorities. The decision whether to recognize minority self-determination claims should not be seen as a purely internal matter. Instead, the international community should intervene in proportionate ways to require member states to grant their minorities autonomous institutions.

Finally, I distinguished my own account of collective self-determination from the one put forward by liberal nationalists. On my view, the value of collective self-determination does not derive from the importance of promoting or protecting national culture(s). In modern pluralist societies, I held that it is unjust for a dominant national group to organize political institutions in ways that preferentially privilege its own history and culture to the exclusion of cultures valued by citizens of different nationalities. This sends the invidious message that political institutions "belong" in a special way to that national group, devaluing those who do not share their identity. My "equal civic status" constraint does not require the state to relegate culture entirely to the private sphere. But it does mean that when government provides valued cultural goods, or supports culture in various ways, it has strong reason to do so in a manner that does not unequally privilege one or more component cultures in society over others. I argued that instead of "nation building," a just state should foster a common commitment to a shared political endeavor that recognizes and affirms the distinctiveness of various minorities.

Finally, Parts III and IV of this book argued that the exclusionary sovereignty rights that can plausibly be justified on the basis of the three core values do not extend to the full complement of claims states currently make. My defense of the territorial state is therefore a qualified one: it does not actually justify the full set of sovereign rights that states now claim, and that are recognized under international law. Instead, I suggest that we ought to work to institutionalize additional limits to sovereignty, significantly qualifying states' exclusionary prerogatives.

Two kinds of limit were discussed. First, there are *morally binding* but *unenforceable* duties of justice, including the duty of cultural neutrality, the duty not to exclude migrants who will not harm the local population, and the duty to more fairly share the economic value of the natural resources situated on a state's territory. I argued that these duties of justice ought to be recognized and implemented by citizens, acting through their domestic political processes. Though citizens generally have the right (within certain limits) to decide their cultural, migration, and resource management policies, this does not mean that there are no moral guidelines as to what they *should* decide. Both citizens and foreigners should attempt to persuade a self-determining people to adopt the policies outlined above. Yet even if citizens decide wrongly in these cases (e.g., by privileging the majority culture or religion, refusing to admit harmless migrants, or refusing to share their resources), I have held that their decisions should be immune from external coercive interference.

Second, I also argued for *morally binding, enforceable* limits to states' sovereignty. While the concept of sovereignty holds that a nation's internal affairs should be the exclusive concern of its government and citizens, this book has problematized what should count as an "internal matter." In particular, I held that states and their citizens have an enforceable duty to respect others' fundamental interests in the earth, a duty that functions as a proviso on states' territorial sovereignty. Decisions that infringe outsiders' fundamental territorial interests do not plausibly count as internal issues that are justifiably insulated against interference.

Securing everyone's fundamental interests in the earth is an essential condition for the legitimacy of a territorial states system. Because the states system is a humanly imposed political institution, those who must live under it have the right to demand a justification for its rules, on the basis of reasons they can accept. Since no one would agree to a social institution that required them to sacrifice fundamental interests in a common resource so that others can enjoy benefits that are not morally urgent, the states system must make provision to secure these fundamental territorial interests for all co-owners of the earth.[1] This requires "building in" certain limits to states' exclusionary prerogatives. Where an exclusionary decision would jeopardize outsiders' fundamental territorial interests, that decision no longer counts as a purely internal affair subject to the authority of a national government. Instead, it becomes a legitimate subject of international

---

[1] This is similar to the argument for allocating the international community secondary responsibilities to protect human rights; otherwise, predictable shortfalls in states' primary responsibilities would mean the international system could not reasonably be accepted by its subjects since they would be trapped in tyrannical regimes. See the discussion in Beitz, *The Idea of Human Rights*, 128–31.

concern. Only if fundamental territorial interests are guaranteed can the global order credibly claim that the core values of occupancy, basic justice, and self-determination have been realized for all the earth's inhabitants. Accepting and institutionalizing these duties to protect fundamental territorial interests is thus a cost of organizing our world as a system of separate states.

To a certain extent—albeit inchoately—international law already recognizes duties to secure fundamental territorial interests. The Refugee Convention provides for an important exception to states' rights to exclude foreigners, and the duty not to cause transboundary harm gives states a responsibility not to cause environmental damage in areas beyond their jurisdiction. But if the states system is to live up to its legitimating ideals, these exceptions must be further extended, and institutionalized in a more binding fashion. I argued in Chapter 6 that we should move beyond the current Refugee Convention, since it excludes from the definition of "refugee" many people whose fundamental territorial interests are at stake, and it fails to provide an adequate remedy for those migrants it does protect. Similarly, I argued in Chapter 8 that we should go beyond the duty not to cause transboundary harm, requiring states to cooperate in international resource comanagement schemes for *global systemic resources*.

The idea that there are nonconventional moral constraints on the appropriation of the globe has its roots in the work of Grotius, who argued that common ownership leaves traces in the form of "residual common rights."[2] One residual common right was the right of refugees to a permanent new home: Grotius holds that "a fixed Abode ought not to be refused to Strangers, who being expelled their own Country, seek a Retreat elsewhere: Provided they submit to the laws of the State" (*DJBP*, 2.2.16).

Grotius saw these common rights as enforceable claims:

> [They are] not founded on what some alledge, that the Proprietor is obliged by the Rules of Charity to give of his Substance to those who want it; but on this, that the Property of Goods is supposed to have been established with this favorable Exception, that in such Cases one might enter again upon the Rights of the primitive Community.   (*DJBP*, 2.2.6)

In arguing for enforceable duties to secure fundamental territorial interests, I have drawn on this tradition of thought about the distributive constraints imposed by common ownership.[3]

Since the duty to secure fundamental territorial interests remains vague and underspecified in our current international system, however, some are tempted to downgrade it to a humanitarian responsibility. Humanitarian duties hold between strangers, when (i) one party is in urgent need and (ii) the risks and costs of

---

[2] Dennis Klimchuk, "Grotius on Property and the Right of Necessity," *Journal of the History of Philosophy* 56, no. 2 (2018): 239–60.

[3] See also Risse, *On Global Justice*, 111.

assisting are relatively low for the other party.⁴ Michael Walzer, for example, suggests that while "on the one hand, everyone must have a place to live, and a place where a reasonably secure life is possible, on the other hand, this is not a right that can be enforced against particular host states."⁵

I disagree. The problems with specificity and directedness that plague the duty to secure fundamental territorial interests are not reason to demote it to an imperfect duty of humanity. Unlike duties of beneficence, which must be performed from a certain sincere motive, the constraints of common ownership are not *in principle* unenforceable. Instead, they are *in practice* difficult to enforce, because they are not yet sufficiently specified and institutionally allocated. States collectively have a duty of justice to act to institutionalize these duties at the global level, and to enforce them collectively, by taking appropriate countermeasures to discourage defaulters. The inhabitants of the globe should place political pressure on their states to create the required international arrangements.

Thus, I believe we all have a common responsibility to work "from the bottom up" to create multilateral institutions that would better specify, allocate, and enforce duties to protect fundamental territorial interests, including conservation reform, national emissions quotas, and a new refugee agreement. Transnational activists should attempt to catalyze "learning processes" on the part of national populations, heightening awareness and sensitizing domestic publics to these common ownership concerns. Civil society groups should mobilize domestic citizenries in favor of such proposals, engaging in publicity campaigns, and organizing boycotts or global protest actions.

In part, this strategy of mobilizing domestic public opinion makes good pragmatic sense: the most feasible means for bringing the United States, say, into a multilateral scheme to better accommodate refugees, address climate change, or encourage resource conservation is to persuade US citizens to support policies that would bind it to accept this regime. Lea Ypi also emphasizes that domestic states have two further advantages as a framework for cosmopolitan reform. First, they allow for legitimate coercion. When cosmopolitan reforms are enacted through domestic procedures, citizens will comply with them not "simply out of fear of coercive mechanisms," but as part of "their allegiance to political institutions to whose development they have contributed."⁶ Second, states possess institutions that may help these cosmopolitan reforms, once enacted, to become stable. Civic education through historically affirmed institutions enables individuals to internalize cosmopolitan requirements, and to become effectively motivated by them. Institutionalizing protections for fundamental territorial interests will thus depend on long-term "learning processes" on the part of domestic citizenries, leading them to see themselves as part of a global community of

---

⁴ Walzer, *Spheres of Justice*, 33.   ⁵ Walzer, *Spheres of Justice*, 50.
⁶ Ypi, *Global Justice and Avant-Garde Political Agency* (Oxford: Oxford University Press, 2012), 152.

shared responsibility. The hope is that this political mobilization will lead prominent states to come together, via multilateral treaty, to enact norms of refugee protection and environmental conservation that protect fundamental territorial interests for all the globe's inhabitants, and that these states will implement these norms in their domestic legal orders, enforce these norms horizontally, and educate their citizens to support them. Only once such duties are reliably allocated and enforced will our territorial states system be fully legitimate.

One might object that while this "bottom-up" strategy is not unattractive, it will ultimately prove ineffective. Why would states voluntarily bind themselves, through multilateral arrangements, in ways that might limit their own sovereign prerogatives? In reply, I note that states have done this several times in the past. In the nineteenth century, state sovereignty was held to include the right to acquire territory through aggressive war. The UN Charter limited this sovereign prerogative, imposing a duty on all member states to "refrain in their international relations from the threat or use of force against the territorial integrity or political independence of any state."[7] Prior to the Universal Declaration and subsequent human rights covenants, a state's treatment of its own subjects was held to be an internal sovereign matter. But today, human rights are widely accepted as providing a standard of legitimate rule, and when states violate these rights, this provokes an international response. At the beginning of the twentieth century, states were held to have the right to subjugate "uncivilized" non-Western peoples. Since 1960, however, imperial rule has been outlawed, and colonial peoples are recognized as having a right to independence. Because states have limited their sovereign prerogatives through multilateral arrangements before, I believe it is not unreasonable to hope that this might happen again.

One might further object that external limitations on states' exclusionary prerogatives are incompatible with state sovereignty. But I doubt this, at least not if the process of institutionalization and enforcement of these limitations is approached in the right way. It is not obvious that the only way to work toward more qualified exclusionary rights is for one powerful state to impose them, or for the world community to submit to a coercive global Leviathan. States have already bound themselves, through multilateral institutions, in ways that limit their sovereign decision-making by norms of human rights, nonintervention, and self-determination. They have also delegated authority over a number of important issues to supranational institutions. So long as this delegation is authorized from within the state's domestic legal system—as it would be, if the envisaged arrangements are established via multilateral treaty—these limitations do not compromise the state's *internal sovereignty*, i.e., the political community's right that its constitutional order be supreme within its territory. As I argued in the introduction,

---

[7] *Charter of the United Nations*, Article 2(4).

sovereignty need not be comprehensive or unlimited: a holder of sovereignty need not be sovereign over all matters.

Further, so long as enforcement proceeds through "horizontal" sanctioning measures (such as imposing tariffs on the goods of noncompliant countries), it need not interfere with the state's *external sovereignty*, i.e., the community's right to immunity from interference by outside powers within its territory. Though horizontal sanctioning measures do exert pressure on a recalcitrant state, they refrain from interfering within its territory. Peoples are still free to make their own decisions, even if they are heavily incentivized to cooperate. As I argued in Chapter 8, in the case of fundamental territorial interests, such horizontal sanctioning measures can plausibly be viewed as a form of collective self-defense.

In holding that cosmopolitan duties are best institutionalized through multilateral cooperation and horizontal sanctioning, I follow Kant, who advocated a league of states, not a world state, as the appropriate framework for law-governed relations internationally. An alternative approach would seek to limit state sovereignty from above, by instituting a world government with executive powers. A "world government," as I define it here, is not a cooperative association among peoples, supplemented by supranational institutions and horizontal sanctioning devices. It is instead a federal super-state with the overriding legal authority and coercive powers usually exercised by domestic regimes.

Several thinkers have argued for a world government. David Held holds that nation-states should be superseded by a cosmopolitan democracy that would disperse various powers and competences to different levels in accordance with their capacity to solve significant problems. On Held's view, a global parliament should be empowered to produce binding cosmopolitan law and to tax the world's citizens. Cosmopolitan law should be entrenched into national constitutions so as to override domestic legislation, and it should be coercively enforced.[8] Catherine Lu argues that a world state is necessary to enforce the minimally just background conditions of global political order, which could support the self-determination of domestic states and render it legitimate.[9] Lu refers to duties to refugees and asylum-seekers and duties to combat climate change as two cases where the need for a world state seems most urgent. Lea Ypi holds that if cosmopolitan principles are to be principles of justice, rather than counsels of charity or humanitarianism, they must be enforceable, and this requires a global political authority capable of doing the enforcement.[10] Finally, Simon Caney defends the establishment of "democratically elected global and regional supra-state political authorities standing over and above 'states'" and argues that these authorities

---

[8] Held, *Democracy and the Global Order*, 276.

[9] Lu, "Cosmopolitan Justice, Democracy, and the World State," in *Institutional Cosmopolitanism*, edited by Luis Cabrera (Oxford: Oxford University Press, 2018), 232–52.

[10] Ypi, "Cosmopolitanism without If and without But," in *Cosmopolitanism versus Non-Cosmopolitanism* (Oxford: Oxford University Press, 2013), 75–91.

should be endowed with significant coercive capabilities, in the form of a "permanent UN volunteer force."[11]

Supporters of world government frequently appeal to Kant as an inspiration for their views, though he did not fully follow (what they see as) the implications of his own ideas. Specifically, they invoke Kant's notion that there is a "second-level" state of nature among states that must be overcome in order for Right to be fully realized.[12] Kant often makes the analogy between individuals and states, holding that both have a duty to exit the state of nature: "a state of nature among nations, like a state of nature among individual human beings," he says, "is a condition that one ought to leave to enter a lawful condition" (6:350). Indeed, Kant frequently argues that a lawful condition will only be brought about once domestic right (justice among cocitizens) is supplemented by international right (justice among states) and cosmopolitan right (justice among citizens of different states) (6:311).

But, though it is true that we should work to overcome the state of nature among states, it is not obvious that law-governed relations among states should be constituted in the same way law-governed relations are constituted domestically. Indeed, if the argument of this book is correct, there are good reasons for thinking international and domestic right should be institutionalized quite differently. I argued in Chapter 4 that our natural duty of justice not only requires us to constitute a minimally just political order, it also requires us to impose that political order in a manner that is respectful of individuals' capacity to make judgments about how, and by whom, they wish to be ruled. So long as the world contains peoples who wish to be ruled by distinct states (i.e., so long as there is no omnilateral will in favor of political authority on a global scale), it will be illegitimate to replace peoples' domestic institutions with a world government.

It was due to such concerns, I believe, that Kant held that the *form* of a law-governed condition between states should be different than it is among individuals. Instead of arguing for a federal world state with coercive powers, Kant advocates a league of states. A rightful condition among states, Kant holds, "would be a league of nations, which however, need not be a state of nations" (8:354). According to him, "this league does not look to acquiring any power of a state but only to preserving and securing the *freedom* of a state itself and of other states in league with it...without there being any need for them to subject themselves to public laws and to coercion under them (as people in the state of nature must do)" (8:356).[13]

---

[11] Caney, *Justice Beyond Borders*, 161–2.

[12] Held, *Democracy and the Global Order*, 276; Lu, "Cosmopolitan Justice, Democracy, and the World State," 240; Ypi, "Cosmopolitanism without If and without But," 80.

[13] There is considerable controversy among Kant interpreters about these views. For interpretations close to mine, see Ripstein, *Force and Freedom*, 225–31; Patrick Capps and Julian Rivers, "Kant's Concept of International Law," *Legal Theory* 16, no. 4 (2010): 229–57; Katrin Flikschuh, "Kant's Sovereignty Dilemma: A Contemporary Analysis," *Journal of Political Philosophy* 18, no. 4 (2010): 469–93; Oliver Eberl and Peter Niesen, *Immanuel Kant: Zum ewigen Frieden* (Berlin: Suhrkamp, 2011). For alternatives, see Louis-Philippe Hodgson, "Realizing External Freedom," *Kant's Political Theory: Interpretations and Applications*, edited by Elisabeth Ellis (University Park: Pennsylvania State

Kant's opposition to a world state, in my view, is not rooted in doubts about the project's feasibility (though there are serious concerns of this kind). Consider briefly two important problems. First, to effectively overcome strong states' resistance, a world government would have to be extraordinarily powerful. It is not clear that it would even be possible to establish a super-state with the necessary overriding powers, given that the United States, Russia, China, France, the UK, India, Pakistan, Israel, and North Korea possess nuclear weapons. To make the project feasible, domestic states would first have to disarm. Second, the world-state project also envisions domestic states becoming something like federal provinces of a global super-state with the final authority to enforce its law over them. Yet given that many domestic states in the world today are not liberal democracies, it is unclear how such a super-state would be constituted. It may prove impossible to structure a global state along liberal-democratic lines, while remaining representative of its subjects. Yet creating an unrepresentative and/or potentially illiberal authority hardly seems a recipe for cosmopolitan progress.

While important, I believe Kant's opposition to a world state is not driven by these feasibility concerns. Instead, it primarily derives from worries about the *legitimacy* of the project. To have the right to make and enforce law for a population, Kant believes an institution must be *collectively authorized* by that population. I have argued that such authorization occurs when cooperators within a territory share a commitment to self-organized procedures that they accept as an appropriate way to establish justice among themselves. When cooperators have that omnilateral will toward a government, the coercion it exerts will not be alienating to them. The worry about a global super-state is that it may not receive the authorization required for its coercive powers to be legitimate.

To claim the right to make and enforce law for a group of people, according to Kant, is to claim a kind of *superiority* over them: the state settles the matter for its subjects, even where they disagree. This claim to superiority can be reconciled with the autonomy and equality of individuals only if it is collectively authorized by cooperators among that state's population. The value of political autonomy therefore supports refraining from imposing cosmopolitan reforms over the objections of subject populations. Instead, we ought to pursue cosmopolitan reforms in ways that are compatible with their self-determination. This is what my "bottom-up" strategy, involving multilateral cooperation and horizontal sanctioning, attempts to do.

While very important, I have emphasized throughout this book that respect for collective self-determination is not absolute. When the essentials of basic justice, security, and public order cannot otherwise be secured, it may become permissible to subject people to illegitimate coercion. As I argued in Chapter 5, uses of alien coercion by occupying forces or humanitarian interveners fall within this

University Press, 2012), 101–34; Otfried Höffe, *Kant's Cosmopolitan Theory of Law and Peace* (Cambridge: Cambridge University Press, 2006), 189–203; Pauline Kleingeld, *Kant and Cosmopolitanism: The Philosophical Ideal of World Citizenship* (Cambridge: Cambridge University Press, 2012), 40–71.

category. At some point, there may arise a case for treating climate change or refugee crises in the same way. In such a scenario, a global hegemon with sufficient power could permissibly subject people to institutions coordinating morally mandatory cooperation, even if they were unwilling to submit to them. This permission to use unilateral force is subject to several qualifications, such as (i) it must be done to protect basic rights or to avert extremely grave social harms; (ii) the harms it threatens must be proportionate to the goods the use of force is likely to achieve; and (iii) unauthorized force must be used only as a last resort. But if the only way to prevent massive death from climate change is to coerce recalcitrant countries into a conservation scheme at the barrel of a gun, this may have to be done.

Still, it is important to recognize that such a course of action would come at very great cost: we should override self-determination only in truly dire circumstances. There is every reason to work first toward climate justice, more extensive refugee rights, and other cosmopolitan reforms via "self-binding" arrangements that will reflect, rather than violate, collective self-determination. Such a strategy may allow for the establishment of multilateral institutions that can limit state sovereignty by enforceable duties to secure fundamental territorial interests.

Bibliography

Law Cases, Conventions, Government Statistics, etc.

Armed Activities on the Territory of the Congo (Democratic Republic of the Congo v. Uganda), Judgment, I.C.J. Reports 2005. Available online at: https://www.icj-cij.org/files/case-related/116/116-20051219-JUD-01-00-EN.pdf.

Crandall v. State of Nevada, 73 U.S. 35 (1867).

Declaration of the United Nations Conference on the Human Environment. Report of the United Nations Conference on the Human Environment. June 1972. Available online at: http://www.un-documents.net/unchedec.htm.

International Commission on Intervention and State Sovereignty. *The Responsibility to Protect.* Ottawa: International Development Research Centre, 2001. doi: https://idl-bnc-idrc.dspacedirect.org/bitstream/handle/10625/18432/IDL-18432.pdf.

Montevideo Convention on the Rights and Duties of States. Seventh International Conference of American States. 26 December 1933. Available online at: https://www.jus.uio.no/english/services/library/treaties/01/1-02/rights-duties-states.xml.

Roberts v. United States Jaycees, 468 US 609 (1984).

"Trail Smelter Arbitration." *United States v. Canada.* Reports of International Arbitral Awards, Vol. 3 (1938/1941). Available online at: http://legal.un.org/riaa/cases/vol_III/1905-1982.pdf.

United Nations. *Charter of the United Nations.* 24 October 1945. Available online at: https://treaties.un.org/doc/publication/ctc/uncharter.pdf.

UN General Assembly. *Convention Relating to the Status of Refugees.* 28 July 1951. Available online at: http://www.unhcr.org/protect/PROTECTION/3b66c2aa10.pdf.

UN General Assembly. *Declaration on the Establishment of a New International Economic Order.* Resolution 3201 (S-VI). 1 May 1974. Available online at: http://www.un-documents.net/s6r3201.htm.

UN General Assembly. *Declaration on the Rights of Indigenous Peoples.* 13 September 2007. Available online at: http://www.un.org/esa/socdev/unpfii/documents/DRIPS_en.pdf.

UN General Assembly. *International Covenant on Civil and Political Rights.* Resolution 2200A (XXI). 16 December 1966. Available online at: https://www.ohchr.org/en/professionalinterest/pages/ccpr.aspx.

UN General Assembly. *International Covenant on Economic, Social and Cultural Rights.* Resolution 2200A (XXI). 16 December 1966. Available online at: https://www.ohchr.org/EN/ProfessionalInterest/Pages/CESCR.aspx.

UN General Assembly. "Permanent sovereignty over natural resources." Resolution 1803 (XVII). 14 December 1962. Available online at: https://www.ohchr.org/Documents/ProfessionalInterest/resources.pdf.

UN General Assembly. *Protocol Relating to the Status of Refugees.* 31 January 1967. Available online at: http://www.unhcr.org/protect/PROTECTION/3b66c2aa10.pdf.

UN General Assembly. *Universal Declaration of Human Rights.* 10 December 1948. Available online at: https://www.ohchr.org/EN/UDHR/Documents/UDHR_Translations/eng.pdf.

Worcester v. Georgia, 31 U.S. (6 Pet.) 515 (1832).

Books, Articles, and Chapters

Abizadeh, Arash, Manish Pandey, and Sohrab Abizadeh. "Wage Competition and the Special Obligations Challenge to More Open Borders." *Politics, Philosophy, Economics* 14, no. 3 (2015): 255–69. doi: https://doi.org/10.1177/1470594X14544286.

Abizadeh, Arash. "Democratic Theory and Border Coercion: No Right to Unilaterally Control Your Own Borders." *Political Theory* 36, no. 1 (2008): 37–65. doi: https://doi.org/10.1177/0090591707310090.

Abizadeh, Arash. "On the Demos and its Kin: Democracy, Nationality, and the Boundary Problem." *American Political Science Review* 106, no. 4 (2012): 121–30. doi: https://doi.org/10.1017/S0003055412000421.

Altman, Andrew, and Christopher Wellman. *A Liberal Theory of International Justice* (Oxford: Oxford University Press, 2009).

Anaya, James. *Indigenous Peoples in International Law* (Oxford: Oxford University Press, 2004).

Anderson, Malcom. *Frontiers: Territory and State Formation in the Modern World* (Cambridge: Polity, 1996).

Anderson, Scott. "Coercion." *The Stanford Encyclopedia of Philosophy* (Winter 2017 edition), edited by Edward N. Zalta. http://plato.stanford.edu/entries/coercion/.

Angeli, Olivero. *Cosmopolitanism, Self-Determination, and Territory* (New York: Palgrave Macmillan, 2015).

Applbaum, Arthur. "Legitimacy without the Duty to Obey." *Philosophy & Public Affairs* 38, no. 3 (2010): 215–39. doi: https://doi.org/10.1111/j.1088-4963.2010.01186.x.

Arhin, Albert, and Joanes Atela. "Forest Carbon Projects and Policies in Africa." In *Carbon Conflicts and Forest Landscapes in Africa*, edited by Melissa Leach and Ian Scoones (Oxford: Routledge, 2015), 43–57.

Armstrong, Christopher. "Against 'Permanent Sovereignty' over Natural Resources." *Politics, Philosophy & Economics* 14, no. 2 (2015): 129–51. doi: https://doi.org/10.1177/1470594X14523080.

Armstrong, Christopher. "Fairness, free-riding and rainforest protection." *Political Theory* 44, no. 1 (2016): 106–30. doi: https://doi.org/10.1177/0090591715594840.

Armstrong, Christopher. *Justice and Natural Resources* (Oxford: Oxford University Press, 2017).

Armstrong, Christopher. "Resources, Rights, and Global Justice: A Response to Kolers." *Political Studies* 62, no. 1 (2014): 216–22.

Atela, Joanes. "Carbon in Africa's Agricultural Landscapes: A Kenyan case." In *Carbon Conflicts and Forest Landscapes in Africa*, edited by Melissa Leach and Ian Scoones (Oxford: Routledge, 2015), 43–57.

Bailey, L. R. *The Long Walk: A History of the Navajo Wars*, 1846-68 (Los Angeles: Westernlore Press, 1964).

Baldwin, Thomas. "The Territorial State." In *Jurisprudence: Cambridge Essays*, edited by Hyman Gross and Ross Harrison (Oxford: Clarendon, 1992), 207–30.

Bayrak, Mucahid, and Lawal Marafa. "Ten Years of REDD+: A Critical Review of the Impact of REDD+ on Forest-Dependent Communities." *Sustainability* 8, no. 7 (2016): 620.

Barry, Brian. "Humanity and Justice in a Global Perspective." *Nomos* 24 (1982): 219–52. doi: https://www.jstor.org/stable/24219453.
Barry, Brian. *Culture and Equality* (Cambridge, MA: Harvard University Press, 2001).
Beitz, Charles. *The Idea of Human Rights* (Oxford: Oxford University Press, 2009).
Beitz, Charles. "The Moral Standing of States Revisited." *Ethics and International Affairs* 23, no. 4 (2009): 325–47. doi: https://doi.org/10.1111/j.1747-7093.2009.00227.x.
Beitz, Charles. *Political Theory and International Relations* (Princeton: Princeton University Press, 1979).
Beitz, Charles. "Tacit Consent and Property Rights." *Political Theory* 8, no. 4 (1980): 487–502. doi: www.jstor.org/stable/190658.
Bentham, Jeremy. "Principles of the Civil Code." In *The Works of Jeremy Bentham*, edited by John Bowring (New York: Russell and Russell, 1962), 297–364.
Blackstone, William. *Commentaries on the Laws of England*, edited by George Sharswood (Philadelphia: Lippincott, 1893).
Blake, Michael. "Distributive Justice, State Coercion, and Autonomy." *Philosophy & Public Affairs* 30, no. 3 (2001): 257–96.
Blake, Michael. "Immigration, Association, and Self-Determination." *Ethics* 122, no. 4 (2012): 748–62. doi: 10.1086/666327.
Blake, Michael. "Immigration." In *The Blackwell Companion to Applied Ethics*, edited by Christopher Wellman and R.G. Frey (Oxford: Blackwell, 2003), 224–37.
Blake, Michael. "Immigration, Jurisdiction, and Exclusion." *Philosophy & Public Affairs* 41, no. 2 (2013): 103–30. doi: https://doi.org/10.1111/papa.12012.
Blake, Michael. "Immigration and Political Equality." *San Diego Law Review* 45, no. 4 (2008): 963–80.
Blake, Michael. *Justice and Foreign Policy* (Oxford: Oxford University Press, 2013).
Blake, Michael. "Territorial Rights: In Defense of the Naïve View." Presented colloquium paper, Eastern-APA, Washington University in St. Louis, 2014.
Bloch, Marc. *Feudal Society* (Chicago: University of Chicago Press, 1961).
Blomfield, Megan. "Global Common Resources and the Just Distribution of Emission Shares." *Journal of Political Philosophy* 21, no. 3 (2013): 283–304. doi: https://doi.org/10.1111/j.1467-9760.2012.00416.x.
Borjas, George R. "The Labor Demand Curve is Downward Sloping: Re-examining the Impact of Immigration on the Labor Market." *Quarterly Journal of Economics* 118, no. 4 (2003): 1335–74. doi: https://doi.org/10.1162/003355303322552810.
Bratman, Michael. *Structures of Agency* (Oxford: Oxford University Press, 2007).
Brezger, Jan, and Andreas Cassee. "Debate: Immigrants and Newcomers by Birth: Do Statist Arguments Imply a Right to Exclude Both?" *Journal of Political Philosophy* 24, no. 3 (2016): 367–78. doi: https://doi.org/10.1111/jopp.12088.
Buchanan, Allen. "Political Legitimacy and Democracy." *Ethics* 112, no. 4 (2002): 689–719. doi: https://doi.org/10.1086/340313.
Buchanan, Allen. "Self-Determination, Revolution, and Intervention." *Ethics* 126, no. 2 (2016): 447–73. doi: https://doi.org/10.1086/683639.
Buchanan, Allen. *Justice, Legitimacy, and Self-Determination* (Oxford: Oxford University Press, 2004).
Burbank, Jane, and Frederick Cooper. *Empires in World History: Power and the Politics of Difference* (Princeton: Princeton University Press, 2009).
Butt, Daniel. *Rectifying International Injustice* (Oxford: Oxford University Press, 2009).
Calloway, Colin. *First Peoples: A Documentary Survey of American Indian History* (Boston: Bedford/Saint Martins, 2007).

Campbell, John. "Climate-Induced Community Relocation in the Pacific." In *Climate Change and Displacement: Multidisciplinary Perspectives*, edited by Jane McAdam (Oxford: Hart, 2012), 57–80.

Caney, Simon. "Cosmopolitan Justice, Responsibility, and Global Climate Change," *Leiden Journal of International Law* 18, no. 4 (2005): 747–75. doi: https://doi.org/10.1017/S0922156505002992.

Caney, Simon. *Justice Beyond Borders* (Oxford: Oxford University Press, 2005).

Capps, Patrick, and Julian Rivers. "Kant's Concept of International Law." *Legal Theory* 16, no. 4 (2010): 229–57. doi: 10.1017/S1352325210000212.

Card, David. "Immigration and Inequality." *American Economic Review* 99, no. 2 (2009): 1–21. doi: 10.1257/aer.99.2.1.

Card, David. "Is the New Immigration Really So Bad?" *Economic Journal* 115, no. 507 (2005): 300–23. https://doi.org/10.1111/j.1468-0297.2005.01037.x.

Carens, Joseph. *The Ethics of Immigration* (Oxford: Oxford University Press, 2013).

Carens, Joseph. "Migration and Morality: A Liberal Egalitarian Perspective." In *Free Movement*, edited by Brian Barry and Robert E. Goodin (University Park: Pennsylvania State University Press, 1992), 25–47.

Casal, Paula. "Global Taxes on Natural Resources." *Journal of Moral Philosophy* 8, no. 3 (2011): 307–27. doi: 10.1163/174552411X591339.

Cassese, Antonio. *Self-Determination of Peoples: A Legal Reappraisal* (Cambridge: Cambridge University Press, 1995).

Cavallar, Georg. *The Rights of Strangers* (Aldershot: Ashgate, 2002).

Christiano, Thomas. "Self-Determination and the Human Right to Democracy." In *Philosophical Foundations of Human Rights*, edited by Rowan Cruft, S. Matthew Liao, Massimo Renzo (Oxford: Oxford University Press, 2015), 459–80.

Cohen, G.A. *Self-Ownership, Freedom, and Equality* (Cambridge: Cambridge University Press, 1995).

Cohen, Jean. *Globalization and Sovereignty: Rethinking Legality, Legitimacy, and Constitutionalism* (Cambridge: Cambridge University Press, 2012).

Cohen, Joshua, and Charles Sabel. "Extra Rempublicam Nulla Justitia?" *Philosophy & Public Affairs* 34, no. 2 (2006): 176–92. doi: https://doi.org/10.1111/j.1088-4963.2006.00060.x.

Cohen, Joshua. "Deliberation and Democratic Legitimacy." In *Philosophy, Politics, Democracy* (Cambridge, MA: Harvard University Press, 2009), 1–17.

Cohen, Joshua. "Is There a Human Right to Democracy." In *The Arc of the Moral Universe* (Cambridge, MA: Harvard University Press, 201), 349–72.

Cole, Phillip, and Christopher Wellman. *Debating the Ethics of Immigration: Is There a Right to Exclude* (Oxford: Oxford University Press, 2011).

Cole, Phillip. *Philosophies of Exclusion* (Edinburgh: Edinburgh University Press, 2000).

Collier, Paul. *Exodus: Immigration and Multiculturalism in the 21st Century* (Oxford: Oxford University Press, 2013).

Crawford, Neta. *Arguments and Change in World Politics: Ethics, Decolonization, and Humanitarian Intervention* (Cambridge: Cambridge University Press, 1996).

Dahl, Robert. *Democracy and Its Critics* (New Haven: Yale University Press, 1989).

Davies, Norman. *God's Playground: A History of Poland* (New York: Columbia University Press, 2005).

Davies, Norman. *Heart of Europe: The Past in Poland's Present* (Oxford: Oxford University Press, 2001).

Dietrich, Christopher. *Oil Revolution: Anticolonial Elites, Sovereign Rights, and the Economic Culture of Decolonization* (Cambridge: Cambridge University Press, 2017).

Du Bois, W. E. B. *Black Reconstruction in America* (New York: Harcourt, Brace and Company, 1935).
Dworkin, Ronald. *Freedom's Law* (Cambridge, MA: Harvard University Press, 1996).
Dworkin, Ronald. *Justice for Hedgehogs* (Cambridge, MA: Belknap Press, 2011).
Dworkin, Ronald. *Life's Dominion* (New York: Vintage Books, 1994).
Dworkin, Ronald. *Sovereign Virtue* (Cambridge, MA: Harvard University Press, 2000).
Dworkin, Ronald. *Taking Rights Seriously* (Cambridge, MA: Harvard University Press, 1978).
Eberl, Oliver, and Peter Niesen. *Immanuel Kant: Zum Ewigen Frieden* (Berlin: Suhrkamp, 2011).
Eisgruber, Christopher, and Lawrence Sager. *Religious Freedom and the Constitution* (Cambridge, MA: Harvard University Press, 2007).
Estlund, David. *Democratic Authority* (Princeton: Princeton University Press, 2008).
Eyal, Nir. "Informed Consent." *The Stanford Encyclopedia of Philosophy* (Fall 2012 edition), edited by Edward N. Zalta. https://plato.stanford.edu/entries/informed-consent/.
Fairhead, James, Melissa Leach, and Ian Scoones. "Green Grabbing: A New Appropriation of Nature?," *Journal of Peasant Studies* 39, no. 2 (2012): 237–61.
Ferracioli, Luara. "The Appeal and Danger of a New Refugee Convention." *Social Theory and Practice* 40, no. 1 (2014): 123–44. doi: 10.5840/soctheorpract20144016.
Fine, Sarah. "Freedom of Association is Not the Answer." *Ethics* 120, no. 2 (2010): 338–56. doi: https://doi.org/10.1086/649626.
Fitzmaurice, Andrew. *Sovereignty, Property, and Empire* (Cambridge: Cambridge University Press, 2014).
Flikschuh, Katrin. "Kant's Sovereignty Dilemma: A Contemporary Analysis." *Journal of Political Philosophy* 18, no. 4 (2010): 469–93. doi: https://doi.org/10.1111/j.1467-9760.2010.00361.x.
Frankfurt, Harry. *The Importance of What We Care about* (Cambridge: Cambridge University Press, 1988).
Freiman, Christopher, and Javier Hidalgo. "Liberalism or Immigration Restrictions, but Not Both." *Journal of Ethics and Social Philosophy* 10, no. 2 (2016): 10–22.
French, Peter. *Collective and Corporate Responsibility* (New York: Columbia University Press, 1984).
Fukuyama, Francis. *The Origins of Political Order* (New York: Farrar, Straus, and Giroux, 2011).
Fung, Archon. "The Principle of Affected Interests: An Interpretation and Defense." In *Representation: Elections and Beyond*, edited by Rogers M. Smith and Jack H. Nagel (Philadelphia: University of Pennsylvania Press, 2013), 236–68.
Gans, Chaim. *A Just Zionism* (Oxford: Oxford University Press, 2011).
Gans, Chaim. *The Limits of Nationalism* (Cambridge: Cambridge University Press, 2003).
Garrison, Tim. *The Legal Ideology of Removal: The Southern Judiciary and the Sovereignty of Native American Nations* (Athens: University of Georgia Press, 2009).
Gellner, Ernest. *Nations and Nationalism* (Ithaca: Cornell University Press, 2009).
Getachew, Adom. *Worldmaking after Empire* (Princeton: Princeton University Press, 2019).
Gilabert, Pablo. *From Global Poverty to Global Equality* (Oxford: Oxford University Press, 2012).
Goodin, Robert E. "Enfranchising All Affected Interests, and Its Alternatives." *Philosophy & Public Affairs* 25, no. 1 (2007): 40–68. doi: https://doi.org/10.1111/j.1088-4963.2007.00098.x.
Goodwin-Gill, Guy S., and Jane McAdam. *The Refugee in International Law*, 3rd ed. (Oxford: Oxford University Press, 2007).

Gorenberg, Gershom. *The Accidental Empire: Israel and the Birth of Settlements, 1967–1977* (New York: Times Macmillan, 2007).

Grainger, Matt, and Kate Geary. "The New Forests Company and its Uganda plantations." Oxfam International. 2011. Available online at: https://www.oxfam.org/en/research/new-forests-company-and-its-uganda-plantations-oxfam-case-study.

Grotius, Hugo. *Commentary on the Law of Prize and Booty*, edited by Martine Julia van Ittersum (Indianapolis: Liberty Fund, 2006).

Grotius, Hugo. *The Rights of War and Peace*, edited by Richard Tuck (Indianapolis: Liberty Fund, 2005).

Habermas, Jürgen. "Struggles for Recognition in the Democratic State." In *Inclusion of the Other*, edited by Ciaran Cronin and Pablo de Greiff (Cambridge, MA: MIT Press, 1998), 203–38.

Harel, Alon. "Whose Home Is It?" *Theoretical Inquiries in Law* 5, no. 2 (2004): 333–66.

Harris, J. W. *Property and Justice* (Oxford: Oxford University Press, 1996).

Haslett, D. W. "Is Inheritance Justified?" *Philosophy & Public Affairs* 15, no. 2 (1986): 122–55. doi: http://www.jstor.org/stable/2265382.

Hathaway, James, and Michelle Foster. *The Law of Refugee Status*, 2nd ed. (Cambridge: Cambridge University Press, 2014).

Hathaway, Oona and Scott Shapiro. *The Internationalists: How a Radical Plan to Outlaw War Remade the World* (New York: Simon and Schuster, 2017).

Hayward, Tim. "Global Justice and the Distribution of Natural Resources." *Political Studies* 54, no. 2 (2006): 349–69. doi: https://doi.org/10.1111/j.1467-9248.2006.00606.x.

Held, David. *Democracy and the Global Order* (Stanford: Stanford University Press, 1995).

Hidalgo, Javier. "Self-Determination, Immigration Restrictions, and the Problem of Compatriot Deportation." *Journal of International Political Theory* 10, no. 3 (2014): 261–82. doi: https://doi.org/10.1177/1755088214539414.

Hinsley, F. H. *Sovereignty* (Cambridge: Cambridge University Press, 1986).

Hobbes, Thomas. *Leviathan*, edited by Richard Tuck (Cambridge: Cambridge University Press, 1996).

Hodgson, Louis-Philippe. "Kant on Property Rights and the State." *Kantian Review* 15, no. 1 (2010): 57–87. doi: 10.1017/S1369415400002375.

Hodgson, Louis-Philippe. "Realizing External Freedom: The Kantian Argument for a World State." In *Kant's Political Theory: Interpretations and Applications*, edited by Elisabeth Ellis (University Park: Pennsylvania State University Press, 2012), 101–34.

Höffe, Otfried. *Kant's Cosmopolitan Theory of Law and Peace* (Cambridge: Cambridge University Press, 2006).

Honoré, Tony. *Making Law Bind* (Oxford: Clarendon Press, 1987).

Hossain, Kamal, and Subrata Roy Chowdhury. *Permanent Sovereignty over Natural Resources in International Law: Principle and Practice* (New York: Saint Martin's, 1984).

Huber, Jakob. "No Right to Unilaterally Claim Your Territory: On the Consistency of Kantian Statism." *Critical Review of International Social and Political Philosophy* 20, no. 6 (2016): 677–96. doi: https://doi.org/10.1080/13698230.2016.1196093.

Huemer, Michael. "Is There a Right to Immigrate." *Social Philosophy and Policy* 36, no. 3 (2010): 429–61. doi: 10.5840/soctheorpract201036323.

Hume, David. *A Treatise of Human Nature*, edited by L. A. Selby-Bigge and P. H. Nidditch (Oxford: Clarendon Press, 1978).

James, Aaron. *Fairness in Practice* (Oxford: Oxford University Press, 2012).

Johnson, Walter. "To Remake the World: Slavery, Racial Capitalism, and Justice." *Boston Review*. February 20, 2018.

Jones, Peter. "Group Rights and Group Oppression." *Journal of Political Philosophy* 7, no. 4 (1999): 353-77. doi: https://doi.org/10.1111/1467-9760.00081.
Jost, John, Laurie Rudman, Irene Blair, Dana Carney, Nilanjana Dasguta, Jack Glaser, and Curtis Hardin. "The Existence of Implicit Bias Is Beyond a Reasonable Doubt." *Research in Organizational Behavior* 29 (2009): 39-69.
Julius, A. J. "Nagel's Atlas." *Philosophy & Public Affairs* 34, no. 2 (2006): 176-92. doi: https://doi.org/10.1111/j.1088-4963.2006.00061.x.
Kant, Immanuel. "Toward Perpetual Peace." In *Immanuel Kant: Practical Philosophy*, edited by Mary J. Gregor (Cambridge: Cambridge University Press, 1996), 311-52.
Kant, Immanuel. "The Metaphysics of Morals." In *Immanuel Kant: Practical Philosophy*, edited by Mary J. Gregor (Cambridge: Cambridge University Press, 1996), 353-604.
Kijazi, Martin. "Climate Emergency, Carbon Capture and Coercive Conservation on Mt. Kilimanjaro." In *Carbon Conflicts and Forest Landscapes in Africa*, edited by Melissa Leach and Ian Scoones (Oxford: Routledge, 2015), 58-79.
Kleingeld, Pauline. *Kant and Cosmopolitanism: The Philosophical Ideal of World Citizenship* (Cambridge: Cambridge University Press, 2012).
Kleinig, John. "The Nature of Consent." In *The Ethics of Consent*, edited by Franklin Miller and Alan Wertheimer (Oxford: Oxford University Press, 2010), 3-24.
Klimchuk, Dennis. "Grotius on Property and the Right of Necessity." *Journal of the History of Philosophy* 56, no. 2 (2018): 239-60.
Kolers, Avery. "Justice, Territory, and Natural Resources." *Political Studies* 60 no. 2 (2012): 269-86. doi: https://doi.org/10.1111/j.1467-9248.2011.00933.x.
Kolers, Avery. *Land, Conflict, and Justice* (Cambridge: Cambridge University Press, 2009).
Kolodny, Niko. "Rule Over None I: What Justifies Democracy." *Philosophy & Public Affairs* 42, no. 3 (2014): 195-229. doi: https://doi.org/10.1111/papa.12035.
Kolodny, Niko. "Rule over None II: Social Equality and the Justification of Democracy." *Philosophy & Public Affairs* 42, no. 4 (2014): 287-336.
Korman, Sharon. *The Right of Conquest* (Oxford: Clarendon Press, 1996).
Korsgaard, Christine. "The Right to Lie: Kant on Dealing with Evil." In *The Kingdom of Ends* (Cambridge: Cambridge University Press, 1996), 133-58.
Krasner, Stephen. *Sovereignty: Organized Hypocrisy* (Princeton: Princeton University Press, 1999).
Kratochwil, Friedrich. "Of Systems, Boundaries, and Territoriality: An Inquiry into the Formation of the State System." *World Politics* 39, no. 1 (1986): 27-52. doi: https://doi.org/10.2307/2010297.
Krisch, Nico. *Beyond Constitutionalism: The Pluralist Structure of International Law*. (Oxford: Oxford University Press, 2010).
Kutz, Christopher. *Complicity* (Cambridge: Cambridge University Press, 2000).
Kymlicka Will, and Keith Banting. "Immigration, Multiculturalism, and the Welfare State." *Ethics and International Affairs* 20, no. 3 (2006): 281-304. doi: https://doi.org/10.1111/j.1747-7093.2006.00027.x.
Kymlicka, Will. *Multicultural Citizenship* (Oxford: Oxford University Press, 1995).
Kymlicka, Will. *Politics in the Vernacular* (Oxford: Oxford University Press, 2001).
Laborde, Cécile, *Liberalism's Religion* (Cambridge, MA: Harvard University Press, 2017).
Lamond, Grant. "The Coerciveness of Law." *Oxford Journal of Legal Studies* 20, no. 1 (2000): 39-62. doi: 10.1093/ojls/20.1.39.
Lear, Jonathan. *Radical Hope* (Cambridge, MA: Harvard University Press, 2006).
Lefkowitz, David. "Autonomy, Residence, and Return." *Critical Review of International Social and Political Philosophy* 18, no. 5 (2015): 529-46. doi: https://doi.org/10.1080/13698230.2014.927117.

Lesch, Ann M. "No Refuge for Refugees: The Insecure Exile of Palestinians in Kuwait." In *Exile and Return: Predicaments of Palestinians & Jews*, edited by Ann M. Lesch and Ian S. Lustick (Philadelphia: University of Pennsylvania Press, 2005), 161–82.

Lewellen, Ted C. *Political Anthropology: An Introduction* (South Hadley: Bergin and Garvey, 1983).

Lister, Matthew. "Immigration, Association, and the Family." *Law and Philosophy* 29, no. 6 (2010): 717–45. doi: https://www.jstor.org/stable/40926338.

Lister, Matthew. "Who Are Refugees?" *Law and Philosophy* 32, no. 5 (2013): 645–71. doi: https://www.jstor.org/stable/24572417.

Locke, John. *Second Treatise of Government*, edited by Donald Cress (Indianapolis: Hackett, 1980).

Lowie, Robert H. "Some Aspects of Political Organization among the American Aborigines." *The Journal of the Royal Anthropological Institute of Great Britain and Ireland* 78, no. 1/2 (1948): 11–24. doi: http://www.jstor.org/stable/2844522.

Lu, Catherine. "Cosmopolitan Justice, Democracy, and the World State." In *Institutional Cosmopolitanism*, edited by Luis Cabrera (Oxford: Oxford University Press, 2018), 232–52.

Lu, Catherine. "Decolonizing Borders, Self-Determination, and Global Justice." In *Empire, Race, and Global Justice*, edited by Duncan Bell (Cambridge: Cambridge University Press, 2019), 251–71.

Lu, Catherine. *Justice and Reconciliation in World Politics* (Cambridge: Cambridge University Press, 2017).

Lyons, David. "The New Indian Claims and Original Rights to Land." In *Reading Nozick*, edited by Jeffrey Paul. (Totowa: Rowman and Littlefield, 1981), 355–79.

MacDonald, Terry. *Global Stakeholder Democracy: Power and Representation Beyond Liberal States* (Oxford: Oxford University Press, 2008).

Macedo, Stephen. "The Moral Dilemma of US Immigration Policy: Open Borders versus Social Justice?" In *Debating Immigration*, edited by Carol M. Swain (New York: Cambridge University Press, 2007), 63–81.

Malanczuk, Peter. *Akehurst's Modern Introduction to International Law* (London: Routledge, 1997).

Mancilla, Alejandra. "Shared Sovereignty over Migratory Natural Resources." *Res Publica* 22, no. 1 (2016): 21–35. doi: 10.1007/s11158-015-9309-7.

Mancilla, Alejandra. "Rethinking Land and Natural Resources, and Rights over Them." *Philosophy and Public Issues* 6, no. 2 (2016): 125–41.

Marchetti, Raffaele. *Global Democracy: For and Against* (New York: Routledge, 2008).

Margalit, Avishai, and Joseph Raz. "National Self-Determination." *Journal of Philosophy* 87, no. 9 (1990): 439–61. doi: jphil199087942.

Massey, Douglas. "Why Does Immigration Occur? A Theoretical Synthesis." In *The Handbook of International Migration: The American Experience*, edited by Charles Hirschman, Philip Kasinitz, and Josh DeWind (New York: Russel Sage, 1999), 34–52.

Mazor, Joseph. "Liberal Justice, Future People, and Natural Resource Conservation." *Philosophy & Public Affairs* 38, no. 4 (2010): 380–408. doi: https://doi.org/10.1111/j.1088-4963.2010.01189.x.

Mazower, Mark. *Dark Continent* (New York: Random House, 1998).

McAdam, Jane. *Climate Change, Forced Migration, and International Law* (Oxford: Oxford University Press, 2012).

McAdam, Jane. "Introduction." In *Climate Change and Displacement: Multidisciplinary Perspectives*, edited by Jane McAdam (Oxford and Portland: Hart Publishing, 2010), 1–8.

McAdam, Jane, and Maryanne Loughry. "We Aren't Refugees." *Inside Story*. 30 June 2009.

McMahan, Jeff. *Killing in War* (Oxford: Oxford University Press, 2009).
Meisels, Tamar. "Can Corrective Justice Ground Claims to Territory?" *Journal of Political Philosophy* 11, no. 1 (2003): 65–88. doi: https://doi.org/10.1111/1467-9760.00167.
Meisels, Tamar. *Territorial Rights*, 2nd ed. (AA Dordrecht, Netherlands: Springer, 2009).
Mele, Alfred. *Autonomous Agents: From Self-Control to Autonomy* (Oxford: Oxford University Press, 1995).
Meyer, Lukas. "Intergenerational Justice." *The Stanford Encyclopedia of Philosophy* (Summer 2016 edition), edited by Edward N. Zalta. Available online at: https://plato.stanford.edu/entries/justice-intergenerational/.
Mill, J.S. *On Liberty and Other Essays*, edited by John Gray (Oxford: Oxford University Press, 1998).
Miller, David. "Democracy's Domain." *Philosophy & Public Affairs* 37, no. 3 (2009): 201–28. doi: https://doi.org/10.1111/j.1088-4963.2009.01158.x.
Miller, David. "Global Justice and Climate Change: How Should Responsibilities Be Distributed?" *The Tanner Lectures on Human Values*. Tsinghua University, Beijing (2008). Available online at: https://tannerlectures.utah.edu/_documents/a-to-z/m/Miller_08.pdf.
Miller, David. "Grounding Human Rights." *Critical Review of International Social and Political Philosophy* 15, no. 4 (2015): 407–27. doi: https://doi.org/10.1080/13698230.2012.699396.
Miller, David. "Immigration: The Case for Limits." In *Contemporary Debates in Applied Ethics*, edited by Andrew Cohen, Christopher Wellman (Malden: Blackwell, 2004), 193–206.
Miller, David. "Is There a Human Right to Immigrate?" In *Migration in Political Theory: The Ethics of Movement and Membership*, edited by Sarah Fine and Lea Ypi (Oxford: Oxford University Press, 2016), 11–31.
Miller, David. "Majorities and Minarets: Religious Freedom and Public Space." *British Journal of Political Science* 46, no. 2 (2016): 437–56. doi: https://doi.org/10.1017/S0007123414000131.
Miller, David. *On Nationality* (Oxford: Oxford University Press, 1997).
Miller, David. *National Responsibility and Global Justice* (Oxford: Oxford University Press, 2007).
Miller, David. "Neo-Kantian Theories of Self-Determination: A Critique." *Review of International Studies* 42, no. 5 (2016): 858–75. doi: https://doi.org/10.1017/S0260210516000115.
Miller, David. "Secession and the Principle of Nationality." *Canadian Journal of Philosophy* 26, Supplementary Volume (1997): 261–82.
Miller, David. *Strangers in Our Midst* (Cambridge, MA: Harvard University Press, 2016).
Miller, David. "Territorial Rights: Concept and Justification." *Political Studies* 60, no. 2 (2011): 252–68 doi: DOI: 10.1111/j.1467-9248.2011.00911.x.
Moellendorf, Darrel. *The Moral Challenge of Dangerous Climate Change: Values, Poverty, and Policy* (Cambridge: Cambridge University Press, 2014).
Moore, Margaret. "Justice and Colonialism." *Philosophy Compass* 11, no. 8 (2016): 447–61. doi: https://doi.org/10.1111/phc3.12337.
Moore, Margaret. *A Political Theory of Territory* (Oxford: Oxford University Press, 2015).
Morris, Benny. *The Birth of the Palestinian Refugee Problem* (Cambridge: Cambridge University Press, 2004).
Morris, Christopher. *An Essay on the Modern State* (Cambridge: Cambridge University Press, 1998).
Moyn, Samuel. *Not Enough: Human Rights in an Unequal World* (Cambridge, MA: Harvard University Press, 2018).

Näsström, Sofia. "The Challenge of the All-Affected Principle." *Political Studies* 59, no. 1 (2011): 116–34. doi: https://doi.org/10.1111/j.1467-9248.2010.00845.x.

Nine, Cara. "Ecological Refugees, States Borders, and the Lockean Proviso." *Journal of Applied Philosophy* 27, no. 4 (2010): 359–75. doi: https://doi.org/10.1111/j.1468-5930.2010.00498.x.

Nine, Cara. *Global Justice and Territory* (Oxford: Oxford University Press, 2012).

Nine, Cara. "When Affected Interests Demand Joint Self-Determination: Learning from Rivers." *International Theory* 6, no. 1 (2014): 157–74. doi: https://doi.org/10.1017/S1752971914000086.

Nordhaus, William. "Climate Clubs: Overcoming Free Riding in International Climate Policy," *American Economic Review* 105, no. 4 (2015), 1339–70.

Nozick, Robert. *Anarchy, State, and Utopia* (New York: Basic Books, 1974).

Nozick, Robert. "Coercion." In *Philosophy, Politics, and Society: Fourth Series*, edited by Peter Laslett, W. G. Runciman, and Quentin Skinner (Oxford: Blackwell, 1972), 101–35.

Oberman, Kieran. "Immigration and Equal Ownership of the Earth." *Ratio Juris* 30, no. 2 (2017): 144–57. doi: https://doi.org/10.1111/raju.12151.

Oberman, Kieran. "Immigration as a Human Right." In *Migration in Political Theory: The Ethics of Movement and Membership*, edited by Sarah Fine and Lea Ypi (Oxford: Oxford University Press, 2016), 32–56.

Oberman, Kieran. "Immigration, Global Poverty, and the Right to Stay." *Political Studies* 59, no. 2 (2011): 253–68. doi: https://doi.org/10.1111/j.1467-9248.2011.00889.x.

Oberman, Kieran. "Reality for Realists: Why Economic Migrants Should not Just 'Go Home and Wait for Assistance'." *European Political Science* 17, no. 4 (2017): 1–18. doi: https://doi.org/10.1057/s41304-016-0095-2.

Orgad, Liav. *The Cultural Defense of Nations* (Oxford: Oxford University Press, 2015).

Ostrom, Elinor. *Governing the Commons: The Evolution of Institutions for Collective Action* (Cambridge: Cambridge University Press, 1990).

Ottaviano, Gianmarco, and Giovanni Peri. "Rethinking the Effects of Immigration on Wages." National Bureau of Economic Research. Working Paper 12497, revised version May 2008.

Overland, Gerhard, and Barry, Christian. "Do Democratic Societies Have a Right to Do Wrong?," *Journal of Social Philosophy*, 42, no. 2 (2011): 111–31. doi: https://doi.org/10.1111/j.1467-9833.2011.01524.x.

Van Parijs, Philippe. "International Distributive Justice." In *A Companion to Contemporary Political Philosophy*, edited by Robert Goodin, Philip Pettit, and Thomas Pogge (Oxford: Blackwell, 2007), 638–52.

Parker, Linda. *Native Estate*. Honolulu: University of Hawaii Press, 1989.

Patten, Alan. "Self-Determination for National Minorities." In *The Theory of Self-Determination*, edited by Fernando Teson (Cambridge: Cambridge University Press, 2016), 120–44.

Patten, Alan. *Equal Recognition* (Princeton: Princeton University Press, 2014).

Perdue, Theda, and Michael Green. *The Cherokee Nation and the Trail of Tears* (New York: Viking Penguin, 2007).

Perrez, Franz. "The Relationship between 'Permanent Sovereignty' and the Obligation not to cause Transboundary Environmental Damage." *Environmental Law* 26, no. 4 (1996): 1187–212. doi: https://www.jstor.org/stable/43267547.

Pettit, Philip, and Christian List. *Group Agency* (Oxford: Oxford University Press, 2011).

Pettit, Philip. "Rawls's Political Ontology." *Politics, Philosophy, and Economics* 4, no. 2 (2005): 157–74. doi: https://doi.org/10.1177/1470594X05052536.

Pettit, Philip. "Responsibility Incorporated." *Ethics* 117, no. 2 (2007): 171–201. doi: https://doi.org/10.1086/510695.
Pettit, Philip. *On the People's Terms* (Cambridge: Cambridge University Press, 2012).
Pevnick, Ryan. *Immigration and the Constraints of Justice* (Cambridge: Cambridge University Press, 2011).
Pevnick, Ryan, and Michael Kates. "Immigration, Jurisdiction, and History." *Philosophy & Public Affairs* 42, no. 2 (2013): 179–94. https://doi.org/10.1111/papa.12030.
Pevnick, Ryan. "Social Trust and the Ethics of Immigration Policy." *Journal of Political Philosophy* 17, no. 2 (2009): 146–67. doi: https://doi.org/10.1111/j.1467-9760.2007.00296.x.
Philpott, Daniel. *Revolutions in Sovereignty* (Princeton: Princeton University Press, 2010).
Pogge, Thomas. "Allowing the Poor to Share the Earth." *Journal of Moral Philosophy* 8, no. 3 (2011): 335–52. doi: 10.1163/174552411X588982.
Pogge, Thomas. "An Egalitarian Law of Peoples." *Philosophy & Public Affairs* 23, no. 3 (1994): 195–224. doi: https://doi.org/10.1111/j.1088-4963.1994.tb00011.x.
Pogge, Thomas. *Realizing Rawls* (Ithaca: Cornell University Press, 1989).
Pogge, Thomas. *World Poverty and Human Rights* (Cambridge: Polity, 2008).
Price, Matthew. *Rethinking Asylum: Its History, Purpose, and Limits* (Cambridge: Cambridge University Press, 2009).
Pufendorf, Samuel. *Of the Law of Nature and Nations*, translated by Basil Kennett (London: Carew, 1729).
Putnam, Robert D. "*E Pluribus Unum*: Diversity and Community in the Twenty-First Century." *Scandinavian Political Studies* 30, no. 2 (2007): 137–74. doi: https://doi.org/10.1111/j.1467-9477.2007.00176.x.
Quong, Jonathan. *Liberalism without Perfection* (Oxford: Oxford University Press, 2011).
Rafanelli, Lucia. "A Defense of Individualism in an Age of Corporate Rights." *Journal of Political Philosophy* 25, no. 3 (2017): 281–302. doi: https://doi.org/10.1111/jopp.12112.
Ranlegh, John. *A Short History of Ireland* (Cambridge: Cambridge University Press, 1983).
Rawls, John. "Social Unity and Primary Goods." In *John Rawls: Collected Papers*, edited by Samuel Freeman (Cambridge, MA: Harvard University Press, 1999), 359–87.
Rawls, John. *A Theory of Justice*, 2nd ed. (Cambridge, MA: Harvard University Press, 1999).
Rawls, John. *Justice as Fairness: A Restatement* (Cambridge, MA: Harvard University Press, 2001).
Rawls, John. "A Kantian Conception of Equality." *Cambridge Review* 96, no. 225 (1975): 94–9.
Rawls, John. *The Law of Peoples* (Cambridge, MA: Harvard University Press, 1999).
Rawls, John. *Political Liberalism*, expanded edition (New York: Columbia University Press, 2005).
Raz, Joseph. "Human Rights without Foundations." In *The Philosophy of International Law*, edited by John Tasioulas and Samantha Besson (Oxford: Oxford University Press, 2010), 321–38.
Raz, Joseph. *The Morality of Freedom* (Oxford: Clarendon Press, 1986).
Ripstein, Arthur. "Beyond the Harm Principle." *Philosophy & Public Affairs* 34, no. 3 (2006): 215–45. doi: www.jstor.org/stable/3876391.
Ripstein, Arthur. *Force and Freedom* (Cambridge, MA: Harvard University Press, 2009).
Risse, Mathias. *On Global Justice* (Cambridge, MA: Harvard University Press, 2012).
Risse, Mathias. "The Right to Relocation: Disappearing Island Nations and Common Ownership of the Earth." *Ethics and International Affairs* 23, no. 3 (2009): 281–300. doi: https://doi.org/10.1111/j.1747-7093.2009.00218.x.

Risse, Mathias. "Taking up Space on Earth: Theorizing Territorial Rights, the Justification of States and Immigration from a Global Standpoint." *Global Constitutionalism* 4, no. 1 (2015): 81–113. doi: https://doi.org/10.1017/S2045381714000161.

Ronzoni, Miriam. "The Global Order: A Case of Background Injustice?" *Philosophy & Public Affairs* 37, no. 3 (2009): 229–56. doi: https://doi.org/10.1111/j.1088-4963.2009.01159.x.

Salter, John. "Grotius and Pufendorf on the Right of Necessity." *History of Political Thought* 26, no. 2 (2005): 284–302. doi: http://www.jstor.org/stable/26221696.

Sangiovanni, Andrea. "Global Justice, Reciprocity, and the State." *Philosophy & Public Affairs* 35, no. 1 (2007): 3–39. doi: https://doi.org/10.1111/j.1088-4963.2007.00097.x.

Scanlon, T. M. *The Difficulty of Tolerance* (Cambridge: Cambridge University Press, 2003).

Scanlon, T. M. "Nozick on Rights, Liberty, and Property." In *Reading Nozick*, edited by Jeffrey Paul (Oxford: Blackwell, 1981), 107–29.

Scanlon, T. M. *What We Owe to Each Other* (Cambridge, MA: Harvard University Press, 1998).

Schrijver, Nico. *Sovereignty over Natural Resources: Balancing Rights and Duties.* (Cambridge: Cambridge University Press, 1997).

Sciaraffa, Stefan. "Identification, Meaning, and the Normativity of Social Roles." *European Journal of Philosophy* 19, no. 1 (2009): 107–28. doi: https://doi.org/10.1111/j.1468-0378.2009.00375.x.

Schotel, Bas. *On the Right of Exclusion: Law, Ethics, and Immigration Policy* (London: Routledge, 2012).

De Schutter, Helder, and Lea Ypi. "Mandatory Citizenship for Immigrants." *British Journal of Political Science* 45, no. 2 (2015): 235–51. doi: https://doi.org/10.1017/S0007123414000568.

De Schutter, Helder. "Non-territorial Jurisdictional Authority: A Radical Possibility in Need of a Critique." In *Recognition and Redistribution in Multinational Federalism*, edited by J. F. Grégoire and M. Jewkes (Leuven: Leuven University Press, 2015), 35–56.

Sen, Amartya. "Equality of What?" *The Tanner Lectures on Human Values.* Stanford University, 22 May 1979. Available at: http://www.ophi.org.uk/wp-content/uploads/Sen-1979_Equality-of-What.pdf.

Shachar, Ayelet. *The Birthright Lottery* (Cambridge, MA: Harvard University Press, 2009).

Shacknove, Andrew. "Who is a Refugee?" *Ethics* 95, no. 2 (1985): 274–84. doi: http://www.jstor.org/stable/2380340.

Shapiro, Scott. *Legality* (Cambridge, MA: Harvard University Press, 2011).

Sharon, Assaf. "Domination and the Rule of Law." In *Oxford Studies in Political Philosophy*: Volume 2, edited by David Sobel, Peter Vallentyne, and Steven Wall (Oxford: Oxford University Press, 2016), 128–55.

Shaw, Malcolm. *International Law* (Cambridge: Cambridge University Press, 2008).

Shue, Henry. "Subsistence Emissions and Luxury Emissions," *Law and Policy*, 15, no. 1 (1993): 39–60.

Shue, Henry. "Limiting Sovereignty." In *Humanitarian Intervention and International Relations*, edited by Jennifer Welsh (Oxford: Oxford University Press, 2004), 11–28.

Shepherd, Todd. *The Invention of Decolonization* (Ithaca: Cornell University Press, 2006).

Sidgwick, Henry. *The Elements of Politics* (London: MacMillan, 1908).

Simmons, A. John. *Justification and Legitimacy: Essays on Rights and Obligations* (Cambridge: Cambridge University Press, 2001).

Simmons, A. John. "On the Territorial Rights of States." *Philosophical Issues* 11, no. 1 (2001): 300–26. doi: https://doi.org/10.1111/j.1758-2237.2001.tb00048.x.

Simmons, A. John. *Boundaries of Authority* (Oxford: Oxford University Press, 2016).

Simmons, A. John. *The Lockean Theory of Rights* (Princeton: Princeton University Press, 1992).
Spruyt, Hendrik. *The Sovereign State and Its Competitors* (Princeton: Princeton University Press, 1996).
Standing Bear, Luther. *My People, the Sioux*, new ed. (Lincoln: Bison Books, 2006).
Steiner, Hillel. *An Essay on Rights* (Oxford: Wiley-Blackwell, 1994).
Steiner, Hillel. "Territorial Justice and Global Redistribution." In *The Political Philosophy of Cosmopolitanism*, edited by Gillian Brock and Harry Brighouse (Cambridge: Cambridge University Press, 2005), 28–38.
Steiner, Hillel. "Territorial Justice and Global Redistribution." *Philosophy & Public Affairs* 38, no. 4 (2010): 28–38.
Stilz, Anna. "Civic Nationalism and Language Policy." *Philosophy & Public Affairs* 37, no. 3 (2009): 257–92. doi: https://doi.org/10.1111/j.1088-4963.2009.01160.x.
Stilz, Anna. "Collective Responsibility and the State." *Journal of Political Philosophy* 19, no. 2 (2011): 190–208. doi: https://doi.org/10.1111/j.1467-9760.2010.00360.x.
Stilz, Anna. "Decolonization and Self-Determination." *Social Philosophy and Policy* 32, no.1 (2015): 1–24. doi: https://doi.org/10.1017/S0265052515000059.
Stilz, Anna. "Is There an Unqualified Right to Leave?" In *Migration and Morality*, edited by Sarah Fine and Lea Ypi (Oxford: Oxford University Press, 2016), 57–79.
Stilz, Anna. "Nations, States and Territory." *Ethics* 121, no. 3 (2011): 572–601. doi: https://doi.org/10.1086/658937.
Stilz, Anna. "Occupancy Rights and the Wrong of Removal." *Philosophy & Public Affairs* 41, no. 4 (2013): 324–56. doi: https://doi.org/10.1111/papa.12018.
Stilz, Anna. "Why Do States Have Territorial Rights?" *International Theory* 1, no. 2 (2009): 185–213. doi: https://doi.org/10.1017/S1752971909000104.
Stilz, Anna. *Liberal Loyalty: Freedom, Obligation, and the State* (Princeton: Princeton University Press, 2009).
Strayer, Joseph. *Medieval Origins of the Modern State* (Princeton: Princeton University Press, 2005).
Tadros, Victor, "The Persistence of the Right of Return." *Politics, Philosophy, and Economics* 16, no. 4 (2017): 375–99. doi: https://doi.org/10.1177/1470594X17736265.
Taylor, Charles. "What's Wrong with Negative Liberty?" *Philosophy and the Human Sciences* 2, no. 8 (1985): 211–29. doi: https://doi/org/10.1017/CBO9781139173490.009.
Trigger, Bruce, ed. *The Handbook of the North American Indians, Vol. 15: Northeast* (Washington, DC: Smithsonian Institution, 1978).
Tuck, Richard. *The Rights of War and Peace* (Oxford: Oxford University Press, 2011).
Tully, James. *A Discourse on Property* (Cambridge: Cambridge University Press, 1980).
Valentini, Laura. "Human Rights, Freedom, and Political Authority." *Political Theory* 40, no. 5 (2012): 573–601. doi: https://doi.org/10.1177/0090591712451721.
Valentini, Laura. "No Global Demos, No Global Democracy? A Systemization and Critique." *Perspectives on Politics* 12, no. 4 (2014): 789–807. doi: https://doi.org/10.1017/S1537592714002138.
Valentini, Laura. "On the Distinctive Procedural Wrong of Colonialism." *Philosophy & Public Affairs* 43, no. 4 (2015): 312–31. doi: https://doi.org/10.1111/papa.12057.
Vanderheiden, Steve. *Atmospheric Justice: A Political Theory of Climate Change* (Oxford: Oxford University Press, 2008).
Vanderheiden, Steve. "Territorial Rights and Carbon Sinks." *Science and Engineering Ethics* 23, no. 5 (2017): 1273–87. doi: 10.1007/s11948-016-9840-8.
De Vattel, Emer. *The Law of Nations*, edited by Béla Kapossy and Richard Whatmore (Indianapolis: Liberty Fund, 1758/2008).

Viehoff, Daniel. "Democratic Equality and Political Authority." *Philosophy & Public Affairs* 42, no. 4 (2014): 337–75. doi: 10.1111/papa.12036.

Vitoria, Francisco. "On the American Indians." In *Political Writings*, edited by Anthony Pagden and Jeremy Lawrence (Cambridge: Cambridge University Press, 1991), 278–84.

Van der Vossen, Bas. "Immigration and Self-Determination." *Politics, Philosophy and Economics* 14, no. 3 (2014): 270–90. doi: https://doi.org/10.1177/1470594X14533167.

Van der Vossen, Bas. "Imposing Duties and Original Appropriation." *Journal of Political Philosophy* 23, no. 1 (2013): 64–85. doi: https://doi.org/10.1111/jopp.12029.

Waldron, Jeremy. *Liberal Rights, Collected Papers 1981–1991* (Cambridge: Cambridge University Press, 1993).

Waldron, Jeremy. "Homelessness and the Issue of Freedom." *UCLA Law Review* 39, no. 295 (1992): 295–324.

Waldron, Jeremy. "Kant's Legal Positivism." *Harvard Law Review* 109, no. 7 (1996): 1535–66. doi: 10.2307/1342024.

Waldron, Jeremy. *Law and Disagreement* (Oxford: Oxford University Press, 1999).

Waldron, Jeremy. "Superseding Historic Injustice." *Ethics* 103, no.1 (1992): 4–28. doi: https://www.jstor.org/stable/2381493.

Waldron, Jeremy. "Two Conceptions of Self-Determination." In *The Philosophy of International Law*, edited by John Tasioulas and Samantha Besson (Oxford: Oxford University Press, 2010), 397–416.

Waldron, Jeremy. *The Right to Private Property* (Oxford: Oxford University Press, 1988).

Walzer, Michael. "The Moral Standing of States." In *Thinking Politically*, edited by David Miller (New Haven: Yale University Press, 2007), 219–36.

Walzer, Michael. "Nation and Universe." In *Thinking Politically*, edited by David Miller (New Haven: Yale University Press, 2007), 183–218.

Walzer, Michael. *On Toleration* (New Haven: Yale University Press, 2008).

Walzer, Michael. *Spheres of Justice* (New York: Basic Books, 1983).

Watson, Gary. "Free Agency." In *The Inner Citadel: Essays on Individual Autonomy*, edited by John Christman (Brattleboro: Echo Point, 1989), 109–21.

Wellman, Christopher, and A. John Simmons. *Is There a Duty to Obey the Law* (Cambridge: Cambridge University Press, 2005).

Wellman, Christopher. "Immigration and Freedom of Association." *Ethics* 119, no. 1 (2008): 109–41. doi: 10.1086/592311.

Wellman, Christopher. "Occupancy Rights and the Right of Return." Unpublished manuscript, 2015.

Wellman, Christopher. "The Rights Forfeiture Theory of Punishment." *Ethics* 122, no. 2 (2012): 371–93. doi: 10.1086/663791.

Wellman, Christopher. *A Theory of Secession* (Oxford: Oxford University Press, 2005).

Wenar, Leif. *Blood Oil* (Oxford: Oxford University Press, 2016).

Wenar, Leif. "Reparations for the Future." *Journal of Social Philosophy* 37, no. 3 (2006): 396–405. doi: https://doi.org/10.1111/j.1467-9833.2006.00344.x.

Witherspoon, Gary. "Navajo Social Organization." In *Handbook of North American Indians* 10 (Washington, DC: Smithsonian Institution, 1983), 524–35.

Woodward, James. "Commentary: Liberalism and Migration." In *Free Movement*, edited by Brian Barry and Robert Goodin (Oxford: Oxford University Press, 2016), 59–84.

Young, Iris Marion. *Global Challenges* (Cambridge: Polity, 2007).

Young, Iris Marion. *Inclusion and Democracy* (New York: Oxford University Press, 2000).

Ypi, Lea. "Cosmopolitanism without If and without But." In *Cosmopolitanism versus Non-Cosmopolitanism*, edited by Gillian Brock (Oxford: Oxford University Press, 2013), 75–91.

Ypi, Lea. *Global Justice and Avant-Garde Political Agency* (Oxford: Oxford University Press, 2012).

Ypi, Lea. "A Permissive Theory of Territorial Rights." *European Journal of Philosophy* 22, no. 2 (2012): 288–312. doi: https://doi.org/10.1111/j.1468-0378.2011.00506.x.

Ypi, Lea. "Structural Injustice and the Place of Attachment." *Journal of Practical Ethics* 5, no. 1 (2017): 1–21.

Ypi, Lea. "What's Wrong with Colonialism." *Philosophy & Public Affairs* 41, no. 2 (2013): 158–91. doi: https://doi.org/10.1111/papa.12014.

Zertal, Idith, and Akiva Eldar. *Lords of the Land: The War over Israel's Settlements in the Occupied Territories, 1967–2007* (New York: Nation Books, 2005).

Zuehl, Jake. *Collective Self- Determination*. PhD dissertation, Princeton University, 2016.

Name Index

Abizadeh, Arash 7
Altman, Andrew 136, 151 and n.66, 152
Armstrong, Chris 183–4, 219, 227, 228 and n.35, 229 and n.43, 230

Barry, Brian 159
Beitz, Charles 159, 228 and n.36
Bentham, Jeremy 38
Bodin, Jean 13
Blackstone, William 61
Blake, Michael 112, 192, 198–9
Buchanan, Allen 25–6, 90, 135, 138n.32
Burbank, Jane 3

Caney, Simon 255
Carens, Joseph 7, 42–3, 187, 202–203, 204n.48, 205, 208n.60, 209
Casal, Paula 228
Cicero 63
Cohen, Joshua 131n.20
Columbus, Christopher 39, 65
Coon-Come, Matthew 231
Cooper, Frederick 3
Cornell, Nicolas 72n.32

Davies, Norman 18
Dworkin, Ronald 161–2

Freiman, Chris 203

Gans, Chaim 53, 143
Goodin, Robert 6–7
Grotius, Hugo 23, 60–4, 67, 71, 73, 84, 225 and n.27, 226, 252
 De Jure Belli ac Pacis 63, 71, 252
 De Jure Praedae 61 and n.6, 62

Held, David 255
Hidalgo, Javier 203
Hobbes, Thomas 13, 36, 38, 124n.7
Honoré, Tony 69
Hossain, Kamal 221
Hume, David 25, 36, 38–9, 226

Kant, Immanuel 23, 54n.38, 59, 68 and n.22, 94–7, 99n.20, 114–15, 117, 118n.51, 119, 131, 134, 148, 153, 255, 256 and n.13, 257

Kates, Michael 198
Kolers, Avery 160, 162–3, 164 and n.26, 167
Kolodny, Niko 99n.21, 107
Kratochwil, Friedrich 4
Krisch, Niko 7
Kymlicka, Will 53, 139–40, 143, 145, 177

Locke, John 23, 26–7, 33, 40n.14, 47, 63, 65, 130, 225n.26
Lu, Catherine 255
Ly, Minh 183n.67

MacDonald, Terry 7
Mancilla, Alejandra 238 and n.61
Margalit, Avishai 139
Mazower, Mark 19
Meisels, Tamar 53
Mill, John Stuart 150 and n.61
Miller, David 28, 53, 136n.28, 162, 169, 177, 180–1, 190–1, 195n.26, 204n.50, 206
Moore, Margaret 29, 53, 80n.49, 151, 169, 233
Morris, Benny 51

Nine, Cara 29, 179, 224, 230, 241–2
Nordhaus, William 245
Nozick, Robert 33, 50, 69

Oberman, Kieran 7, 203, 208n.60

Patten, Alan 177
Pevnick, Ryan 198
Philpott, Daniel 14
Pogge, Thomas 159, 162n.19, 234–5
Pufendorf, Samuel von 23, 64–5, 67, 69, 225 and n.27

Rawls, John 8 and n.37, 9 and n.37, 38, 46n.24, 70n.27, 89, 93 and n.15, 111, 114n.47, 128n.14, 130n.19, 131n.20, 150 and n.61, 153, 161n.11, 165n.30, 204–205, 207
 Law of Peoples 8n.37, 114n.47
 Theory of Justice 8
Raz, Joseph 48n.26, 139, 204, 207
Ripstein, Arthur 70n.28

Risse, Mathias 159–60, 161 and n.11, 162, 169
Ross, John 75
Rousseau, Jean-Jacques 106, 127

Scanlon, T.M. 47n.25
Schrijver, Nico 220, 239n.64
Sen, Amartya 161n.11
Shacknove, Andrew 171n.45
Sidgwick, Henry 25
Simmons, A. John 33, 40n.14, 79, 157
Stalin, Josef 178
Steiner, Hillel 159, 161–2
Strayer, Joseph 5

Tadros, Victor 81

Valentini, Laura 132n.21
De Vattel, Emer 225
Viehoff, Daniel 70n.29, 99n.21

Waldron, Jeremy 40n.14, 66, 68, 79n.46
Walzer, Michael 105n.33, 110–11, 141–2, 190–1, 253
Weber, Max 14, 131
Wellman, Christopher 136, 151 and n.66, 152, 191 and n.15, 193
Wenar, Leif 25, 236

Ypi, Lea 59, 253, 255

Zuehl, Jake 99n.21

Subject Index

absolutism 13, 130
accountability 232
adjudication 68, 90, 95–6
aesthetics 163–4, 174
Africa 20, 91, 172, 247
agencies 239, 244
agency 110, 114, 124–5, 191
  collective 120, 125, 127
  self-directed 105–106, 109, 152
agriculture 3
Algeria 20, 102–104, 105n.33, 235
alienation 100, 117, 127, 134–5, 137, 141, 145,
  153, 158, 195–6, 227, 231, 250 *see also*
  coercion, alien *and* non-alienation
  and rights, to alienate
  avoidance of *see* non-alienation
All-Affected Interests Principle 6
All-Subjected Principle 7
Amazon, the 45
Amish, the 44
anarchism 115
annexation 91–2, 102–104, 117–19, 132, 148,
  151 and n.66
  colonial 95, 117–18
Antarctica 229, 233
apartheid 133–4
appropriation 63–4, 67–8, 71, 91
  unilateral 64–6, 84
Arab States, the 51, 167
Arabs 192
Arctic, the 41, 57, 233
asylum seekers 171
attitudes 141, 150, 196–7, 201–202
Australia 76, 178–81
Australian Aborigines 2
Austria 18
authority 1, 3–4, 14, 66–8, 96–8, 100, 126, 130–1,
  164, 189, 214, 232, 236–7, 250, 255–7
  allocation of 10
  channels for revoking 128, 130–1
  global/international 7, 59
  legitimacy of 20, 68, 95, 110, 124n.7, 188,
    236, 257
  omnilateral 68 *see also* legitimacy, omnilateral
  political 10, 100, 128, 182, 256–7
  public 100
  of the state 95–6

autonomy 12, 20, 60–2, 64, 67–9, 80, 90, 94,
  99–101, 104–107, 110–15, 117–18,
  128, 138 and n.32, 151, 153, 175, 177,
  179, 181–2, 207, 215, 226, 232, 248
  see also self-governance
  of individuals/personal 11, 23, 29, 41–2, 67,
    71, 99–102, 105–107, 110–11,
    113–15, 117, 128, 131, 141, 152, 167,
    191, 193, 195, 204–205, 207, 229,
    232, 241, 249, 257
  internal 117–18, 120, 133, 134 and n.25, 137,
    139, 224, 232, 251
  political 23–4, 84, 94, 99n.21, 104,
    106–107, 110, 112, 114–20, 126–7,
    131–2, 134n.25, 135, 138 and n.32,
    140–1, 149–50, 152, 158, 179, 182,
    189, 193–5, 197–8, 240–1, 250
  territorially based *see* self-determination
  thinking component of 105–106
  threats to 107, 194

backlash 201, 212
bands 2–3, 38n.10
basic justice *see* justice, basic
Bedouins, the 167–8, 192
Black Hills (South Dakota) 41, 43, 223
Blue Lake (New Mexico) 41, 43, 83
borders 7, 19, 22, 104, 197, 203, 207
  control of 1, 22, 170, 199, 201–204, 207, 215
  interaction across 207
  open 6–8, 209
"bottom up" strategy, the 253–4, 257
boundaries 2, 4–5, 8–9, 18–19, 25, 27, 55, 104,
  152, 165, 197, 209–210 *see also* borders
  and transboundary issues
  current 18, 20, 23
  drawing of 9, 103–104, 127 *see also*
    boundaries, redrawing of
  establishment of 57n.40
  jurisdictional 210, 249
  legitimacy of 9 and n.37, 12, 17, 20, 210
  redrawing/renegotiation of 20n.58, 127, 132,
    134, 175
  theories of 29
British Empire, the 115, 235
burdens 48, 178, 199, 243–4
Burma 160

Canada 54, 137, 205
  native peoples of *see* Native North Americans
  territories/provinces of
    Nunavut 137
    Quebec 231
"cantilever argument", the 202–203
Catalonia 20 and n.58
Catholicism 54, 148–9, 165
causal processes 109
Ceteris paribus clause, the 47
checks and balances 13
children 35, 81, 206, 214
Chile 221
China 20, 193–4
choice 46–7, 71, 92, 107, 191, 204–206, 207
    and n.59, 237, 241
  control of 204
  lack of 121, 123
citizens 197–8, 256
  second-class *see* "denizens"
citizenship 197 and n.31
citizenship education 197–8, 253
civil disobedience 1
clans 38n.10
climate change 6, 14, 16, 22, 24, 158, 164–5, 169,
    179, 182, 185, 212, 220, 238, 258
  mitigation of 242, 244–8, 258
climate justice 178n.56, 220, 243–4
coercion 1, 3, 23–4, 51–2, 95, 99–100,
    106–107, 109, 111, 115, 117–18,
    121–3, 125–6, 138, 141, 149, 152–3,
    203, 236, 241, 245–6, 254, 257–8
    see also coercive power *and*
    enforcement, coercive
  alien 23, 100, 141, 153
    avoidance of/protection from 11, 23, 100,
      126, 209–210
  border 52
  legitimacy of 153, 253, 257–8
  omnilateral 109
  political 109, 126, 153
  social 130
  unilateral 99, 109, 211, 258
    avoidance of 23, 99–101, 110, 258
coercive power 3, 7, 21n.59, 25, 152–3
collective action 6, 16, 67 *see also* agency,
    collective *and* coordination *and* duties,
    to contribute to morally mandatory
    collective action
collective self-determination *see*
    self-determination, collective
collectivism 34 and n.4, 36, 133, 151 and
    n.66, 152

colonialism 9, 15, 18, 20, 23, 38, 77–8, 90–2, 95,
    101–104, 115, 117–18, 135, 151,
    187n.3, 193, 236, 254 *see also* colonial
    settlement *and* decolonization
  benign 23, 91–2
  wrongs of 101–104, 118, 131
colonial settlement 20, 23, 73–4, 193
commitments 47, 57–8, 71, 94, 98, 109, 112,
    114, 116, 123, 144, 153, 174, 190
  second-order 108
  shared 110, 117, 123, 129, 193
common sympathies 150, 152–3
communities 39, 110–11, 113, 129, 179, 181,
    183, 190, 230, 233–4, 237, 247–8
  of character 190
  local 233–4, 247–8
  political 89, 108, 110–11, 143, 146, 158–9,
    163, 166–7, 183, 190–1, 232, 240, 254
compensation 76–7, 222 and n.11, 228, 243–5
competition 21, 64, 129, 161, 188 *see also*
    interests, competing
complexity 121
comprehensive aims 230
compulsion 50–2, 90
conflict 49, 116, 122, 175 *see also* disputes
conquest 9, 18–20, 25, 58, 74, 91, 142
consent 27, 65, 123, 125
  collective 64
  global 226
  invalidation of 125
conservation 243–8, 258 *see also* climate change,
    mitigation of *and* environment, the
    and land, preservation of
consumption 164n.26, 228n.36
constraint 65–6, 109, 116 *see also* governments,
    constraint of
contract 10, 36–7, 56, 71, 95
conventions
  international 39, 233, 237, 247
  social 39, 69
cooperation 98, 100–101, 112–13, 115,
    120–4, 126, 128n.14, 132–3, 141,
    150, 152, 195, 237, 239, 241, 243–6,
    252, 255, 257–8 *see also* duties, of
    cooperation and comanagement
    and partnership
  collective 133
  economic 16
  lack of 94
  political 135, 152
  social 93
cooperators 94, 98, 100–101, 104, 110–13, 117,
    119–20, 152, 257 *see also* noncooperators

coordination 6, 16, 96–8, 246, 258 *see also* collective action
core values 10–12, 14–15, 18, 21–2, 24, 157, 185, 212, 214, 250, 252
  basic justice *see* justice, basic
  collective self-determination *see* self-determination, collective
  occupancy *see* occupancy
corporations 221–2, 240
correspondence 107, 110–11, 126, 141, 190 *see also* willing participation
cosmopolitanism 5, 6 and n.22, 7–9, 12, 14, 17, 59–60, 64, 153, 159, 219, 228 and n.35, 229, 234, 247, 253, 255–8
  moral 6n.22, 9
costs 48, 199, 202, 207–208, 211, 243–5
Crimea 20, 178
Cuba 54
cultural neutrality 147–9, 241, 251
culture 28, 43, 83, 111, 122, 124, 139–46, 147 and n.58, 148–50, 158, 162, 164, 174–5, 177, 179–81, 183, 190–2, 196, 200, 205, 213, 230, 232, 240, 250 *see also* nations, cultural *and* practices, cultural *and* rights, cultural
  national 139–40, 143–5, 147, 191–2, 196, 250
  protection and promotion of 140–2, 149–50, 190–1, 196, 200, 213
  shared 140, 150, 196
Czechoslovakia 20n.58, 137

"decency" 167–8
decentralization 29, 250
decisions 44, 68, 98–9, 104, 106, 109, 119, 121, 124–6, 129, 137, 152, 186–7, 189–90, 205–206, 242, 255
  collective 109, 152, 189, 241
  political 6, 101, 108, 189
decolonization/anticolonialism 20n.58, 104, 221–2, 230, 235–6
delegation 129
democracy 98, 102–104, 106, 127–30, 131 and n.20, 133, 198, 248, 255, 257 *see also* elections *and* institutions, democratic
  deliberative 140, 249
  global 6–7
  "stakeholder" 7
democratic incorporation 102–103
demography 19, 160
"denizens" 197
Denmark 132, 194
developed countries 243, 248

developing countries 222 and n.11, 243–4, 247–8 *see also* Global South, the
difference principle, the 89
dislocation 53, 78
displacement 58, 79, 178
dispossession 23, 38, 80, 84
  past 74, 85
disputes/disagreements 54n.38, 68, 90, 95–6, 116, 175
  settlement of 14, 55n.38, 95–6
distribution 22, 48, 65–6, 74, 101, 103, 158, 161, 163, 164 and n.26, 165, 173–4, 176–7, 180, 183–5, 200, 207–208, 233–5, 237, 245–6, 252 *see also* fair shares
diversity 53, 191–2, 195 *see also* pluralism
division of labor 2
Doctrine of Right 68
domains 225
Druze, the 192
duties 16, 48 and n.26, 49, 63, 67–8, 71–2, 91, 101, 111, 115, 170, 185, 199, 238 and n.63, 239, 241, 245–6, 252–3, 255, 258 *see also* duty to allow harmless migration *and* duty to not interfere with occupancy rights *and* duty to permit permanent settlement
  basic 62, 113, 195
  to contribute to morally mandatory collective action 16
  of cooperation and comanagement 237–9, 241, 243–6, 252
  of corrective justice 16–17
  distributive 17, 245
  to ensure fair background conditions for self-determination 16
  to ensure fair terms of economic cooperation 16
  grounding of 72
  imposed 48, 59, 199 *see also* burdens
  of justice *see* justice, duties of
  moral 37n.9, 60, 63, 67 and n.20, 68–70, 74, 79, 195–6, 229, 251
  natural 95, 98, 116 *see also* justice, duties of, natural
  of poverty eradication 15
  self-imposed 67
  of states 13
  sufficientarian 15
duty to allow harmless migration 170–2, 186–8, 197, 211, 215, 241, 251–2
duty to permit permanent settlement 188
duty to not interfere with occupancy rights 51n.32, 186 *see also* freedom, from interference *and* rights, of others, respect for

economic development 173
economics 49–50, 71, 91, 172, 180, 200, 208, 221–3, 231, 237, 245 *see also* cooperation, economic *and* practices, economic
effective control (principle of) 24–6
egalitarianism 2, 98, 149, 159, 161, 165, 191n.15 *see also* equality
elections 104, 106, 129, 131, 133
empires 3–4
enforcement 1, 67–8, 89–90, 96, 101, 113, 118, 130, 152–3, 185, 241, 245–6, 251, 253, 257–8
  coercive 3, 106–107, 257–8 *see also* coercion
  legitimacy of 96, 113, 132, 153, 245, 257–8
  omnilateral 97, 99
  temporarily permissible 113, 115, 126, 132
  unilateral 23, 97–9, 258 *see also* coercion,unilateral
  vigilante 90
environment, the 147, 160, 162, 166–7, 171, 187, 220, 223, 227, 231, 233, 239, 242, 244–8 *see also* climate change *and* justice, environmental *and* policy, environmental *and* regulation, environmental
envy test, the 161
equality 62, 68, 111, 115, 145, 149, 158, 161, 163, 165, 173, 184, 195n.26, 197, 222n.14, 229, 250, 257 *see also* egalitarianism
  of distribution *see also* fair shares
  global 15
  lack of *see* inequality
  social 98, 99 and n.21, 102
  of states 13
ethnicity 45, 54, 143, 166, 195
ethnogeography 166
Europe 4, 193n.21, 205
  Eastern 78
European Union (EU), the 2n.5, 57, 187
exchange 2, 71, 163n.20, 164
exclusion 1, 12, 69–70, 72–4, 157, 164–5, 176, 185–92, 193 and n.21, 194–202, 207–208, 211–15, 226–7, 230, 232, 237, 246, 250–1
  from citizenship 197
  conditional model of 60, 69–70, 72–4, 186–9, 191, 194–6, 198–9, 207, 211–15, 234 *see also* rights, to exclude, conditional
  discretionary *see* rights, to exclude, conditional
  justifications for 188, 195–7, 200–202, 208, 211–14
    ideal reasons for 199–201, 211–13
    non-ideal reasons for 196, 201–202, 212
  neutralist model of 192 and n.18
  rights *see* rights, to exclude
  from territory 197
  unjustifiability of *see* duty to allow harmless migration *and* duty to not interfere with occupancy rights
"Exclusive Economic Zones" 223
exploitation 16, 91, 101, 132, 162 and n.19, 231 *see also* resources, exploitation of
expulsion 19–20, 23, 44–5, 53, 74–6, 80–2, 85, 92
external objects 62–3, 68n.22, 72 *see also* goods *and* possessions *and* resources

fair shares 159, 161, 165, 173, 176, 181–5, 207–208, 233, 237, 241, 251
fair use proviso, the 21, 47–9, 57, 63, 69, 74, 157–8, 185–6, 234 *see also* full proviso *and* minimalist proviso
family and friends 44, 49, 123, 203, 205–206, 214
facists 18, 40n.15, 195–6
federalism 137
force 25, 48, 50–1, 91, 99, 106–107, 115, 245, 258 *see also* removal forced
foundational title 27, 33–5, 58, 73
France 4, 20, 102–104, 194, 225, 235
fraud 19
freedom 47, 50, 64, 70n.28, 90, 114, 121, 128, 131, 135, 191, 199, 202–203, 204 and nn.48 and 50, 205–206, 208, 232, 249, 256 *see also* liberty
  of association 191–4
  bare 204 and n.50
  basic 204 and n.50, 208
  of expression 203
  infringement of 64, 198–9
  from interference/restriction 61–4, 80, 95, 203, 204 and n.47, 205, 240, 249
  lack of *see* unfreedom
  limits to 240
  of movement *see* movement, freedom of
  political 221
full proviso, the 173–5, 182, 185
functionalism 90–4 *see also* territory, theories of, functionalist
  maximizing variants of 91
  threshold variants of 91

genocide 92
geographic locations *see* locations
Germany 4, 18–19, 78, 80, 92
  Nazi 18, 40n.15
global resource dividend (GRD) 234–5

SUBJECT INDEX 281

Global South, the 16, 248 *see also* developing countries
goals 43–4, 69, 71–3, 76, 83–4, 95, 123, 140, 146, 184–5, 208, 213–14
 comprehensive 42 and n.18, 48, 63
 peripheral 42, 48, 64
goods 16, 53, 66, 68 and n.22, 69–72, 101, 147n.58, 158, 161n.11, 162, 163 and n.20, 165, 167, 174, 183, 209, 221, 223, 226, 237, 258 *see also* fair shares
 basic 208n.60
 material 60, 62, 64, 101, 162, 226
 nondistributable 163
 public 174, 200, 209, 214, 233 *see also* public benefits
governance 21–2, 90–4, 110, 117, 129–30, 152, 173, 210, 237, 255
 global 12 *see also* world state
 oppressive 167
 provision of 21
 self- *see* self-governance
 systems of 29
 temporary 21
governments 89–90, 110, 120, 130–1, 133, 135, 145, 177, 180, 257
 constraint of 109
 ousting of 131 *see also* authority, channels for revoking *and* intervention
groups 34, 49, 53, 54 and n.38, 55, 80 and n.49, 93, 104, 108–109, 116–17, 123–4, 126–7, 129, 131–2, 135–6, 140, 142–4, 148–51, 164, 175, 178, 180, 182–4, 191, 196, 209
 alienated 134–5, 137 *see also* alienation
 "encompassing" 139
 as holders of rights 36, 53, 80 and n.49 *see also* rights, of groups
 homeland 54, 158, 178–9
 interests of *see* interests, of groups
 membership of 132–3, 150
 non-homeland 54
 transboundary 57n.40
 unification of 108

harms 12, 60, 75–6, 82n.52, 187, 198–200, 211, 213–15, 230, 238–9, 258 *see also* inhabitants, harm caused to
 balancing 74
 lack of 70
 social 101, 230, 258
hierarchy 105, 121–2, 131n.20, 197, 222 *see also* relationships, hierarchical
Hispaniola 39, 65
history 9, 15, 60, 124, 131, 150, 162, 177, 180–2, 192n.18, 236, 246

homelands 55, 77, 142, 177–8, 182 *see also* groups, homeland *and* return
human nature 40n.13
humanity 59, 99n.20, 158–9, 223, 228–9, 238
Hutterites 54
 Gaza Strip, the 52, 84
 geography 41, 48, 166, 180
 Guam 19

Iceland 145
ideals 111
identity 80 and n.49, 115, 145, 148, 150–1
 civic 149
 collective 53, 151
 cultural 143–4, 150, 190–1
 national 79, 140, 143, 190
 personal 29, 42, 101
 political 145, 150
 preservation of 190
immigrants 53–4, 133, 143, 179, 191–2, 194–6, 197 and n.31, 198–202, 214–15
immigration 7, 77, 142, 188, 192–6, 198, 200–202, 207 and n.59, 214–15
 limiting 22, 190–2, 194–6, 198–203, 207, 211–13, 215
income 227, 228n.35 *see also* money *and* wealth *and* work
incommensurability 185
independence 70, 92–3, 95, 97, 99–100, 111–13, 117, 128, 135–6, 138, 254
indigenous peoples 2, 57n.40, 75, 83, 91, 118, 133n.24, 135, 137, 138 and n.32, 145, 176, 180, 192, 231–2, 238, 240–1, 248 *see also* Native North Americans
 self-determination of 12, 118, 134, 138 and n.32, 231, 241
individuals 4–6, 10–11, 23, 25–6, 36, 40–1, 43–7, 53–6, 62, 67–8, 70 and n.28, 73, 76, 89, 96–7, 99 and n.20, 100, 105–110, 112, 114, 116, 123–9, 141, 151n.66, 152, 160, 184, 189 and n.6, 190–1, 193–4, 196, 209, 222n.14, 240, 247, 256–7
 autonomy of *see* autonomy, of individuals
 interests of *see* interests, of individuals
 lives of 10–11, 43–51, 53, 55, 62–3, 69, 71–3, 76, 79, 84, 102, 106, 117, 123, 140, 161, 163, 174–5, 184–5, 191, 201, 203, 205–206, 208, 213–14, 230, 247 *see also* goals *and* located life plans
 and nations 28
 opportunities for 2, 71, 169, 183–4, 187, 208, 214
 plans of 71–3 *see also* goals *and* located life plans

282　SUBJECT INDEX

individuals (*cont.*)
　priorities of 189
　as holders of rights 36, 53 *see also* rights, of individuals
　security of 52, 73, 101, 113–14, 116–17, 128, 174
　self-determination of *see* self-determination
　state protection of 11, 25–6, 47, 56, 90–3, 113, 205, 209
Indonesia 235
inequality 16, 98, 102, 200, 213, 248
　regulating 16–17
　between states 6, 17
infrastructure 180
inhabitants 22–3, 34, 58, 61, 73–4, 80, 90–1, 113, 149, 164–6, 176, 179, 181–2, 187, 190–3, 198, 208–212
　harm caused to 12, 60, 176, 187–9, 194–5, 198–200, 208, 211–15
inheritance/bequeathment 73, 79–81, 83, 111, 189n.6
injustice 6, 50, 85, 135, 136 and n.26, 150
　colonial 74
institutional alternatives
　lack of 56, 117, 157
institutionalism 36, 37 and n.9, 38, 39 and n.12, 65, 124 *see also* peoplehood, institutional view of *and* preinstitutionalism
　hybrid 39
　legal 36, 38
　limits of 36
　social 36, 38–9
institutions 8–9, 11, 14–15, 23–4, 37–9, 47, 71, 109, 112, 114, 116, 118, 120, 123–4, 126–7, 130–7, 145, 149–51, 153, 172, 174, 178, 181, 183, 192–3, 195–6, 199, 205, 209–210, 212, 246–7, 253, 255–6 *see also* institutionalism *and* preinstitutionalism
　arrangement of 11, 127, 141
　changes to 196–7, 199 *see also* institutions, usurpation/subversion of
　choosing 92–3, 114
　coercive 23, 29, 107, 141
　common set of 11, 194, 253
　control of 130
　democratic 7, 59
　feasible 117, 174
　functioning of 210
　global 14, 60, 69
　imposition of 91, 130–1, 194
　international 16, 29, 186, 246
　just 135–6, 167
　legal 39
　legitimacy of 23, 68, 118
　making/design of 23, 29, 37, 93, 114, 127, 135, 143, 253
　political 11, 24, 60, 64, 69, 92–3, 109, 112, 116, 124–7, 133, 141, 146, 148, 166, 174, 179, 189 and n.6, 194–6, 198–9, 201, 212, 240
　representative 135, 193
　selection of 9
　shared 37n.9, 111–12, 133, 194
　social 36, 40, 152, 193
　state 112, 126, 141, 150, 153, 192, 250
　structure of 58, 126, 133, 143, 183, 192, 197
　support for 109, 195
　supranational/multilateral 6, 16, 253–5, 258
　usurpation/subversion of 196, 199, 211
intentions 70
　shared 112, 126
interests 40, 64, 93, 110, 124, 158, 166–9, 178, 181, 188, 192–4, 203–204, 210, 212–13, 215, 232, 235, 240–2, 251
　basic 158, 167–8 *see also* territorial interests, basic
　competing 188, 192
　control-based 44, 58, 76, 182, 190, 193
　correspondence 136
　fundamental 204, 251–2
　of future generations 238n.63
　of groups 53, 152
　of individuals 10, 43–4, 46, 53, 55, 63–4, 74, 76, 109–110, 190, 192–4, 204–205, 207, 209, 250
　legitimate 188
　material 166
　of others 21, 48, 63–4, 181, 251
　of outsiders 219, 238–41
　plan-based 44, 58, 63, 71, 76
　practice-based 158 *see also* territorial interests, practice-based
　"property-like" 72 *see also* "property-like" entitlement
　shared 227–8 *see* shareable-interest approach, the
　of states *see also* territorial interests
　territorial *see* territorial interests
interference 70, 90, 111, 186, 188, 237 *see also* duty to not interfere with occupancy rights *and* freedom, from interference
　legitimate 66 *see also* intervention
Intergovernmental Panel on Climate Change 164
international aid 178
international community, the 139, 169, 172, 250, 251n.1
International Monetary Fund (IMF) 223

SUBJECT INDEX

international order, the 17, 24, 29, 142, 153, 185, 209, 226, 237, 250, 254–6
international relations 5, 14
International Seabed Authority 223
intervention 102 and n.24, 131–2, 138, 250
  coercive 114n.47
  humanitarian 21, 92, 131, 252, 255, 257
  justification of 102 and n.24, 131
Inuit 2
invasion 58
Islam 165 *see also* Muslims
Israel 20, 51–2, 77–8, 82–4, 192–4
  Law of Return 192 and n.18

Japan 52, 145, 205, 235
Jews/Judaism 18–19, 40n.15, 54, 76, 77 and n.44, 78, 80, 192 and n.18
joint endeavors 120 and n.2, 121–2 *see also* cooperation
Jordan 52
judgement(s) 68, 78, 90, 96, 99, 102, 105–111, 114–15, 117, 124–5, 128–9, 141, 152–3, 189, 256
jurisdictional exclusivity 4–5
just cause 97
justice 9, 25, 89–91, 96–7, 99, 101, 110, 113, 115–16, 131, 146, 148, 152, 158–9, 169, 173, 176, 188, 192, 209–211, 230, 236–7, 251, 256–7 *see also* injustice
  basic 10–11, 13–14, 21, 23, 56, 90, 112–16, 118, 126–7, 131, 134–5, 149, 157, 166–7, 197, 232, 240, 249, 252, 257
  climate *see* climate justice
  corrective 16, 236
  distributive 15–17, 38, 163, 174
  duties of 6n.22, 246, 251, 253
    natural 11, 55n.38, 94–6, 98, 116–17, 130
  egalitarian 159
  environmental 221, 233, 246 *see also* climate justice
  global 15, 17, 256
  obstacles to 17
  political 190
  principles of 8 and n.37, 9, 68, 255
  provision of 23, 91, 93, 134
  requirements of 95, 99, 113, 117–18, 127, 131, 135, 167, 192
  socioeconomic 17
  sufficientarian 234

Kenya 248
kinship 3
Kiribati 178–82
Kosovo 81
Kurds 157

land 27–8, 38, 68, 70–1, 73–6, 80–1, 158, 161–2, 164 and n.26, 165–6, 180, 183–4, 225n.27, 226, 231–2, 243, 248 *see also* property *and* space
  improvements to 228n.35
  loss of 238
  preservation of 162, 240, 244
  public 179
  relating to the 162–3, 166
  use of 69, 158, 161–2, 165, 174, 181, 231–2 *see also* resources, use of *and* shareable-interest approach, the *and* space, use of *and* territory, use of
  usefulness of 161–2
language 111, 124, 140, 145–8, 150, 179–82, 191–2
  English 45
  I-Kiribati 182
  official 146
  Somali 54
  Spanish 54
  Swahili 55
Latin America 247
law 10, 13, 21, 27, 36–7, 39, 113, 133, 157, 181, 190, 203, 220, 230, 236, 255–7 *see also* legal systems *and* legislation
  contract 37, 56
  criminal 83n.54
  enforcement of 1, 89, 94, 257 *see also* enforcement
  inheritance 37
  international 24, 119, 133, 137, 138n.32, 164, 170, 219, 223–5, 232, 246, 251–2, 255
  interpretation of 1
  making of 1, 7, 14, 23, 94
  natural 62
  obedience to the 106, 120
  positive 36–8
  post-national 7
  property 55n.38, 56, 89, 230
  supranational 2n.5, 255
  systems of 36, 38, 56, 95
  tort 10, 37, 56
leaders/leadership 2–3
learning processes 253
Lebanon 52, 81
legal systems 69, 256
legislation 59, 67, 99n.21
legitimacy 9, 18, 21, 23, 26, 56, 58, 77, 89–95, 97, 104, 113, 114 and n.47, 119, 124n.7, 130, 132, 148–9, 166, 183, 188, 236–7, 241, 248–52, 254, 257–8 *see also* authority, legitimacy of *and* legitimation *and* territorial claims,

legitimacy (*cont.*)
    legitimacy of *and* territorial jurisdiction, legitimate conditions for 56–7, 114 and n.47
    democratic 103
    external 114n.47
    internal 1–2
    "liberal principle of" 111
    "maker" 93 and n.15, 94
    omnilateral 68 *see also* authority, omnilateral
    political 1, 111, 232
        weak notion of 21n.59
    "taker" 93–4
legitimation 137
liberal nationalism *see* nationalism, liberal
liberalism 90, 201–202, 212, 257
libertarianism 191n.15, 194
liberty 70nn.27–8, 89, 101, 203–205, 208, 240–1 *see also* freedom
    basic 204–205, 208
    negative 204
    of residence 35, 58
    to travel 35
Libya 102 and nn.24–5, 103, 194
located life plans 11, 40–5, 46 and n.24, 47–53, 55, 57 and n.40, 59, 62, 69, 79, 83–4, 117, 166, 174–5, 183, 197, 200, 230, 240 *see also* goals
locations 11, 34–5, 40–1, 43–4, 46–8, 50, 53, 55, 75, 83, 164, 166, 168, 173–5, 177, 179, 183, 208, 234 *see also* located life plans
    attachment to 43, 46, 163, 168 *see also* staying put
Lu, Catherine 57n.40
Lviv 19
Ly Minh 56n.39

majority, the 94, 103–104, 117, 119, 129, 140–1, 147–8, 180, 200, 240
market, the 159, 162, 163n.20, 164–5, 173
mergers 195
Mexico 3, 19, 205
Miami 54
Middle Ages, the 4
migrants 46, 74, 77, 157, 162, 164, 170, 172, 176, 181, 185–8, 190–1, 193–8, 202, 205–215, 234, 237, 241, 246 *see also* immigrants
    compensatory 187n.3
    number of 196, 200–202
    opportunity 187, 214–15
migration 7, 46, 57n.40, 164–5, 172–3, 176, 179, 181, 188–9, 191, 193, 197–206, 207 and n.59, 208–215, 241, 246 *see also* duty to allow harmless migration *and* immigration *and* relocation
    out of necessity 24, 50, 178–9, 187
minimalist proviso, the 169–73, 175–6
minorities 24, 117, 133–4, 136–9, 141, 143, 144 and n.54, 145–6, 148–50, 177–8, 181, 192, 232, 250 *see also* autonomy, internal
mobility 46n.24, 208
monarchs 129
money 37, 200, 205–206, 213, 223, 244, 248
Montevideo Convention (1933) 1
moral/ethical issues 5, 9, 15, 17, 25, 29, 37n.9, 40nn.13 and 15, 46–7, 49, 52, 57, 63, 65, 67, 68 and n.22, 70–2, 74, 76, 81, 91, 96, 106, 111–12, 114–15, 128, 133–6, 138, 146–7, 152, 157, 165, 188, 195–6, 199, 204–205, 211, 227, 229–30, 232, 240–1 *see also* rights, moral *and* values, moral
movement *see* people, movement of 7, 19, 193, 202
multilateral authorization 97 and n.18
Muslims 193n.21
mutual aid 190

national defense 51n.32
nationalism 28, 34, 124, 139, 141–4, 148 *see also* nations *and* territory, theories of, collectivist, nationalist view
    cultural 141, 143
    liberal 8, 29, 53, 111, 120, 139–45, 149–50, 177, 250
nationality 148
nations 28, 53–5, 81, 140, 142–6, 148, 180–1, 212 *see also* identity, national *and* nationalism *and* nation-states
    building of 140, 144, 146
    cultural 28, 139, 143–4 *see also* culture, national
    security of 199, 211, 257
nation-states 28, 142–4, 150 *see also* nation-states
Native North Americans 19, 20 and n.58, 38, 43, 137, 176, 179
    Apache 38
    Cherokee 20, 75–6
    Cree 231
    Navajo 38 and n.10, 39–41, 162, 163 and n.20, 240
    Pueblo 41, 43, 83, 231
    Sioux 41, 43, 223
naturalism 60
"near unanimity" 130n.19
Netherlands, the 235
networks 7, 43

SUBJECT INDEX   285

newcomers 77, 181, 193, 201, 214 see also
    outsiders
New Forests Company 247
New International Economic Order (NIEO) 222
    and n.14, 223
New Zealand 178
Nigeria 225
nomadism 3, 167–8, 183
non-alienation 10, 109, 190, 250
noncooperators/dissenters 110, 112–13, 115–16,
    130, 134n.25, 135–6
nonintervention 1, 13, 254
non-refoulement 170–1
non-state organizations 7, 16, 21, 43, 121–3,
    139, 245–6
non-usurpation 26
North America 2
North Korea 121, 125, 206–207
Norway 20n.58, 137, 194

obligations 1, 4, 198, 200, 212–13, 215
occupancy 10–11, 14, 22, 35–6, 38, 40–2, 44, 50,
    52–4, 58–9, 76–7, 79–81, 83, 91, 117,
    174–5, 197, 200, 224, 225 and n.27,
    231, 233–4, 238, 246, 249, 252
    see also rights, occupancy
  blameless 74
  challenges to 59
  claims 57 see also territorial claims
  concept of 34, 54, 58
  control-based interest in see interests,
      control-based
  deprivation of 51–3 see also removal and
      rights, occupancy, deprivation of
  distribution of 177
  plan-based interest in see interests, plan-based
  present day 85
  restoration of 52n.32 see also return
  rightful 21, 38, 56, 75, 85, 89, 94, 249
  and territory 55
occupancy rights see rights, occupancy
occupation 131 see also occupancy
  foreign 133
  military 92, 133
omnilateralism 95–7, 99 see also authority,
    omnilateral *and* coercion, omnilateral
    and enforcement, omnilateral *and* will,
    omnilateral
OPEC 222
other people 47, 49, 68, 71–2, 115–17, 158, 185,
    199, 235, 241, 252
  respect for 21, 48, 60–4, 67–8, 70–1, 90, 94–5,
      97, 100, 112–13, 115, 117, 135, 181,
      185, 224, 226, 229, 238, 240–1, 249,
      251 see also freedom, from interference
      and rights, of others, respect for
Ottoman Empire, the 4
outsiders/foreigners 12, 90, 113, 131, 143, 148,
    159, 164–5, 175–6, 185, 193, 209–211,
    214, 225n.27, 237–40, 249, 252 see also
    newcomers
  burdens placed upon 9
  exclusion of 1, 12, 60, 70, 72–4, 157, 165, 185,
      187–90, 201, 230, 234, 237, 246 see also
      exclusion *and* rights, to exclude
  interests of see interests, of outsiders
  rights claimed against 1, 9, 165
ownership 22, 39, 58, 61, 69, 71, 158, 179,
    189n.6, 224, 226, 235–6, 246 see also
    property, ownership of *and* resources,
    natural, ownership of *and* territory,
    ownership of
  common 59, 61–2, 64–6, 69–70, 73, 84, 162,
      165, 173, 177, 229, 252–3
  full liberal 69, 70n.28, 71–2, 162

Pacific Islanders 178–80
Palestine 19–20, 51–2, 76–7, 83
Palestinians 77 and n.44, 81–2, 83 and n.54,
    84, 194
Paris Climate Change Treaty 242, 247
participation 135
  civic 141
  political 204–205
  willing 91, 125–7
  reasonable 125
partnership 108
Pennington (New Jersey) 55
people 23–4, 29, 43, 45, 51, 53, 90–1, 93, 99 and
    n.20, 100, 112, 121, 124, 127, 131n.20,
    133, 150–1, 153, 163, 178, 184, 224n.20,
    226, 232, 237, 248, 255 see also
    peoplehood *and* territory, theories of,
    collectivist, peoplehood view
  beliefs of 11, 195–6 see also culture
  definition of the 24, 126–7, 150 and n.61
  differences between 183, 185
  experience of 184
  institutionalist view of 38, 39 and n.12, 124
  movement of 7, 19, 193, 202–206, 207 and n.59,
      208, 212–14, 246 see also migration *and*
      movement *and* relocation
    domestic 202–203
    forced 44, 193 see also removal, forced
    freedom of 57, 202–206
  non-political view of 124, 129
  stateless 38–9
  will of the see will

peoplehood *see also* territory, theories of, collectivist, peoplehood view
  institutional view of 124
    endogenous theory of 24, 123–6, 153
  non-political view of 124
permanent sovereignty over natural resources *see* resource sovereignty, permanent
persecution 170, 192n.18
personal ties 4
persuasion 100, 193, 241
Philadelphia 55
Philippines 91–2
plebiscites 136
plenitude 163–4
pluralism 7, 12, 17, 29, 41, 45, 94, 118, 120, 142, 145, 192, 195–6, 198, 232, 250
Poland 18–20, 78, 82
policy 91, 109, 113, 147–8, 193, 213, 241–2
  environmental 116, 242
  immigration 188, 192 and n.18, 214
  language 147–8, 182
  making 23
  monetary 37
  political 196
  public 196
  undermining 196
political organization 2–5, 8–10, 12–13, 15, 17, 23
  polycentric 7, 12 *see also* pluralism
politics 23, 26, 59, 79, 94, 106–109, 120 and n.2, 124, 128n.14, 134–5, 138–9, 145–6, 150, 152–3, 172, 175, 177, 179, 193–4, 197, 204, 209, 236, 254
Pomerania 19
poor, the 200, 212–13, 215, 248
possessions 63, 71–2
poverty 173, 247
  global 234–5
    duty to eradicate 15
power 16, 111, 197
  abuse of 122
  coercive *see* coercive power
  economic 104
  political 26, 91, 102–104, 111, 153, 207n.59
  of the state 25–6, 107
practices 58, 116, 146, 166, 168, 177, 179, 181, 183, 232
  cultural 35, 39, 49, 54, 73, 81–4, 146, 185, 200, 214, 230
  economic 35, 39, 43, 49, 73, 82, 84, 179, 183, 185, 230
  political 49, 54, 179, 183, 185
  shared 42, 49
  social 35–6, 39, 42, 53–4, 73, 82, 84, 183, 185, 200, 230

preferences 148, 173, 180, 183, 188, 191, 195, 232
  shared 104, 194
preinstitutionalism 36–7, 39 and n.12, 40
prejudice 195–6
Presbyterianism 165
Princeton 55–6, 133
principle of right 59
privacy 70, 90, 98, 147
privileges 148
procedures 122 *see also* will, procedural
property 10, 22, 33–7, 39 and n.12, 56, 60–1, 64, 67–8, 70n.28, 72–3, 79, 90, 95, 157, 162, 225 and n.27, 226–9 *see also* ownership *and* territory, theories of, proprietarian
  confiscation of 19
  forms of 37
  ideas about/theories of 36–7, 73 *see also* institutionalism *and* preinstitutionalism
  intellectual 37
  institutionalist versus preinstitutionalist theories of
  law *see* law, property
  ownership of 35, 39, 158 *see also* ownership
  personal 70n.27
  private 2, 34–5, 61
  rights to *see under* rights
  rules 33–4, 90, 226–7
"property-like" entitlement 22, 33–4, 58, 72
proprietarian theories *see* territory, theories of, proprietarian
Prussia 18
public benefits 200, 209–211, 213–14, 227–8, 233, 237
public opinion 125, 128, 253
public order 101, 116, 132, 138, 257
public services 199, 211–12
public sphere, the 149, 181, 190
Puerto Rico 19

Qaddafi, Muammar Al 102 and n.25
Quebec 20 and n.58, 55, 134–5

racism 101, 195–6
reasoning 105–106, 111
redistribution 17, 22, 24, 57, 60, 157–8, 161, 177–8, 180, 228
referenda 103
reflection 105
refugee crises 6, 16, 24, 258
refugees 51–4, 81–2, 83 and n.54, 84, 143, 158, 164–6, 170, 171 and n.45, 172–4, 179 and n.60, 181–2, 186–7, 252, 258

climate 24, 158, 164–5, 169, 174, 179, 182, 185, 212
  resettlement of 14, 24
regulation 16, 69, 220, 227, 239 *see also* inequality, regulating
  environmental 37, 162, 231
relationships 29, 40, 43–6, 49, 51, 53, 100, 114, 121, 123, 139, 168, 184, 208 *see also* social ties
  hierarchical 98, 105
  social 98
religion 43, 54, 83, 111, 114, 148–9, 165, 168, 203, 205, 213–14
relocation 22, 75, 164, 169, 173, 178–9, 185, 205–206, 211, 213–15
  "pure" 45
removal 37, 48–53, 75 *see also* colonial settlement *and* dispossession *and* expulsion *and* return and repatriation
  forced 33, 38, 40, 45, 48, 50–2
  freedom from 58 *see also* rights, occupancy, respect for
  process of 45
representation 116, 119, 182
resettlement 14, 24, 82, 165, 171, 180, 182–3
residence 55, 57, 171–2 *see also* rights, residency
resistance 1, 130
resource sovereignty 215, 219–24, 227–9, 231–7, 242, 244, 246–8 *see also* resources
  discarding idea of 220, 229
  limited 228–9, 231–8, 247
  permanent 219–22, 224–7, 229, 232, 239n.64
  and forest carbon sinks 220–1, 227–9, 238–8, 241–7
resources 1, 48, 61, 64, 147 and n.58, 161 and n.11, 162 and n.19, 163, 165–6, 169, 176, 182–3, 207, 215, 219–27, 228 and n.36, 229 and n.43, 230–9, 241–7, 251–2 *see also* global resource dividend
  auction of 161–2
  claims to 159, 165, 182, 222, 226, 228n.35, 233–4, 236–7, 241, 244–5
  distribution of 228, 235, 237, 246
  equality of 15–16, 159, 161 *see also* equality *and* fair shares
  exploitation of 162n.19, 221, 231, 233, 243–4
  global systemic 238, 246, 252
  material 27, 54n.38, 60–1, 234, 239
  natural 12, 22, 158, 162 and n.19, 163n.20, 169, 219 and n.1, 220–39, 241–8, 251
    control of 231, 238
    jurisdiction over 221, 224, 225 and n.27, 227, 229, 231, 233–6, 246

  management of 220, 227, 229, 231, 234, 237, 239, 241–6
  nationalization of 220, 222, 224, 231, 233, 236
  ownership of 22, 59, 220–7, 229, 233, 235–7, 246 *see also* ownership
  regulation of 220, 227, 236, 239
  shared/sharing 60–4, 66, 161, 165, 173, 181–3, 207, 228–9, 239n.64, 241, 245, 251 *see also* fair shares
  sovereignty over *see* resource sovereignty
  uncreated 159
  use of 46, 61–4, 72, 159–60, 162 and n.19, 176, 182, 234, 237, 248 *see also* land, use of *and* shareable-interest approach, the *and* space, use of *and* territory, use of
  usurpation of 59, 64, 132, 248
return and repatriation 52, 58, 75–85, 192 *see also* Israel, Law of Return *and* non-refoulement
  of subsequent generations 76–9, 82–5, 249 *see also* rights, of return, for subsequent generations *and* territorial claims, of subsequent generations
rights 2, 13, 25, 36, 39, 48–9, 56, 61, 65, 68, 71, 73–4, 79, 89–92, 95–6, 101, 110, 112–16, 128, 130–2, 135, 138, 158, 169, 174, 179, 185–6, 198, 209, 223, 226, 232, 256, 258
  to alienate 71–2
  autonomy 113–14, 117, 128, 131
  to avoid unwanted obligations 187, 189, 198–9
  basic 114 and n.47, 128–9, 131–2, 135, 149, 209, 258
  bearers of 36
  civil 134n.25
  to closure 210
  to collective self-determination 113–14, 117, 119, 133n.24, 134–7, 138 and n.32, 139, 167, 177, 185, 187, 189–90, 209–210, 224, 249
  contract 95
  core personal autonomy 167
  cultural 24, 158, 175, 177, 191
  democratic 102, 130
  economic 245
  enforcement of 10, 56, 67–8, 95–7, 100, 132
  equal 115, 143, 165
  establishment of 59, 75, 116
    unilateral 58
  to exclude 1, 24, 35, 48, 70, 72–3, 157, 165, 176, 181, 189–90, 191 and n.15, 194–6, 207–208, 211–15 *see also under* exclusion

rights (cont.)
    conditional 187, 189, 194, 198–9,
        211–14, 234
    discretionary 69, 73, 187, 190–1,
        195n.26, 198
    limited 60, 69–70, 72–4, 176, 182, 185–9,
        211, 215, 251–2, 254 see also
        duty to allow harmless migration and duty to
        not interfere with occupancy rights
    exclusive 61
        limited 60
    to use force 3
    fundamental 10, 65
    of groups 53–5, 80 and n.49, 149 see groups,
        as holders of rights
    human 13, 26, 91–2, 114n.47, 119, 128n.14,
        138 and n.32, 170, 187, 189, 198,
        202–203, 206, 208, 251n.1, 254
        abuses of 101–102, 171
        respect for 26, 128n.14
    of individuals 2, 10, 26, 36, 53–5, 58, 169,
        193–4 see also individuals, as holders
        of rights
    interest-based theories of 40
    interpretation of 56, 67–8, 115
    land-tenure 243
    limits to 67–70, 73–4, 181, 250–1
    to migrate 173, 178, 189, 191n.15, 195,
        202–203, 204 and n.47, 205, 207 and
        n.59, 208 and n.60, 209, 215
    of minorities 144n.54, 149
    moral 37n.9, 39, 47, 52, 61, 64, 68, 74, 89, 100,
        157, 181
    natural 27, 33, 39, 40n.13, 72, 226
    occupancy 10, 22, 34–6, 38–40, 46–60, 74–5,
        78–81, 84–5, 96, 117, 157–8, 181, 185,
        200, 224, 243, 249 see also occupancy
        "core" preinstitutional 57
        deprivation of 51n.32, 52
        infringement of 49, 51, 91
        justification of 47–8, 76–7, 85, 250
        limits of 249
        non-transmissability of 60, 80–1, 84, 249
        transmission of 79, 81
    of others 48 and n.26, 49, 60–1, 63–4, 67–8,
        70–2, 90, 94–5, 117, 135, 158
        respect for 48 and n.26, 49, 51n.32, 58,
            60–2, 67, 90, 97, 100, 112–13, 115,
            117, 128, 135, 229, 238, 249
    against outsiders 1, 12, 74
    political 134n.25
    preinstitutional 39, 40 and n.13, 57, 84
    primitive 60–74, 78–80, 84–5, 158, 226, 249
        extent of 69–74

objections to 64–8, 72
    interpretation and enforcement 67–8
    unilateralism 64–6
private 98, 112–13, 117, 232, 249
property 22, 26–7, 33–9, 60–1, 68, 72, 78, 85,
    90, 95, 116, 162, 189n.6, 224, 225 and
    n.26, 226–7, 230, 236–7
property-like 58 see also property-like
    entitlement
protection of 90–3, 128 and n.14, 129, 131–2,
    198, 209, 258
reciprocal 10, 61
representation 182, 232
residency 35, 46, 48, 50, 53, 55, 57, 197
residual common 252
    over resources 27, 61, 215, 219–20, 223–6,
        228n.35, 229, 233, 237, 248 see also
        resources
    of return 52, 76–9, 80 and n.49, 81–5, 192, 249
        for subsequent generations 76–9, 81–5,
            249 see also return, of subsequent
            generations and territorial claims, of
            subsequent generations
scope of 63
security 113–14, 117, 128, 131, 166, 169, 174,
    183, 232, 249
settlement 172
social 134n.25
sovereignty 223, 250–1
of states see states, rights claimed by
subsistence 113–14, 117, 128, 131, 166,
    168–9, 172–3, 183, 187, 206, 232, 249
systems of 110
territorial 2, 8, 12–15, 21–2, 25, 26n.64, 35,
    59, 68, 73–4, 117, 157, 181, 185, 227
    limits of 13–14, 22, 61, 73–4, 164n.26, 181,
        249–51
use 22, 60–4, 72, 249
violation of 78, 91–2, 135, 138, 171–2
to do wrong 195, 237, 240
Roman Empire, the 4
rule 21, 23, 27, 90, 92, 101, 120, 125, 197, 210,
    232, 254
    domestic 23, 256
    foreign 23, 131–3
    just 25, 127
    justified 21n.59, 25, 90–2, 131, 232, 254
    political 106
    non-unilateral 94 see also will, omnilateral
Russia 18–20 see also Soviet Union, the

Saami people, the 83, 230
sachems 3
San Francisco 56

SUBJECT INDEX   289

sanctions 138, 245–6, 255
Scandinavia 83, 230
Scotland 20 and n.58, 134–5
sea levels 165, 238
secession 20, 133, 136–8
    unilateral 136–8
self, the 191
    definition of 119
self-defense 131, 245
self-determination 7, 10–12, 21, 29, 54, 90, 92–4, 98, 101, 106, 111–12, 114–15, 119–24, 127, 130, 131 and n.20, 132–5, 136 and nn.26 and 28, 137–42, 149–53, 172, 174n.51, 191–6, 198, 209–210, 222n.14, 224, 231, 233, 237–8, 240–2, 246, 250–2, 254, 257–8 *see also* self-governance
    accounts of 23, 93, 119–21, 136, 221
        liberal nationalist theory 120, 139–45, 149–50
        peoplehood theory 120, 150–2
        political autonomy theory 23, 94, 120
    claims to 134–5, 136 and n.28, 138–9, 195, 250 *see also* territorial claims
        moralized 195, 232
    collective 10–11, 14, 23–4, 90, 94, 98, 113–14, 117, 119–20, 128–30, 131 and n.20, 151–2, 157, 189–91, 197–8, 209–210, 224, 229–30, 232–4, 249–50 *see also* rights, to collective self-determination *and* shared political will
    conditions for 16, 128–30
    denial of 195
    expressions of 224
    granting of 139
    limits to 135, 136 and n.26, 241, 258
    overriding 258
    political 139, 142, 167, 178
    respect for 112–13, 237, 258
    right of *see* rights, to collective self-determination
    value of 120, 127, 140
    violation of 92, 132, 258
self-direction 10, 105–106, 109, 153, 190, 250 *see also* agency, self-directed
self-governance 12, 24, 28–9, 92, 116, 151–2, 250
    desire for 29
    nonterritorial 116
    political 179
self-preservation 60–2, 67–70, 80, 84, 207n.59, 226, 229
separation of powers 13
separatism 20, 145 *see also* secession

Serbs 81
settlement 9, 18, 60, 74, 78, 157, 164, 172, 175–6, 179 and n.60, 188–9, 193, 196, 200, 205, 209 *see also* colonial settlement *and* resettlement
    undoing 23
    wrongful 23, 75–8, 80, 84–5, 91–2, 132, 193
settlers 73–7
"Seven Sisters" (oil companies) 221
shaming 138
shareable-interest approach, the 165–8, 228
shared intention *see* intentions, shared
shared political will 10–11, 21, 56, 90, 94, 100, 104, 108–109, 116–17, 120n.2, 121, 126–7, 129, 132–3, 149, 152, 157, 209, 250 *see also* preferences, shared *and* will, actual popular *and* will, omnilateral
    dissent from 56, 94, 112–17, 130, 136, 157, 167 *see also* institutional alternatives, lack of *and* noncooperators/dissenters
Sierra Leone 205
Silesia 19
social cohesion 201–202, 212–14
social conventions 64
social divisions 142
social entrepreneurs 153
social life 49
social mobility 146
social needs 184–5
social ties 45–6, 53, 107
society 36, 41, 43, 93n.15, 94, 98, 99 and n.21, 101, 107, 124, 128n.14, 129, 130n.19, 131, 140, 142, 145, 147–8, 153, 164, 166, 172, 179, 181, 191, 193, 196, 198, 200–201, 204–205, 208–209, 212–15, 231, 233, 236, 240–1, 248 *see also* practices, social
    international 131n.20, 153
    organization of 45, 99, 101, 193
    political 27
    rules of 36–7, 94, 101, 106, 125, 168, 237
South America 3
sovereign wealth funds 229
sovereignty 13, 22, 179n.60, 185, 215, 219, 236, 250–1, 255, 258
    external 13–14, 255
    internal 8–9, 13, 25, 251, 256
    limits to 13, 186, 219, 251, 254, 258
    over resources *see also* permanent sovereignty over natural resources *and* resource sovereignty
    reciprocal 14

sovereignty (cont.)
  territorial 2, 12–15, 17–18, 22, 24, 166, 170
    see also rights, territorial and
    territorial jurisdiction
    justification of 18–19, 24–5, 27, 250
      see also territory, theories of
    revisionist view of 22, 182
Soviet Union, the 19
space 10, 12, 18, 27, 34–5, 39–40, 48, 50, 58–60, 63, 66, 70, 72, 74, 84, 157, 160–1, 164–5, 169, 174–6, 178–9, 182–4, 198, 231, 234 see also locations
  entitlement to 35, 39n.12, 60, 72–4, 79n.46, 84, 165, 181–2, 249 see also foundational title and "property-like" entitlement and territorial claims and territory, theories of
  rights of occupancy 35 see also occupancy and rights, occupancy
  rights of private ownership 35
    see also property, private
    and rights, property
  rights of territorial jurisdiction 35
    see also rights, territorial and
    territorial jurisdiction
  public 55, 74, 174, 177, 179, 230
  use of 69–70, 72, 74, 80, 160, 176, 249
    see also land, use of and resources, use of and
shareable-interest approach, the and territory, use of
value of 160, 165
state, the 2–4, 6, 14, 17, 22, 54 and n.38, 56, 58, 89, 95–8, 104, 112–13, 115, 120, 125–6, 131–2, 136–9, 144–6, 147 and n.58, 148–50, 153, 177–8, 185–6, 191–4, 203–204, 206, 212–15, 245, 256–7
    see also territorial states system, the
  "absorptive capacity" of 212–13
  authority of see authority, of the state
  civic 144
  definition of 2, 4, 14
  domestic affairs of 16, 256
  external relations of 4, 255–6
  interference with 90
  necessity of 10
  legitimacy of see legitimacy
  nature of 95–8, 112, 119, 121, 123, 131, 152, 190, 198, 254
    as impersonal 121, 123
    as involuntary 121, 123
  responsibilities/things required of 82, 83 and n.54, 84, 93, 113–14, 117, 125, 127–8, 135, 209–211, 215, 219, 226, 234, 249–50

  rights claimed by 1, 8–9, 12–15, 21–5, 90–1, 157, 170, 187, 193–4, 251
    to control their borders 1, 170, 215 see also borders, control of
    nonintervention 1 see also non-intervention
    resource 1, 215 see also permanent sovereignty over natural resources and resources
    territorial jurisdiction 1, 8, 56, 157, 215
      see also territorial claims and territorial jurisdiction
  role of 11, 25, 93, 95–8, 124, 177, 190
  structure of 13, 24, 57, 126–7
    unitary 12
  and its subjects 1, 11, 22–6, 56–8, 90–3, 96, 101, 107, 109–110, 112–13, 121, 124n.7, 125–8, 130–1, 141, 149, 190, 193, 195–6, 206, 207n.59, 210–11, 249–50, 256–7 see also inhabitants
"state of nature" 40, 71–2, 96, 99, 256
states 15–18, 33, 124, 132, 136–7, 142, 144, 149, 178, 185–6, 187n.3, 193, 209–210, 212, 224n.20, 245–6, 251, 254, 256–8 see also state, the and territorial states system, the
  bureaucratic 14
  establishment of 68
  independence of 136
  interdependence of 16, 256–7
  league of 255–7
  liberal 144n.54, 145
  multinational 141, 143–4
  pluralistic 192
  self-determining 193–4
  welfare see welfare state, the
staying put 46 see also rights, of residence
Stockholm Declaration on the Human Environment 239
sustainability 164n.26, 166, 227, 246
suum, the 62
Sweden 20n.58, 52, 105n.33, 132, 137, 194
Switzerland 43
symbols/symbolism 147
Syria 52, 157

taxation 162, 163n.20, 228–9, 235, 237, 245
technology 223
territorial claims 13, 18, 21, 27, 34, 40, 54, 57–60, 81–5, 90, 157, 164–5, 176, 182, 226, 232 see also occupancy, claims
  broadened 57
  "clean" 60
  group 80 and n.49
  legitimacy of 19–22, 58, 60, 85, 176, 181, 254
    see also rule, justified

SUBJECT INDEX 291

limits to 176, 181–2, 249–51
particularized 40
of subsequent generations 77–85, 249 see also return, of subsequent generations and rights, of return, for subsequent generations
territorial interests 13, 22, 158, 166–79, 181, 183, 185, 214, 237, 240, 252–4, 258
 basic 158, 167–9, 171–2, 174–7, 179, 183, 234
 fundamental 157, 188, 238–9, 242, 245–6, 252–4
 practice-based 158, 167–9, 173–9, 181, 183
 protection of 253–4
 threats to 170–1, 187, 237, 246
 unfulfilled/unmet 171, 185, 187
territorial jurisdiction 1, 5, 8–9, 21–2, 34–5, 56–8, 157, 198
 legitimate 21–3, 26, 56–8, 89–90, 157, 249 see also rule, justified
territorial membership 33, 123
territorial removals see removal
territorial states system, the 2, 5, 13–14, 17–18, 95, 118–19, 185, 249, 251, 255
 criticism of 5–6, 8–9, 14, 17, 60
 moral justification for 5, 8–12, 14–15, 17–18, 24, 119, 185, 209, 250
  see also core values, the
 institutionally conservative 8 and n.37, 9
 reforming 5, 8–9, 12–15, 17, 253, 258
territories 94
 distinct 3
territory 18–19, 21, 25, 28, 33, 54, 58, 73–4, 94, 102, 112, 116–17, 142, 157–61, 163–4, 167, 169, 173, 177–85, 192, 197, 211, 213, 228n.35, 234–5, 251 see also land
 access to 12, 60, 245
 acquisition of 18–20, 132
 ancillary 56–8
 annexation of see annexation
 assignment to a particular 6
 claims to see territorial claims
 configuration of 152
 core 56, 58
 distribution of 173–4, 177, 184–5, 208, 246 see also distribution
 exclusion from see exclusion
 as full 164–5
 new 74, 171
 and occupancy 55
 ownership of 34 see also ownership
 redistribution of see redistribution
 shared 78, 181, 183
 theories of 25, 27–30

collectivist 27–9, 34 and n.4, 151 and n.66
 see also collectivism
nationalist view 28–9, 34 see also self-determination, accounts of, liberal nationalist theory
peoplehood view 28–9 see also self-determination, accounts of, peoplehood theory
functionalist 25, 26 and n.64, 91 see also functionalism
proprietarian 22, 26–7, 29, 33–4, 73 see also property
Lockean 27, 33–4
unoccupied 179n.60, 180, 182, 225n.27, 233
use of 159–60 see also land, use of and resources, use of and shareable-interest approach, the and space, use of
theft 66
threats 100, 107, 211–13, 235, 238, 246
Tibet 20, 194
Tokyo 160–1, 183–5
toleration 143
Toronto 205
Trail Smelter, the 239
transboundary issues 221, 239 and n.64, 245
tribes 3, 38, 129, 131, 160, 167–8, 231
Turkey 157
Tuvalu 179

Ukraine 18
unfreedom 6
unilateralism 95–9, 102, 135–7 see also appropriation, unilateral and coercion, unilateral and enforcement, unilateral and rights, establishment of, unilateral and rights, primitive, objections to, unilateralism
 wrong of 98–101, 104
United Kingdom, the 76, 103, 235, 247 see also British Empire, the
United Nations, the 13, 97, 221, 224n.20, 254
 Charter of 13, 119, 254
 Convention on the Law of the Sea (UNCLOS) 223
 Convention Relating to the Status of Refugees 170–3, 252
 Declaration of the Rights of Indigenous Peoples 133n.24, 138 and n.32, 232
 High Commissioner for Refugees 164
 General Assembly of 219 and n.1, 222
 Reduced Emissions for Deforestation and Forest Degradation Program (REDD+) 247–8
 Universal Declaration of Human Rights 13, 254

United States of America 3, 19–20, 34–5, 37–8, 41, 57, 75, 77–8, 89, 91–2, 104, 137, 159, 176, 178–9, 205–206, 225, 231, 239, 253
    Indian Reorganization act 20n.58, 137
    Indian Territory of 20 and n.58, 75–6
    native peoples of *see* Native North Americans
    states of
        Alaska 19, 55, 57, 168
        Arizona 38, 40
        Georgia 20, 75–6
        Hawaii 19–20, 55
        Kentucky 55
        Montana 231
        New Jersey 34, 55, 224
        New Mexico 38, 41, 55, 240
        Oklahoma 20, 75
        Texas 19
    Supreme Court of 75

value 28, 48, 158, 160–2, 164–5, 173, 184, 234–5, 246
values 94, 105, 108–109, 111, 113, 115, 127, 132, 143, 146, 150–1, 153, 163–4, 168, 178, 181, 190, 193, 195, 210, 212, 237, 241, 250 *see also* core values
    cultural 181, 232
    moral 17
    personal 79
    political 150, 198
    social 45, 100, 134
Vilnius 19
violence 20 and n.58, 25

war 5–6, 14, 91, 97, 137
Washington 75
ways of life 163, 164n.26, 165, 168, 173–6, 180–1, 183, 200
    "downsizing" 176 and n.52, 181
    protecting 200, 212–13
wealth 16, 200, 202, 205, 213, 219n.1 *see also* sovereign wealth funds
welfare 15 *see also* welfare state, the
    aggregate 49
welfare state, the 200, 212
well-being 41, 91, 151, 184–5, 187, 193, 208
West Bank, the 20, 52, 77, 84, 193
wilderness 56–7
will 67, 98, 100, 120n.2, 132, 210
    actual popular 23, 94, 119, 150
    omnilateral 23, 94–5, 119, 153
    of the people 97–8, 130, 150 *see also* shared political will
    procedural 11
    shared 108–110, 116–17, 121, 123, 126–7, 129, 133, 150, 152, 157 *see also* shared political will
willing participation *see* participation, willing
withdrawal 227
work 201, 203, 205, 207, 213
world state 6, 95, 118 and n.51, 119, 153, 173, 255–8
World War I 18
World War II 18–19, 92, 137

Yom Kippur War, the 222

Zimbabwe 235